Quantitative
Methods
for Management

31

Quantitative Methods for Management

ROSS H. JOHNSON

PAUL R. WINN

Illinois State University

HOUGHTON MIFFLIN COMPANY · BOSTON

Atlanta   Dallas   Geneva, Ill.   Hopewell, N.J.   Palo Alto   London

Library of Congress Catalog Card Number: 75-25239

ISBN: 0-395-20633-2

To Marjorie
R. H. J.

To Susan and my parents
P. R. W.

Contents

6/Dynamic Programming and Decision Diagrams   107

7/Network Concepts and Techniques   129

8/Game Theory   159

9/Inventory Concepts   179

Preface

One of the difficulties facing many college students has been the task of mastering quantitative analysis. Many students insist that they just can't deal with anything that even looks like higher mathematics, and some find they have a real dislike for quantitative analysis. Other students demonstrate an interest and ability to handle the material from the start. The predicament might be solved if we could just omit quantitative material from the study plans of those who thought they didn't like it, and offer it to those who had a self-professed ability in the area.

Realistically, quantitative analysis provides such an important set of tools for students of business and other disciplines that it just cannot be omitted. There are two types of benefits the student derives from the study of the quantitative techniques included in this text. The first pertains to *content*: the student learns a body of material, some of which is directly applicable to situations in business and government. The second, and perhaps the more important, benefit involves the *processes* of quantitative analysis. Through the study of the material in this text, the student will become more proficient in solving problems. Because of the way the material is presented, the student should learn to think more analytically. This will be one of the valuable carry-overs into later college courses and career experiences.

To help motivate the student, and to help him or her become a better problem solver, we have attempted to do two things not done in similar texts. First, whenever possible we have avoided proofs, theorems, abstract notation, and much of the technical jargon common to other approaches. Since in some cases it is impossible to present the material without notation, the book is not devoid of formulas. However, we have attempted to avoid the "symbol shock" often caused by this type of book.

Second, we have tried to make extensive use of examples, diagrams, and illustrations drawn from business contexts to assist the student in understanding problem formulation, step-by-step solution, and interpretation. Except in the very few instances in which they are applicable, we have eliminated the trite card games, dice, urns, and coins. The simple reason for their elimination is that they are difficult to relate to real business problems (except over the lunch hour, perhaps).

The text is oriented to an undergraduate or graduate course beyond basic algebra and statistics. In one instance in which calculus may be helpful, this material has been set off as a chapter appendix. Because business applications and examples are emphasized, only basic algebra and probability theory are necessary for comprehension. For those students who are weak in probability theory and matrix algebra, Chapters 2 and 3 provide a brief review of the material necessary for comprehension of later chapters. The text is organized in some places so that either matrix algebra or other approaches can be used, depending upon the preference of the instructor.

The proper approach to problem resolution includes learning how to identify problems, how to select useful techniques, how to solve the problems, and how to interpret the results. To help the student master these steps, we have included a number of business problems at the end of chapters. It is our hope that after the student has analyzed and solved these, he or she can extend the abilities acquired to other problem-solving and decision-making business situations.

In terms of physical structure, the book can be divided into modules to fit various situations.

1. A one-semester undergraduate introductory course could cover all of the material or, if the instructor wished to concentrate on some of the early material, Chapters 11, 12, 16, and 17 could be omitted.

2. A basic M.B.A. course might skip over the first four or five chapters, allowing the student to review the material if some brushing up was necessary.

3. A two-quarter undergraduate business or engineering sequence could take nine chapters per quarter.

4. A one-quarter course in programming methods could use Chapters 6, 7, 10 through 13, 16, and 17.

In this text the chapters covering dynamic programming (6), network concepts and techniques (7), game theory (8), inventory concepts (9), transportation (13), queuing (14), and Markov analysis (15) are fairly flexible and can be read in any sequence after Chapter 4.

In the writing of a text of this sort, there are a multitude of people who play a vital role. One author (P. R. W.) wishes to thank Donald G. Frederick, then at the University of Illinois, for motivating him to become a student of the area to start with, and for being so patient during his studies. Both authors wish to acknowledge the special contribution of Dr. Don Robinson at Illinois State University to the preparation and innovative presentation of the material in Chapters 10 through 13, as well as the preparation of the Instructor's Manual that accompanies this text. Dr. Edwin C. Hackleman of the University of Connecticut is acknowledged for his contribution of material in the business simulation area. Myron Cox of Wright State University, C. L. Hubbard of Georgia State University, and Nesa Wu of Eastern Michigan University provided invaluable review comments throughout the writing of the book and demonstrated exemplary professional competence and diligence. Their efforts have helped to improve the book and are greatly appreciated. We are also indebted to John Evans of the University of North Carolina, Wayne Meinhart of Oklahoma State University, Robert Pickhardt of the University of North Florida, and Andrew Thacker of the University of Houston for their most helpful reviews in the difficult early stages of the text.

Thanks also go to Mrs. Mary Lou Travers for her sense of humor and exceptional accuracy demonstrated while typing the material. Graduate students John Beem, Terry Pemberton, Joe Provost, and Larry Wade provided very useful input, as did Terry Childers of State Farm Insurance. And, as is most often the case in an undertaking of this type, it is the motivation and patience of a spouse that makes the entire venture possible, so most profound thanks to Marjorie and Susan.

Ross H. Johnson
Paul R. Winn

Quantitative
Methods
for Management

1/The Scientific Method

THE SCIENTIFIC approach to the analysis and solution of managerial problems is the major point to be examined in this book. Essentially, this approach involves the systematic, controlled analysis of possible alternative courses of action and the selection of the alternative that best allows the firm to achieve its desired outcomes, or objectives. The use of the terms *systematic* and *controlled* distinguishes the scientific approach from more haphazard methods. These terms imply that the results of the analysis of alternatives can be treated with confidence, and more importantly, that the findings could be duplicated under the same conditions or constraints.

The scientific approach to the analysis and solution of managerial problems involves (1) collection of information, (2) specific definition of the problem, (3) selecting alternative courses of action, (4) testing the selected alternatives, (5) selecting the best alternative(s), and (6) implementation. Because the scientific method is so important in quantitative analysis, each of the six steps in this approach will be treated individually.

COLLECTION OF INFORMATION

Even prior to the specific definition of the problem, the decision maker must become concerned with the *topic* of the problem. This involves the collection of a body of information pertinent to the impending decision. For example, in a problem situation involving improper selection of salespeople's routes, a decision maker might talk to the salespeople involved, collect reports from the sales managers, and obtain information on the actual routes. There are two types of information the decision maker might collect. The first is *primary* information, which refers to new material that has not been collected and recorded before. The second is *secondary* information that is currently on file, in books or in other sources, and needs merely to be compiled. Most of the information to be collected at this stage falls into the "secondary" category.

SPECIFIC DEFINITION OF THE PROBLEM

If, after preliminary investigation, the decision maker concludes there is a problem, he or she should prepare for specific definition of the elements in the problem and an exact statement of what the problem is.

When correctly defined, a problem takes the form of a question involving the relationships between two or more variables. For example, a problem might be: Do sales-routing plans lead to increased sales? Another problem might be: Does inventory-control system A lead to lower costs for our firm than inventory-control system B? Although problems can be much more complicated than these, they all should meet at least two criteria. First, they should be clearly stated, and second, they should allow for alternative courses of action. It is the allowance for alternative courses of action that makes this step in the scientific method the most important, because it implies the solution or solutions. We should note that although the steps appear to progress sequentially, they are actually very interdependent. Because of this interdependence, the whole decision-making framework must be examined prior to analysis of specifics.

Failure to execute the problem-definition step properly early in the problem-resolution process represents one of the most serious pitfalls in scientific decision making. A situation may be incorrectly regarded as a problem when it is actually only a symptom of a problem. Many firms treat declining sales as a problem when the true problem may be, for example, an ineffective employee-compensation program. Even worse, many decisions are made without *ever* correctly stating the problem, a fact which attests to the difficulty of proper definition.

SELECTING ALTERNATIVE COURSES OF ACTION

A search for and selection of potential solutions to the problem constitutes the next stage in the decision-making process. For example, in order to solve the sales-routing problem, two alternative courses of action could be specified. One could be selection of a group of sales territories in which operations would continue under the current sales-routing plan. In a second group of territories, fairly well matched to the first, salespeople could be allowed to make calls wherever their judgment dictated, with no prespecified routing plan. These alternative approaches could then be tested for effectiveness.

Quite often there are multiple courses of action that can be employed to solve the problem. Although the manager may have a single solution that appears to be best, the scientific approach calls for testing this approach against other reasonable alternatives. If the list of alternatives does not include the best solution, the selected solution cannot be optimum. An optimum decision can mean many things, but, in general, it should be the one that, when compared to the goals of the firm, will be most beneficial.

TESTING THE SELECTED ALTERNATIVES

Before starting discussion of the next step in decision making, it is necessary to comprehend how the word *test* is used. *Test* does not necessarily imply that quantitative analysis must be performed to solve a problem. Many management decisions are made using rules of logic and verbal information only. The major part of this book will be devoted to the quantitative approach to testing alternatives, but this in no way implies that this is the only way to proceed in the problem-resolution process.

In the usual case, the decision maker is faced with having to collect information regarding the potential effectiveness of various alternatives. There are a number of ways to collect this information.

Experimentation

Experimentation is defined as the controlled manipulation of one or a set of independent variables and the measurement of their impact on a dependent variable. In the sales-routing example, the manager would be manipulating routing strategies (independent variable) and measuring the impact on sales (dependent variable).

There are, in general, two types of experimental approaches. One is the *laboratory experiment*, which involves isolating the decision situation from its real-world setting and manipulating one or more independent variables under tightly controlled conditions. Another is the *field experiment*, which is conducted in a realistic setting with the independent variables manipulated under conditions that are as tightly controlled as possible.

The laboratory experiment suffers from a lack of realism but benefits from the manager's ability to control such potential influences on the dependent variable as changes in attitude, selection of a preferred product, and so forth. The field experiment, because it is set in a realistic situation, is often affected by external influences. For example, a field experiment involving sales routes may suffer from changes in the competition in one of the groups of territories. If this were not specified as an independent variable, accurate evaluation of changes in sales could be difficult.

Often, because of the complexity or setting of the problem, experimentation may be cumbersome or even impossible. As a result, the decision maker must rely on other methods of testing alternatives.

Types of Models

A model can be defined as an abstract generalization of real-world phenomena. It involves specifying the relationships within a set of variables in order to explain or describe some system or process. Although there has perhaps been an overextensive attempt to classify models, three generally accepted classes are *physical*, *analogue*, and *symbolic* models.

Physical Models A physical model is an actual physical representation of some object or situation. A road map is a good everyday example, as are model cars, blueprints, and photographs.

Analogue Models Analogue models do not physically depict phenomena. They are more abstract in nature, representing one element by use of a different element. An organization chart is an analogue model, as is a demand curve. Although analogue models do not physically replicate the real world, they may behave as the real-world system does.

Symbolic Models Symbolic models may take two forms: *verbal* and *mathematical*. Verbal models involve a collection of statements describing a situation or pertaining to the thought processes of managers. They allow managers to use words to specify the relationships between concepts before making a decision.

Mathematical models also involve the specification of the relationships within a set of variables, but differ from other models in their use of mathematical symbols. Because of this use of mathematical language, they lend themselves to manipulation more readily than other types of models. It is this manipulation that allows the decision maker to test alternative solutions to a problem.

Since this book will concentrate on mathematical models, further discussion of the types of mathematical models should prove useful. We should first note, however, that there are two broad classes of mathematical models: *deterministic* and *stochastic*. Deterministic models are those in which uncertainty plays no part. Transportation models, break-even models, and linear programming models are usually deterministic. On the other hand, Bayesian decision models, queuing models, and dynamic programming models, all of which involve uncertainty, fall into the category of stochastic models.

Mathematical Models

Queuing Models Queuing models are used for input-output sequence problems. A person or entity is ready to be served, and the problem revolves around the waiting time for this service. Classic examples of this are waiting lines at grocery stores and hold patterns at airports, and other situations that involve the balancing of the opposing costs of providing the service and losing business.

Allocation Models Allocation models have been devised to aid in selecting the correct course of action when there is a set of resources which have to be allocated simultaneously but which can be divided into a multitude of different levels. The model aids in allocating the resources in such a manner that the objective is achieved. Linear programming, dynamic programming, and integer programming models deal with allocation problems.

Inventory-Control Models Inventory-control models involve the balancing of the supply of a product (or service) with demand for that product. The basic objective of the inventory model is to match the inventory level to the demand in such a way that the combination of the cost of handling stock and the cost of being out of stock will be minimized. In passing, we should note that the whole area of inventory management serves as fertile ground for increased profits for business; however, it is often treated as an unproductive area of analysis.

Sequence and Routing Models Sequence models are more pervasive than those discussed so far. They are used when the manager is seeking a sequential course of action that best meets the stated objectives. Examples of sequence models are critical path, which may well be treated stochastically, sales routing, and job scheduling. Although these models may be verbal models in some cases, recent additions to modeling literature have introduced sequence models that involve uncertainty and other mathematical concepts.

Simulation Models Simulation models deal with abstractions of real-world decision settings. One of the more popular applications is business games. There are simulations of marketing processes, production systems, and financial decision situations, as well as many others. In these games the objective is to depict real-world processes as well as possible, including periodic human intervention for the purpose of making decisions. These games are often less precise than the other quantitative techniques. However, simulation is often necessary because of the complexity of the decision framework. For example, decisions may be necessary regarding expenditures on research, advertising, and inventory, as well as regarding production levels and the hiring of new employees. The outcomes of simulation are often more easily generalized than those of analytical models. In addition, simulation, because it attempts to depict business situations, can be used for executive development and employee training.

A major limitation of simulation is that, as the decision situation becomes more complex, it is more difficult to simulate all interactions accurately. As a result, simulations may become unwieldy and inaccurate as they are extended to more complicated decisions.

Game Models In game models, strategies are evaluated by comparing their potential outcomes with the possible actions of competitors. Game models are less realistic than simulation models and are usually more limited in scope. For example, a simulation may take into account each competitor in the industry, while a game model may account for only two firms or two people. Despite these limitations, some of the processes involved in game models provide valuable experience in learning to deal with aggressive competitors.

The types of models discussed so far make up a major portion of this book. Additional decision models such as Bayesian decision theory and Markov models are discussed. All of these models serve as aids to the decision maker in solving a problem or a set of problems.

SELECTING THE BEST ALTERNATIVE(S)

After proper definition of the problem and proper testing of alternative solutions through experimentation, logic, or some form of model, the decision maker should be able to select the alternative that best allows the firm to obtain its objectives (such as sales, profits, growth, or market share). Although the process appears to be simple, it may not be, for complex problems. The simplest situation involves the testing of only one alternative, and the answer is yes or no. In the case of complex decisions, such as many allocation decisions, there may be several alternatives that are nearly equal. Then the decision maker must use good, sound judgment to match these alternatives to the objectives of the firm.

IMPLEMENTATION

It might seem that selection of a course of action would be the final step in the problem-resolution process. But this assumption has led to many non-implemented decisions. Once the action is selected, it must be actually carried out before the problem can be resolved. The effective business manager will then verify that the decision has been correctly implemented and that it is, in fact, the best alternative.

A WORD OF CAUTION

Before proceeding to the next chapter, the student should be warned about two of the pitfalls of quantitative analysis. First, definition of the problem often lies outside the domain of the person employing a quantitative technique to help solve the problem. However, the success of the quantitative analysis depends on correct definition at the outset. Second, no amount of quantitative analysis, model building, simulation, or use of any other technique will substitute for sound business judgment. These techniques are used solely as aids in making decisions. Their misuse can often lead to an erroneous decision.

In the end, it is the decision maker, not the technique, that makes the decision. The student should learn how to recognize the conditions under which quantitative techniques can be correctly used.

STUDY SUGGESTIONS

1. Try to define the following terms in such a manner that a subordinate who works in your firm would know exactly what you mean.

   (a) Demand
   (b) Share of market
   (c) Risk
   (d) Control
   (e) Subjective

2. Now that you have defined each term, exchange papers with a classmate who has defined them also (without consultation). Examining his or her answers, can you see how uncertainty in definitions can lead to complications in solving problems?

3. Write down a message pertaining to any topic. (The message should contain three or four different events.) Pass this to a classmate who will verbally pass the message to someone else, who in turn will pass it on. After about six or seven people have passed on the message, stop the process and have the message stated by the person who just received it.

   (a) What implications does the distortion of the message have for management decision making?
   (b) As a message or task becomes more complex, how adequate do you feel verbal communications will be?

SUPPLEMENTARY READINGS

Braithwaite, R. *Scientific Explanation.* Cambridge University Press, Cambridge, U.K., 1955.
Cohen, M. *A Preface to Logic.* Meridian, New York, 1957.
Dewey, J. *Logic: The Theory of Inquiry.* Holt, Rinehart and Winston, New York, 1938.
Fisher, R. *The Design of Experiments*, 6th ed. Hafner, New York, 1951.
Kemeny, J. *A Philosopher Looks at Science.* Van Nostrand Reinhold, New York, 1959.

2/Probability

PROBABILITY concepts have many exciting and useful applications in business management. In the constantly changing areas of marketing, finance, and production, decisions often have to be made under conditions of uncertainty or risk. Wrong decisions can have unfortunate impacts upon firms as well as upon participants in the decisions.

In many decision situations, it is possible to specify the probabilities of particular occurrences and outcomes. The decision maker can then use these probabilities in conjunction with estimates of profits and costs as an aid to scientific problem resolution.

The objective of this chapter is to provide an introduction to probability that will serve as a basis for concepts treated in later chapters. Probability is usually covered in a basic statistics course, and more extended treatments of probability can be found in the supplementary readings at the end of this chapter.

PROBABILITY CONCEPTS

Definitions

Before we discuss different types of probabilities and how they can be used, definitions of some commonly used terms will be helpful.

Set Any collection of objects or symbols can be considered a set. For example, if the possible outcomes in a vote for mayor of a town were

Decker (X), Childers (Y), and Lutz (Z), we could describe the set of possible outcomes as

$$\{\text{Decker, Childers, Lutz}\},$$

or using symbols,

$$\{X, Y, Z\}.$$

In some instances this set of all possible outcomes is called the *sample space*.

Event   In the voting example, an event is any individual element in the set. For instance, the election of Decker is an event. Statistically, this type of event would be called a *simple event*. Using the language of sets, each event could be called a *subset* of the entire space. There are also *complex events*, which are made up of more than one simple event. An example is drawing a red king from a deck of cards.

Population   If we were interested in finding out the attitudes of students toward beer drinking in the student union at a university with 10,000 students, this entire group of 10,000 would be viewed as a population. If we had the time, money, and facilities we could question each student, the result being a census of the student body. The population, then, is the entire group of interest in any study. The reader should be careful to note that *population* does not necessarily refer to people; a population can consist of any group of entities, such as elephants, ball bearings, or cars.

Sample   Recognizing that it is often too time consuming, too costly, or flatly impossible to take a census (or measure) of the entire population, we may take a sample. A sample can be viewed as a subset of the population. For example, we may wish to select 500 of the students, obtain their views about beer in the union, and then make statements (inferences) about what the entire population thinks, based upon the results from this sample of 500.

Random Sample   Making statements about the entire student body from a sample of 500 students may appear to be dangerous. To minimize the danger of making a mistake, it is common practice in scientific studies to select random samples. When large enough, random samples generally insure an accurate representation of the population. The simplest random sample is one in which each member of the population, each student in this case, has an equal chance (probability) of being selected in the sample. This kind of sample is called an *unrestricted* random sample.

In more complicated sample designs, a manager may wish to sample a little more heavily from one group than from another, or may want to concentrate interviews in a certain geographic area. This type of sample is a *restricted* random sample. For example, in the student sample we may wish to include more juniors and seniors than freshmen and sophomores.

In any type of scientific random sample it is very important that we *know* what the chances are of selecting any member for the sample, so that we can weigh the results and arrive at an accurate representation of the population.

Continuous Versus Discrete Data Data can take on many forms, and often we have to treat different types in different ways. *Continuous* data can have any values over a range of values. Examples are the weights of eighth-grade students, the distances college students live from the union, or—to use other examples—the diameters of ball bearings, and the speeds of race cars.

Discrete data are those that can take on only certain distinct values, with no intermediate possibilities. For example, the answers yes and no to the question of beer in the union can be coded as 1 and 0. There are no intermediate values such as .50 or .77. Items that can be classified into two or more discrete groups are often called *attributes*, such as yes-no, male-female, or high-medium-low.

Relative Frequency
A probability is represented by a number between zero and one, inclusive. It expresses the chance that an event will occur. An event that is unlikely to happen will have a probability close to zero. As the event becomes more likely, the probability will move closer to one. A probability of zero means that an event cannot occur; when the probability is one, on the other hand, the event is certain to occur.

If a probability P is defined as the relative frequency of success, based on data collected from past experiments, it can be written as:

$$P(N) = \frac{\text{Number of successes}}{\text{Total number of trials}},$$

where $P(N)$ is the notation for the probability that N will happen. For example, past data can be evaluated to estimate the probability that an order for a product can be filled from stock.

$$P(\text{Filling order from stock}) = \frac{\text{Number of orders filled from stock}}{\text{Total number of orders processed}}.$$

If a firm had 1,000 total orders over the last year and 750 of these were filled from stock, the probability of filling an order from stock would be:

$$P = \frac{750}{1,000} \quad \text{or} \quad .75.$$

In addition to this fundamental definition of probability, there are two other methods of defining or calculating probability.

Probability Distributions

Often the probability of an event's occurrence is known or can be determined without experiment, because the process is already well known. Dice, cards, or coins are familiar examples. We can accurately estimate the probability of drawing an ace from a complete deck of cards without resorting to experimental trials: $P(\text{Ace}) = 4/52 = 1/13$. Even in more complicated situations, there are special probability distributions, such as the binomial distribution or the Poisson distribution, that can be utilized without recourse to an experiment. For example, the probabilities of obtaining yes-no responses to a public poll are treated much differently than the probabilities of obtaining a certain diameter of ball bearing from a production line. The proper use of the special distributions requires the matching of the decision situation and the characteristics of the numbers to the assumptions of the distributions. These distributions and assumptions will be discussed later.

Subjective Estimates

A subjective probability is a decision maker's estimate of the likelihood of an event's occurrence. There are many situations in which one cannot determine a relative frequency or use a probability distribution. When a new product is being introduced, the decision maker may wish to know the probability of the competition's reacting in a certain way. Because this behavior is in the future, information for relative frequency estimates is lacking, and because of the uniqueness of the situation, a standard probability distribution would not apply.

The decision maker must estimate the probability of each competitive action. It should not be inferred that this estimate is a wild guess, since it could be based upon sound judgment, collection of information, or past experience. The decision maker usually has been involved previously in calculating the chances of competition's reacting in a certain way. The combination of this prior experience with information pertaining to the current decision can often yield a sound estimate of the probabilities of competitive actions. Once a probability has been estimated, even though it has less of a scientific basis, the value can be used much like more objective probability estimates.

THREE TYPES OF PROBABILITY

Consider a random sample of 100 people who have been polled concerning their reading of our magazine last month. The breakdown of the collected data is given in Table 2-1. These data will be utilized in illustrating three different types of probability: *marginal, joint,* and *conditional.*

Marginal Probability

In the random sample, the marginal or simple (the terms will be used synonomously here) probability of selecting a reader can be written as:

$$P(R) = \frac{51}{100} = .51.$$

The term *marginal probability* is used because this value is located in the margin of a probability table. The $P(NR)$ is 49/100 or .49. A marginal probability gives information only about the basic category, in this case reader or nonreader, without regard to other categories.

Joint Probability

A joint probability represents the chance that a respondent (or entity) has two or more characteristics. In this case, the probability of selecting a woman who is also a reader, a joint probability, can be found in the body of Table 2-1.

$$P(W \cap R) = \frac{41}{100} = .41,$$

when we use the symbol $\cap$ to represent "and." Similarly, the probability of drawing a male nonreader, $P(M \cap NR)$, is 30/100 or .30. The joint probabilities are found within the body of the table, while the marginal probabilities are found by summing these joint probabilities. A joint probability refers to two or more characteristics, while a marginal probability refers to the total for one characteristic only.

Table 2-1 Reading behavior of 100 men and women

	Men (M)	Women (W)	
Readers (R)	10	41	51
Nonreaders (NR)	30	19	49
	40	60	100

Conditional Probability

If we wish to know the probability that a person is a reader, given that the person is a woman, this is a conditional probability. The probability of selecting a reader is conditioned upon the premise that the selection is being made from the women.

The conditional probability of R given W can be expressed as $P(R|W)$ and is equal to

$$\frac{\text{Joint probability of } R \text{ and } W}{\text{Marginal probability of } W} \quad \text{or} \quad \frac{P(R \cap W)}{P(W)}.$$

With the data from Table 2-1,

$$P(R|W) = \frac{.41}{.60} = .68.$$

Using this same method, we can calculate the probability of selecting a nonreader, given that he is a man:

$$P(NR|M) = \frac{P(NR \cap M)}{P(M)} = \frac{.30}{.40} = .75.$$

To calculate $P(M|NR)$, the probability of selecting a man, given that he is a nonreader, we can write

$$P(M|NR) = \frac{P(M \cap NR)}{P(NR)} = \frac{.30}{.49} = .61.$$

Note that $P(NR|M) \neq P(M|NR)$.

SETS OF EVENTS

Collectively Exhaustive Events

If a set of events contains all possible outcomes or occurrences, it is collectively exhaustive. The set of events {man, woman, reader, nonreader} is collectively exhaustive. Similarly, in an experiment involving the colors of cards, the only possible outcomes are red and black. If a die is cast, the collectively exhaustive set of events is $\{1, 2, 3, 4, 5, 6\}$.

Mutually Exclusive Events

Events are mutually exclusive if the occurrence of one precludes the occurrence of the other. In other words, if one event occurs the other event cannot occur. If only one item is to be selected, the selection of a red card precludes the selection of a black card on the same trial. In this case, the events are mutually exclusive. In the previous example, the selection of a woman did *not* preclude the selection of a reader. These events were not mutually exclusive and could occur together; however, selection of a woman did preclude selection of a man, and selection of a reader precluded a nonreader, so these pairs of occurrences are mutually exclusive.

Addition Rules

For events that are mutually exclusive, the probability of one *or* the other event's occurring is found by summing the probabilities of the events' occurring individually:

$$P(A \text{ or } B) = P(A) + P(B).$$

If a coin is tossed,

$$P(\text{Head or tail}) = P(\text{Head}) + P(\text{Tail}).$$

From this addition rule, it can be noted that the sum of the probabilities for the set of all mutually exclusive and collectively exhaustive events equals one.

If the two events are not mutually exclusive, there will be an overlap between them, since both could occur at the same time. In Figure 2-1, besides the independent occurrences of *A* and *B*, there is also simultaneous

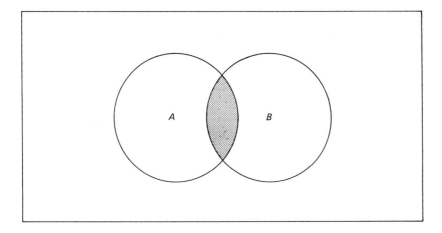

Figure 2-1 Venn diagram of nonmutually exclusive events

occurrence of A and B, which would not be the case for mutually exclusive events. This leads to the addition rule for nonmutually exclusive events.

The probability of one or the other event's occurring is found by summing the probabilities of the events' occurring individually and subtracting the probability of their joint occurrence.

$$P(A \text{ or } B) = P(A) + P(B) - P(A \cap B).$$

In the example shown in Table 2-1, the probability of a man or a reader is

$$P(M) + P(R) - P(M \cap R) = .40 + .51 - .10 = .81.$$

Again referring to Figure 2-1, we can see that when we include the probability of A, or $P(A)$, moving from left to right in the figure, we have included the overlap area, and when we include $P(B)$, moving from right to left in the figure, we have added in the overlap area once again. Therefore, we have to subtract the overlap to avoid double counting. The overlap in the magazine-reading example is $P(M \cap R)$.

Multiplication Rules

For dependent events, meaning when the $P(A|B) \neq P(A)$, conditional probabilities are often used to derive joint probabilities. From the section on conditional probabilities, we know that

$$P(A|B) = \frac{P(A \cap B)}{P(B)}.$$

Solving for $P(A \cap B)$, we find that

$$P(A \cap B) = P(A|B) \times P(B).$$

In the example of Table 2-1,

$$P(NR) = .49 \quad \text{and} \quad P(M|NR) = .61.$$

Therefore,

$$P(M \cap NR) = P(M|NR) \times P(NR) = .61 \times .49 = .30.$$

Solving for $P(NR \cap M)$ in the same way, we calculate that

$$P(NR \cap M) = P(NR|M) \times P(M) = .75 \times .40 = .30.$$

To determine the joint probability, a conditional probability is multiplied by a marginal probability. The marginal probability used will correspond to the given information in the conditional probability. Thus, the probability of a nonreader given male is multiplied by the probability of a male.

Table 2-2 Summary of probability formulas

Independent events

$P(A \text{ or } B) = P(A) + P(B)$
$P(A \cap B) = P(A) \times P(B)$

Dependent events

$P(A \text{ or } B) = P(A) + P(B) - P(A \cap B)$
$P(A \cap B) = P(A|B) \times P(B)$
$\qquad\qquad = P(B|A) \times P(A)$
$P(A|B) = \dfrac{P(A \cap B)}{P(B)}$

The same result comes from the probability of a male given nonreader multiplied by the probability of a nonreader: $P(M|NR) \times P(NR)$. Knowledge of this procedure for determining the joint probability is important in later applications.

When we are dealing with independent events, $P(A|B) = P(A)$. Therefore, when events are independent,

$$P(A \cap B) = P(A) \times P(B).$$

As an example, the probability of tossing a tail in a valid coin flip is independent of the results of prior tosses. Because a coin has no memory or conscience (although the flipper does), the probability of getting three tails in a row would be $1/2 \times 1/2 \times 1/2 = 1/8$, and so on.

A summary of the various formulas used to this point can be found in Table 2-2. When we work probability problems, it is usually very helpful to set them up using a table similar to Table 2-2. Once we have inserted all the known information into appropriate positions in the table, later computations become easier.

PROBABILITY TREES

Probability trees, which can be used to portray many problems, can help a person follow the logic of a problem. For example, for three flips of a fair coin, the potential outcomes and their probabilities can be represented in graphic form with a probability tree as in Figure 2-2.

Figure 2-2 represents a rather straightforward problem. Because the events are independent, the probability of a head or a tail remains constant. As the number of trials increases, the tree becomes more and more cumbersome, but in many situations the use of a tree simplifies a problem and

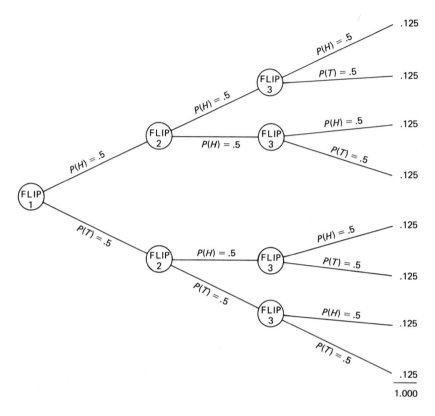

Figure 2-2 Probability tree for fair coin flip experiment

helps to show the type of probability—marginal, joint, or conditional—with which we are dealing. A practical business problem can be analyzed using similar techniques, as in the following example.

Imagine that our firm, the Proctor Company, is considering the development of a new deodorant, Wisp. We currently have 30 percent of the deodorant market, and our major competitor has 70 percent. Given certain technical breakthroughs in the chemical formulation of the product, our laboratory researchers estimate that they are 80 percent sure of developing this new deodorant. If the new product breakthrough is made, Wisp will be used as a new entrant in the market, which consists of our current offerings as well as our competitor's.

In our decision on whether or not to market Wisp, we need to be very careful to make estimates of how our competitor, Meyer Brothers, will react. We estimate that there is a .60 chance that Meyer Brothers will introduce a new product to counteract a new Proctor product. If this happens, there is a .30 chance that Proctor will have a 70 percent market share, a .40 chance that Proctor will have a 50 percent market share, and a .30 chance that Proctor will have a 40 percent market share. The marketing research department also estimates that if Meyer Brothers is unable to react with a new product, Proctor will have a .80 chance of obtaining an 80 percent market share, a .10 chance of obtaining a 50 percent market share, and a .10 chance of obtaining a 40 percent market share. In the event that we decide not to market Wisp, Proctor will maintain its current 30 percent market share.

As a marketing manager you are interested in the chances that Proctor will gain at least a 50 percent market share. This problem can best be depicted on a probability tree. From Figure 2-3 we can see the procedure for solving this problem. The As in the figure are alternative courses of action by Proctor, the Zs are competitive reactions by Meyer Brothers, and the Ss are states of nature or market reactions. In this special case, the As are not strictly controllable alternatives, because marketing is dependent upon the success of the development. In most cases, these As would be treated as controlled decision variables. To find the chance of gaining at least a 50 percent market share, we are interested in each combination of events that leads to a 50 percent or greater market share. States of nature S_1 and S_2 qualify. Therefore combinations $A_1 \cap Z_1 \cap S_1$, $A_1 \cap Z_1 \cap S_2$, $A_1 \cap Z_2 \cap S_1$, and $A_1 \cap Z_2 \cap S_2$ should be included. The solution—in other words, the probability of any one of these four combinations—is:

$$P = .144 + .192 + .256 + .032 = .624.$$

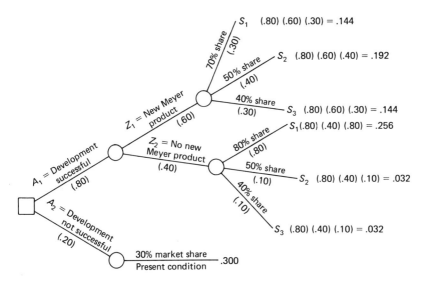

Figure 2-3 Probability tree for Wisp introduction

Probability trees are very useful in management decision making. They graphically portray a situation that, because of the interaction of events, may be quite complex. In addition to simplifying the problem, trees can often make a decision process more scientific by forcing concise specification of alternative courses of action as well as of potential outcomes for each decision. Although probability trees can become somewhat cumbersome as the number of alternatives and potential outcomes increases, this limitation can be overcome by graph theory, which will be discussed in Chapter 7.

THE BINOMIAL DISTRIBUTION

Consider families that have three children. Assuming that the occurrences of male or female children are independent, equally likely events, we could represent the probability distribution of the various numbers of females as in Table 2-3.

Table 2-3 expresses the relationship between the variable R and the probabilities of each value of R. The column labeled R in this case can be called a *sample space*, since it represents all possible situations or outcomes. Although the families always consist of exactly three children, there are four (or $n+1$) events in this sample space. The possibility of *zero* females represents the fourth possibility. Because we are dealing with independent events, the occurrence of a female or a male child can be considered a *random variable*, which is a variable free to take on any value. In this case the variable is random because we cannot predetermine which event will take place on any trial. Using our previous definitions, the probabilities listed are mutually exclusive, collectively exhaustive, and are all between zero and one, inclusive. The sum of all probabilities is also one.

Table 2-3 Probabilities of numbers of females in a family with three children

Number of females, R	Probability, P (R)
0	1/8 = .125
1	3/8 = .375
2	3/8 = .375
3	1/8 = .125
	1.0

Using the Binomial Distribution to Calculate Probabilities

When we are dealing with independent events having stable probabilities, and when there are only two possible outcomes of a trial, we can use the binomial distribution to calculate the probabilities for samples of a given size. In the family example, we were calculating the probabilities of outcomes of 0, 1, 2, and 3 females from a sample of three persons (children). In the entire population, the probability of a female birth is assumed to be stable at .5.

Consider the example of a neighborhood poll, in which 60 percent of the people are in favor of a leash law for dogs and 40 percent are against it. Assuming that the responses are independent, we can evaluate the probabilities of various outcomes of a sample using the binomial distribution. In a sample of four people, the probability of four yes answers (people in favor of the leash law) is calculated as follows:

$$P(4 \text{ yes}) = .6 \times .6 \times .6 \times .6 = .1296.$$

The probability of four no answers can be found in the same manner:

$$P(4 \text{ no}) = .4 \times .4 \times .4 \times .4 = .0256.$$

For other combinations of yes-no answers, it is necessary to perform additional calculations, because there is a variety of possible combinations of yesses and noes. In the present illustration, there are sixteen possible outcomes.

YYYY	NNNN	NNYY	YNYN	YNNY
YYYN	NNNY	YYNN	NYNY	NYYN
YYNY	NNYN			
YNYY	NYNN			
NYYY	YNNN			

In order to count possible combinations, we could make up a list like this each time we encountered a binomial situation. But as a short cut we could use a mathematical method.

The following formula can be used to calculate the number of combinations of successes (or yes answers in this case) in n trials.

$$_nC_r = \frac{n!}{r!(n-r)!}$$

where $n!$ (n factorial) is $4 \times 3 \times 2 \times 1$, r stands for the number of successes, and C is the number of combinations. The number of combinations of three yes answers in four trials is found as follows:

$$C = \frac{4 \times 3 \times 2 \times 1}{3 \times 2 \times 1(4-3)!} = \frac{4 \times 3 \times 2 \times 1}{3 \times 2 \times 1 \times 1} = 4.$$

We can verify this answer by counting the number of outcomes having three Ys in our list of combinations. When dealing with factorials, remember that, by definition, $0! = 1$, so when $n - r = 0$ calculations of the factor are still possible.

Letting p stand for the probability of a yes answer and $1 - p$, or q, for the probability of a no answer, then the probability of three yesses in four trials is equal to $_nC_r p^r q^{(n-r)}$, or:

$$_4C_3(.6)^3(.4)^1 = 4(.6)^3(.4) = .3456.$$

As a substitute for this procedure, the *binomial expansion* can be used by listing all possible outcomes and combinations of outcomes in an experiment. For our example, the binomial expansion is:

$$_4C_4 p^4 q^{(4-4)} + {}_4C_3 p^3 q^{(4-3)} + {}_4C_2 p^2 q^{(4-2)} + {}_4C_1 p^1 q^{(4-1)} + {}_4C_0 p^0 q^{(4-0)}$$

Combining terms, we obtain

$$p^4 + {}_4C_3 p^3 q + {}_4C_2 p^2 q^2 + {}_4C_1 pq^3 + q^4.$$

As a rule, the formula $\frac{n!}{r!(n-r)!}$ can be used to calculate each individual combination of n events taken r at a time.

In dealing with the binomial probability model, the following general statements apply, allowing a short cut for establishing the terms in the expansion.

1. There are always $n+1$ points in the binomial expansion, since it corresponds to the sample space.
2. The exponents of p are $n, n-1, n-2, ..., 1, 0$.
3. The exponents of each term always sum to n.
4. The expansion is symmetrical, and the coefficients for terms in similar positions are equal. For example, the coefficient of the second term from the beginning is the same as that of the second term from the end. The coefficients ascend to the middle of the series and then descend.
5. The coefficient of each term can be obtained by the following steps.
   (a) Number each term in the expansion from 1 to $n+1$. In our example, there are five positions in the sample space:

$$\underset{1}{p^4} + \underset{2}{p^3 q} + \cdots + \underset{5}{q^4}.$$

(b) Multiply any term's coefficient by the exponent of p and divide by the number of the term to obtain the coefficient of the next term. To obtain the coefficient of the second term in our example, we would calculate that

$$\frac{1 \times 4}{1} = 4,$$

which completes the second term,

$$4p^3q.$$

The coefficient of the third term would then be:

$$\frac{3 \times 4}{2} = 6.$$

and the completed term would be:

$$6p^2q^2.$$

(c) Complete this operation for all terms in the expansion:

$$p^4 + 4p^3q + 6p^2q^2 + 4pq^3 + q^4 = (.6)^4 + 4(.6)^3(.4) + 6(.6)^2(.4)^2$$
$$+ 4(.6)(.4)^3 + (.4)^4.$$

From this completed binomial expansion, any probabilities or combination of probabilities from the polling can be calculated. There are two types of solutions generally sought to a binomial problem. The first is an *individual-term* probability. For example, what is the probability of two yes answers and two no answers? The third term in the expansion corresponds to this question.

$$P(2 \text{ yes}, 2 \text{ no}) = 6p^2q^2 = 6(.6)^2(.4)^2 = .3456.$$

Second, a *cumulative* probability may be needed. If the question were, "What is the probability of two or more yes answers?" we would be referring to the first three terms in the expansion, which represent four, three, and two yes answers, respectively. To solve this problem, we would add these terms:

$$P(2 \text{ or more yes}) = p^4 + 4p^3q + 6p^2q^2$$
$$= (.6)^4 + 4(.6)^3(.4) + 6(.6)^2(.4)^2$$
$$= .1296 + .3456 + .3456 = .8208.$$

Because the expansion is collectively exhaustive and the sum of all terms in the expansion equals 1.0, we could solve this problem by calculating and summing the last two terms—which represent the probability of less than two yes answers—and subtracting this sum from 1.0:

$$P(0 \text{ or } 1 \text{ yes}) = 4(.6)(.4)^3 + (.4)^4 = .1536 + .0256 = .1792,$$
$$P(2 \text{ or more yes}) = 1.0 - .1792 = .8208.$$

Assumptions of the Binomial Distribution

1. There are only two possible outcomes or attributes in the experiment, such as success or failure, yes or no. The probability of a success (yes) can be represented by p, and the probability of failure can be represented by $1-p$, or q. For example, when the probability of a yes answer (p) is .6, the probability of a no answer ($1-p$, or q) equals $1-.6$, or .4.

2. The trials and measurements are independent of one another. For instance, if we are dealing with the gender of children at birth, the sex of the first child has no influence on the sex of later children. If we are collecting opinions from four randomly selected people, the measurements are assumed to be independent.

3. The probability of a success or failure remains constant over the time period of the experiment. This means that opinions do not change because of changing conditions, the coin does not become bent, and the deck of cards does not become so worn that it causes differing results.

Using Tables of the Binomial Distribution

Using $_nC_r p^r q^{n-r}$ or the binomial expansion, the evaluations are almost impossible to perform by hand as the number of trials, n, becomes very large. In this situation we must resort to the binomial distribution tables shown in Appendices B and C. Appendix B lists the individual-term probabilities, and Appendix C lists the cumulative probabilities. The cumulative distribution refers to the probability of r or more successes for a given value of r, given the values for n and p.

EXAMPLE 1

In a small rural town it is known that 40 percent of the population favors retention of a law prohibiting drinking on Sunday. In a sample of ten people, what is the probability of six answers favoring retention? From Appendix B we find that

$$P(r = 6 \mid n = 10, p = .40) = .1115.$$

What is the probability of four or more answers favoring retention? This probability is found in the cumulative binomial probability table in Appendix C:

$$P(r \geq 4 \mid n = 10, p = .40) = .6177.$$

What is the probability of three or fewer yes answers? This cannot be found directly from the table; but from our previous experience with the binomial expansion, we know that the probability of three or fewer yes answers is the same as 1 minus the probability of four or more yes answers:

$$P(r \leq 3 \,|\, n = 10, p = .40) = 1 - P(r \geq 4 \,|\, n = 10, p = .40) = .3823.$$

EXAMPLE 2

In a complex process for making tractor tires, the probability of producing a correct part is .70, and the probability of producing a defective part is .30. We wish to determine the probability of selecting 8 correct tires in a sample of 12 tires drawn from a large batch. When working with situations such as this, it is important to ascertain that the assumptions of the binomial distribution apply.

First, there are only two possible outcomes: correct and defective. Second, to comply fully with the requirement that the trials be independent, each time we select a part we should note whether it is defective and then return it to the batch. If we are taking a small sample from a large batch of items, as in this case, failure to replace each part may not have much impact. But when the sample is more than 15 to 20 percent of the population, we should be very careful to sample with replacement; if we don't, each trial will have an influence on later trials. Third, the probability of selecting a correct part remains constant over the period of the experiment, because we are sampling from a fixed lot of parts. The assumptions appear to be reasonably met in this case.

Reading directly from Appendix B, we obtain the probability of 8 correct parts in the sample of 12:

$$P(r = 8 \,|\, n = 12, p = .70) = .2311.$$

The probability of 8 *or more* correct parts is found in Appendix C:

$$P(r \geq 8 \,|\, n = 12, p = .70) = .7237.$$

The probability of 3 or fewer successes, for example, could also be found:

$$1 - P(r \geq 4 \,|\, n = 12, p = .70) = 1 - .9983 = .0017.$$

Our examples of binomial distribution applications have been an opinion poll and a production operation; however, any problem that involves two outcomes and that meets the necessary assumptions may be solved as a binomial distribution—for instance, the number of people passing or failing a course, or watching or not watching a particular television program.

Often in practical decision situations samples are taken from large batches, such as in the tire example, and items are not replaced as the sampling proceeds. This method is called sampling without replacement. Theoretically, since it violates the assumptions of the binomial distribution, another distribution, called the hypergeometric distribution, should be used. But as a rough rule, if the sample is less than 20 percent of the population, the binomial is an adequate approximation of the hypergeometric.

THE POISSON DISTRIBUTION

When the value of p is very small and the sample size n is large, the binomial distribution can be approximated very closely by the Poisson distribution. The basic assumptions underlying the Poisson distribution are very much the same as those for the binomial distribution.

1. There are two possible outcomes to the experiment.
2. Each trial has the same probability of success as any other. In the case of the Poisson distribution, this probability is very small.
3. Each trial is independent of earlier and later trials.

Poisson Probability Calculations

For cases in which np is constant, the sample size n is large, and the value of p approaches zero, the probability of X successes in n trials is approximated by

$$P(X) = \frac{e^{-np}(np)^X}{X!} = \frac{e^{-m}m^X}{X!},$$

where $m = np$ and e, a constant that is the base of natural logarithms, is 2.71828.

As an example of the use of the Poisson distribution, suppose that a new brand of cigarette lighter is guaranteed to light 98 out of 100 times. In an experiment of 100 tries, we wish to know the probability of 0, 1, 2, and 3 failures to light. In this case, m is $100 \times .02$, or 2.00. From the formula or from Appendix D, which lists the individual-term Poisson probabilities, we find that

$$P(X = 0 \mid m = 2) = \frac{e^{-2}2^0}{0!} = .1353,$$

$$P(X = 1 \mid m = 2) = \frac{e^{-2}2^1}{1!} = .2707,$$

$$P(X = 2 \mid m = 2) = \frac{e^{-2}2^2}{2!} = .2707,$$

$$P(X = 3 \mid m = 2) = \frac{e^{-2}2^3}{3!} = .1804.$$

These figures represent probabilities of exactly X occurrences. What if we wanted to determine the probability of X or fewer occurrences? We could obtain the probability of 3 or fewer occurrences by summing the values we have just calculated:

$$P(X \leq 3 \mid m = 2) = .1353 + .2707 + .2707 + .1804 = .8571.$$

Appendix E contains the cumulative Poisson probabilities for X or more occurrences for various values of m. Using the individual and cumulative Poisson tables in Appendices D and E is very similar to using the binomial tables. For instance,

$$P(X = 2 \mid m = 3) = .2240,$$
$$P(X \geq 3 \mid m = 3) = .5768,$$
$$P(X < 3 \mid m = 3) = 1 - P(X \geq 3) = 1 - .5768 = .4232.$$

Applications of the Poisson Distribution

The Poisson distribution is widely used to estimate probabilities in queuing or waiting-line problems, such as check-outs at supermarkets, landings at airports, and arrivals at shipping ports. For example, a manager of a discount department store, knowing he can lose business if customers have to stand in long lines, may wish to estimate the probabilities of various line lengths in order to determine how many check-out lanes to have and how to staff them. The Poisson is also useful for problems involving defects in a manufactured product, the movement of goods or materials, machinery breakdowns, clerical errors, and inventory control.

Situations in which the Poisson distribution is applicable often deal with a rate or frequency. Examples are aircraft arrivals per hour, defects per square yard, and errors per page of a manuscript. The value of p must be very low and must remain constant. The trials also must be independent; if errors on a machine occurred successively and were causally related, the Poisson distribution would not apply.

THE NORMAL DISTRIBUTION

When n, the number of trials, increases, the binomial distribution can be well approximated by the normal distribution. The normal distribution, shown in Figure 2-4, has the following distinctive characteristics.

1. The equation for the normal curve is:

$$\frac{1}{\sigma\sqrt{2\pi}} e\left(-\frac{(X-\mu)^2}{2\sigma^2} \right),$$

where μ (the Greek letter mu) is the *mean*, σ (the Greek letter sigma) is the *standard deviation*, π (the ratio of the circumference of a circle to its diameter) equals 3.14159, and e equals 2.71828. The mean μ and standard deviation σ completely describe a normal distribution.

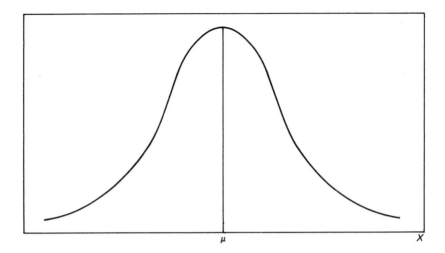

Figure 2-4 The normal curve

2. The normal curve involves data that are continuous, as previously described, unlike the binomial distribution, which involves discrete data.

3. The normal curve is bell-shaped and symmetric about the mean axis, labeled μ in Figure 2-4.

4. The area under the normal curve represents probability, and each half contains 50 percent of the possible outcomes. In other words, the entire area under the curve contains 100 percent of the possible outcomes; in terms of probability, the total area is 1.0.

5. The normal curve is asymptotic; that is, its tails gradually approach, but never reach, the base line.

Uses of the Normal Distribution

Values or data in many real situations tend to form normal distributions. Examples are test scores, diameters of ball bearings, heights of boys aged 12, and so on. In addition, the normal distribution is used to represent the distributions of sampling statistics, which are called sampling distributions. The arithmetic mean, for example, tends to be normally distributed as the sample size increases, and this is only minimally influenced by the shape of the population.

Standard Deviation Units

Appendix A contains a table of areas under the normal curve. Because the total area under the curve equals one, the area under a portion of the curve can be expressed as a fraction of one. The two measures that are typically used in dealing with this curve are the mean and the deviation of a point from the mean. The mean can be calculated from figures that have many differing units of measure, such as pounds, dollars, inches, miles, or points. In order to standardize these units of measure so that a single table can be used, standard deviation units (SDUs) are employed. In the first column of the table in Appendix A, the deviation $X - \mu$, indicating the distance of a point X from the mean μ, is divided by the standard deviation σ. The resulting value, Z, is called a *normal deviate* and can be written as:

$$Z = \frac{X - \mu}{\sigma}.$$

In Figure 2-5, since $\mu = 100$ and $X = 150$, $X - \mu = 50$. If $\sigma = 40$, then

$$Z = \frac{X - \mu}{\sigma} = \frac{50}{40} = 1.25.$$

Appendix A shows that the area under the normal curve corresponding to 1.25 SDUs is .3943. This means that .3943 of the area under the normal curve is between the center or mean and $+1.25$ SDUs. Note that although the table lists values only up to .4998, the normal curve is symmetric and, therefore, $+1.25$ will contain the same area as -1.25. As a result,

$$\mu \pm 1.25 \text{ SDU} = .7886.$$

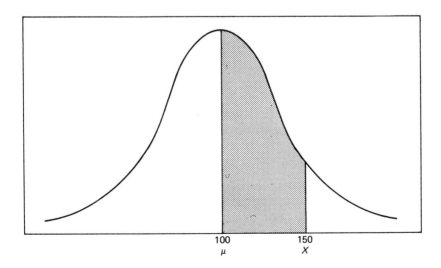

Figure 2-5 An area under the normal curve

EXAMPLE 1

A teacher has 100 test scores that are normally distributed, with a mean of 70 and a standard deviation of 8. How many test scores are between 70 and 82 (as illustrated in Figure 2-6)?

$$Z = \frac{82 - 70}{8} = \frac{12}{8} = 1.5.$$

From Appendix A we see that 1.5 SDUs = .4332, so .4332 × 100 or approximately 43 of the test scores fall between 70 and 82.

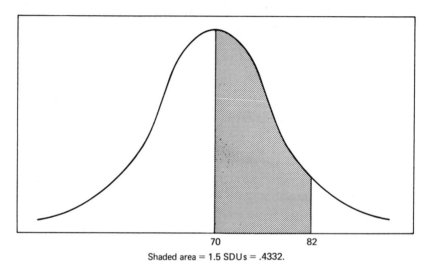

70   82

Shaded area = 1.5 SDUs = .4332.

Figure 2-6 Test scores for example 1

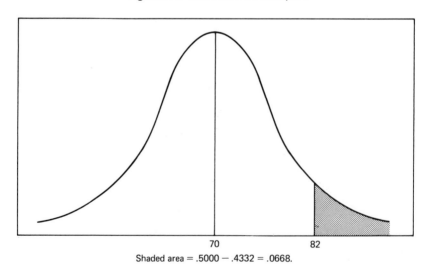

70   82

Shaded area = .5000 − .4332 = .0668.

Figure 2-7 Test scores for example 2

EXAMPLE 2

How many of the test scores in the previous example are above 82? Since the total area under one half of the normal curve is .5000, we know that the area beyond 82, as illustrated in Figure 2-7, is .5000 minus the portion of the area from 70 to 82.

$$.5000 - .4332 = .0668.$$

Then $.0668 \times 100$ or approximately 7 test scores are above 82.

EXAMPLE 3

We can make use of information from both sides of the curve to determine the number of tests between 65 and 78. Each side of the curve is dealt with separately, as illustrated in Figure 2-8.

$$\frac{78 - 70}{8} = +1.0 \text{ SDU} = .3413,$$

$$\frac{65 - 70}{8} = -.63 \text{ SDU} = .2357,$$

Area between 65 and 78 $= .3413 + .2357 = .5770.$

Each side of the curve was considered separately. Although we can add and subtract areas under the normal curve as shown in examples 2 and 3, we *cannot* add or subtract standard deviation units, since the area represented by an SDU differs depending upon where on the curve it is.

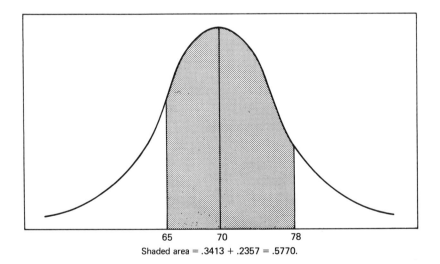

65   70   78
Shaded area $= .3413 + .2357 = .5770.$

Figure 2-8 Test scores for example 3

EXAMPLE 4

If we want to know what proportion of the scores falls between 75 and 80, we are looking for the area under the curve shown in Figure 2-9. To solve this problem, we can subtract areas under the normal curve. We determine the area between 70 and 80, and then subtract from that the area between 70 and 75; the remainder is the area between 75 and 80:

$$\frac{80-70}{8} = 1.25 \text{ SDU} = .3943,$$

$$\frac{75-70}{8} = .63 \text{ SDU} = .2357, \cdot$$

Area between 75 and 80 = .3943 − .2357 = .1586.

There are approximately 16 tests (100 × .1586) with scores between 75 and 80.

The uses of the normal distribution demonstrated in these examples apply in many real situations. All three of the distributions we have discussed—the normal, binomial, and Poisson—are very useful in business. To employ them effectively, the decision maker must know the assumptions of the distributions as well as the characteristics of the relevant data. Proper use requires a matching of these assumptions and characteristics with the decision situation.

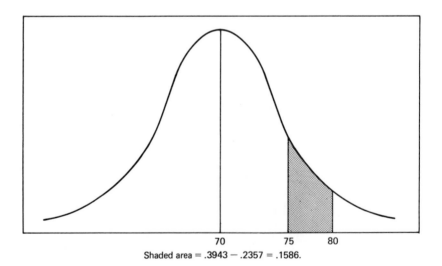

Shaded area = .3943 − .2357 = .1586.

Figure 2-9 Test scores for example 4

PROBLEMS

1. The characteristics of a sample of students at a midwestern university are as follows:

Males	100
Females	90
Male undergraduates	65
Male graduates	35
Female undergraduates	65
Female graduates	25

(a) Set up a frequency table to show the relationships.
(b) What are the marginal probabilities?
(c) What are the joint probabilities?
(d) What are the conditional probabilities?
(e) Are sex and type of student independent of one another?

2. The Marketing Corporation of America has established that 60 percent of the students at a large university own cars. Of the students who own cars, 10 percent own Volkswagens, 7 percent own Pintos, and 8 percent own Vegas. A random sample of ten students was taken.

(a) What is the probability that at least three students in the sample own Volkswagens?
(b) What is the probability that at least two students in the sample own a Volkswagen, a Pinto, or a Vega?
(c) What is the probability that the students in the sample own: (1) no Volkswagens? (2) no Pintos? (3) no Vegas? (4) no Pintos or Vegas? (5) no Pintos or Volkswagens? (6) no Vegas or Volkswagens?

3. Assume that 40 percent of the voters in a town of 80,000 people are in favor of establishing a junior college there. A sample survey is made with $n = 4$. The questionnaire asks, "Do you favor the establishment of a junior college in your town?" Yes or no answers are obtained.

(a) What probability model should be used to evaluate the possible outcomes of this experiment? What are these outcomes?
(b) Select any two of the possible outcomes and compute the probability of each of them—assuming random sampling.
(c) What is the probability of one or more yes answers under the conditions given?

4. The charge accounts at a certain department store have an average balance of $110 and a standard deviation of $40. If the account balances are normally distributed:

(a) what proportion of the accounts is over $150?

(b) what proportion of the accounts is between $100 and $150?

(c) what proportion of the accounts is between $60 and $90?

5. An auditor selects accounts for inspection at random from the file of accounts receivable. Accounts that are less than six months old are termed new accounts. The accounts are classified as follows.

	Current (C)	Delinquent (D)
New accounts (N)	108	12
Old accounts (O)	792	88

Let N denote the selection of a new account; O, the selection of an old account; C, the selection of an account that is current; and D, the selection of an account that is delinquent. Calculate the following probabilities.

(a) $P(N|C)$

(b) $P(D \cap O)$

(c) $P(N \text{ or } D)$

(d) $P(N|C \text{ or } D)$

6. A sales manager's records at a store specializing in selling used televisions indicate that 30 percent of the TV sales are of color sets; that 40 percent are of the larger (23-inch and over) tube sizes; and that of those who purchase sets with larger tubes, about 70 percent buy color sets. Indicate which of the following four statements are correct and support your answers.

If a purchase is selected at random:

(a) the probability is .60 that the set will have a smaller tube (less than 23 inches) and .70 that it will be black-and-white rather than a color set.

(b) the probability is .28 that the set will be a color model with a larger tube.

(c) the probability is .72 that the set will be a small-tube set, a black-and-white set, or a set with both of these characteristics.

(d) the probability is .93 that a person who selects a small-tube set will buy black-and-white instead of color.

7. A person who sells farm implements classifies tractor sales over a year according to the customers' methods of payment, listing the proportion of the total sales for each payment method.

	Method of payment	
Type of tractor	Cash	Credit
New	.04	.20
Used	.32	.44

(a) What is the simple probability of a new-tractor purchase if the salesperson selects a buyer at random?

(b) What is the conditional probability that a buyer of a used tractor will pay in cash?

(c) What is the joint probability of selling a used tractor on credit?

(d) Are the type of tractor and the method of payment statistically independent?

8. If 45 percent of the freshman class at a local university has portable electric typewriters and 25 percent has electric calculators, and if 33 percent of those who have electric typewriters have electric calculators, what proportion of those who have electric calculators also have electric typewriters?

9. A newspaper girl is considering using a list of subscribers for door-to-door advertising of Christmas cards. She knows that 35 percent take the *weekly* paper only, 15 percent take just the *Sunday* paper, and 20 percent take both. Another 30 percent take neither the weekly nor the Sunday, but rather the *daily* paper. If a subscriber takes the weekly paper, what is the probability that he or she also subscribes to the Sunday paper?

10. Suppose for a moment that you are the manager of the computer-manufacturing division of QMB. You have just had a phone call from a supplier of transistors, who says that he has cleaned his warehouse and inadvertently mixed several cases of transistors of various types in one large bin. He is willing to sell this mixed bin at a discount; however, some of the transistors are of a type that you no longer use. Your job is to ascertain the various probabilities of extracting usable transistors from this bin, given the following data.

The mixed bin contains the following transistors, which have been coded by color.

300	Green
400	Green with a white star
500	Green with white rings
500	Blue
200	Blue with a white star
100	Blue with white rings

(a) What is the probability that a transistor is green, given that it has white rings?

(b) What is the probability that the transistor has a white star, given that it is blue?

(c) What is the name of the type of probability you have calculated in parts (a) and (b)?

(d) If the only usable transistors are green, what is the probability of selecting a usable transistor from the bin in a random draw?

11. Using Appendices B and C, evaluate the following binomial probabilities.

(a) $P(r = 2 \mid n = 7, p = .10)$

(b) $P(r = 6 \mid n = 10, p = .60)$

(c) $P(r \geq 9 \mid n = 12, p = .70)$

    (d) $P(r \leq 3 \mid n = 7, p = .30)$

    (e) $P(r < 6 \mid n = 10, p = .35)$

12. Using Appendices D and E, evaluate the following Poisson probabilities.

    (a) $P(X = 2 \mid m = 4)$

    (b) $P(X \geq 3 \mid m = 6)$

    (c) $P(X \leq 5 \mid m = 7)$

    (d) $P(X < 3 \mid m = 5)$

SUPPLEMENTARY READINGS

Drake, Alvin W. *Fundamentals of Applied Probability Theory*. McGraw-Hill, New York, 1967.

Feller, W. *An Introduction to Probability and Its Applications*, 2d ed. Wiley, New York, 1957, vol. I.

Goldberg, Samuel. *Probability: An Introduction*. Prentice-Hall, Englewood Cliffs, N.J., 1960.

Hays, W. L., and R. L. Winkler. *Statistics*. Holt, Rinehart and Winston, New York, 1970, pp. 38–143.

Levinson, H. C. *Chance, Luck, and Statistics*. Dover, New York, 1963.

Lindgren, B. W., and G. W. McElrath. *Introduction to Probability and Statistics*. Macmillan, New York, 1959.

Meyer, P. L. *Introductory Probability and Statistical Applications*. Addison-Wesley, Reading, Mass., 1965.

Mosteller, F., R. E. Rourke, and G. B. Thomas, Jr. *Probability with Statistical Applications*, 2d ed. Addison-Wesley, Reading, Mass., 1970.

Parzen, E. *Modern Probability Theory and Its Applications*. Wiley, New York, 1960.

Peters, W. S., and G. V. Summers. *Statistical Analysis for Business Decisions*. Prentice-Hall, Englewood Cliffs, N.J., 1968.

Schlaifer, R. *Probability and Statistics for Business Decisions*. McGraw-Hill, New York, 1959, pp. 2–21, 160–180, 194–208.

Spurr, William A., and Charles P. Bonini. *Statistical Analysis for Business Decisions*. Irwin, Homewood, Ill., 1973.

Yamane, Taro. *Statistics: An Introductory Analysis*, 3d ed. Harper and Row, New York, 1973.

3/Matrix Operations

MANY of the quantitative methods discussed in later chapters of this book can be simplified through the use of matrices. Numerous problems in game theory, Markov analysis, and linear programming, for example, can best be solved using matrices because a matrix aids the manager in organizing and classifying sets of values. The purpose of this chapter is to explain basic matrix operations.

DEFINITION OF A MATRIX

A matrix is a rectangular array of numbers arranged in rows and columns. In symbolic form, a matrix can be written as:

$$A = \begin{bmatrix} a_{11} & a_{12} & \cdots & a_{1n} \\ a_{21} & a_{22} & \cdots & a_{2n} \\ \vdots & & & \\ a_{m1} & a_{m2} & \cdots & a_{mn} \end{bmatrix}.$$

In this notation, A is an $m \times n$ matrix, where m stands for the number of rows and n stands for the number of columns. When a matrix has the same number of rows as columns, it is called a *square matrix*. Otherwise, it is called a *rectangular matrix*. In an actual problem, each position in the matrix would be a number, as in the following:

$$A = \begin{bmatrix} 4 & 5 & 3 \\ 3 & 7 & 2 \\ 4 & 2 & 1 \end{bmatrix}.$$

In the numerical example, A is a 3×3 square matrix. When referring to the size of a matrix, we place the number of rows first and the number of columns second. If A had three rows and four columns, it would be called a 3×4 matrix. In addition, we can have an $m \times 1$ matrix, called a *column vector*, such as

$$\begin{bmatrix} 1 \\ 2 \\ 3 \end{bmatrix},$$

or a $1 \times n$ matrix, called a *row vector*, such as

$$[1 \quad 2 \quad 3].$$

ADDITION AND SUBTRACTION OF MATRICES

Matrices can be added or subtracted only if they are of the same *order*. This means that they must contain equal numbers of elements. In addition, they must have the same numbers of rows and columns. When these conditions are met, two matrices can be added as follows:

$$\underset{A_1}{\begin{bmatrix} a_{11} & \cdots & a_{1n} \\ \vdots & & \\ a_{m1} & \cdots & a_{mn} \end{bmatrix}} + \underset{A_2}{\begin{bmatrix} b_{11} & \cdots & b_{1n} \\ \vdots & & \\ b_{m1} & \cdots & b_{mn} \end{bmatrix}} = \underset{A_3}{\begin{bmatrix} a_{11}+b_{11} & \cdots & a_{1n}+b_{1n} \\ \vdots & & \\ a_{m1}+b_{m1} & \cdots & a_{mn}+b_{mn} \end{bmatrix}}.$$

If the following two matrices, each 3×3, are added, the resulting matrix is also a 3×3.

$$\underset{A_1}{\begin{bmatrix} 4 & 5 & 3 \\ 3 & 7 & 2 \\ 4 & 2 & 1 \end{bmatrix}} + \underset{A_2}{\begin{bmatrix} 5 & 3 & 2 \\ -3 & 4 & 1 \\ 2 & 1 & 0 \end{bmatrix}} = \underset{A_3}{\begin{bmatrix} 9 & 8 & 5 \\ 0 & 11 & 3 \\ 6 & 3 & 1 \end{bmatrix}}.$$

If two 2×2 matrices are added, the resulting matrix will be a 2×2.

The procedure for subtraction of matrices is similar:

$$\underset{A_1}{\begin{bmatrix} 4 & 5 & 3 \\ 3 & 7 & 2 \\ 4 & 2 & 1 \end{bmatrix}} - \underset{A_2}{\begin{bmatrix} 5 & 3 & 2 \\ -3 & 4 & 1 \\ 2 & 1 & 0 \end{bmatrix}} = \underset{A_3}{\begin{bmatrix} -1 & 2 & 1 \\ 6 & 3 & 1 \\ 2 & 1 & 1 \end{bmatrix}}.$$

In subtraction of matrices, as in addition, the resulting matrix will have the same number of rows and columns as the original matrices.

MULTIPLICATION OF MATRICES

For multiplication of two matrices, one condition must always be met. The number of columns in the first matrix *must* equal the number of rows in the second matrix. For example, a 2×5 matrix can be multiplied by a 5×2 matrix, or a 2×3 matrix can be multiplied by a 3×1, but a 2×5 matrix cannot be multiplied by a 3×6 matrix. As a check, then, the second number given for the first matrix, $2 \times ③$, must be equal to the first number given for the second matrix, $③ \times 1$.

We perform the multiplication as follows:

$$\begin{bmatrix} 3 & 1 & 2 \\ 3 & 6 & 1 \end{bmatrix} \times \begin{bmatrix} 4 \\ 0 \\ 1 \end{bmatrix} = \begin{bmatrix} 3 \times 4 + 1 \times 0 + 2 \times 1 \\ 3 \times 4 + 6 \times 0 + 1 \times 1 \end{bmatrix} = \begin{bmatrix} 14 \\ 13 \end{bmatrix}.$$

$$2 \times ③ \leftarrow = \rightarrow ③ \times 1 \qquad\qquad\qquad 2 \times 1$$
$$\rule{1cm}{0pt} 2 \times 1 \rule{1cm}{0pt}$$

The total number of rows and columns of the product matrix can be determined from the size of the original matrices. We were multiplying a 2×3 by a 3×1. The outside elements, 2 and 1, determine the size of the new matrix: It will be a 2×1.

It is important to note that, in contrast to operations involving single numbers (scalars), the order in which two matrices are multiplied does make a difference. For example, if

$$A = \begin{bmatrix} a_{11} & a_{12} & a_{13} \\ a_{21} & a_{22} & a_{23} \end{bmatrix} \quad \text{and} \quad B = \begin{bmatrix} b_{11} & b_{12} \\ b_{21} & b_{22} \\ b_{31} & b_{32} \end{bmatrix},$$

AB will be a 2×2 matrix:

$$AB = \begin{bmatrix} a_{11}b_{11} + a_{12}b_{21} + a_{13}b_{31} & a_{11}b_{12} + a_{12}b_{22} + a_{13}b_{32} \\ a_{21}b_{11} + a_{22}b_{21} + a_{23}b_{31} & a_{21}b_{12} + a_{22}b_{22} + a_{23}b_{32} \end{bmatrix}.$$

BA, however, is a 3×3 matrix:

$$BA = \begin{bmatrix} b_{11}a_{11} + b_{12}a_{21} & b_{11}a_{12} + b_{12}a_{22} & b_{11}a_{13} + b_{12}a_{23} \\ b_{21}a_{11} + b_{22}a_{21} & b_{21}a_{12} + b_{22}a_{22} & b_{21}a_{13} + b_{22}a_{23} \\ b_{31}a_{11} + b_{32}a_{21} & b_{31}a_{12} + b_{32}a_{22} & b_{31}a_{13} + b_{32}a_{23} \end{bmatrix}.$$

In AB, A is *premultiplying* B, or B is *post*multiplying A. This is very different from premultiplying A by B. We can make the point clearer by substituting numbers for the symbols:

$$
\begin{array}{ccc}
A & B & AB
\end{array}
$$

$$
\begin{bmatrix} 4 & 3 & 6 \\ 2 & 1 & 1 \end{bmatrix} \times \begin{bmatrix} 1 & 2 \\ 5 & 1 \\ 4 & 2 \end{bmatrix} = \begin{bmatrix} 43 & 23 \\ 11 & 7 \end{bmatrix},
$$

$$
2 \times ③ \leftarrow = \rightarrow ③ \times 2 \qquad 2 \times 2
$$
$$
\underline{\qquad 2 \times 2 \qquad}
$$

$$
\begin{array}{ccc}
B & A & BA
\end{array}
$$

$$
\begin{bmatrix} 1 & 2 \\ 5 & 1 \\ 4 & 2 \end{bmatrix} \times \begin{bmatrix} 4 & 3 & 6 \\ 2 & 1 & 1 \end{bmatrix} = \begin{bmatrix} 8 & 5 & 8 \\ 22 & 16 & 31 \\ 20 & 14 & 26 \end{bmatrix}.
$$

$$
3 \times ② \leftarrow = \rightarrow ② \times 3 \qquad 3 \times 3
$$
$$
\underline{\qquad 3 \times 3 \qquad}.
$$

RULES FOR ADDITION AND MULTIPLICATION

1. $AB \neq BA$, except for special cases that will be discussed later. This means that the commutative law of multiplication does not usually apply to matrices. In the multiplication of $A \times B$ in the previous example, AB was a 2×2 matrix, while BA was a 3×3. When the original matrices are of the same order, both of the resulting matrices will also be of that order but will generally not be equal. As another example, if

$$
A = \begin{bmatrix} 4 & 6 \\ 2 & 2 \end{bmatrix} \quad \text{and} \quad B = \begin{bmatrix} 1 & 2 \\ 3 & 4 \end{bmatrix},
$$

then

$$
AB = \begin{bmatrix} 22 & 32 \\ 8 & 12 \end{bmatrix} \quad \text{and} \quad BA = \begin{bmatrix} 8 & 10 \\ 20 & 26 \end{bmatrix}.
$$

2. $A+B = B+A$. The commutative law of addition holds; however, the original matrices must be of the same order. For example,

$$
\begin{bmatrix} 1 & 3 \\ -6 & 0 \end{bmatrix} + \begin{bmatrix} 1 & 2 \\ 3 & 4 \end{bmatrix} = \begin{bmatrix} 1 & 2 \\ 3 & 4 \end{bmatrix} + \begin{bmatrix} 1 & 3 \\ -6 & 0 \end{bmatrix} = \begin{bmatrix} 2 & 5 \\ -3 & 4 \end{bmatrix}.
$$

3. $(A+B)+C = A+(B+C)$. The associative law of addition holds. Since addition of matrices involves addition of corresponding elements,

it does not matter in which order the operation takes place. For example,

$$\left(\begin{bmatrix} 1 & 3 \\ -6 & 0 \end{bmatrix} + \begin{bmatrix} 1 & 2 \\ 3 & 4 \end{bmatrix} \right) + \begin{bmatrix} 1 & 3 \\ 0 & 1 \end{bmatrix} = \begin{bmatrix} 1 & 3 \\ -6 & 0 \end{bmatrix}$$
$$+ \left(\begin{bmatrix} 1 & 2 \\ 3 & 4 \end{bmatrix} + \begin{bmatrix} 1 & 3 \\ 0 & 1 \end{bmatrix} \right),$$

$$\begin{bmatrix} 2 & 5 \\ -3 & 4 \end{bmatrix} + \begin{bmatrix} 1 & 3 \\ 0 & 1 \end{bmatrix} = \begin{bmatrix} 1 & 3 \\ -6 & 0 \end{bmatrix} + \begin{bmatrix} 2 & 5 \\ 3 & 5 \end{bmatrix}$$
$$= \begin{bmatrix} 3 & 8 \\ -3 & 5 \end{bmatrix}.$$

4. $(AB)C = A(BC)$. The associative law of multiplication holds. We can form AB and postmultiply by C, or form BC and premultiply by A. For example,

$$\left(\begin{bmatrix} 1 & 3 \\ -6 & 0 \end{bmatrix} \times \begin{bmatrix} 1 & 2 \\ 3 & 4 \end{bmatrix} \right) \times \begin{bmatrix} 1 & 3 \\ 0 & 1 \end{bmatrix} = \begin{bmatrix} 1 & 3 \\ -6 & 0 \end{bmatrix}$$
$$\times \left(\begin{bmatrix} 1 & 2 \\ 3 & 4 \end{bmatrix} \times \begin{bmatrix} 1 & 3 \\ 0 & 1 \end{bmatrix} \right),$$

$$\begin{bmatrix} 10 & 14 \\ -6 & -12 \end{bmatrix} \times \begin{bmatrix} 1 & 3 \\ 0 & 1 \end{bmatrix} = \begin{bmatrix} 1 & 3 \\ -6 & 0 \end{bmatrix} \times \begin{bmatrix} 1 & 5 \\ 3 & 13 \end{bmatrix}$$
$$= \begin{bmatrix} 10 & 44 \\ -6 & -30 \end{bmatrix}.$$

SPECIAL TYPES OF MATRICES

Unit or Identity Matrix
The following is a square identity matrix with ones (or units) in the *main diagonal* and zeros in all other, or *off-diagonal*, positions.

$$I = \begin{bmatrix} 1 & 0 & 0 \\ 0 & 1 & 0 \\ 0 & 0 & 1 \end{bmatrix}.$$

This type of matrix will assume particular importance in our linear programming work. This matrix I is one of those special cases in which pre- and postmultiplication yield the same result:

$$IA = AI = A.$$

Symmetric Matrix

The following matrix is referred to as a symmetric matrix, because of the position matching and value matching of all off-diagonal elements.

$$S = \begin{bmatrix} 4 & 1 & 3 \\ 1 & 2 & 2 \\ 3 & 2 & 1 \end{bmatrix}.$$

The elements to the right of the main diagonal replicate the elements to the left of the main diagonal.

OTHER MATRIX OPERATIONS

Transposition

The transposition of a matrix A can be accomplished by interchanging the rows and columns to produce a new matrix A':

$$A = \begin{bmatrix} 3 & 4 & 1 \\ 1 & 2 & 3 \end{bmatrix} \qquad A' = \begin{bmatrix} 3 & 1 \\ 4 & 2 \\ 1 & 3 \end{bmatrix}.$$

Matrix A is a 2×3 matrix, and the transpose matrix A' is a 3×2. For a symmetric matrix, like the one shown in the previous section, the transpose is identical to the original, or $S = S'$.

Determinants

A determinant is a scalar quantity associated with any complete *square* matrix. The notation $|A|$ is used to represent the determinant of matrix A. Care should be taken not to confuse this symbol with the one for absolute value. In this chapter it will stand for the determinant of a matrix.

In the case of a 2×2 matrix, the determinant is formed by subtracting the product of the off-diagonal elements from the product of the main-diagonal elements. For the matrix

$$\begin{bmatrix} 3 & 3 \\ 6 & 7 \end{bmatrix}$$

the determinant is calculated as follows:

$$\begin{vmatrix} 3 & 3 \\ 6 & 7 \end{vmatrix} = (3)(7) - (6)(3) = 3.$$

As another example,

$$\begin{vmatrix} 4 & 1 \\ 0 & 3 \end{vmatrix} = (4)(3) - (1)(0) = 12.$$

The method for calculating the determinant of a 3×3 matrix is somewhat similar:

$$\begin{vmatrix} 2 & 3 & 2 \\ 4 & 6 & 1 \\ 2 & 1 & 1 \end{vmatrix} = 2 \begin{vmatrix} 3 & 2 \\ 6 & 1 \end{vmatrix} - 1 \begin{vmatrix} 2 & 2 \\ 4 & 1 \end{vmatrix} + 1 \begin{vmatrix} 2 & 3 \\ 4 & 6 \end{vmatrix}$$
$$= 2(3-12) - 1(2-8) + 1(12-12)$$
$$= -18 + 6 + 0 = -12.$$

This determinant is calculated by the following steps.

1. Select some row or column of the matrix that contains numbers easy to multiply. We selected the third row.

2. For each of the elements in the third row, find the 2×2 matrix containing no components from that element's row or column. For example, in

$$\begin{vmatrix} 2 & ③ & ② \\ 4 & ⑥ & ① \\ 2_{31} & 1_{32} & 1_{33} \end{vmatrix},$$

   where the subscripts represent the row and column of the element, respectively, the circled elements are those not in the same row or column as element 2_{31}.

3. Find the determinant of this new 2×2 matrix, in this case $3 - 12$, or -9.

4. Multiply the result by the original element (2), and change the sign of the result if the original element is in an odd-numbered position. We determine whether a position is odd or even by adding the subscripts. For example, 2_{31} is in an even-numbered position, because the sum of the subscripts, 3 and 1, equals 4. The result, then, is 2×-9, or -18, and we leave the sign unchanged.

5. Follow the same procedure for each other element in the row or column selected. In

$$\begin{vmatrix} ② & 3 & ② \\ ④ & 6 & ① \\ 2 & 1 & 1 \end{vmatrix}$$

   the circled elements are those corresponding to 1_{32}. We calculate that

$$(2)(1) - (4)(2) = 2 - 8 = -6$$

and $1(-6) = -6$. Because this is an odd-numbered position $(3+2=5)$, we change the sign and the result is $+6$.

For the last element in the row the result is $1(12-12) = 0$. Although it doesn't matter in the case of zero, the original element is in an even position and the sign stays the same.

6. Add the results. In this case, the sum $-18+6+0$ equals -12. The same result of -12 will be obtained if any other row or column is selected as the starting point.

Using Determinants to Solve a Set of Simultaneous Equations

Assume that we have a set of simultaneous linear equations to be solved:

$$5X - 4Y + Z = 8,$$
$$-2X + 6Y + 4Z = -14,$$
$$X - 7Y - 3Z = 9.$$

In basic algebra, a solution is obtained by multiplying through to get one variable to cancel out and solving for the remaining two variables before substituting back in to solve for the third. Determinants prove useful on certain occasions to solve these equations. Using general notation, these simultaneous equations can be written as:

$$\begin{bmatrix} C_{X_{11}} & C_{Y_{12}} & C_{Z_{13}} \\ C_{X_{21}} & C_{Y_{22}} & C_{Z_{23}} \\ C_{X_{31}} & C_{Y_{32}} & C_{Z_{33}} \end{bmatrix} = \begin{bmatrix} W_1 \\ W_2 \\ W_3 \end{bmatrix},$$

where $C_{X_{11}}$ stands for the coefficient of X_{11}, $C_{Y_{12}}$ is the coefficient of Y_{12}, and so on. The Ws to the right of the equality stand for the values to the right of the equality in the original set of equations. With the matrix to the left of the equality labeled A, the equations can be solved as follows:

$$X = \frac{\begin{vmatrix} W_1 & C_{Y_{12}} & C_{Z_{13}} \\ W_2 & C_{Y_{22}} & C_{Z_{23}} \\ W_3 & C_{Y_{32}} & C_{Z_{33}} \end{vmatrix}}{|A|},$$

$$Y = \frac{\begin{vmatrix} C_{X_{11}} & W_1 & C_{Z_{13}} \\ C_{X_{21}} & W_2 & C_{Z_{23}} \\ C_{X_{31}} & W_3 & C_{Z_{33}} \end{vmatrix}}{|A|},$$

$$Z = \frac{\begin{vmatrix} C_{X_{11}} & C_{Y_{12}} & W_1 \\ C_{X_{21}} & C_{Y_{22}} & W_2 \\ C_{X_{31}} & C_{Y_{32}} & W_3 \end{vmatrix}}{|A|}.$$

We then write in the actual numbers from the three simultaneous equations:

$$X = \frac{\begin{vmatrix} 8 & -4 & 1 \\ -14 & 6 & 4 \\ 9 & -7 & -3 \end{vmatrix}}{|A|},$$

$$Y = \frac{\begin{vmatrix} 5 & 8 & 1 \\ -2 & -14 & 4 \\ 1 & 9 & -3 \end{vmatrix}}{|A|},$$

$$Z = \frac{\begin{vmatrix} 5 & -4 & 8 \\ -2 & 6 & -14 \\ 1 & -7 & 9 \end{vmatrix}}{|A|}.$$

Solving for $|A|$, we find that

$$|A| = \begin{vmatrix} 5 & -4 & 1 \\ -2 & 6 & 4 \\ 1 & -7 & -3 \end{vmatrix} = 66,$$

$$X = \frac{148}{66} = 2.242,$$

$$Y = \frac{10}{66} = .151,$$

$$Z = \frac{-172}{66} = -2.606,$$

where 148, 10, and -172 are the values of the determinants shown in the numerators for X, Y, and Z, respectively. These results can be verified by substitution into the original equations.

METHODS OF MATRIX INVERSION

The inverse of a matrix is written in the same way as the reciprocal of a scalar in basic mathematics. For any square matrix A, such as a 2×2 or a 3×3, the inverse is labeled A^{-1}, and when it is multiplied by A, it forms an identity matrix I. The matrix I performs the same role in matrix operations that 1 does in scalar operations. In testing to see whether we have formed the correct inverse of a matrix, we will rely on the following relationship, which always holds.

$$A^{-1}A = I = AA^{-1}.$$

The inverse of a matrix may not always exist, even though the original matrix is square. The existence of the inverse matrix depends upon whether the matrix has a nonzero determinant. Under special conditions when the determinant is zero, the matrix cannot be inverted.

Row or Column Procedures

The inversion of a matrix using row and column procedures is one of the more time-consuming operations in matrix algebra. Computer programs are available to ease the computational burden. However, a basic knowledge of the procedures is necessary for later applications of matrix techniques to linear programming.

The inversion consists of placing an identity matrix next to the matrix that is to be inverted and then converting the original matrix to an identity matrix. If an inverse does not exist, this conversion is not possible. All operations performed on the original matrix are performed on the matrix by its side, and when the process is finished the latter is the inverse of the original. In any single inversion operation, either row or column procedures may be used, but not both. The following list represents the acceptable procedures for matrix inversion with row or column methods.

1. One row can be interchanged with another row.

2. One column can be interchanged with another column.

3. A row can be multiplied by a constant.

4. A column can be multiplied by a constant.

5. One row can be added to or subtracted from another row.

6. One column can be added to or subtracted from another column.

7. A multiple of a row can be added to or subtracted from another row.

8. A multiple of a column can be added to or subtracted from another column.

For instance, for the matrix A,

$$\begin{bmatrix} 1 & 3 \\ 4 & 2 \end{bmatrix},$$

the inversion steps are as follows.

1. Place an identity matrix next to the original, to the right of the dashed line.

$$\begin{bmatrix} 1 & 3 & \vdots & 1 & 0 \\ 4 & 2 & \vdots & 0 & 1 \end{bmatrix}$$

2. Multiply the second row by $\frac{1}{2}$ (procedure 3).

$$\begin{bmatrix} 1 & 3 & \vdots & 1 & 0 \\ 2 & 1 & \vdots & 0 & \frac{1}{2} \end{bmatrix}$$

3. Multiply the first row by 2 and subtract it from the second row (procedure 7).

$$\begin{bmatrix} 1 & 3 & \vdots & 1 & 0 \\ 0 & -5 & \vdots & -2 & \frac{1}{2} \end{bmatrix}$$

4. Multiply the second row by $\frac{3}{5}$ (procedure 3).

$$\begin{bmatrix} 1 & 3 & \vdots & 1 & 0 \\ 0 & -3 & \vdots & -\frac{12}{10} & \frac{3}{10} \end{bmatrix}$$

5. Add the second row to the first row (procedure 5).

$$\begin{bmatrix} 1 & 0 & \vdots & -\frac{2}{10} & \frac{3}{10} \\ 0 & -3 & \vdots & -\frac{12}{10} & \frac{3}{10} \end{bmatrix}$$

6. Multiply the second row by $-\frac{1}{3}$ (procedure 3).

$$\begin{bmatrix} 1 & 0 & \vdots & -\frac{2}{10} & \frac{3}{10} \\ 0 & 1 & \vdots & \frac{4}{10} & -\frac{1}{10} \end{bmatrix}$$

The matrix

$$\begin{bmatrix} -\frac{2}{10} & \frac{3}{10} \\ \frac{4}{10} & -\frac{1}{10} \end{bmatrix}$$

represents the inverted form of the original matrix A and is called A^{-1}. As mentioned before, $A^{-1}A = I$, and this serves as a good check to see if we have correctly formed A^{-1}:

$$\begin{bmatrix} -\frac{2}{10} & \frac{3}{10} \\ \frac{4}{10} & -\frac{1}{10} \end{bmatrix}\begin{bmatrix} 1 & 3 \\ 4 & 2 \end{bmatrix} = \begin{bmatrix} -\frac{2}{10}+\frac{12}{10} & -\frac{6}{10}+\frac{6}{10} \\ \frac{4}{10}-\frac{4}{10} & \frac{12}{10}-\frac{2}{10} \end{bmatrix} = \begin{bmatrix} 1 & 0 \\ 0 & 1 \end{bmatrix}.$$

In a later chapter we will want to use these procedures in the solution of linear programming problems. For example, if we have a set of equations,

$$9x_1 + 6x_2 + 12x_3 = 720,$$
$$3x_1 + 14x_2 + 10x_3 = 600,$$
$$2x_1 + 4x_2 + 15x_3 = 460,$$

we may need to reduce the matrix of coefficients to the left of the equality to an identity matrix. Because we have to treat the elements to the right of the equal sign in an equation in the same way as those to the left, we are dealing with a 3×4 matrix:

$$\begin{bmatrix} 9 & 6 & 12 & \vdots & 720 \\ 3 & 14 & 10 & \vdots & 600 \\ 2 & 4 & 15 & \vdots & 460 \end{bmatrix}.$$

To reduce the 3×3 matrix of coefficients to an identity matrix, we can utilize row or column procedures. Using row procedures, we progress by the following steps.

STEP 1

(a) Multiply the first row by $\frac{1}{9}$ (procedure 3).

$$\begin{bmatrix} 1 & \frac{2}{3} & 1\frac{1}{3} & \vdots & 80 \\ 3 & 14 & 10 & \vdots & 600 \\ 2 & 4 & 15 & \vdots & 460 \end{bmatrix}$$

(b) Subtract 3 times the first row from the second row (procedure 7).

$$\begin{bmatrix} 1 & \frac{2}{3} & 1\frac{1}{3} & \vdots & 80 \\ 0 & 12 & 6 & \vdots & 360 \\ 2 & 4 & 15 & \vdots & 460 \end{bmatrix}$$

(c) Subtract 2 times the first row from the third row (procedure 7).

$$\begin{bmatrix} 1 & \frac{2}{3} & 1\frac{1}{3} & \vdots & 80 \\ 0 & 12 & 6 & \vdots & 360 \\ 0 & 2\frac{2}{3} & 12\frac{1}{3} & \vdots & 300 \end{bmatrix}$$

STEP 2

(a) Multiply the second row by $\frac{1}{12}$ (procedure 3).

$$\begin{bmatrix} 1 & \frac{2}{3} & 1\frac{1}{3} & \vdots & 80 \\ 0 & 1 & \frac{1}{2} & \vdots & 30 \\ 0 & 2\frac{2}{3} & 12\frac{1}{3} & \vdots & 300 \end{bmatrix}$$

(b) Subtract $\frac{2}{3}$ times the second row from the first row (procedure 7).

$$\begin{bmatrix} 1 & 0 & 1 & \vdots & 60 \\ 0 & 1 & \frac{1}{2} & \vdots & 30 \\ 0 & 2\frac{2}{3} & 12\frac{1}{3} & \vdots & 300 \end{bmatrix}$$

(c) Subtract $2\frac{2}{3}$ times the second row from the third row (procedure 7).

$$\begin{bmatrix} 1 & 0 & 1 & \vdots & 60 \\ 0 & 1 & \frac{1}{2} & \vdots & 30 \\ 0 & 0 & 11 & \vdots & 220 \end{bmatrix}$$

STEP 3

(a) Subtract $\frac{1}{11}$ times the third row from the first row (procedure 7).

$$\begin{bmatrix} 1 & 0 & 0 & \vdots & 40 \\ 0 & 1 & \frac{1}{2} & \vdots & 30 \\ 0 & 0 & 11 & \vdots & 220 \end{bmatrix}$$

(b) Subtract $\frac{1}{22}$ times the third row from the second row (procedure 7).

$$\begin{bmatrix} 1 & 0 & 0 & \vdots & 40 \\ 0 & 1 & 0 & \vdots & 20 \\ 0 & 0 & 11 & \vdots & 220 \end{bmatrix}$$

(c) Multiply the third row by $\frac{1}{11}$ (procedure 3).

$$\begin{bmatrix} 1 & 0 & 0 & \vdots & 40 \\ 0 & 1 & 0 & \vdots & 20 \\ 0 & 0 & 1 & \vdots & 20 \end{bmatrix}$$

Although row or column procedures are useful in some applications, use of the cofactor method of matrix inversion is sometimes faster, especially in the case of a 2×2 matrix.

Inversion Using Cofactor and Adjoint Matrices

A *cofactor matrix* can be formed from any 2×2 or larger matrix. A cofactor is an element or group of elements remaining when a row and a column have been removed from a matrix. In the case of the 2×2 matrix A,

$$\begin{bmatrix} a_{11} & a_{12} \\ b_{21} & b_{22} \end{bmatrix},$$

the cofactor matrix, A_{cof}, is:

$$\begin{bmatrix} b_{22} & -b_{21} \\ -a_{12} & a_{11} \end{bmatrix}.$$

The process of forming this new 2×2 cofactor matrix consists of the following steps.

1. Exchange elements on the same diagonal.

2. Change the sign of those exchanged elements that are not on the main diagonal. (Or change the sign if the element is in an odd-numbered position.)

For example, if

$$A = \begin{bmatrix} 6 & 5 \\ 2 & 1 \end{bmatrix}, \quad \text{then} \quad A_{cof} = \begin{bmatrix} 1 & -2 \\ -5 & 6 \end{bmatrix}.$$

The elements in odd positions have their signs changed. As another example, if

$$B = \begin{bmatrix} 6 & -9 \\ 9 & 0 \end{bmatrix}, \quad \text{then} \quad B_{cof} = \begin{bmatrix} 0 & -9 \\ 9 & 6 \end{bmatrix}.$$

We have previously discussed how to transpose a matrix. The *adjoint matrix* is simply the transpose of the cofactor matrix. For our two examples,

$$A_{adj} = \begin{bmatrix} 1 & -5 \\ -2 & 6 \end{bmatrix} \quad \text{and} \quad B_{adj} = \begin{bmatrix} 0 & 9 \\ -9 & 6 \end{bmatrix}.$$

We can use both cofactor and adjoint matrices in forming inverses. First, though, we should see how to find the cofactor matrix of a matrix larger than 2×2.

The procedure for finding the cofactor matrix for a 3×3 matrix involves determinants. If our original matrix, A, is

$$\begin{bmatrix} 5_{11} & 3_{12} & 0_{13} \\ 1_{21} & 6_{22} & 1_{23} \\ 4_{31} & 3_{32} & 2_{33} \end{bmatrix},$$

we work through the following steps.

1. For each element in the original matrix, find that group of elements remaining after elimination of the row and column containing the element. For example, the group of elements remaining after eliminating the row and column of element 5_{11} is:

$$\begin{bmatrix} 6 & 1 \\ 3 & 2 \end{bmatrix}.$$

2. Find the determinant of this remaining group of elements:

$$(6)(2) - (3)(1) = 9.$$

3. Change the sign of this determinant if the sum of the subscripts for the element involved (5_{11}) is an odd number.

4. Place this new element in the cofactor matrix in the same position that 5_{11} occupied in the original matrix:

$$\begin{bmatrix} 9 & \\ & \end{bmatrix}.$$

Using this procedure, we derive the complete cofactor matrix.

Element with row and column to be removed	Cofactors		Value to be placed in cofactor matrix
$\begin{bmatrix} ⑤ & 3 & 0 \\ 1 & & \\ 4 & & \end{bmatrix}$	$\begin{bmatrix} 6 & 1 \\ 3 & 2 \end{bmatrix}$	$\begin{vmatrix} 6 & 1 \\ 3 & 2 \end{vmatrix} = 9$	$1+1 =$ even; sign not changed
$\begin{bmatrix} 5 & & \\ ① & 6 & 1 \\ 4 & & \end{bmatrix}$	$\begin{bmatrix} 3 & 0 \\ 3 & 2 \end{bmatrix}$	$\begin{vmatrix} 3 & 0 \\ 3 & 2 \end{vmatrix} = -6$	$2+1 =$ odd; sign changed
$\begin{bmatrix} 5 & & \\ 1 & & \\ ④ & 3 & 2 \end{bmatrix}$	$\begin{bmatrix} 3 & 0 \\ 6 & 1 \end{bmatrix}$	$\begin{vmatrix} 3 & 0 \\ 6 & 1 \end{vmatrix} = 3$	$3+1 =$ even; sign not changed
$\begin{bmatrix} 5 & ③ & 0 \\ & 6 & \\ & 3 & \end{bmatrix}$	$\begin{bmatrix} 1 & 1 \\ 4 & 2 \end{bmatrix}$	$\begin{vmatrix} 1 & 1 \\ 4 & 2 \end{vmatrix} = 2$	$1+2 =$ odd; sign changed
$\begin{bmatrix} & 3 & \\ 1 & ⑥ & 1 \\ & 3 & \end{bmatrix}$	$\begin{bmatrix} 5 & 0 \\ 4 & 2 \end{bmatrix}$	$\begin{vmatrix} 5 & 0 \\ 4 & 2 \end{vmatrix} = 10$	$2+2 =$ even; sign not changed
$\begin{bmatrix} & 3 & \\ & 6 & \\ 4 & ③ & 2 \end{bmatrix}$	$\begin{bmatrix} 5 & 0 \\ 1 & 1 \end{bmatrix}$	$\begin{vmatrix} 5 & 0 \\ 1 & 1 \end{vmatrix} = -5$	$3+2 =$ odd; sign changed
$\begin{bmatrix} 5 & 3 & ⓪ \\ & 1 & \\ & 2 & \end{bmatrix}$	$\begin{bmatrix} 1 & 6 \\ 4 & 3 \end{bmatrix}$	$\begin{vmatrix} 1 & 6 \\ 4 & 3 \end{vmatrix} = -21$	$1+3 =$ even; sign not changed

Element with row and column to be removed (cont.)	Cofactors (cont.)		Value to be placed in cofactor matrix (cont.)

$$\begin{bmatrix} & & 0 \\ 1 & 6 & ① \\ & & 2 \end{bmatrix} \qquad \begin{bmatrix} 5 & 3 \\ 4 & 3 \end{bmatrix} \qquad \begin{vmatrix} 5 & 3 \\ 4 & 3 \end{vmatrix} = -3 \qquad \begin{matrix} 2+3 = \text{odd}; \\ \text{sign changed} \end{matrix}$$

$$\begin{bmatrix} & & 0 \\ & & 1 \\ 4 & 3 & ② \end{bmatrix} \qquad \begin{bmatrix} 5 & 3 \\ 1 & 6 \end{bmatrix} \qquad \begin{vmatrix} 5 & 3 \\ 1 & 6 \end{vmatrix} = 27 \qquad \begin{matrix} 3+3 = \text{even}; \\ \text{sign not changed} \end{matrix}$$

Substituting all the values into the new matrix, we find that

$$A_{\text{cof}} = \begin{bmatrix} 9 & 2 & -21 \\ -6 & 10 & -3 \\ 3 & -5 & 27 \end{bmatrix}.$$

To form A^{-1}, there are only three additional steps. First, formulate the adjoint matrix, which is the transpose of the cofactor matrix:

$$A_{\text{adj}} = \begin{bmatrix} 9 & -6 & 3 \\ 2 & 10 & -5 \\ -21 & -3 & 27 \end{bmatrix}.$$

Second, find the value of the determinant of the *original* matrix,

$$\begin{vmatrix} 5 & 3 & 0 \\ 1 & 6 & 1 \\ 4 & 3 & 2 \end{vmatrix}.$$

The value is 51. Third, divide each element in the adjoint matrix by the value of the determinant of the original matrix. This forms the inverse of the original matrix:

$$A^{-1} = \frac{A_{\text{adj}}}{|A|},$$

$$A^{-1} = \begin{bmatrix} \frac{9}{51} & -\frac{6}{51} & \frac{3}{51} \\ \frac{2}{51} & \frac{10}{51} & -\frac{5}{51} \\ -\frac{21}{51} & -\frac{3}{51} & \frac{27}{51} \end{bmatrix}.$$

To test whether the correct inverse of the original matrix A has been formed, multiply the inverse matrix by the original matrix; the product must be an identity matrix:

$$A^{-1} \qquad \times \qquad A \qquad = \qquad I$$

$$\begin{bmatrix} \frac{9}{51} & -\frac{6}{51} & \frac{3}{51} \\ \frac{2}{51} & \frac{10}{51} & -\frac{5}{51} \\ -\frac{21}{51} & -\frac{3}{51} & \frac{27}{51} \end{bmatrix} \times \begin{bmatrix} 5 & 3 & 0 \\ 1 & 6 & 1 \\ 4 & 3 & 2 \end{bmatrix} = \begin{bmatrix} 1 & 0 & 0 \\ 0 & 1 & 0 \\ 0 & 0 & 1 \end{bmatrix}.$$

This result is an identity matrix and, therefore, the inverse A^{-1} is correct.

PROBLEMS

1. You are given the following matrices.

$$A \qquad\qquad\qquad B$$

$$\begin{bmatrix} -1 & 2 & 3 \\ 2 & -3 & 1 \\ 3 & 1 & -2 \end{bmatrix} \qquad \begin{bmatrix} 4 & 5 & 6 \\ 5 & 6 & 4 \\ 6 & 4 & 5 \end{bmatrix}.$$

(a) Add A to B to form C.
(b) Subtract A from C.
(c) Subtract B from C.
(d) Multiply $A \times B$.
(e) Multiply $B \times A$.

2. Multiply

$$\begin{bmatrix} 3 & 2 \\ 6 & 0 \\ 4 & 1 \end{bmatrix} \times \begin{bmatrix} 0 & 1 & -4 \\ 2 & 0 & 1 \end{bmatrix}.$$

3. Multiply

$$\begin{bmatrix} 0 & 1 & -4 \\ 2 & 0 & 1 \end{bmatrix} \times \begin{bmatrix} 3 & 2 \\ 6 & 0 \\ 4 & 1 \end{bmatrix}.$$

4. Find the determinants of the following matrices.

$$W \qquad\qquad X \qquad\qquad Y \qquad\qquad Z$$

$$\begin{bmatrix} -1 & -2 \\ -3 & -4 \end{bmatrix} \quad \begin{bmatrix} 1 & -3 & 1 \\ 4 & 1 & -3 \\ -4 & 5 & 3 \end{bmatrix} \quad \begin{bmatrix} 1 & 0 & 0 \\ 0 & 1 & 0 \\ 0 & 0 & 1 \end{bmatrix} \quad \begin{bmatrix} -1 & 2 & 3 \\ 2 & 3 & -1 \\ 3 & -1 & 2 \end{bmatrix}$$

5. Find the cofactor matrix for each of the following matrices.

$$X \qquad\qquad Y \qquad\qquad Z$$

$$\begin{bmatrix} 1 & 2 \\ 3 & 7 \end{bmatrix} \quad \begin{bmatrix} -1 & 2 & 3 \\ 2 & 3 & -1 \\ 3 & -1 & 2 \end{bmatrix} \quad \begin{bmatrix} 1 & 2 & 3 \\ 1 & 2 & 3 \\ 1 & 2 & 3 \end{bmatrix}$$

6. Solve the following set of simultaneous equations.

$$3X + 0Y + Z = 3,$$
$$2X + Y + 3Z = 2,$$
$$X + 0Y + 2Z = 1.$$

7. Solve the following set of simultaneous equations.

$$2X + 3Y + Z = 0,$$
$$6X + Y - Z = 0,$$
$$4X - 8Y - 6Z = 2.$$

8. (a) Invert the following matrices using the cofactor method.

$$X \qquad\qquad Y$$
$$\begin{bmatrix} 1 & 2 \\ 3 & 7 \end{bmatrix} \qquad \begin{bmatrix} -1 & 2 & 3 \\ 2 & 3 & -1 \\ 3 & -1 & 2 \end{bmatrix}$$

(b) Invert matrix X using row or column procedures.

9. Using row or column procedures, convert the following matrix to an identity matrix.

$$\begin{bmatrix} 1 & 0 & 2 \\ 5 & 4 & 2 \\ -4 & -3 & -1 \end{bmatrix}$$

10. WRW, Inc., in Huttington Beach sells residential air conditioning equipment. The market in the area is broken down into seven territories. The following row vector represents the average sales per territory.

$$[\$1,100 \quad 1,200 \quad 1,000 \quad 1,450 \quad 950 \quad 750 \quad 1,175]$$

The seven salesmen have been given the following quotas for sales in the upcoming month.

$$Q = \begin{bmatrix} 3 \\ 6 \\ 9 \\ 4 \\ 6 \\ 2 \\ 5 \end{bmatrix}$$

(a) Using vector multiplication, compute the total dollar sales if each salesman sells his quota.
(b) What will sales be if the firm performs at a rate 15 percent over quota?

11. A pharmaceutical saleswoman often needs to make estimates of sales of pills in an upcoming market period so as to assist her firm in scheduling production. This particular saleswoman has kept accurate records of sales per trip to various accounts, and has revised the past records to indicate future buying patterns. These estimates are shown in the following volume matrix.

Type of account / Type of pills	Doctors' offices	Hospitals	Pharmacies	Nursing homes
Antibiotics	900	900	800	600
Analgesics	700	400	800	400
Sedatives	400	900	300	900
Antihistamines	800	200	400	200

In addition, she has planned her sales calls for the upcoming month as shown in the following call vector.

$$\begin{array}{l} \text{Doctors' offices} \\ \text{Hospitals} \\ \text{Pharmacies} \\ \text{Nursing homes} \end{array} \begin{bmatrix} 6 \\ 5 \\ 7 \\ 3 \end{bmatrix}$$

(a) Taking the volume matrix in conjunction with the number of calls the saleswoman plans to make for each type of account over the next month, estimate the total demand for drugs.

(b) Given the vector of pill sales, the saleswoman could then estimate dollar sales by transforming unit sales to dollars. Assume that the dollar prices are as follows.

Antibiotics	$9 per 100
Analgesics	7 per 100
Sedatives	6 per 100
Antihistamines	5 per 100

Estimate dollar sales for each type of pill and total dollar sales of pills for the upcoming month.

(c) Estimate the total number of pills that will be sold to each type of account.

SUPPLEMENTARY READINGS

Aitken, A. C. *Determinants and Matrices*, 8th ed. Interscience, New York, 1954.
Bellman, R. *Introduction to Matrix Analysis*. McGraw-Hill, New York, 1960.

Campbell, H. C. *An Introduction to Matrices, Vectors, and Linear Programming*. Appleton-Century-Crofts, New York, 1965.

Finkbeiner, D. T. *Matrices and Linear Transformations*. Freeman, San Fransisco, 1960.

Gantmacher, F. R. *The Theory of Matrices*. Chelsea, New York, 1959, vols. I–II.

Hadley, G. *Linear Algebra*. Addison-Wesley, Reading, Mass., 1961.

Pipes, L. *Matrix Methods for Engineering*. Prentice-Hall, Englewood Cliffs, N.J., 1962.

Schwartz, J. T. *Introduction to Matrices and Vectors*. McGraw-Hill, New York, 1961.

Turnbull, H. W. *The Theory of Determinants, Matrices, and Invariants*. Dover, New York, 1960.

4/Decision-Making Strategies

THE GENERAL framework of a decision contains three elements. The first element is a *state of nature* or a potential influence on a decision. The state of nature may or may not be predictable and is generally not under the control of the decision maker. Weather and market demand are two examples of states of nature that may affect the outcome of a decision. As a second element, the decision framework must also include *alternative courses of action* that can be taken. Finally, there must be a *decision rule* that is used to guide the selection of one of the alternatives. The extent and complexity of these elements in the decision framework often depend upon the conditions under which the decision is being made.

In conditions of *certainty*, the outcome or state of nature for each alternative is singular and known. If there is more than one state of nature, and the probability distribution for their occurrence is known, we are dealing with decision making under *risk*. For example, insurance premiums are established under conditions of risk; mortality tables are used to reflect the probabilities of particular occurrences covered by the insurance. A football team captain is dealing with a risk situation when he calls the coin flip at the beginning of a game. He knows the chance of each outcome but does not know which will occur.

When no information is available about the probabilities of outcomes, or when the information is only partial, the decision maker is operating under conditions of *uncertainty*. Examples are pricing decisions and introductions of new products.

Under some conditions of uncertainty, the manager may wish to estimate probabilities of states of nature. In this case the manager will have to assign his or her own subjective probabilities. Care must be taken to differentiate between *objective* and *subjective* probabilities. Objective probabilities, which apply most often in decision making under risk conditions, involve a known probability distribution. (See Chapter 2 for discussion of probability distributions.) Subjective probabilities are used when the probability distribution is not available or is only partially available. This does not imply that subjective probabilities are hit-or-miss estimates; they should be carefully thought out and based upon the best information that can be found.

In this chapter decisions made under varying conditions of risk and uncertainty will be explored, and the use of various decision rules for probability, *expected monetary value* (*EMV*), and *expected opportunity loss* (*EOL*) will be investigated.

DECISIONS AND PROBABILITY

Typically, the decision maker is dealing with a decision framework that can be functionally stated as

$$R = f(A_j, S_i),$$

where

$R =$ the return to the decision maker, measured on a scale such as monetary value or utility,

$A_j =$ a set of alternative courses of action that can be controlled by the decision maker,

$S_i =$ a set of events that can occur independently of the selection of a particular course of action. These events, or states of nature, are not under the control of the decision maker.

The process for arriving at a decision would consist of specification of which alternative courses of action are feasible and what the reaction might be to each course of action, along with some statement of the potential return based upon the combinations of A_j and S_i.

Weighted Averages

The decision maker frequently may know the true probability of occurrence of each state of nature. For example, in the situation illustrated in Table 4-1, assume that the probabilities of states of nature S_1 and S_2 are,

Table 4-1 Payoff matrix

Alternative strategies / Potential outcomes	A_1	A_2
S_1	10	-3
S_2	-4	7

respectively, .4 and .6. We assume that money has a constant or un-changing value; in other words, the ten thousandth dollar of a return is worth just as much as the first dollar. We are not dealing with the situation of diminishing returns, which is so common in economic theory. Our decision maker does realize that there is no guarantee of the occurrence of a state of nature. As a result, his or her selection of an appropriate strategy will be based upon the combination of the chances of each state of nature's occurring and the payoffs (or losses) of these occurrences. Calculating the chance and payoff combinations, we find that if the decision maker selected A_1, the expected return, R, would be:

$$R_1 = .4(10) + .6(-4) = 1.60.$$

If alternative A_2 were selected, the expected return would be:

$$R_2 = .4(-3) + .6(7) = 3.00.$$

Since R_2 is larger, the decision maker would choose alternative course of action A_2. Under this decision rule the manager has used the chances for the different states of nature as *weighting* factors in the calculation. The resulting figures, 1.60 and 3.00, are *weighted averages* of the pertinent payoffs. The payoffs shown in Table 4-1 are called conditional payoffs because each is conditioned upon the occurrence of a particular state of nature.

Expected Opportunity Loss

Rather than use the maximum expected payoff, or largest expected mone-tary value (EMV), as the objective, the decision maker could select the objective of minimizing the opportunity loss. The expected opportunity loss (EOL) is defined as the difference between the expected monetary value of a decision and the expected monetary value of the best decision that could have been made under the circumstances. In common-sense terms, this means that a manager should try to make the best of a situation by keeping the losses as small as possible or the gains as large as possible. If a grocer stocks ten cases of milk and sells only nine, the opportunity loss is the difference between the profit if nine were stocked and nine sold and the actual profit when ten were stocked and nine sold. The cost of the extra case of milk that had to be thrown away (or sold at a loss) is the opportunity loss. As another example of opportunity loss, assume that the grocer stocked eight cases but could have sold nine. In this instance, the opportunity loss is the profit the grocer did not make on the ninth case.

Consider a situation in which the warehouse manager for an automobile parts distributor has been asked to provide an estimate of probable lost profits for the next month because all styles of an auto muffler will be out of stock. This product has been under heavy demand, and economic conditions have caused raw material shortages, resulting in reduced production. Therefore out-of-stock conditions have been quite common. Since a muffler is required immediately when a garage mechanic is in the process of completing repairs, the customer goes elsewhere when an order cannot be filled promptly. No orders are carried over to a subsequent day. The warehouse manager has kept accurate records over the last 100 days showing the number of orders that could not be filled and were therefore canceled and lost. He has compiled the exact number of lost orders for each day resulting from stockouts, as shown in Table 4-2.

By using the probabilities, $P(S)$, and the numbers of lost orders, S, the manager can calculate that the average number of orders lost per day was 6.40, as shown in Table 4-3. This weighted average is useful here because the sample was adequate and conditions for the upcoming month appear to be similar to those of the previous 100 days.

The next step is to calculate the expected opportunity loss, or the loss in profit that can be expected to result from the lost orders. The number of orders lost can be converted into expected dollar losses, as shown in Table

Table 4-2 Orders lost because of out-of-stock conditions over a 100-day period

Number of lost orders	Number of days	Proportion of days
0	0	.00
1	0	.00
2	5	.05
3	5	.05
4	5	.05
5	10	.10
6	25	.25
7	25	.25
8	10	.10
9	10	.10
10	5	.05
	100	1.00

Table 4-3 Use of probabilities to calculate the average number of orders lost per day

S (Lost orders)	P(S)	S × P(S) (Average number lost per day)
0	.00	.00
1	.00	.00
2	.05	.10
3	.05	.15
4	.05	.20
5	.10	.50
6	.25	1.50
7	.25	1.75
8	.10	.80
9	.10	.90
10	.05	.50
		6.40

Table 4-4 Expected opportunity loss

S	P(S)	L (Loss)	P(S) × L (Expected opportunity loss)
1	.00	$ 0	$ .00
2	.05	10	.50
3	.05	15	.75
4	.05	20	1.00
5	.10	25	2.50
6	.25	30	7.50
7	.25	35	8.75
8	.10	40	4.00
9	.10	45	4.50
10	.05	50	2.50
			$32.00

4-4, in which we have assumed that each lost sale results in a loss of $5 potential profit. The daily EOL caused by the mufflers' being out of stock is $32.

Using Payoff Tables

A grocery store with a bakery department is faced with the problem of how many cakes to buy in order to meet the day's demand. The grocer prefers not to sell day-old goods in competition with fresh products; leftover cakes are therefore a complete loss. On the other hand, if a customer desires a cake and all of them have been sold, the disappointed customer will buy elsewhere and the sale will be lost. The grocer has therefore collected information on past cake sales for a selected 100-day period, as shown in Table 4-5.

The wholesale price paid by the store is $.80 per cake and the selling price is $1.00. The payoff estimates in Table 4-6 show the profits for each combination of demand and amount of stock carried. The alternative decisions (numbers of cakes to stock) given across the top of the table are under the control of the decision maker. The possible daily demands listed down the left side of the table represent states of nature not under the control of the decision maker. The values in the body of the table represent the payoffs for each decision–state of nature combination. And the circled elements in the main diagonal represent optimal conditions.

How are these payoffs calculated? And how does the grocer use them to determine what number of cakes to stock? Consider the decision to stock 25 cakes at the beginning of each day. Table 4-7 shows how we arrive at the expected profits for this course of action. Assume first that the actual demand turns out to be 25. Since all 25 items are sold, the profit or payoff is 25 items × $.20 profit per item, or $5.00. Since the probability of a demand of 25 is .10, the expected profit is .10 × $5.00, or $.50. If 25 were stocked and the demand turned out to be 26, the store would sell the 25

Table 4-5 Cake sales per day for a 100-day period

Sales per day (cakes)	Number of days	Probability
25	10	.10
26	30	.30
27	50	.50
28	10	.10
	100	1.00

Table 4-6 Payoffs for bakery decisions

Alternative actions / Possible demands	25	26	27	28
25	($5.00)	$4.20	$3.40	$2.60
26	5.00	(5.20)	4.40	3.60
27	5.00	5.20	(5.40)	4.60
28	5.00	5.20	5.40	(5.60)

Table 4-7 Expected profits when 25 cakes are stocked

Actual demand	Probability	Payoff	Expected profit (probability × payoff)
25	.10	$5.00	$ .50
26	.30	5.00	1.50
27	.50	5.00	2.50
28	.10	5.00	.50
			$5.00

Table 4-8 Expected profits when 26 cakes are stocked

Actual demand	Probability	Payoff	Expected profit
25	.10	$4.20	$ .42
26	.30	5.20	1.56
27	.50	5.20	2.60
28	.10	5.20	.52
			$5.10

available for a payoff of $5.00 and the twenty-sixth customer would be turned away. The expected profit is .30 × $5.00, or $1.50. The calculations for demands of 27 or 28 are performed in a similar manner, with customers in excess of 25 being turned away. The expected profits are summed to obtain the total expected profit of $5.00 if the decision is to stock 25 cakes.

Table 4-8 shows the payoffs and expected profits if the decision is to stock 26 items per day. When the actual demand is 25, there will be a profit of .20 × 25, or $5.00 on the 25 sold; however, since the one cake left over will represent a loss of $.80, the net payoff is $4.20. The expected profit for this combination is $4.20 × .10, or $.42. If 26 items were stocked and the demand were also 26, the payoff would be 26 × $.20, or $5.20, resulting in an expected profit of $1.56. Continuing the calculations and summing the expected profits, we find that the total expected profit is $5.10 when the decision is to stock 26 cakes. This is greater than the $5.00 expected profit if 25 were stocked.

The other two possible actions (to stock 27 or 28) are evaluated in Tables 4-9 and 4-10. The action of stocking 26 items results in a greater expected profit than any other of the alternative actions, and therefore the optimum decision is to stock 26 cakes.

Table 4-9 Expected profits when 27 cakes are stocked

Actual demand	Probability	Payoff	Expected profit
25	.10	$3.40	$ .34
26	.30	4.40	1.32
27	.50	5.40	2.70
28	.10	5.40	.54
			$4.90

Table 4-10 Expected profits when 28 cakes are stocked

Actual demand	Probability	Payoff	Expected profit
25	.10	$2.60	$ .26
26	.30	3.60	1.08
27	.50	4.60	2.30
28	.10	5.60	.56
			$4.20

Using Tables for Expected Opportunity Loss

Our bakery example has involved decision making based on selecting the alternative showing the greatest expected profit. We can now analyze the same problem with the objective of selecting the alternative having the lowest expected opportunity loss. The losses for the different combinations of action and demand are compiled in Table 4-11.

Table 4-12 shows the calculations for the action of stocking 25 cakes. If 25 items are stocked and the actual demand is 25, there is no action that would have yielded a better profit; the opportunity does not exist to make a better profit. If 25 items are stocked and the demand is actually 26, the grocer could have made $.20 more by stocking 26; the lost opportunity is therefore $.20. When the $.20 is weighted by the .30 probability of its

Table 4-11 Opportunity losses for bakery decisions

Alternative actions / Possible demands	25	26	27	28
25	($ .00)	$.80	$1.60	$2.40
26	.20	(.00)	.80	1.60
27	.40	.20	(.00)	.80
28	.60	.40	.20	(.00)

Table 4-12 Expected opportunity losses when 25 cakes are stocked

Actual demand	Probability	Opportunity loss	Weighted expected opportunity loss
25	.10	$.00	$.00
26	.30	.20	.06
27	.50	.40	.20
28	.10	.60	.06
			$.32

occurrence, the expected opportunity loss becomes $.20 × .30, or $.06. Similar calculations for demands of 27 and 28 provide the rest of the figures in the last column of the table; when summed the figures equal a total expected opportunity loss of $.32.

Next, consider the possible results if the decision were to stock 26 items at the beginning of each day. The calculations are shown in Table 4-13. If the actual demand were 25, one item would be left over. Since this reduces profit by $.80, the opportunity to make $.80 more was lost. Since the probability of a demand of 25 is .10, the weighted expected opportunity loss is $.80 × .10, or $.08, which appears in the last column of the table. In each case, the opportunity loss is the extra profit that could have been earned by a different decision. The summation of the expected values is $.22 for the decision to purchase and stock 26 items per day. This is less than the expected opportunity loss if 25 cakes were stocked; therefore stocking 26 is the better decision.

However, stocks of 27 and 28 must be considered before the optimum action is determined. These two possible decisions are evaluated in Tables 4-14 and 4-15. When we examine these tables, it still appears that to

Table 4-13 Expected opportunity losses when 26 cakes are stocked

Actual demand	Probability	Opportunity loss	Weighted expected opportunity loss
25	.10	$.80	$.08
26	.30	.00	.00
27	.50	.20	.10
28	.10	.40	.04
			$.22

Table 4-14 Expected opportunity losses when 27 cakes are stocked

Actual demand	Probability	Opportunity loss	Weighted expected opportunity loss
25	.10	$1.60	$.16
26	.30	.80	.24
27	.50	.00	.00
28	.10	.20	.02
			$.42

Table 4-15 Expected opportunity losses when 28 cakes are stocked

Actual demand	Probability	Opportunity loss	Weighted expected opportunity loss
25	.10	$2.40	$.24
26	.30	1.60	.48
27	.50	.80	.40
28	.10	.00	.00
			$1.12

minimize expected opportunity loss the grocer should purchase 26 cakes. This is the same action that we recommended to maximize expected profit. In general, maximizing profit or expected monetary value (EMV) and minimizing expected opportunity loss (EOL) will yield the same optimal strategy; they are simply on different ends of the decision-strategy continuum. In the case of EMV, we are dealing with a situation in which we can expect a profit, and we wish to select the alternative yielding the largest return. In the case of EOL, we are dealing with a loss and wish to keep it at a minimum.

Subjective Probabilities and Uncertainty

In recent years business has become increasingly concerned with decision making under conditions of uncertainty. Often referred to rather loosely as decision theory, various decision models assist management in selecting the most appropriate or the optimal course of action when the firm is confronted with incomplete information.

Imagine that the designer and producer of a new automatic drapery pleater is attempting to evaluate the market demand for her new product.

Because this product has not been sold previously, she does not have prior data to evaluate, as we did in the previous problems in this chapter. Even though prior information is lacking, a decision must be made regarding the number of pleaters to manufacture and to have ready for sale.

The designer's situation is somewhat unique, but not uncommon; the firm consists of one person, and she has a one-time decision as to how many pleaters to manufacture. She must make this decision before introducing the marketing program, which will take all of her time once it is begun. She feels that there are only two types of market conditions (states of nature) facing her: high demand and low demand. In determining the amount to manufacture, she decides that there is a choice between producing 25 units (A_1) and producing 75 units (A_2). From her business judgment, discussion with potential customers, and analysis of market figures, she feels that the chance of obtaining a high demand is .70 and the probability of a low demand is therefore .30. She has made some estimates of the various consequences of decisions and market reactions, and the values in Table 4-16 show the results of these estimates. Figures 4-1 and 4-2 present the same information in the form of decision trees, showing the various alternative courses of action, states of nature, and payoffs.

Table 4-16 Payoff matrix for drapery pleaters

States of nature / Alternative actions	A_1 (Produce 25 units)	A_2 (Produce 75 units)
S_1 (High demand)	$3,500	$9,000
S_2 (Low demand)	2,000	−7,000

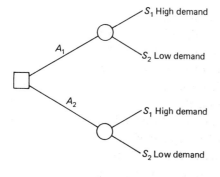

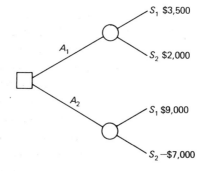

Figure 4-1 Decision tree for drapery pleaters

Figure 4-2 Completed decision tree for drapery pleaters

From Figure 4-2 the expected monetary values or weighted average payoffs for A_1 and A_2 can be calculated as follows:

$$\text{EMV}(A_1) = .70(\$3,500) + .30(\$2,000) = \$3,050,$$
$$\text{EMV}(A_2) = .70(\$9,000) + .30(-\$7,000) = \$4,200.$$

Selecting the strategy offering the highest expected monetary value, the businesswoman would pick A_2 and would produce 75 units. Note that the EMV is simply a weighted average of conditional payoffs for actions A_1 and A_2; it differs from a standard arithmetic mean only because S_1 and S_2 were not equally probable.

The differences between a situation such as this and the previous examples can be further elaborated at this point. In the auto warehouse and the bakery problems, a set of *objective* probabilities existed, derived from data that had been collected over 100 days. But in our drapery example, it was necessary to make use of *subjective* probability estimates, because there were no past data upon which to base probabilities. Thus, the earlier decisions were made under conditions of risk, while the drapery decision was made under uncertainty.

The Expected Value of Perfect Information (EVPI)

Perfect information is at the other extreme from no information. The value of perfect information is considered here not because we expect to be able to obtain it; rather, it is considered as a limit to the value of data that might be obtained. If we are thinking of collecting more data before making a decision, the value of perfect information would be the upper boundary on expenditure to obtain this added data. Since we recognize that perfect information will not be achieved, we would certainly not consider an expenditure of funds equal to or greater than the value of perfect information.

The expected value of perfect information (EVPI) can be determined rather easily. It can be defined as the difference between the payoff expected when the best decision is made on the basis of available data and the payoff expected when perfect information is available.

Consider again the bakery problem whose payoffs are shown in Table 4-6. If perfect information were available, the grocer would always stock the quantity of cakes that equaled the actual demand, and the payoffs or profits would be the circled ones on the diagonal of the table. The expected profits under these conditions are listed in Table 4-17. If perfect information were available and the grocer knew exactly how many cakes to stock, the total expected profit would be $5.32.

With the information that the grocer actually had, the best decision was

Table 4-17 Expected profits from cake sales when perfect information is available

Actual demand	Probability	Payoff	Expected profit
25	.10	$5.00	$ .50
26	.30	5.20	1.56
27	.50	5.40	2.70
28	.10	5.60	.56
			$5.32

to stock 26 cakes, which yielded a profit of $5.10. Therefore the expected value of perfect information is $5.32 – $5.10, or $.22. Any efforts on the grocer's part to collect better data could increase the profits by only $.22 per day. If someone offered to provide better data at a cost of $2.00 per week, the grocer should refuse it, since perfect data would improve the weekly profit by only $7 × $.22$, or $1.54—if the store were open 7 days a week.

In the drapery pleater example, we will recall that the expected payoff for A_2 was $4,200. Under conditions of perfect information we would always make the right decision. Therefore, if the information told the designer that high demand was the condition expected, she would select A_2; if low demand was the condition expected, she would choose A_1. We should be careful to note, however, that $P(S_1) = .70$ and $P(S_2) = .30$. Taking these probabilities into account,

$$.70(\$9,000) + .30(\$2,000) = \$6,300 + \$600 = \$6,900.$$

This figure represents the expected *payoff* of perfect information. The expected *value* of perfect information would be the net difference between this figure ($6,900) and the EMV of the best alternative selected without perfect information, which was A_2 where EMV = $4,200. Therefore, the EVPI would be $6,900 – $4,200, or $2,700. The designer could then afford to pay up to $2,700 for perfect information, assuming that it was possible to collect.

BAYESIAN DECISION THEORY

In many decision situations it becomes necessary to compare the costs of making an erroneous decision with the expense of collecting new information. Bayesian decision concepts provide a means to handle such problems. These concepts are a logical extension of decision theory into conditions of uncertainty in which there is only partial information. Bayesian decision theory involves a set of decision-making steps that deal with progressive improvements in the information needed to make a decision. The provision of new information is done at a cost, and the business manager must decide whether the value of the information makes up for the cost of securing it.

Bayesian decision theory provides a scientific approach to selecting the best course of action when the outcome depends upon a state of nature. Again, the state of nature is unknown and not under the control of the decision maker; however, it is possible to derive information about it from judgment or experimentation.

Types of Bayesian Analysis

Prior Analysis In prior analysis, the decision maker specifies states of nature, their probabilities, and payoffs of alternative decision–state of nature combinations. He or she makes the selection from alternative courses of action on the basis of this information. An entrepreneur will often have to make this type of decision when time or resources do not permit the collection of additional information.

Preposterior Analysis Sometimes the availability of time or the importance of the decision calls for the decision maker to delay his decision pending the collection and analysis of additional information. The firm must pay for this information, and it will almost never be entirely accurate. The decision maker will have to weigh the cost of the information against its value to the firm—against the risks or potential results of a decision based on prior analysis. Therefore this kind of analysis, known as preposterior, involves whether or not to collect the information in the first place.

Posterior Analysis Once the new information is known, the decision maker incorporates it into the analysis, calculates the expected payoffs of alternative actions, and selects that action leading to the highest expected payoff, given the information then available. This incorporation of new information and revision of prior probabilities is called posterior analysis. The process of revision of prior notions on the basis of new information is one of the strengths of Bayesian analysis.

Sequential Analysis Decision situations involving multistage information collection and evaluation are within the domain of sequential analysis. It involves a series of preposterior analysis steps in which decisions are made regarding the value to the firm of possible sequences of action, such as information collection over a period of time.

Prior Analysis

In Chapter 2, we imagined that our firm was considering the introduction of the deodorant Wisp. Now we can return to that example and use Bayesian analysis in the decision-making process. Assume that considerable use of logic has resulted in the conditional payoff matrix shown in Table 4-18.

In this table, each A_j represents an alternative course of action for the firm, while the S_i values represent the potential market reactions. The firm can choose between introducing Wisp and not introducing it; if Wisp is abandoned, the company will spend more on promotion of current products. The states of nature are assumed to be mutually exclusive, collectively exhaustive events. (In many cases, of course, there would be more than two states of nature and two alternative courses of action.) Assume that the payoffs are net profits (or losses) in the tens of thousands of dollars, with zero dollars omitted. If the company introduces Wisp and the market is good, the profit will be $80,000, while if the market reaction is poor the net loss will be $30,000. If A_2 is selected and there is a good market, the loss will be $40,000, because of sunk costs and potential competitive successes. If the market for the new product is poor and the firm promotes its current line, the expected gain is $100,000.

We could conduct a prior analysis now and make a final decision. To do this we would calculate the expected monetary value of each alternative and choose the alternative with the highest EMV. If we assume that the probabilities of states of nature S_1 and S_2 are .60 and .40, respectively, the respective EMVs are as follows:

$$\text{EMV}(A_1) = .60(8) + .40(-3) = 3.6,$$
$$\text{EMV}(A_2) = .60(-4) + .40(10) = 1.6.$$

Action A_1 would be selected.

Table 4-18 Conditional payoff matrix for Wisp deodorant

Alternative actions / Market reactions	A_1 (Introduce Wisp)	A_2 (Do not introduce Wisp; promote current products)
S_1 (Good)	8	-4
S_2 (Poor)	-3	10

Table 4-19 Opportunity loss matrix for Wisp deodorant

Alternative actions / Market reactions	A_1 (Introduce Wisp)	A_2 (Do not introduce Wisp; promote current products)
S_1 (Good)	0	12
S_2 (Poor)	13	0

Table 4-19 shows the problem formulated according to expected opportunity losses. Applying the same methodology used for the EMV calculations, we find that alternative A_1 has an EOL of 5.2, while alternative A_2 has an EOL of 7.2. Once again, A_1 would be selected. In this case, both methods yielded the same decision, and the differences between the EMVs for A_1 and A_2 and the EOLs for A_1 and A_2 were both 2.0.

We have noted that both methods led to the selection of A_1, the introduction of Wisp, as the better alternative. The question may come up: How small would $P(S_1)$ have to be before we shifted our decision from A_1 to A_2? This type of question introduces *indifference probabilities*. An indifference probability is the probability of occurrence that gives the two alternatives an equal EMV, so that one alternative would be just as good as the other. The indifference probabilities in our example can be determined by equating the expected losses of the two actions in the opportunity loss table. If

$$P_1 = \text{indifference probability of state of nature } S_1,$$
$$(1 - P_1) = \text{indifference probability of state of nature } S_2,$$

then

$$P_1(0) + (1 - P_1)(13) = P_1(12) + (1 - P_1)(0),$$
$$13 - 13P_1 = 12P_1,$$
$$25P_1 = 13,$$
$$P_1 = 13/25 = .52.$$

Therefore, if $P(S_1)$ is greater than .52, A_1 will lead to a lower EOL than A_2. But when $P(S_1)$ is less than .52, the decision maker will select A_2. In a practical situation, when we are dealing with two outcomes, all we have to do is estimate whether the $P(S_1)$ is greater or less than the indifference value, which in this case is .52. Note that we could have calculated the same indifference probabilities from the conditional payoff matrix.

In summary, prior analysis begins with specification of a set of mutually exclusive, collectively exhaustive alternative strategies and states of nature. Given the estimated probabilities for the states of nature, we select a strategy that maximizes expected monetary value or minimizes expected opportunity loss.

Preposterior Extensive Form Analysis

The method of prior analysis does not demonstrate the true "power" of Bayesian decision theory, because it does not include examination of the advisability of collecting additional information and of the potential payoffs of this information. Preposterior analysis, in contrast, deals with a decision-making situation in which a judgment is made as to *whether or not it is economically desirable to collect additional information.* Thus, in the Wisp example, if we were not satisfied with the information used in our prior evaluation, we could make an evaluation to determine whether or not to collect additional information. We would be asking, "How much is it worth to our firm to collect additional information?"

Consider how this concept might be applied to the Wisp example. On the basis of past experience with market surveys, a firm's marketing research department can often estimate how accurate a survey of consumer attitudes will be. The analysts know that in no sense can a survey be entirely accurate. Table 4-20 presents some assumed conditional probabilities of obtaining survey results that match the true states of nature. Remember that this analysis is taking place before actual collection of the information.

From the probabilities shown in the table, it can be seen that the marketing research department feels that the results will be slightly more accurate when the market is good than when it is bad. In addition, the researchers feel that there is a possibility of obtaining inconclusive results to the survey.

Although we need the information in Table 4-20, we are still interested in what the probabilities are for the two states of nature *given* potential survey results. This statement makes it appear that we are dealing with another conditional probability; this is, in fact, the case. We are looking for $P(S_1|Z_j)$ and $P(S_2|Z_j)$, which will become our revised prior probabilities; what we have available is $P(Z_j|S_1)$ and $P(Z_j|S_2)$. It is here that

Table 4-20 Conditional probabilities of survey results given states of nature: $P(Z_j|S_i)$

Survey results Market reactions	Z_1 (Market good)	Z_2 (Market poor)	Z_3 (Inconclusive results)
S_1 (Good) S_2 (Poor)	.80 .10	.10 .75	.10 .15

Bayesian analysis is introduced. Bayes' rule states that

$$P(S_1 | Z_1) = \frac{P(Z_1 | S_1) \cdot P(S_1)}{P(Z_1 | S_1) \cdot P(S_1) + P(Z_1 | S_2) \cdot P(S_2)},$$

where we would include all $P(Z_1 | S_i)$ in the denominator. Although this formula may appear to be complicated, we can easily relate it to the probability material we covered in Chapter 2. The probability of $S_i | Z_j$ is a conditional probability, and as Chapter 2 explains, a conditional probability is a joint probability divided by a marginal probability. The denominator is simply a summation of all joint probabilities containing the Z of interest; the result of this summation of joint probabilities is the marginal probability of the Z we are dealing with, which in this case could be Z_1, Z_2, or Z_3. The numerator is the joint probability containing the elements that correspond to those of the conditional probability we are seeking. For example, $P(S_1 | Z_1)$ could be written in this way:

$$P(S_1 | Z_1) = \frac{P(S_1 \cap Z_1)}{P(Z_1)}.$$

Using Bayes' rule in combination with our prior probabilities—$P(S_1) = .60$, $P(S_2) = .40$—we can establish a table of revised prior probabilities. In Table 4-21, we have calculated joint probabilities by multiplying the conditional probabilities shown in Table 4-20 by the respective prior probabilities. The marginal probabilities of Z are derived by summing down the joint probabilities, as demonstrated in Chapter 2, and the marginal $P(S_i)$ are verified by summing across. Table 4-22 shows the revised prior probabilities, found by dividing each joint probability by the appropriate marginal probability of Z, according to Bayes' rule.

For example,

$$P(S_1 | Z_1) = \frac{\text{Joint probability of } S_1 \text{ and } Z_1}{\text{Marginal probability of } Z_1} = \frac{P(S_1 \cap Z_1)}{P(Z_1)} = \frac{.48}{.52} = .923.$$

Table 4-21 Joint and marginal probabilities for Wisp deodorant

Survey results Probability	Z_1	Z_2	Z_3	$P(S_i)$
$P(Z_j | S_1) \cdot P(S_1)$ or $P(S_1 \cap Z_j)$	$.80 \times .60 = .48$	$.10 \times .60 = .06$	$.10 \times .60 = .06$	.60
$P(Z_j | S_2) \cdot P(S_2)$ or $P(S_2 \cap Z_j)$	$.10 \times .40 = .04$	$.75 \times .40 = .30$	$.15 \times .40 = .06$	.40
$P(Z_j)$	.52	.36	.12	1.00

Table 4-22 Revised prior probabilities for Wisp deodorant

Survey results / Probability	Z_1	Z_2	Z_3
$P(S_1 \mid Z_j)$	$.48/.52 = .923$	$.06/.36 = .167$	$.06/.12 = .500$
$P(S_2 \mid Z_j)$	$.04/.52 = .077$	$.30/.36 = .833$	$.06/.12 = .500$

Each posterior probability in Table 4-22 represents the probability of a particular state of nature, S_i, conditioned upon the occurrence of a particular survey result, Z_j. In other words, it indicates the chances that S_i will occur if some particular Z occurs.

Having set up the information shown in Table 4-22, we are ready to answer the question about the value of collecting additional information. Figure 4-3 is a decision tree that incorporates all the needed information. A thorough examination of this decision tree illustrates the process of working with trees in general.

First, a decision tree usually involves a process called *backwards induction*, because the computational process works from right to left. Second, there are two types of nodes on the decision tree. One is a *probabilistic node*, which is a point at which the decision maker faces uncontrollable factors, such as states of nature or potential survey outcomes. These nodes are indicated by circles on the decision tree. In the situations represented by these nodes, the manager must accept an expected value because he or she is dealing with a probabilistic event. The other type of node is a *decision node*, at which the manager is to make a choice from among the alternative strategies. These nodes are indicated by squares on the tree. Since this choice is under the decision maker's control, he or she should choose the maximum gain or minimum opportunity loss, as the case may warrant.

We should be careful to treat the Z_j values as uncontrollable outcomes, since we have no control over the results of a scientific market survey. For this reason, the 6.84 EMV was obtained by multiplying each selected strategy's payoff by the marginal probability of the survey outcome:

$$.52(7.153) + .36(7.66) + .12(3.00) = 6.84.$$

Before we proceed to normal form analysis, another way to view the same problem, two additional things should be noted. First, examine how different the conditional $P(S_i \mid Z_j)$ are from the prior probabilities. For example, $P(S_1 \mid Z_1)$ is .923, while in prior analysis $P(S_1)$ was .60. The .923, a revised prior probability, is so much larger than the original probability

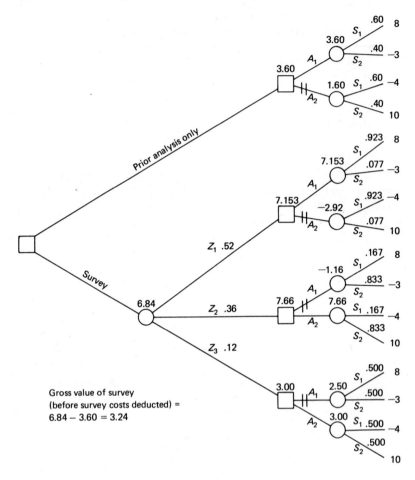

Figure 4-3 Decision tree for Wisp deodorant

because the assumed given information (Z_1) corresponds to S_1: the survey indicates that market conditions are good, and they *are* good. Each of the other results can be reasoned out in a similar manner.

Second, the result of the analysis is a *gross* result; no costs of the survey have been incorporated. Theoretically, the decision maker could pay as much as 3.24 units for the survey information, but more realistically, he or she would want to pay less than this in order to get a *net* benefit from collecting the survey information. Paying more than 3.24 units for the survey would be irrational behavior, because the manager could obtain a larger payoff by simply selecting the optimal prior strategy and proceeding.

Preposterior Normal Form Analysis

In order to demonstrate the versatility of Bayesian analysis, we can use another approach, normal form analysis, which does not involve Bayes'

Table 4-23 Normal form strategies for Wisp deodorant

Strategies	Z_1	Z_2	Z_3
C_1	A_1	A_1	A_1
C_2	A_1	A_1	A_2
C_3	A_1	A_2	A_1
C_4	A_1	A_2	A_2
C_5	A_2	A_1	A_1
C_6	A_2	A_1	A_2
C_7	A_2	A_2	A_1
C_8	A_2	A_2	A_2

rule. As is the case for extensive form analysis, either expected monetary value or expected opportunity loss can be calculated; the same set of decision rules will result. Regardless of which value is selected, the outcomes of normal form analysis will be identical to those of extensive form.

Table 4-23 lists all the possible combinations of alternative actions and survey results in the Wisp example. Each possible combination can be called a *strategy*, or C. From Tables 4-19 and 4-20, we can calculate the conditional expected opportunity loss (CEOL) of each of these strategies, given the respective true states of nature S_1 and S_2:

$$\text{CEOL}(C_1 \,|\, S_1) = .80(0) + .10(0) + .10(0) = 0,$$
$$\text{CEOL}(C_1 \,|\, S_2) = .10(13) + .75(13) + .15(13) = 13.0,$$
$$\text{CEOL}(C_2 \,|\, S_1) = .80(0) + .10(0) + .10(12) = 1.2,$$
$$\vdots$$
$$\text{CEOL}(C_8 \,|\, S_1) = .80(12) + .10(12) + .10(12) = 12.0.$$

The rest of the conditional expected opportunity losses are found in Table 4-24. From these computations, we can see the EOL of each feasible combination of strategy and state of nature.

Convex Set Solution In Figure 4-4, the losses have been plotted, and they form what is called a polyhedral convex set.* Use of this figure requires only limited experience with convex sets. Note that the extreme points on the convex set (C_1 and C_8) are pure strategies: C_1 consists of always choosing action A_1, while C_8 consists of always choosing action A_2. The strategies between these extreme points are mixed strategies, combinations of A_1 and A_2. As we saw from the decision tree, it may not be best

---

* The student who has had no prior work with convex sets can skip this section and continue with the section entitled "Tabular Solution." For those who have had experience with convex sets, the graphic presentation here should prove useful.

Table 4-24 Conditional expected opportunity losses for Wisp deodorant

States of nature	C_1	C_2	C_3	C_4	C_5	C_6	C_7	C_8
S_1	0	1.2	1.2	2.4	9.6	10.8	10.8	12.0
S_2	13.0	11.05	3.25	1.3	11.7	9.75	1.95	0

always to take A_1 or always to take A_2. Depending upon outcomes, we may want to take A_1 in some instances and A_2 in others.

Because we are dealing with losses, intuition tells us that we should select the decision strategy that is closest to the lower left in Figure 4-4. But before making the final selection of the best strategy, we should look back at Table 4-24. In this table we can observe that there are some

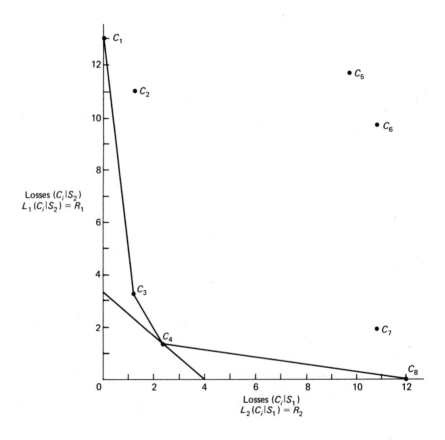

Figure 4-4 Convex set of conditional expected opportunity losses for Wisp deodorant

strategies that have larger EOLs for both states of nature than other strategies. For example, we can see that

$$C_3 \ (1.2, \ 3.25) < C_5 \ (9.6, \ 11.7),$$
$$C_4 \ (2.4, \ 1.3) < C_6 \ (10.8, \ 9.75),$$
$$C_4 \ (2.4, \ 1.3) < C_7 \ (10.8, \ 1.95).$$

In this situation, we can say that C_6 and C_7 are *dominated* by C_4, and that C_5 is dominated by C_3. Because they are dominated by other strategies, C_5, C_6, and C_7 are *inadmissible* strategies. The subset of *admissible* strategies consists of those lying on the lower boundary of the convex set: C_1, C_3, C_4, and C_8. It is from this subset of four strategies that we wish to select the optimum strategy. Because we are dealing with only two states of nature, we can establish a straight line that reflects the prior probabilities of the states of nature and the expected losses:

$$.60(R_1) + .40(R_2) = L.$$

Extending this line, which reflects prior probabilities, from the origin in a left-to-right fashion, we find that the optimum solution occurs at the intersection of the line and the convex set. We will select that intersection which is in the lower portion of the convex set; it is at C_4.

Tabular Solution As an alternative to using the convex set for solving the problem, we can set up a table such as Table 4-25. From examination of the table, we can determine the strategy that has the lowest expected opportunity loss, irrespective of which survey outcome takes place. In this table the conditional expected opportunity losses from Table 4-24 are multiplied by the prior probabilities of the states of nature. In this case, C_4 has the smallest *unconditional* expected opportunity loss.

A comparison of the results of this approach with the results of the extensive form analysis shows that the decision rules provided by the two methods are the same. The choice of which method to use in Bayesian analysis is made on the basis of preference only. Although normal form analysis calls for, at least initially, specification of all feasible strategies, a task which may be cumbersome, the decision trees used in extensive form analysis can also become unwieldy.

Table 4-25 Unconditional expected opportunity losses of C_i for Wisp deodorant

$$C_1 = .60 \,(0) + .40 \,(13.0) = 5.2$$
$$C_3 = .60 \,(1.2) + .40 \,(3.25) = .72 + 1.3 = 2.02$$
$$C_4 = .60 \,(2.4) + .40 \,(1.3) = 1.44 + .52 = 1.96$$
$$C_8 = .60 \,(12.0) + .40 \,(0) = 7.2$$

Sequential Analysis

The Proctor Company, the producer of Wisp, is considering the purchase of a multistage survey. This is often the case under conditions of uncertainty; the first stage is exploratory, and later stages give progressively more precise examinations of the problem. Assume that Proctor is thinking of a two-stage study, the first stage of which is 70 percent reliable and the second stage of which is 80 percent reliable. The research department feels that neither survey will yield inconclusive results; there are only two potential survey outcomes, indicating that either S_1 or S_2 is going to take place. The respective survey reliabilities can be expressed as indicated in Table 4-26.

The research department has estimated the cost of survey 1, the first stage, to be .70, or $70,000; survey 2, because of the ground breaking done on survey 1, will cost only .50, or $50,000. The probabilities of states of nature S_1 and S_2 remain .60 and .40, respectively. Management wants to decide which of the following decisions to make:

D_0 to purchase no survey;

D_1 to purchase only the first, or 70 percent reliable (30 percent unreliable), survey for $70,000;

D_2 to purchase both surveys, the second being 80 percent reliable (20 percent unreliable) and costing $50,000.

This problem can be set up in a probability table, very similar to the ones for preposterior analysis, that includes the appropriate joint, marginal, and conditional probabilities. The left side of Table 4-27 shows the now-familiar calculation of the probabilities for survey 1. For example, the joint probability for Z_1 and S_1 is found in this way:

$$P(Z_1 | S_1) \cdot P(S_1) = .70 \times .60 = .42.$$

In our calculation of the probabilities for survey 2, the conditional probabilities found for survey 1 become the *prior* probabilities. The entry .62

Table 4-26 Conditional probabilities of survey
results for Wisp deodorant

	Survey 1	Survey 2
$P(Z_1 | S_1)$	.70	.80
$P(Z_2 | S_2)$	.70	.80
$P(Z_1 | S_2)$	.30	.20
$P(Z_2 | S_1)$	.30	.20

Table 4-27 Preposterior sequential analysis probabilities for Wisp deodorant

	Survey 1		Survey 2			
	Z_1	Z_2	$Z_1 \cap Z_1$	$Z_2 \cap Z_1$	$Z_1 \cap Z_2$	$Z_2 \cap Z_2$
S_1	.42	.18	.62	.16	.31	.08
S_2	.12	.28	.04	.18	.12	.49
	.54	.46	.66	.34	.43	.57
$P(S_1 \| Z_j)$	.78	.39	.94	.47	.72	.14
$P(S_2 \| Z_j)$	.22	.61	.06	.53	.28	.86

in the upper left-hand corner of the right side of the table was derived
as follows:

$$P(S_1 | Z_1) \cdot P(Z_1 | S_1) = .78 \times .80 = .62.$$

$P(S_1 | Z_1)$ is a conditional probability from survey 1, and $P(Z_1 | S_1)$
represents the 80 percent survey reliability. We can directly multiply these
because they are assumed to be independent: The survey reliability and the
revised prior probability from the first stage are assumed to have no
interaction. As another illustration, the entry .49 in the right-hand column
of the lower part of the table was found as follows:

$$P(S_2 | Z_2) \cdot P(Z_2 | S_2) = .61 \times .80 = .49.$$

Once the appropriate joint, marginal, and conditional probabilities have
been calculated, the problem can be placed in a decision tree. Figure 4-5
illustrates the two alternatives, D_0 and D_1, in the standard preposterior
analysis format. With the given information, strategy D_1 would be selected
over strategy D_0, since the payoffs are 4.40 (after the survey cost of .70 is
deducted) and 3.60, respectively.

Figure 4-6 represents the sequential analysis component of the decision.
Because D_1 was preferred to D_0, D_0 has been dropped from the admissible
alternative strategies. There are two types of branches in Figure 4-6:
branches representing strategy D_2, in which both stages of the survey are
purchased, and branches illustrating D_1, the decision to stop collecting
information after the first stage. We can see that this decision tree can be
a great aid to the decision maker, because there is no *pure strategy* evident;
no one decision rule is sufficient for guidance on all branches. For example,
if the result Z_1, which indicates favorable market conditions, is obtained
on survey 1, the decision maker should elect to stop collecting information
and should choose action A_1. Decision sequence $D_1–A_1$ would be the best
choice. However, if result Z_2, which indicates unfavorable market conditions, is obtained on survey 1, then strategy D_2 should be followed,

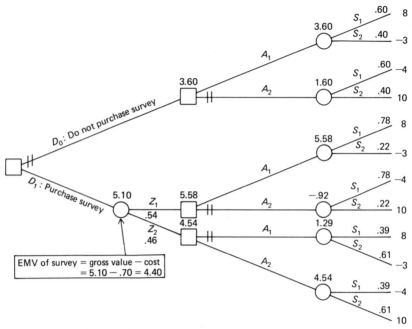

Figure 4-5 Preposterior decision tree for Wisp deodorant

since it yields a higher expected monetary value. If a Z_1 result on the *second* survey is found after a Z_2 result on the first survey, action A_1 (introducing the product) should be selected. However, a sequence of Z_2, Z_2 should lead the decision maker to select A_2 (not introducing the product). This represents one of the few instances in decision theory in which the actual value or cost of collecting information is calculated.

Benefits of Bayesian Analysis

Any method used in quantitative analysis can be viewed as having two components; the first is the *content* or results and the second is the *procedure* or processes used. Bayesian decision theory yields the following content benefits.

1. The results, when used in conjunction with other information, can be a useful aid in strategy selection in prior analysis.

2. The technique allows flexibility in making decisions on the usefulness of collecting additional information. In traditional or classical statistical analysis, the costs of information and even the costs of making a wrong decision are often ignored.

Procedurally, Bayesian decision theory is perhaps even more useful, providing the following benefits.

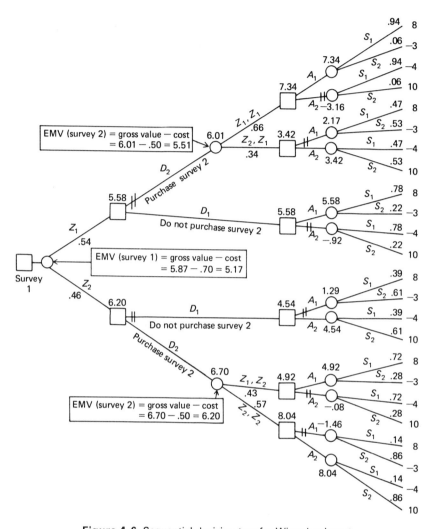

Figure 4-6 Sequential decision tree for Wisp deodorant

1. The decision maker is forced to specify alternative decisions that are available to solve the particular problem at hand. This may seem rather trivial, but it is actually a major benefit of Bayesian analysis. Many decisions are made before proper specification of alternative courses of action; as a result, some feasible strategies are never considered.

2. Once the alternative courses of action (D_i, A_j) have been specified, their potential outcomes must be evaluated for all possible combinations of variables (S_i, Z_j). When this is done, decision making becomes more scientific.

3. Bayesian theory allows us to incorporate subjective probabilities into the analysis. Some might argue that this is one of the major weaknesses of the technique, but it is also one of the strengths. In many situations of uncertainty (partial ignorance), it is impossible to specify objectively the probabilities of particular outcomes. This is especially true in marketing and financial problems. The incorporation of subjective probabilities simply formalizes what would be done anyway in a more haphazard fashion, in "seat-of-the-pants" decisions.

Limitations of Bayesian Analysis

Several deficiencies, both theoretical and procedural, are found in Bayesian analysis.

1. The probabilities used are subjective, and many people feel that they should not be treated in the same manner as objective probabilities.

2. For a complex decision the procedure can become computationally difficult.

3. The estimation of prior distributions and conditional payoffs is difficult and in some cases arbitrary. Although the decision is being made under conditions of uncertainty, the conditional payoffs, once they are estimated, are treated as fixed and are not subject to later adjustment. Essentially, this means that an extensive amount of work goes into revising probabilities, but the estimation of payoffs for particular outcomes is assumed to be correct.

To remedy the first deficiency, much work is being done to combine the more traditional methods and Bayesian techniques. For example, work is being done in the areas of Bayesian regression analysis, Bayesian approaches to sampling, and multistage Bayesian pricing models. The pure statistician might simply argue that the use of a subjective probability distribution makes the technique unscientific. We share this concern to a limited extent, but we see no way to avoid the problem in many decision-making situations.

Regarding the second deficiency, the introduction of computerized procedures has greatly simplified the computational task, although in situations with many possible actions and states of nature the procedure is still complex.

The estimation of prior distributions and conditional payoffs requires an extensive amount of managerial expertise. If there is much disagreement among managers, the specification of prior probabilities may yield relatively "informationless" prior distributions, and the collection of any additional information, such as in preposterior analysis, will simply override the prior probabilities. But this may, in fact, be a benefit, because what was to be an "informationless" decision will have been transformed into one that is more scientific.

In many problems we do not see a way to avoid the difficulties of Bayesian analysis, short of not making the decision or blindly applying traditional statistical methods that do not examine the costs of information or the costs of making a wrong decision. The solution appears to lie in sound management practices—in other words, in following the scientific procedures described in Chapter 1.

PROBLEMS

1. Explain:

   (a) Bayes' rule
   (b) conditional probability
   (c) sequential analysis
   (d) extensive form analysis
   (e) EVPI
   (f) posterior analysis

2. In a local auto body shop 65 percent of "towed in" automobiles cost more to repair this year than a year ago. Thirty-five percent of the "drive in" automobiles needing repair cost more to repair this year than last. Automobiles towed in comprise 70 percent of all the business for this repair shop.

   (a) If an automobile in need of repair is selected at random, what is the probability that the repair will cost more than a year ago?
   (b) If an auto is selected and is noted to cost more to repair than a year ago, what is the probability that it had to be towed in?

3. The median age of players on a professional football team is 25 years. Of the athletes under 25, 65 percent played college football. Of those above the median age, 45 percent played only sand-lot ball. There are no players who played both sand-lot and college ball.

   If a football player is selected at random and if he did not play college football, what is the probability that he will be older than the median age of 25?

4. The Wipe Clean Sponge Company produces a variety of sponges. Some are made from synthetic material, and others are natural, or come from the sea. Both must be shaped by machines into usable sizes. This shaping process produces certain defects in the sponges. The lots show the following frequency distribution.

Proportion of lot defective	Frequency
.04	.40
.05	.44
.08	.11
.13	.02
.19	.03
	1.00

As the plant manager, you take periodic spot samples; today's sample of 15 from one lot has produced no defects. What posterior probabilities could you assign to the events labeled "proportion of lot defective"? (*Note:* Information from the binomial distribution discussed in Chapter 2 should be used in solving this problem.)

5. As the new manager of an auto tire dealership, one of your responsibilities is supervising the tire retreading department. You have gathered information about the process, and it reveals that there are some tires that do not retread properly and must be discarded. Five trucks containing tires for retreading have arrived, and the contents have been assigned the following frequency distribution.

Proportion of lot defective	Frequency
.04	.30
.16	.25
.18	.08
.05	.06
.06	.31
	1.00

You must sample the finished batch of retreaded tires, and today you sample a lot of 20 tires. In doing so you discover that there is one defect in this sample lot. You must ascertain the posterior probabilities in order to decide whether to take another sample lot and/or make complete payment to the supplier.

6. The MCA data collection firm has been a leader in the field of market panel data collection. One of the persistent problems faced by management is the accuracy of the personal interview that is used to screen for participants in the panel. When participants have been interviewed by Shirley Thomas, .15 of them show inaccurate responses. When Ted Williams interviews, .30 of the participants' responses are inaccurate. As a manager you know that Thomas interviews 60 percent of the participants and Williams interviews the rest.

Recently one respondent came in to talk to you and you found that her response was inaccurate. However, she did not remember who interviewed her and your records did not indicate either. What is the probability that this respondent was interviewed by Thomas?

7. When a machine in a complex production process is correctly set up by an operator, .20 of the items produced are defective. When the machine is set up incorrectly, .60 of the production is defective. The manufacturer knows from past experience that the probability of a machine's being set up correctly is .50, but he is uncertain whether to proceed with the current setup. To reduce the uncertainty, he decides to obtain additional information by taking a sample of one piece. This piece is defective. What is the probability that this particular setup is incorrect?

8. A small business firm is in a situation where it is forced to introduce a new product that is certain to lose money. Management has wisely decided that the strategy to follow is to attempt to lose as little money as possible. The following payoff matrix describes the situation.

Market reactions	A_1	A_2
S_1	-10	-4
S_2	-5	-12

$$P(S_1) = .60 \quad \text{and} \quad P(S_2) = .40$$

The losses are in thousands of dollars.

(a) From prior analysis, which course of action should the management follow?

(b) A local business firm has volunteered to conduct a survey of 70 percent reliability at a cost of $400. Should the managers buy the survey even though it requires an additional outlay of money?

9. J. M. McDolands Restaurants, Inc., a hamburger restaurant chain, is considering selling fried chicken in addition to its regular line of hamburgers. The company's marketing research department has been asked to come up with some information that will aid McDolands executives in making the decision. The executives, with the marketing research department, have constructed the following payoff matrix.

Market reactions	A_1 (Sell chicken)	A_2 (Stay with regular line)
S_1 (Favorable)	$1,400,000	0
S_2 (Unfavorable)	$-700,000	0

$$P(S_1) = .70 \quad \text{and} \quad P(S_2) = .30$$

The marketing research department has three possible decisions:

D_0 It can select an alternative now, on the basis of current information.

D_1 It can conduct a survey of 70 percent reliability on its own. $P(Z_1|S_1) = P(Z_2|S_2) = .70$, and $P(Z_1|S_2) = P(Z_2|S_1) = .30$; the survey cost is $50,000.

D_2 It can purchase from MCA Corporation a two-stage survey that is 65 percent reliable in the first stage and 70 percent reliable in the second stage. McDolands may stop after the first stage at a cost of $25,000, or it may proceed with the second stage at an additional cost of $55,000.

(a) What would be the prior payoffs of not taking a survey (decision D_0)? What is the expected value of perfect information?
(b) Compute the expected payoffs for D_1 and D_2 by using decision trees.
(c) Which of the three strategies (D_0, D_1, or D_2) should be selected?

SUPPLEMENTARY READINGS

Bierman, H., C. P. Bonini, and W. H. Hausman. *Quantitative Analysis for Business Decisions*, 4th ed. Irwin, Homewood, Ill., 1973.

Chernoff, H., and L. E. Moses. *Elementary Decision Theory*. Wiley, New York, 1959.

Churchman, C. W., R. Ackoff, and E. L. Arnoff. *Introduction to Operations Research*. Wiley, New York, 1957.

Green, P. E. "Bayesian Statistics and Product Decision." *Business Horizons*, 5 (Fall 1962), 101–109.

Hirshleifer, J. "The Bayesian Approach to Statistical Decision." *Journal of Business*, 34 (October 1961), 471–489.

Kaufmann, A. *Methods and Models of Operations Research*. Prentice-Hall, Englewood Cliffs, N.J., 1963.

Miller, D. W., and M. K. Starr. *Executive Decisions and Operations Research*. Prentice-Hall, Englewood Cliffs, N.J., 1960.

Raiffa, H. *Decision Analysis*. Addison-Wesley, Reading, Mass., 1968.

Savage, L. J. "Business Statistics." In *Recent Developments in Information and Decision Processes*. Macmillan, New York, 1962.

Schlaifer, R. *Analysis of Decisions Under Uncertainty*. McGraw-Hill, New York, 1969.

Schlaifer, R. *Probability and Statistics for Business Decisions*. McGraw-Hill, New York, 1959, pp. 330–354, 508–518, 590–602.

5/Discrete Analysis and Trade-Offs

THIS CHAPTER presents some of the more traditional decision-making approaches used in financial management. These approaches often utilize *discrete analysis*, the evaluation of specific points or values. This chapter provides an opportunity to review these traditional techniques and at the same time to delve into problems involving simple schematic and mathematical models before going into the techniques usually considered part of operations research. This chapter is not, however, intended to cover all of the many approaches to financial decision making. Two general types of problems will be considered. The first deals with replacement of equipment, and the second involves break-even analysis and the associated profit, pricing, and facilities decisions.

In any manufacturing or service organization, continuous evaluation of facilities and equipment is necessary in order to ferret out facts needed in making decisions to retain or replace equipment. These equipment-replacement decisions involve economic comparisons between alternatives. The need for replacement arises primarily from two factors:

1. Decreased reliability of the equipment, and the associated increase in costs of operation and maintenance.

2. Technological obsolescence.

These two factors, which result in increasing cost as equipment ages, must be traded off against decreased costs resulting from greater efficiency, improved productivity, and the spread of the capital costs over a longer period.

COSTS AND RELIABILITY

Reliability is defined as the probability that a piece of equipment will operate for a specified period of time without failure. As an example, the reliability for an automatic machine in a production line could be specified as .90 for one year. This would mean that there was a probability of .90 that the equipment would operate for one year without failure.

A piece of equipment would typically have a failure rate curve similar to Figure 5-1. To begin with, there are early-life failures during the initial operating period. The purchaser of a new automobile, for example, usually finds a number of things to be fixed within the first ninety days after purchase. In electronic equipment and some other products, this low reliability in early life can be improved by operation of the product in the factory (burn-in) to reveal defects for correction before shipment. Following these early-life failures, the equipment settles down to a relatively low and fixed failure rate over most of its normal life span. But as the equipment becomes older, the failure rate increases (the reliability decreases); parts wear out and start to fail. This increase in failure rate can be reduced by overhaul, but otherwise it will steadily increase until the equipment is discarded.

The decrease in reliability as equipment ages will result in increased costs, because of greater maintenance and increased downtime. When equipment breaks down or is out of use for any reason, the firm must endure not only the costs of labor and parts to repair the equipment, but also the costs associated with downtime, such as idle workers, a shut-down production line, and failure to meet schedules. The older equipment may also consume more power, fuel, or lubricants as it becomes worn, which will in turn increase operating costs.

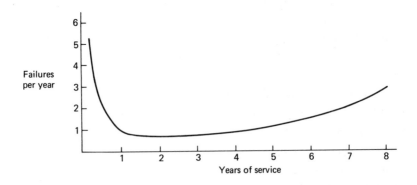

Figure 5-1 Failure rate over equipment life span

TECHNOLOGICAL OBSOLESCENCE

Equipment can become obsolete even if there is no decrease in reliability or increase in the costs of maintenance. This obsolescence takes place simply because newly developed competitive equipment can do the same task at lower cost. If the costs per unit of production of operating and maintaining the new equipment are lower enough to justify the cost of acquiring it, then the old equipment is technologically obsolescent. Usually technical improvements are made gradually, so most replacement decisions involve a combination of the wearing-out and technical-change factors. Often a manufacturing facility will be subject to replacement because of a number of technological and other factors combined with considerations of wear.

PRESENT VALUE

A thousand dollars received today is worth more than a thousand dollars received a year from today. A thousand dollars received two years from today is worth less than either of these. We are not referring to the effects of inflation, but to the time value of money. The thousand dollars received today, invested at 6 percent interest, would bring in $60 income, so that at the end of the year there would be $1,060. Therefore we might say that $1,060 received a year from today has a *present value* of $1,000. The farther in the future the receipt of the money, the less its present value becomes. Similarly, an expenditure in the future has less impact on the firm's budget than an expenditure today. The impact of inflation is, of course, also a factor to be considered; however, it is much less predictable than the effect of time upon value. The present-value concept deals with a certainty, although the percentage value may be uncertain.

If $1,000 were received a year from today, its present value would be calculated in this way if its interest rate were 6 percent.

$$1.06 \times PV = \$1,000,$$

$$PV = \frac{\$1,000}{1.06} = \$943.40.$$

In the same manner, the present value of $1,000 received two years from today would be the value of the $943.40 one year later:

$$PV = \frac{\$943.40}{1.06} \quad \text{or} \quad \frac{\$1,000}{(1.06)(1.06)} = \$890.$$

The present value of $1,000 received n years from now would be:

$$PV = \frac{\$1,000}{(1.06)^n}.$$

if the interest rate is generalized to i and the amount to A,

$$PV = \frac{A}{(1+i)^n}.$$

As a specific example, the present value of $1,000 payable in 10 years, where i is 5 percent compounded annually, would be:

$$PV = \frac{\$1,000}{(1.05)^{10}} = \$613.91.$$

Several other relationships between time and money value are presented in the following table, for interest rate i and number of years n.[*]

Objective	Equation
To find the present value PV, given the future worth of a single amount A.	$PV = \dfrac{A}{(1+i)^n}$
To find the future value FV, given the present amount A.	$FV = A(1+i)^n$
To determine the value of annuity payments Y, given the present value PV.	$Y = \dfrac{PV(1+i)^n \times i}{(1+i)^n - 1}$
To determine the value of annuity payments Y, given the future value FV.	$Y = \dfrac{i(FV)}{(1+i)^n - 1}$
To determine the future value FV, given the annuity payments Y.	$FV = Y\dfrac{(1+i)^n - 1}{i}$
To determine the present value PV, given the annuity payments Y.	$PV = Y\dfrac{(1+i)^n - 1}{i(1+i)^n}$

---

[*] Instead of the equations shown here, a decision maker can use tables of present values and annuities; see J. L. Riggs, *Production Systems*, Wiley, New York, 1970, chapter 4 and appendix B.

A METHOD OF ANALYSIS FOR REPLACEMENT

A piece of equipment is to be considered for replacement by a similar but newer model. In this case, technological obsolescence is not involved. The costs of increasing unreliability and increased maintenance, as well as growing operating costs, are to be traded off against the acquisition cost of the newer equipment. We are searching for the point at which the sum of these costs is a minimum. Consider a concrete-mixer truck that costs $21,000 and that reaches a relatively constant trade-in value of about $3,000 after its normal four-year life period. The time value of money will be ignored initially, and the optimum point for replacement will be selected on the basis of average annual cost. The costs are compiled for a five-year use period; the total costs are then determined and divided by the years in use to obtain the average cost over the period. These costs are tabulated in Table 5-1. By comparison of the values in the last column, we observe that the minimum yearly average total cost occurs when the equipment is replaced after the third year of use. This is a discrete analysis, since we are considering replacement only at one-year intervals. If the time of replacement were considered as a continuous variable, the optimum replacement time could be in any year or part of a year. Again, the assumption here was that the equipment design did not change significantly and that replacement is by an item of a similar design.

So far we have not considered the time value of money. An analysis of the same problem is presented in Table 5-2 using a 10 percent interest rate to represent the time value of money. In this case, all quantities are converted to a present value. The decision will be based upon the annual costs in the last column of the table, which are calculated in the same way as annuity payments. The decision, then, is to select the years of service that will minimize the yearly "payment." In this problem, a four-year replacement cycle yields the minimum annuity equivalent. This is in contrast to the three-year decision when the time value of money was not considered. When the time value of money is considered, the yearly cost is, of course, higher. It can be observed, however, that the difference in yearly cost between three-year replacement and four-year replacement is less than 1 percent of the value itself. This is true in both Table 5-1 and Table 5-2. When the annual costs are plotted as curves in Figure 5-2, the minimum point on either curve shows the optimum replacement age. But the curves are rather flat close to the optimum age, again showing that a year more or less does not make a great deal of difference. Thus, the analysis that did not consider the time value of money provided a good estimate of the

Table 5-1 Tabular analysis for replacement of a concrete-mixer truck at minimum average cost

(1) Years in service	(2) Initial price or trade-in value at year's end	(3) Loss of value to date	(4) Operating cost per year	(5) Maintenance cost per year	(6) Operating and maintenance costs for year: (4)+(5)	(7) Cumulative operating and maintenance costs	(8) Average capital cost per year: (3)/(1)	(9) Yearly average operating and maintenance costs: (7)/(1)	(10) Yearly average total costs: (8)+(9)
0	$21,000								
1	11,400	$ 9,600	$ 9,000	$1,800	$10,800	$10,800	$9,600	$10,800	$20,400
2	6,300	14,700	10,800	2,400	13,200	24,000	7,350	12,000	19,350
3	3,600	17,400	12,600	3,600	16,200	40,200	5,800	13,400	19,200
4	3,000	18,000	14,400	4,800	19,200	59,400	4,500	14,850	19,350
5	3,000	18,000	16,200	6,000	22,200	81,600	3,600	16,320	19,920

Table 5-2 Tabular analysis for replacement of a concrete-mixer truck, assuming a 10 percent interest rate

(1) Years in service	(2) Present value of trade-in	(3) Initial price $21,000 minus present value of trade-in	(4) Present value of yearly operating and maintenance costs	(5) Cumulative present value of operating and maintenance costs	(6) Total present values: (3)+(5)	(7) Equivalent annuity or annual cost*
1	$11,400/(1+.10) = $10,364	$10,636	$10,800/(1+.10) = $9,818	$ 9,818	$20,454	$20,454 × 1.1 = $22,499
2	$ 6,300/(1+.10)^2 = $5,207	15,793	$13,200/(1+.10)^2 = $10,909	20,727	36,520	$36,520 × .576 = $21,036
3	$ 3,600/(1+.10)^3 = $2,705	18,295	$16,200/(1+.10)^3 = $12,171	32,898	51,193	$51,193 × .402 = $20,580
4	$ 3,000/(1+.10)^4 = $2,049	18,951	$19,200/(1+.10)^4 = $13,114	46,012	64,963	$64,963 × .315 = $20,463
5	$ 3,000/(1+.10)^5 = $1,862	19,138	$22,200/(1+.10)^5 = $13,780	59,792	78,930	$78,930 × .264 = $20,838

* This is equal to the value in column (6) multiplied by $i(1+i)^n/(1+i)^n - 1$.

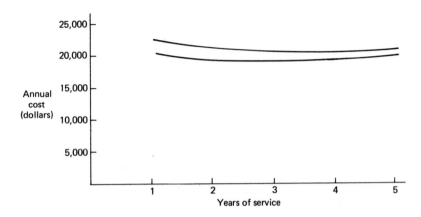

Figure 5-2 Continuous plots of annual costs for concrete-mixer truck

optimum service life. If the interest rate were higher, however, the results would show a greater difference. A good rule is to consider the time value of money if the interest rate is over 15 percent, and neglect it when the rate is less than 15 percent; in the latter case the answer will almost always be similar with either method.

BREAK-EVEN MODELS

Break-even models deal with profits, costs, and prices under varying production volume. Their basic application is in determining the volume of production at which the costs exactly equal the revenue, resulting in neither a profit nor a loss. This is called the *break-even point*. This basic traditional model is expanded to perform evaluations that help to answer questions such as the following:

1. What increase in sales expenditures is justified to increase sales?
2. How will price changes affect profits?
3. Will sales at a higher price be sufficient to produce a greater profit?
4. Will sales volume sustain current operating costs?

The break-even approach helps to provide answers to these and other decision-making questions. Break-even analysis techniques are introduced here not only because of their general application to business situations, but also as illustrations of schematic and mathematical models.

Schematic Models

The traditional break-even chart shown in Figure 5-3 is a schematic model. Production volume is shown on the horizontal axis and dollars on the

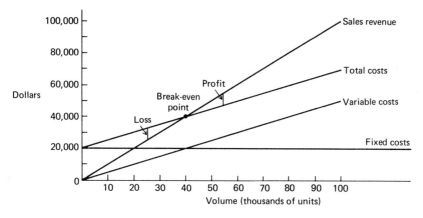

Figure 5-3 Traditional break-even chart

vertical axis. The lines on the chart represent the fixed costs, variable costs, total costs, and sales revenues. The decision is made in terms of resulting profits or losses at the various volumes.

The fixed costs are represented as a horizontal line because they are constant over some given range of production volume. These costs include rent, property taxes, executive salaries, and other factors that do not vary as production increases or decreases.

Variable costs are those directly related to volume. Materials used in the product and direct labor to make the product are ordinarily considered variable costs, since they increase or decrease in proportion to the quantity produced. These costs are represented in Figure 5-3 by a slanting line starting at the origin. Some types of costs are semivariable, but these can usually be divided into fixed and variable components.

The sum of the fixed costs and the variable costs is represented as the total cost line in Figure 5-3. The sales revenue line starts at the origin and rises in proportion to the quantity produced. The point where the sales revenue line crosses the total cost line is the break-even point. When the volume is higher than at this point, there is a profit, since the sales revenue line is above the total cost line. Likewise, a loss occurs when the volume is lower than at the break-even point.

Mathematical Models

The data given in the break-even chart of Figure 5-3 can also be represented by equations, or mathematical models.

The following example corresponds to the chart in Figure 5-3. Fixed costs are $20,000, variable costs are $.50 per unit, and the selling price is

$1.00 per unit. These equations represent the problem:

$$R = P \times V,$$

Revenue	Price per unit	Volume

$$TVC = V \times C,$$

Total variable costs	Volume	Variable cost per unit

$$TC = F + TVC.$$

Total costs	Fixed costs	Total variable costs

The break-even point occurs when total costs equal revenue, so that

$$R = F + TVC$$

or

$$P \times V = F + V \times C.$$

Solving for V, we find that

$$V(P - C) = F,$$

$$V = \frac{F}{P - C}.$$

Now we substitute in the values for this example:

$$V = \frac{20,000}{1.00 - .50} = 40,000 \text{ units.}$$

This is the intersection point on the schematic model in Figure 5-3.

VARIATION OF PARAMETERS ·

The elementary use of a break-even model is to determine the volume above which a profit accrues to the firm. Decisions, however, often involve effects of variations in one or more of the parameters—costs, price, or volume—when the other factors are held constant.

Price Changes

A firm wishes to consider the effect of a change in the selling price of its product from $1.00 to $1.10 when the other parameters are held constant. Figure 5-4 shows the original chart along with a modified revenue line R_1

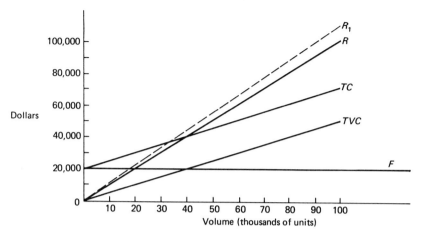

Figure 5-4 Effect of price variation on break-even point

showing the effect of the contemplated price increase. The apparent conclusion from Figure 5-4 is that with the increased price the break-even point will be at a lower volume. If the volume remained at the same number of units and the price were increased, the profits would be higher. A more realistic view, however, would be that the sales volume would decrease if the price were raised. We should compare the profit at the present price and sales volume with the profit at the higher price and probable lower sales volume. This process could be continued by testing several prices and their corresponding expected sales volumes. A discrete analysis of this type is shown in Table 5-3. From this analysis, the decision would be to set the price at $1.10 in order to obtain the total profit of $13,000, which is larger than any other expected profit listed.

Cost Changes

The next step is to evaluate the effect of cost changes upon the profit. Figure 5-5 shows the reduced total cost line TC_1 with the revenue line

Table 5-3 Effect of price changes on profit

Price	Expected sales volume	Total costs (fixed and variable)	Expected revenue	Expected profit
$ .90	70,000	$55,000	$63,000	$ 8,000
1.00	60,000	50,000	60,000	10,000
1.10	55,000	47,500	60,500	13,000
1.20	42,000	41,000	50,400	9,400
1.30	30,000	35,000	39,000	4,000

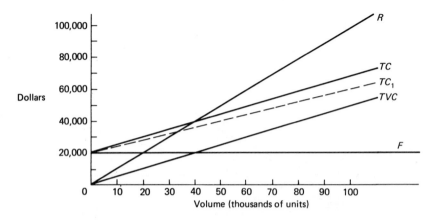

Figure 5-5 Effect of reduced variable costs on break-even point

unchanged; the break-even point appears to be lower. But, in this case, it might be expected that a reduction in cost could be achieved only by detracting from some of the sales features or from product quality, and this would probably result in reduced sales volume. The approach is then to estimate the effect upon sales volume of the reduced cost. Sometimes costs might be reduced without affecting the sales features of the product. In these cases, cost reductions would be taken without question. When the cost reduction affects the potential sales, however, a decision-making situation presents itself. The effect of various cost reductions on sales and profits would be estimated, as in Table 5-4. In this case, the highest profit of $10,160 occurs when the cost is reduced to $.48 per unit, resulting in a decrease of the sales volume to 58,000 units. This is higher than the profit at any other combination of cost and sales volume.

Profit Goals

Another approach to this profit-cost-price-volume problem would be to set a desired profit level and then attempt to determine alternative price-volume combinations that would achieve this profit goal. In Figure 5-6,

Table 5-4 Effect of cost changes on profit

Variable cost per unit	Price	Expected sales volume	Expected revenue	Total costs (fixed and variable)	Expected profit
$.44	$1.00	50,000	$50,000	$42,000	$ 8,000
.46	1.00	55,000	55,000	45,300	9,700
.48	1.00	58,000	58,000	47,840	10,160
.50	1.00	60,000	60,000	50,000	10,000
.52	1.00	61,000	61,000	52,000	9,000

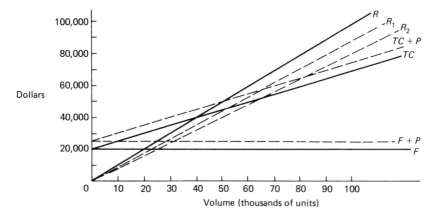

Figure 5-6 Analysis with a set profit goal

the original chart has been altered by considering the profit goal as a fixed goal and adding it to the fixed cost. The line labeled $TC+P$ contains the total costs plus the profit goal. Prices can be varied in the model, resulting in a set of revenue lines, labeled R, R_1, and R_2. Each revenue line inter-sects the $TC+P$ line at the volume that achieves the desired profit. The manager can compare his present volume and price to any of these and select the combination that he views as most readily achievable.

Sales Effort Trade-Offs

Refinements in the break-even model can also be useful in comparing the merits of proposed increases in marketing expenditure aimed at increasing the profits. The basic model in Figure 5-7 identifies the present profit as P. Increased sales are required to boost profits to P_1. The question at hand is the benefits of alternative advertising or sales-emphasis proposals.

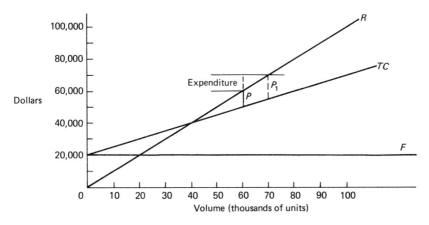

Figure 5-7 Evaluation of sales expenditure proposals

Table 5-5 Effect of sales efforts on profit

Proposal	Cost of effort	Expected revenue	Revenue change	Profit increase
Current	$ 0	$60,000	$ 0	$ 0
A	5,000	68,000	8,000	3,000
B	7,000	69,000	9,000	2,000
C	2,000	62,000	2,000	0
D	6,000	65,000	5,000	−1,000

Estimates of the costs and results of each proposal could be evaluated as in Table 5-5. In this instance, proposal A would be selected as providing the greatest net profit increase.

Concurrent Variation in Two Parameters

The analyses so far have considered the effect of variation in one parameter or variable upon another. Many decision-making situations require the consideration of simultaneous variations in more than one variable. When we considered a reduction in cost, we evaluated the effect upon sales with price held constant. A further alternative would involve a concurrent reduction in price. The analysis in Table 5-3 pinpointed the price that would yield the greatest profit for a given fixed and variable cost structure. A set of similar tables could be prepared for the discrete costs from $.44 per unit to $.54 per unit. Then each chart would locate the best price-quantity combination for a particular cost level. A comparison of the best combinations would indicate the desired overall strategy.

Multiproduct Break-Even

Most plants produce more than one product. The analysis so far has applied to a single-product firm, or has assumed that a firm has allocated costs to each product before the break-even analysis. Now we can consider a multiple-product company, for which the break-even analysis involves the allocation of costs to the various products. Imagine that a fertilizer plant produces four types of fertilizer, as shown in Table 5-6, with fixed costs of $800,000 per year. After the calculations of Table 5-7, we can determine the break-even point, which equals the fixed costs divided by the sum of the weighted contributions:

$$\text{Break-even point} = \frac{\text{Fixed costs}}{.559} = \frac{\$800,000}{.559} = \$1,431,000 \text{ (approx.)}.$$

Table 5-6 Data for four types of fertilizer

Type	Selling price per carload	Variable cost per carload	Percentage of sales volume
A	$300	$150	40
B	400	160	20
C	360	160	25
D	300	100	15

Table 5-7 Weighted contributions for fertilizer sales

Type	Contribution per sales dollar	Revenue as proportion of sales	Weighted contribution
A	$\dfrac{300-150}{300} = .50$	.40	.200
B	$\dfrac{400-160}{400} = .60$	.20	.120
C	$\dfrac{360-160}{360} = .555$	.25	.139
D	$\dfrac{300-100}{300} = .667$	.15	.100
			.559

SUMMARY OF BREAK-EVEN ANALYSIS

We have approached break-even analysis with the traditional break-even chart to find the point at which costs exactly match revenue and the profit is zero. We have expanded this basic model to determine profits at various volumes of production and how these profits vary as other parameters are changed. This discrete analysis procedure helps us to find prices, costs, and quality levels that approach an optimum or desired profit level.

PROBLEMS

1. The original cost of a piece of equipment is $3,000. The cost of operation is estimated to be $5,000 for the first year and to increase by $50 per year thereafter. The costs for eight years, assuming that there is no salvage value, are summarized on the following page.

Year	Cost of operation	Cost of maintenance
1	$5,000	$ 500
2	5,050	550
3	5,100	650
4	5,150	850
5	5,200	1,100
6	5,250	1,400
7	5,300	1,750
8	5,350	2,350

If the time value of money is neglected, determine the best time for replacement.

2. In problem 1, assume an interest rate of 10 percent per year and determine the best replacement time.

3. Fixed costs are $400 and variable costs are $4.00 per unit. Sales price is $9.00 per unit. Plot a break-even chart and compute the break-even point by use of an equation. Compute the profit at a volume of 50 units and at a volume of 200 units.

4. A firm manufactures a line of pumps. Type E in this line shows a loss; however, the firm continues to carry the model because of customer demands for a complete line. Assume that fixed cost is $90,000, variable cost $16 per unit, wholesale price $20 per unit, and current volume 12,000 units of type E.

(a) Determine the present loss on this item.
(b) List some alternatives for alleviating the loss on this item.

5. In problem 3, if fixed costs are held at $400 and variable costs at $4.00 per unit, determine the best price based on the following sales forecasts.

Price	Expected sales volume
$8.60	260
8.75	240
9.00	200
9.30	170
9.50	140

6. The Sigma Company has developed a new attachment for one of its products and is attempting to set a price that will maximize profits. Variable costs are $6 per item, and the fixed costs allocable to the product are $16,000. The sales manager, who is considering four alternative prices, has made the following estimates of sales volumes.

Price	Expected sales volume
$16	4,000
15	5,000
12	6,000
9	10,000

What price should be selected?

7. A computer that can be purchased for $600,000 would have a salvage value of $200,000 five years later. Operating costs are $200,000 per year, including the salaries of programmers and operators and the cost of maintenance. The company can also negotiate a lease, in which case the maintenance is furnished, reducing operating costs to $140,000 per year. If the time value of money is 15 percent, what is the break-even point at which cost of lease is equivalent to cost of purchase?

8. On the traditional break-even chart, draw a line that represents corporate income taxes, so that the chart can be used to assess net profits after taxes.

9. The Beta Manufacturing Company produces stepladders that sell for $7.00 each. The production capacity is limited to 20,000 units per year. Fixed costs are $50,000 and variable costs are $2.00 per item. Compute the break-even point in number of stepladders. How many items must be sold to provide a profit of $30,000? What is the allocation of fixed costs per stepladder at 75 percent capacity?

10. A firm produces four models of tool sets. The fixed costs are $42,000 and the other data are as follows:

Model	Yearly volume	Price	Variable cost per set	Sales revenue
S	4,000	$20	$16	$ 80,000
T	5,000	32	28	160,000
U	1,000	60	50	60,000
V	2,000	50	45	100,000
				$400,000

Determine the break-even point in dollars.

SUPPLEMENTARY READINGS

Barish, N. N. *Economic Analyses for Engineering and Managerial Decision-Making.* McGraw-Hill, New York, 1962.

Bierman, H., and S. Smidt. *The Capital Budgeting Decision.* Macmillan, New York, 1966.

Grant, E. L., and W. G. Ireson. *Principles of Engineering Economy.* Ronald Press, New York, 1970.

Haynes, W. W. *Managerial Economics: Analysis and Cases.* Business Publications, Dallas, 1969.

Mayer, R. R. *Financial Analysis of Investment Alternatives.* Allyn and Bacon, Boston, 1964.

Riggs, J. L. *Production Systems.* Wiley, New York, 1970, chapter 4 and appendix B.

Roberts, N. H. *Mathematical Methods in Reliability Engineering.* McGraw-Hill, New York, 1964.

6/Dynamic Programming and Decision Diagrams

DYNAMIC programming is a technique applicable to certain types of problems involving sequences of interrelated decisions. It provides a systematic process for determining the sequence and combination of decisions that will result in the optimum overall policy or approach. It is useful when future decisions are influenced by decisions in earlier stages of a sequence and when the impact of all stages must be considered before early decisions are made. Dynamic programming is one of the newer operations-research techniques. It is presented early in this text because it can be applied to later material and also because it promotes logical and systematic thinking.

Dynamic programming differs from linear programming and other operations-research techniques that utilize a standard mathematical formulation to solve a class of problems. A standard solution method does not exist for dynamic programming problems. Rather, dynamic programming provides a rationale or logical thinking procedure for arriving at the optimum result; it often makes use of diagrams or graphs to represent the various stages. The level of mathematics needed for making a decision tree is adequate for formulating and solving a dynamic programming problem. Thus, the use of dynamic programming requires ingenuity and insight rather than knowledge of higher mathematical formulas. This chapter presents a variety of dynamic programming problems to help the reader learn to recognize situations in which dynamic programming can be applied and learn to select an appropriate format and approach.

A ROUTING PROBLEM

We will begin with a shipment-routing problem that illustrates the basic concepts and approach of dynamic programming. A shipment of heavy equipment is to be made from a manufacturing plant in Pittsburgh to a destination near Bonn, West Germany. Within the United States, the shipment can be made over three alternative rail routes, to either New York, Baltimore, or Norfolk. From there the equipment can be transported by ship to one of three alternative European ports. From any of the three ports it will be moved to one of two inland cities, where it must be reloaded and transported by truck to its final destination. Figure 6-1 presents a diagram showing all of the possible legs of the journey and their costs. This diagram will be used not only to lay out the problem but also to find the optimum route. The objective, of course, is to minimize the total shipping costs. We could enumerate the cost for every possible combination of ports and depots; however, in many real situations, there could be more alternative paths in each step of the sequence, and enumeration would be very inefficient. We are lucky that the diagram, combined with dynamic programming, provides a systematic method of weeding out nonoptimum paths and bringing the problem into manageable bounds.

Before proceeding with the solution, we should examine the nature of

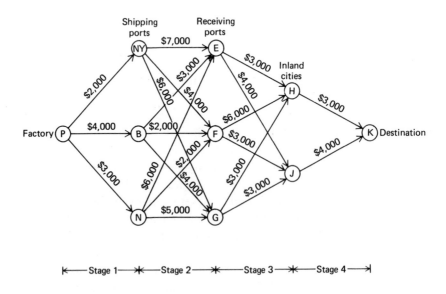

Figure 6-1 Diagram of a shipping problem, showing the cost for each possible leg of the journey

this problem and other problems that can be solved by dynamic programming. First, the problem can always be divided into stages—in this particular case, stages of the journey. The stages of the journey are:

Stage 1   Factory to shipping port.
Stage 2   Shipping port to European receiving port.
Stage 3   Receiving port to inland city.
Stage 4   Inland city to final destination.

In other cases, the stages might be time periods or merely sequential steps in decision making. A policy decision is required at each stage; in our shipping problem, at any place the shipment may be, there are alternative routes for the remainder of the trip. However, the whole system must be considered before any decisions are made.

A second characteristic of the dynamic programming problem is that at each stage there are a number of "states." At the end of the first stage of the shipping problem, for example, the shipment can be in any of three states (or at any of three shipping ports); at disembarkation, it can again be in any of three states (at any of the three European ports). The states, then, are the various possible conditions in which the system might be found at any stage.

A third characteristic of dynamic programming problems is that, given any stage and state, there will be an optimum policy for completing the mission, regardless of how the system arrived at that position. In other words, the optimum policy at any point is independent of the policies formulated at prior decision-making points. For example, in our routing problem, if the shipment has arrived at E, one of the three alternative European ports, there is a single best way to proceed to the destination, and it does not depend upon how the shipment got to E.

Finally, in solving a dynamic programming problem, we begin by finding the optimum policy at the beginning of the last stage. We continue the solution by working backwards through the various stages; the first stage is solved last. (In some problems, a forward solution may also yield the correct answer.)

Returning to Figure 6-1, we start our solution with the decision points of the last stage, namely the depots H and J. The costs associated with each leg of the route are shown on the diagram. But once a shipment has arrived at either H or J, there are no alternatives for decision, so we must move to the previous stage. Figure 6-2 shows the two possible routes that can be taken if the shipment is at port E. Since route E-H-K can be traversed at less cost than route E-J-K, the latter route is nonoptimum. The lowest cost for reaching the destination from port E is entered in circle E; in this

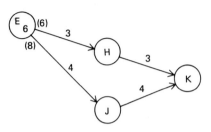

Figure 6-2 Determination of optimum subroutes, with costs indicated in thousands of dollars. The numbers in parentheses are totals for the different routes. Since route E-J-K costs $8,000, while E-H-K costs only $6,000, E-J-K is eliminated.

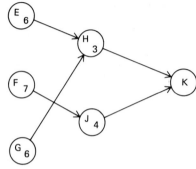

Figure 6-3 First level of simplification. The optimum routes to K from each receiving port (E, F, and G) are identified.

case, the 6 is entered in the circle to represent the $6,000 cost of shipping over path E-H-K. Receiving ports F and G are evaluated in the same manner, and the best cost is entered in each circle. Figure 6-3 identifies the best decision at each of these three points (E, F, and G), regardless of how the shipment may have reached that point. In Figure 6-3 three of the paths originally present in Figure 6-1 have been eliminated.

Now we determine the optimum subpolicy for each of the departure ports, N, B, and NY. Figure 6-4 shows the evaluation for NY, where there are three possible alternatives. If the route to E were selected, the total cost for the remainder of the trip would be 7 (representing $7,000) plus 6 (representing $6,000, the best cost from E to the end), or a total of 13. Each of the three alternatives for NY-to-destination is evaluated as follows:

$$NY\text{-}E\text{-}K = 7 + 6 = 13,$$
$$NY\text{-}F\text{-}K = 4 + 7 = 11,$$
$$NY\text{-}G\text{-}K = 6 + 6 = 12.$$

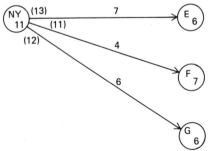

Figure 6-4 Evaluation of shipping ports. The cost for any route is equal to the cost incurred on the first leg plus the optimum cost from the receiving port onward.

This reveals that the best subpolicy from port NY would be to go to F, which would result in a total cost of 11. B and N are evaluated in a similar manner. In this case, the lowest costs from B to K and from N to K are both 9. The value 9 is entered in the circles for B and N in Figure 6-5.

We proceed next to the initial stage; we want to select the route from the original shipping point P that will put us on the minimum cost path for the whole network. The alternative costs from P are:

$$P\text{-}NY\text{-}K = 2 + 11 = 13,$$
$$P\text{-}B\text{-}K = 4 + 9 = 13,$$
$$P\text{-}N\text{-}K = 3 + 9 = 12.$$

The cost of going to N (3) plus the cost from N to the destination (9) is less than the cost of either of the other two choices. Therefore the route P-N-F-J-K, at a cost of $12,000, is the optimum routing for the shipment. Figure 6-5 shows the final solution.

As an extension of the problem, imagine that a New York shipper desires to reduce the shipping cost from that port in order to compete with the present optimum route through Norfolk. What should the New York shipper do? The cost to NY is 2 and the lowest cost from NY to K is 11, giving a total of 13, one more than the optimum solution of 12. If the cost from NY to F were reduced from 4 to 3, the path P-NY-F-J-K would also have a cost of 12; a reduction of the NY-F cost to 2 would make this the optimum path.

This procedure of finding the optimum policy for each decision point, starting with the last stage, is typical of dynamic programming problems. There could have been two or more routes offering identical minimum costs, in which case the decision maker would have an option. A similar problem might involve determination of the shortest distance through a network or determination of the critical path in a PERT network, as

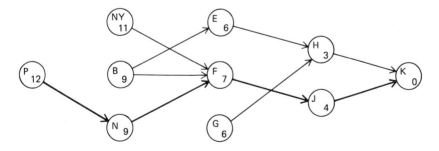

Figure 6-5 Successive identification and elimination of nonoptimum routes narrows available choices until the optimum route is finally determined.

discussed in Chapter 7. Distances through a network can be evaluated in the same manner as costs in this shipment-routing example.

A PRICING-STRATEGY PROBLEM

A company that has developed a new type of office calculator is attempting to determine a pricing strategy. The marketing manager is attempting to decide how to set the price of the new product over the next five years. He has determined that it would be unwise to change the price more than $5.00 from any year to the next; this is a matter of customer relations policy and company image. Thus the price selected for the initial year will constrain prices in the next year, and so on. He is considering four prices of $30, $35, $40, and $45 for the purpose of determining strategy, although in actuality he may deviate one or two dollars from the level he chooses. After an analysis of competitive practices, he has prepared Table 6-1 to show the expected profit in each year for each possible price. The problem is to select a price for the initial year and each subsequent year, subject to the $5 change constraint, so as to maximize the total profits over the five-year period. Comparing this problem to the typical characteristics of a dynamic programming problem, we see that the years are the stages or periods in which the decisions are to be made and the price levels are the possible states of the system.

The dynamic programming solution is obtained by starting at the fourth year and determining the best possible price level at that time. For example, if $35 were the price in year 4, it would be possible under the constraint

Table 6-1 Payoffs for pricing strategies (in thousands of dollars)

Price \ Year	1	2	3	4	5
$30	85	25	40	50	80
$35	70	40	80	20	40
$40	55	35	90	70	30
$45	85	75	25	60	35

1   2   3   4   5
Points for decision

to select either $30, $35, or $40 for year 5. Selection of a price of $30 in year 5 would yield the highest profit (100) for the combined period of years 4 and 5. The 100 is thus entered in the box shown in Table 6-2, and each possible price for year 4 is evaluated in a similar manner. Moving back to year 3, if we take a price level of $35, the optimum policy is to change the price level to $30 in year 4. The total payoff for this strategy is $80 + 130$, or 210, for the total period of years 3 through 5; the other two alternatives would yield only $80 + 100 = 180$ and $80 + 110 = 190$. Therefore the 210 is placed in the box that identifies the best profit outcome for a price of $35 in year 3. All other prices are evaluated in a similar manner for every year, moving from right to left, giving the results shown in Table 6-3.

Table 6-2 Optimum pricing strategies for year 4 and their payoffs

Price \ Year	1	2	3	4	5
$30	85	25	40	[130] 50 →	[80] 80
$35	70	40	80	[100] 20	[40] 40
$40	55	35	90	[110] 70	[30] 30
$45	85	75	25	[95] 60 →	[35] 35

Table 6-3 Optimum pricing strategies

Price \ Year	1	2	3	4	5
$30	[335] 85	[235] 25	[170] 40 →	[130] 50 →	[80] 80
$35	[320] 70 →	[250] 40 →	[210] 80	[100] 20	[40] 40
$40	[330] 55	[245] 35	[200] 90 →	[110] 70	[30] 30
$45	[360] 85 →	[275] 75	[135] 25	[95] 60 →	[35] 35

Examination of the values in the boxes for year 1 shows that 360 is the largest possible profit for the five-year period. Therefore, $45 would be selected as the price in the first year, followed by $45 in year 2, $40 in year 3, $40 in year 4, and $35 in year 5. Although this dynamic programming problem has taken on a different form from the previous one, the basic characteristics are the same.

UNCERTAINTY IN DYNAMIC PROGRAMMING

The first two examples were deterministic, in that the solution provided a single policy for the initial period and for each subsequent period. Next we will consider a situation in which, after each decision is made, conditions of uncertainty intervene. The analysis will follow a pattern of reasoning similar to that for solving a decision tree.

Buying Under Uncertainty

The buyer for a canning company has been notified that a commodity must be purchased within five days because the factory will run out at that time. A study has shown that the price of the commodity fluctuates from day to day, independently of prior prices, in accordance with the following table.

Price	Probability
$9	.4
8	.3
7	.3

By 3:00 P.M. of any day, the buyer can decide to buy the commodity at the prevailing daily price, or she can wait. If she delays the purchase, she must obtain the commodity at a later day at the prevailing price, which may be higher. She can continue postponing the purchase from day to day through the fourth day; if the purchase is not made then, she must buy at the price available on the fifth day. What is the optimum strategy for the buyer to follow? (Interest costs will be ignored here because of the short period involved; however, if the period were longer, interest would be taken into account by adjusting prices to present values.) In this problem, the days represent the stages characteristic of a dynamic programming problem. The states are the prevailing prices, and the decision variable is BUY or WAIT. The difference between this purchasing problem and the previous problems is that, after each decision, uncertainty intervenes; the price level at the subsequent stage is not known.

The search for a solution begins with the fifth day, or last period, as with any dynamic programming approach. If the buyer arrives at period 4 without having made the purchase, she must decide, on the basis of the prevailing price, whether to buy or to wait until the next day. The expected price E for the next day, period 5, will be:

$$E_5 = .4(9) + .3(8) + .3(7) = 8.1.$$

Her decision by 3:00 P.M. of day 4 should then be:

BUY if the price is 7 or 8.
WAIT if the price is 9 (since 9 is greater than E_5).

Next consider the situation if the buyer arrives at day 3 without having made the purchase. At what prices should she buy in period 3, knowing the expected price in period 4? The expected price in period 4 is:

$$E_4 = .4(8.1) + .3(8) + .3(7) = 7.74.$$

The value 8.1 has been substituted for 9 in the equation, since if the price in period 4 is 9 the buyer will wait until period 5, for which the expected price is 8.1. Thus, at the end of period 3 her strategy should be:

BUY if the price is 7 (since this is less than
the expected price of 7.74 in period 4).
WAIT if the price is 8 or 9 (since these are
greater than 7.74).

The remaining evaluations are as follows:

$$E_3 = .4(7.74) + .3(7.74) + .3(7) = 7.518,$$
$$E_2 = .4(7.518) + .3(7.518) + .3(7) = 7.3626,$$
$$E_1 = .7(7.3626) + .3(7) = 7.25382.$$

In each case, the buyer compares the present price to the expected price if she waits, and selects the one with the smaller value. The overall optimum policy is:

If the price is 7 on any of the first three days,
BUY; otherwise, WAIT (since E_1, E_2, E_3,
and E_4 all lie between 7 and 8).

If no purchase is made by day 4, BUY at 7
or 8; otherwise, WAIT and buy on day 5
(since E_5 is between 8 and 9).

If this policy is followed, the expected price is 7.25382, which is lower than for any other policy.

A Farming-Strategy Problem

The essence of dynamic programming under uncertainty is illustrated by the following situation, consisting of three sequential stages. A farmer owns several plots of farm land. He requires $5,000 to pay off a loan in three years. He is able to borrow up to $3,000 against the land. It requires $1,000 for seed and labor to plant and harvest each plot, and it will return $2,000 per plot if weather and pest conditions are favorable. Data show that there are favorable conditions in two years out of three. If conditions are not favorable, the $1,000 investment is completely lost. The objective is to maximize the probability that he will have $5,000 at the end of the three-year period to pay off the loan. This problem can be likened to a gambling situation in which the player has an initial stake of three chips. In each of three plays, the player can bet up to the number of chips he holds at that time. Each play consists of throwing a die; if the die shows 1, 2, 3, or 4, he wins the number of chips bet on that play and keeps his bet; otherwise, he loses all of the chips he bet. If, after three plays, the player holds five or more chips, he wins the game; otherwise, he loses. The probability of winning any one play is 4/6 or 2/3.[1]

In the farming-strategy problem, it can be seen that the three years correspond to the stages of a dynamic programming format. The state of the system is the cash held at each stage, and the decision variable is the amount to invest in planting for each year. Uncertainty is involved in the form of the weather conditions that intervene between the decisions.

Since the dynamic programming method evaluates the stages by working backwards, the chances of being successful in the third year are determined first. The probabilities in the third year are shown in Table 6-4 for any

Table 6-4 Probabilities of achieving objective as year 3 starts

Investment in year 3 / Amount held	0	$1,000	$2,000	$3,000	$4,000
$ 0	0				
1,000	0	0			
2,000	0	0	0		
3,000	0	0	2/3*	2/3	
4,000	0	2/3*	2/3	2/3	2/3
5,000	1*	2/3	2/3	2/3	2/3
6,000	1*	1	2/3	2/3	2/3

* An optimum strategy.

---

[1] This gambling problem is presented in F. S. Hillier and G. J. Lieberman, *Introduction to Operations Research*, Holden-Day, San Francisco, 1974, chapter 6.

amount of money held. It can be seen that, if $2,000 or less is held at the start of year 3, the farmer cannot achieve the desired result of having $5,000 at the end. The alternatives remaining are clear. If the farmer holds $3,000 at the start of year 3, he can achieve the objective by investing $2,000 or more. But there is no point in investing more than $2,000, since the game objective is satisfied by having $5,000. If he holds $4,000, he should invest $1,000. If he already holds $5,000 or more, he has achieved the objective and any investment will reduce his chances of succeeding. The strategy for year 3 can be summarized as follows:

> If $2,000 or less is held, he cannot win.
> If $3,000 is held, invest $2,000; $P(\text{Win}) = 2/3$.
> If $4,000 is held, invest $1,000; $P(\text{Win}) = 2/3$.
> If $5,000 (or more) is held, invest nothing; the
> objective has been achieved.

Each of these optimum strategies is marked by an asterisk (*) in Table 6-4.

Next, the strategies for the second year are determined. Table 6-5 displays the probability of winning the game for each combination of amount held and amount invested during the year. Each of the chance values reflects the evaluation of two possible events. Consider, for example, the case in which $4,000 is held at the start of year 2 and $1,000 is invested. The probability of reaching the objective can be calculated as follows, using the tree in Figure 6-6.

The probability of having a successful year and
reaching the objective: $2/3 \times 1 = 2/3$
The probability of losing the year's investment
and then being successful in year 3 to achieve
the objective: $1/3 \times 2/3 = 2/9$
The total probability of achieving the objective: $\overline{8/9}$

Table 6-5 Probabilities of achieving objective as year 2 starts

Investment in year 2 / Amount held	0	$1,000	$2,000	$3,000	$4,000
$ 0	0				
1,000	0	0			
2,000	0	4/9*	4/9*		
3,000	2/3*	4/9	2/3*	2/3*	
4,000	2/3	8/9*	2/3	2/3	2/3
5,000 or more	1*				

* An optimum strategy.

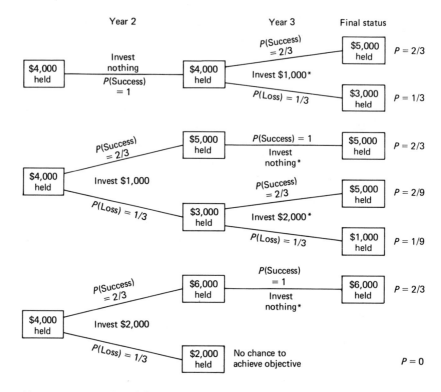

*Strategy dictated by Table 6-4.

Figure 6-6 Evaluation of several alternatives when $4,000 is held at the start of year 2

This value of 8/9 is placed in Table 6-5 in the location corresponding to $4,000 held and $1,000 invested. The other values in Table 6-5 are assigned similarly. Note that the largest probability value of each row in Table 6-5 is asterisked to identify the corresponding strategy as optimum. In two cases, there is more than one optimum strategy. Just as the evaluation of year 2 utilized the asterisked values from year 3 (Table 6-4), the evaluation of year 1 will utilize the asterisked values from year 2. The optimum strategies at each stage are used in considering the previous stage.

The dynamics of the game are concluded by determining the strategies and values for year 1. Recalling that the farmer originally held $3,000, we see that only four courses of action are possible in the first year. The farmer can invest nothing, $1,000, $2,000, or $3,000. The calculation of the chance values related to investing $1,000 is illustrated in the tree of Figure 6-7. But to simplify matters, we could calculate as follows.

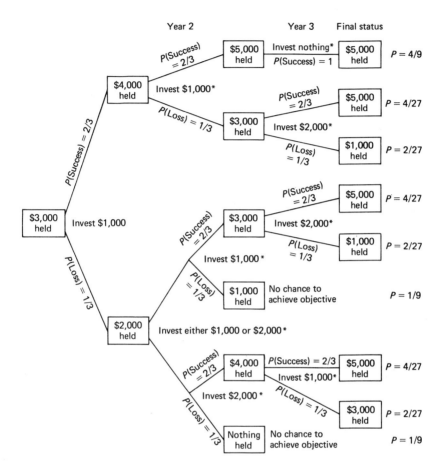

*Strategy dictated by Table 6-4 or 6-5.

Figure 6-7 Calculation of chance values in year 1 when $3,000 is held and $1,000 is invested

The probability of making a successful investment in year 1 and achieving the ultimate
objective: $2/3 \times 8/9 = 16/27$

The probability of losing the investment in
year 1 and achieving the objective afterwards: $1/3 \times 4/9 = \quad 4/27$

The total probability of achieving the objective: $\overline{20/27}$

The other values in Table 6-6 are calculated in a similar manner. Since the best chance in Table 6-6 is represented by 20/27, this value is identified with an asterisk; it corresponds to the optimum strategy for year 1.

Table 6-6 Probabilities of achieving objective as year 1 starts

Investment in year 1 / Amount held	0	$1,000	$2,000	$3,000
$3,000	2/3	20/27*	2/3	2/3

* Optimum strategy.

The optimum policy for the game, then, is to invest $1,000 in the first year. If the first year is successful, then invest $1,000 in the second year also. If the second year is successful, the objective is achieved. If the second year is not, invest $2,000 in the third year.

If the first year's investment is lost, invest either $1,000 or $2,000 in the second year. If $1,000 is invested and the year is successful, invest $2,000 in the third year. If $2,000 is successfully invested in the second year, invest $1,000 in the third year.

The total strategy for years 1, 2, and 3 is found from the asterisked positions in Tables 6-6, 6-5, and 6-4. This strategy will yield the greatest likelihood of achieving the $5,000 goal in the three years allowed.

Uncertainty in Inventory Planning

Let us consider a further example in which factors of uncertainty intervene between decisions. In this situation, inventory level is the variable adjusted by decision, and it is also the variable whose change is uncertain. Decisions concerning the quantity to reorder are made at periodic points by an air-conditioning service firm. Demand over the subsequent period then determines the inventory level at the end of the period.

This service facility for commercial air conditioning stocks a small number of each model of compressor, in order to provide rapid service for customers when units fail. The price of model 941 is $250 per unit, and space is allocated to store up to three units of this model. Selling price is $350, so there is a markup of $100 per unit on replacements. If orders are placed at the beginning of the year, the costs of ordering and of delivery from the manufacturer are $30 for a single unit, $40 if two are ordered together, and $50 for three ordered together. Special orders, however, have a $100-per-unit ordering and delivery charge.

A three-year period is considered in this problem, since units of this model are expected to become obsolete after that time. The service charges for returning units are $40 for one, $60 for two, and $80 for three. The objective is to maximize profit while providing adequate service, and the problem is to determine the optimum inventory strategy for achieving this objective. The data for expected sales are as follows for any year.

Yearly sales or demand	Probability
0	.2
1	.5
2	.3

Carrying costs are ignored for simplicity, although they could be incorporated into the solution by using present values. The information given is diagrammed in Figure 6-8. If the same information were used to construct a probability tree, the tree would require 1,396 branches. A diagram of this form is often much more efficient than a tree in displaying information.

Considering the diagram in Figure 6-8 we see that initially, at the beginning of the first year, the inventory is zero and a decision is required as to how many units to order. The inventory can be brought to as many as three units by payment of the appropriate ordering cost. The price of the

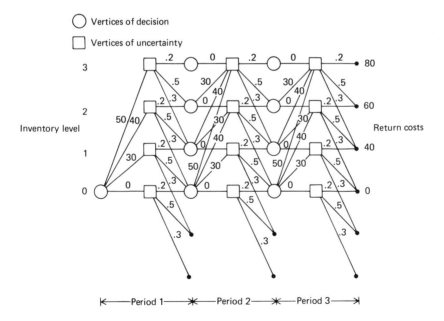

Figure 6-8 Diagram of costs and demand probabilities (SOURCE: Ross H. Johnson, "Decision and Action Diagrams For Inventory Policy," *Journal of the American Production and Inventory Control Society,* 14, No. 2 [1973]. Reprinted by permission of the publisher.)

compressor itself does not enter the calculation, since it is recovered later in the sale. Only ordering costs, return costs, and profits need to be considered. At the beginning of the second year and of the third year, decisions again must be made as to the quantity to order. All decision points in the diagram are represented by circles.

Sales for each year are uncertain, and the points or *vertices* in the diagram where uncertainty takes over are represented by squares. Diverging from each square are branches identified with the probability that the sales for the year will lower the inventory to a particular level. When a branch carries the inventory to a minus level, it is assumed that a special order is placed for each individual unit in order to provide service to the customer, even though the special-order costs may negate the profit.

We can now solve the problem by using a standard dynamic programming approach. To obtain an overall optimum strategy, we start by finding the optimum policy for each inventory level at the beginning of the third year. The strategy for the second and first years will incorporate the optimum subpolicies for the subsequent year or years.

Each value at the extreme right of the diagram is the return cost if that level of inventory remains at the end of the third year. We must calculate the value of each vertex of uncertainty (square) in the third year; for example, if $U(2, 3)$ represents the value of the uncertainty vertex at level 2, period 3, then

$$U(2, 3) = .2(-60+0) + .5(-40+100) + .3(0+200)$$
$$= -12 + 30 + 60 = 78.$$

The values in parentheses represent return costs and profits, respectively, for each sales level. The parenthetical value is multiplied by the probability for reaching that level of demand. In our sample calculation, the inventory was 2 at the beginning of the period. There was a probability of .2 that no items would be used, in which case there would be no profits from sales and an outlay of $60 would have to be made to return the two leftover items. The second term in the equation represents the .5 probability of selling one item, resulting in a profit of $100 and an outlay of $40 to return the one item left over. The third term represents the probability of selling both items, resulting in a profit of $200 and no return costs. The three terms are summined to obtain the expected profit if the vertex $U(2, 3)$ is arrived at.

As another example,

$$U(1, 3) = .2(-40+0) + .5(0+100) + .3(200-100) = 72.$$

The third term represents the probability of .3 that two items are sold, one from inventory, and one requiring a $100 special-order cost; the profit is $200 on the two items. For each vertex of uncertainty in the third period, a value is calculated in this manner and entered in Figure 6-9.

Next, each decision (circle) vertex at the beginning of the third period is evaluated, on the basis that the decision maker will select the course of action having the greatest expected profit. Consider the decision vertex at inventory level 1 at the beginning of period 3; the notation $D(1,3)$ represents the expected value of being at this decision point. The value is the maximum of the three possible decision choices:

1. A decision to order 2 items results in an ordering cost of $40 and an expected profit of $52.

2. A decision to order 1 item results in an ordering cost of $30 and an expected profit of $78.

3. A decision to order 0 items results in no ordering cost and an expected profit of $72.

Therefore

$$D(1,3) = \text{Max}(52-40; 78-30; 72-0) = 72.$$

The largest of the three values is 72, so the optimum strategy at this decision vertex is to purchase no additional items. A heavy line is drawn along that path in Figure 6-9, and the circle is identified by the value of 72.

After each decision vertex at the beginning of period 3 has been assigned

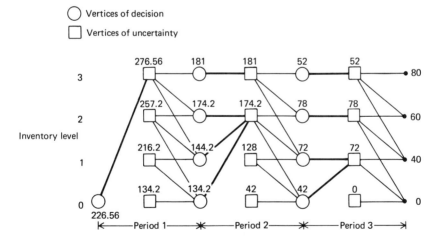

Figure 6-9 Optimum inventory strategies (SOURCE: Ross H. Johnson, "Decision and Action Diagrams For Inventory Policy," *Journal of the American Production and Inventory Control Society*, 14, No. 2 [1973]. Reprinted by permission of the publisher.)

a value, the next step is to evaluate each uncertainty vertex in period 2. The following calculation is for inventory level 3 at the uncertainty vertex in period 2:

$$U(3,2) = .2(52) + .5(100+78) + .3(200+72) = 181.0.$$

From right to left, all vertices in the diagram are assigned values, and all optimum strategies are identified by heavy lines as shown in Figure 6-9. The figure shows the expected value for each vertex and the actions for the decision maker to take to achieve the maximum expected profit at each possible decision point.

The diagram in Figure 6-9 is now ready for use by the decision maker. At the beginning of period 1, the optimum policy in this example is to order three items. Assuming that two were sold in period 1, the inventory level would then be one, and the optimum decision at that point would be to order one additional item. At the beginning of the third year, the optimum strategy is not to order any additional items unless the inventory is zero.[2]

PROBLEMS

1. In the routing problem of Figure 6-1, determine the optimum path and cost if the cost of H-K were reduced from $3,000 to $2,000 and the cost of G-H were increased from $3,000 to $4,000.

2. A sales manager in San Francisco plans to return to the main office in New York. In order to prepare for a meeting, she desires to visit one western office (either Denver, St. Louis, or Phoenix) and one eastern office (either Pittsburgh, Washington, D.C., Atlanta, or Milwaukee). From the airline ticket prices on this and the following page, select the route with minimum cost.

San Francisco to		To New York from	
Denver	$ 60	Atlanta	$180
Phoenix	90	Milwaukee	150
St. Louis	120	Washington, D.C.	80
		Pittsburgh	80

---

[2] This type of portrayal can be used only in those cases in which the variable of decision and the quantity varying with uncertainty are the same. In the case illustrated, this variable is the inventory level. If the variables are different, another method is called for. See R. H. Johnson, "A Simplified Portrayal for Certain Decision Making Problems," *Management Science*, 18 (June 1972), B600–B607; and R. H. Johnson and P. Winn, "Utilization of Graph Theory and Dynamic Programming as Substitutes for Decision Trees," *Journal of the Academy of Marketing Science*, 1 (Fall 1973), 119–127.

To From	Atlanta	Milwaukee	Washington, D.C.	Pittsburgh
Denver	$ 70	$120	$150	$160
Phoenix	110	160	180	190
St. Louis	84	140	166	180

3. In the pricing-strategy example in the text, a review of the data shows that the payoff for price $35 in year 4 should be $50 instead of $20. Compute the resulting revised strategy.

4. An air-freight company has the opportunity to provide a regular service for three shippers. The capacity of the aircraft is 10 tons and the weight and shipping fee for each product are as follows.

Product	Weight (tons)	Fee
X	1	$20
Y	2	50
Z	2	60

Utilize dynamic programming to select the proper combination of products, assuming that at least one of each type will be taken. (*Hint:* Let each stage be the number of a product to be taken; decide first how many of X to take. The states will be the amount of unused capacity still available.)

5. A purchasing agent for a bakery has been advised by the production department that a quantity of flour is needed within six weeks. From past data, he knows that the price fluctuates as follows from week to week.

Price	Probability
$11	.0
10	.2
9	.5
8	.3

The price prevails for a week, so that the purchasing agent can decide to buy on Friday or to wait. Determine an optimum strategy. At what point in the solution process is the optimum strategy obvious?

6. In the farming-strategy problem in the text, assume that $6,000 (or 6 chips) is required to win. What strategy should be followed, and what is the probability of winning?

7. A truck has a weight limitation of 9 tons. The following items are available at the shipping fees shown on the following page.

Item	Weight (tons)	Fee
A	3	$40
B	5	85
C	4	60
D	2	25

Determine the cargo allocation to maximize the total fee for the trip.

8. The weight of a box must be at least 13 pounds. Determine how to allocate the following items so that the total cost will be minimized.

Item	Weight (lbs.)	Cost
A	4	$4.00
B	5	1.50
C	3	3.00
D	2	1.00
E	4	2.50

9. A company has the chance to bid on a research and development program with a net profit of $40,000, exclusive of the cost of preparing a bid, which is $20,000. The probability of winning the contract is estimated as .5. If the contract is won by the company, it will have a chance at the following contract for production, which will have a net profit of $100,000. The chance of obtaining the production contract depends on the level of effort expended during the research and development phase. The following estimates have been made.

Level of effort	Cost	Probability of winning production contract
I	$12,000	.6
II	20,000	.7
III	32,000	.8

If the research and development contract is bid on and lost, the company can still bid on the production contract, with an expenditure of $10,000, but the probability of winning the production contract will then be only .4. A further alternative is to wait and bid only on the production contract, at a cost of $30,000; then there will be only a .2 probability of winning it.

Prepare a decision tree showing the stages, and determine the best strategy.

10. A business-machine company has decided to add six salespeople to increase its sales of three major products. At least one salesperson will be added to each product line. The market research department has calculated expected profits from various allocations of salespeople to products.

| | Profits (millions of dollars) | | |
Salespeople allocated	Product A	Product B	Product C
0	2.0	4.0	3.0
1	4.0	4.2	3.2
2	5.4	4.4	3.4
3	6.6	4.5	3.6
4	6.8	4.6	4.2

Recommend an allocation of salespeople to various products that will maximize expected profits.

11. A company manufactures earth-moving equipment, and a customer has requested that a particular model be designed to provide a four-year service life. At the end of that period, the equipment is to be salvaged or sold. The problem at hand involves an electric motor used on the earth mover. A new motor can be selected at a cost of $880, or a rebuilt motor can be used at a cost of $600. After each year of service, the motor has a certain failure probability and a certain maintenance cost, as shown in the following table.

Age of motor (years)	Cost or salvage value	Probability of failure	Maintenance cost for keeping motor in service
0 (new)	$880	0.1	—
1	600	0.3	$30
2	400	0.5	50
3	200	1.0	70
4	0	—	—

The cost of replacing a motor—either after field failure or at the yearly maintenance period—is $50. A rebuilt motor has the same reliability and the same maintenance costs as an ordinary motor that is one year old; for instance, a two-year-old rebuilt motor exhibits the reliability of an ordinary three-year-old motor.

Specify either a new or a rebuilt motor for the equipment and prescribe a maintenance program so that costs are minimized over the four-year life span. Also, prescribe the type of motor that is to be installed if field failure or maintenance procedures dictate that a replacement is necessary. (Use a graph to solve this problem.)

SUPPLEMENTARY READINGS

Bellman, R. *Dynamic Programming*. Princeton University Press, Princeton, N.J., 1957.

Bellman, R., and S. Dreyfus. *Applied Dynamic Programming*. Princeton University Press, Princeton, N.J., 1962.

Hadley, G. *Nonlinear and Dynamic Programming*. Addison-Wesley, Reading, Mass., 1964.

Hillier, F. S., and G. J. Lieberman. *Introduction to Operations Research*. Holden-Day, San Francisco, 1974, chapter 6.

Howard, R. A. *Dynamic Programming and Markov Processes*. M.I.T. Press, Cambridge, Mass., 1960.

Johnson, R. H. "A Simplified Portrayal for Certain Decision Making Problems." *Management Science*, 18 (June 1972), B600–B607.

Johnson, R. H., and P. Winn. "Utilization of Graph Theory and Dynamic Programming as Substitutes for Decision Trees." *Journal of the Academy of Marketing Science*, 1 (Fall 1973), 119–127.

Shamblin, J. E., and G. T. Stevens, Jr. *Operations Research*. McGraw-Hill, New York, 1974, chapter 13.

White, D. J. *Dynamic Programming*. Holden-Day, San Francisco, 1969.

7/Network Concepts and Techniques

NETWORK methodology can be applied to a variety of problems, which can be placed in two categories. The first category includes situations in which the physical layout is actually in the form of a network; examples are communications lines, roads, rail lines, and pipelines. The second category consists of problems which do not involve an actual network but which can be laid out so that network concepts, such as PERT and critical path scheduling, can be applied.

In either of these categories, the objective might be to determine the fastest or shortest route, the longest or critical path, the maximum flow capacity, or the configuration of interconnections with the least cost.

TERMS USED IN NETWORK THEORY

A *network* can be defined as a special type of graph. A *graph*, such as Figure 7-1, consists of a number of points or vertices connected by lines or *links*. If a vertex is connected to another vertex by a single link, they are said to be adjacent vertices. If the line or link connecting two vertices is oriented, it is referred to as an *arc* and the arrow shows the direction of orientation.

A network is a graph of vertices and links without any *loops* (arcs with both ends incident upon the same vertex). Also, in a network, any vertex must be accessible from any other vertex. In a network with oriented arcs, a vertex is often referred to as a *node*. A *path* (or route) is a series of adjacent arcs providing access from one vertex to another. A path can be described by the vertices it contains or by the arcs it contains. In a communications or transportation network, any of the input or output vertices can be referred to as a *station*. The path of minimal length between two vertices is often called a *track*. The *critical path* is the longest path that must be completed in the network to go from the initial vertex to the final vertex. A *tree* is defined as a group of vertices and arcs that does not consist of a cyclic path. These terms will be expanded upon as they are utilized in examples.

SHORTEST PATH THROUGH A NETWORK

Consider a problem in which the objective is to determine the shortest route from town S to town P through a network of roads and intervening towns, as shown in Figure 7-1. The numbers in the figure show highway distances between towns along the possible legs of the journey. Although this problem does not have stages and states as does a conventional dynamic programming problem, the dynamic programming approach can be used here to arrive at the shortest path through the network of roads. As in other dynamic programming problems, the solution procedure starts at the end point, which is P in Figure 7-1. Starting at P, the distance from P to each town in the network is identified and entered alongside the appropriate vertex, as in Figure 7-2. At any vertex, the smallest figure (marked with an asterisk) represents the shortest path from that vertex

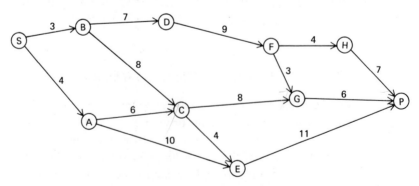

Figure 7-1 Network of roads, towns, and distances

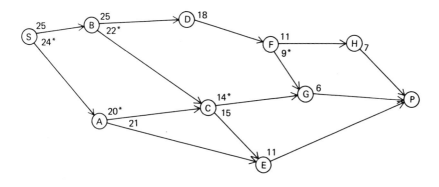

Figure 7-2 Calculations to determine solution (shortest path from S to P) of Figure 7-1

to the end. As each vertex is evaluated, the new arc distance is added to the smallest of the remaining distances from that vertex to the end. In this manner the calculations proceed back toward the start, S. The smallest figure at the initial vertex S then represents the distance along the shortest path; in this case the value is 24 along path S-A-C-G-P. In following the path, the smallest remaining distance is selected at each vertex in turn.

In the network of Figures 7-1 and 7-2, the links are oriented (in the direction of the arrows), although in this case the result would be the same if they were not oriented. Figure 7-3 represents a section of a map with

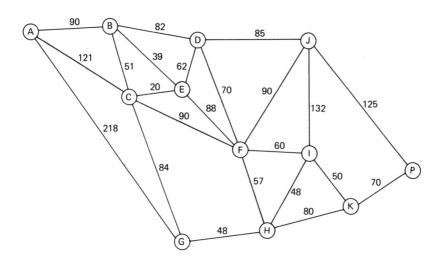

Figure 7-3 Map showing distances without orientation

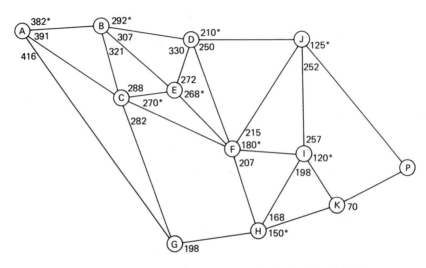

Figure 7-4 Dynamic programming solution for Figure 7-3

unoriented links. The problem is to locate the shortest path from A to P using the available roads. The solution proceeds in the same manner as for Figure 7-1, except that more paths require evaluation at each vertex since travel can be in either direction. The calculations are shown in Figure 7-4. In this case, the minimum distance is 382 over the path A-B-D-J-P.

MINIMUM INTERCONNECTING DISTANCE

A second type of problem is to connect a number of vertices by links at the minimum cost. Consider the six-station layout in Figure 7-5. The distance between each pair of vertices is shown on the graph. The objective is to lay out a set of telephone lines (or it could be roads) so that any vertex can be reached from any other vertex. Assuming that cost is proportional to length of lines laid, the problem becomes one of finding the set of interconnecting links that can be built at the least cost.

A solution is derived from work done by J. B. Kruskal,* who developed an algorithm that can be stated as follows.

1. Select the link that has the least value and make that connection. In Figure 7-5, this would be the link of 30 from vertex 3 to vertex 4; it is identified as step 1 in Figure 7-6.

---

* J. B. Kruskal, "On the Shortest Spanning Subtree of a Graph," *Proceedings of the American Mathematical Society*, 1956.

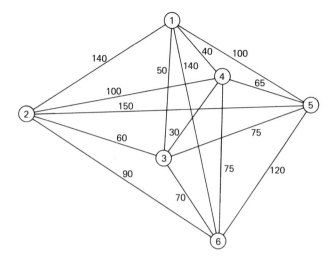

Figure 7-5 Network showing alternative lines of communication and distances

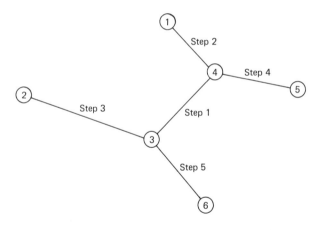

Figure 7-6 Tree of minimum total interconnecting distances

2. Next choose the link that has the next-lowest value and that does not form a cycle with those links already connected. The new link need not necessarily start from an already linked vertex. The next link selected in Figure 7-5 would be the link of 40 from vertex 1 to vertex 4, shown as step 2 in Figure 7-6. Now the 50 from vertex 1 to vertex 3 is the next lowest, but it would form a cycle (in other words, the link from 1 to 3 would not add any new vertex to the existing tree). The third link selected would therefore be 60, from vertex 2 to vertex 3.

3. Repeat this process as necessary. Terminate the procedure when all vertices are part of the tree.

Figure 7-6 illustrates the optimum layout formed from this procedure. This concept has applications in a variety of problems related to transportation or communications.

FLOW AND CAPACITY

Concepts of flow and capacity can be applied to problems that can be represented by networks of links and nodes. Some typical applications would include the following.

1. A network of railroads connects a set of cities. It is desired to determine the maximum rate at which material can be shipped from one particular city to another.

2. A network of pipelines with intermittent stations is available between an origin and a destination. What is the maximum flow between the origin and destination?

3. In application 2, what effect is there on the result if flow is restricted to one direction in each pipeline?

4. In application 2, what is the effect if the station (such as a pumping station) also has a capacity limitation?

Some relatively simple examples will be explored to illustrate concepts related to flow and capacity in a network. Figure 7-7(a) on page 136 shows a simple network with the capacity of each link written above it. Node 1 is the source and node 7 the sink, and the problem is to determine the maximum flow from 1, the source, to 7, the sink.

Assume first that the nodes have unlimited capacity, so that the flow into a node will equal the flow out. In this model, it is also assumed that there are no losses in the network: The flow into the sink, or final destination, will be equal to the flow out of the source.

Flow Restricted to One Direction

For the initial example, assume that the arrows in Figure 7-7(a) indicate the direction of flow for the given capacities. The following procedure now determines the maximum flow through the network from source to sink.

1. Starting at the source, select any path through the network with unused capacity. Initially, all capacities are defined as unused and are shown above the link. As flow is assigned, used capacity is marked below the link. In Figure 7-7(a), path 1-2-5-7 is taken as the starting path.

2. Determine the maximum flow along this path, which is set by the link with the smallest capacity. In this case, it is the 30 on link 5-7 that limits the flow. Direct that amount through the path by entering 30 under each link and subtracting 30 from the unused capacity above the link. Figure 7-7(b) shows the flow below each link and the remaining unused capacity above the link.

3. Repeat steps 1 and 2 until no path remains, as in Figure 7-7(c). The paths were considered here in the following sequence: 1-2-5-7, then 1-4-6-7, then 1-2-7. Other sequences could have been taken, however, and the result would have been the same.

4. Total the capacities either out of the source $(50+0+32)$ or into the sink $(20+30+32)$, yielding a sum of 82. The flow at this point, however, is not yet the maximum.

5. Test other paths by *decreasing* flow in a path without violating the direction-of-flow constraints symbolized by the arrows. Consider the path 1-3-5-2-7. The apparent backwards flow through 5-2 is actually only a reduction in the flow for 5-2 shown in Figure 7-7(c). The flow through this path can be made 16 (limited by path 2-7) by reducing the flow in path 2-5 by 16 from 30 to 14, resulting in Figure 7-7(d). The resulting flow in all paths is still in the direction of orientation.

   Also consider path 1-3-5-2-6-7; the flow through that path is now limited by link 5-2, which can be reduced to 0. If this step is taken, Figure 7-7(e) results.

   The total flow capacity is now 112, and no further paths can be located with unused capacity, since any path tried will have at least one link with 0 remaining capacity.

Direction of Flow Not Restricted

As a continuation of the example, assume that the network system imposes no restriction on the direction of flow in any link. If this is the case, the path 1-3-5-2-6-7 can be used for an additional flow of 6, which would increase the network capacity to 118, as shown in Figure 7-7(f). All flow is still in the direction of the arrows except the flow of 6 units through link 5-2. Evaluation of Figure 7-7(f) will show that none of the paths can handle further flow and that a maximum flow for the network has been found.

Vertex Limitations on Capacity

Consider a further refinement of the original problem in Figure 7-7(a). Assume that each vertex or node has a capacity limitation as listed on page 138, in addition to the link capacities.

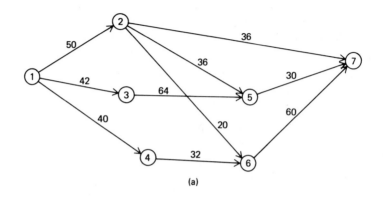

(a)

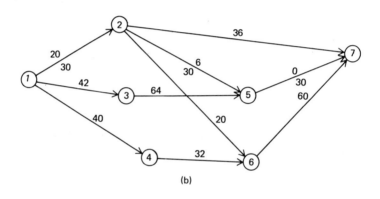

(b)

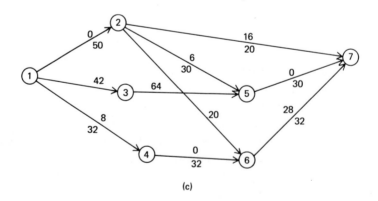

(c)

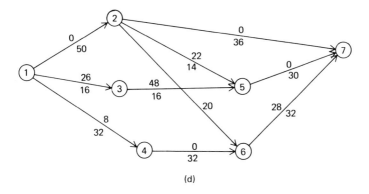

(d)

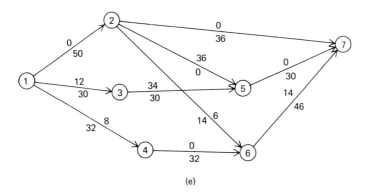

(e)

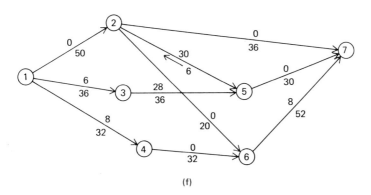

(f)

Figure 7-7 (a) Network showing flow capacities of links. (b) Initial step showing flow along path 1-2-5-7. (c) Tentative solution. (d) Increase in capacity by reducing flow in link 2-5. (e) Final solution for oriented flow. (f) Solution when flow is permitted in any direction.

Vertex	Capacity
1	160
2	46
3	50
4	30
5	40
6	40
7	140

Now, what is the maximum capacity in the network, assuming flow only in the direction of the arrows? In order to perform the analysis, we must draw the revised diagram of Figure 7-8(a) in such a way that a new, artificial link is added to simulate each vertex. At the same time, an artificial vertex is used to terminate the artificial link. The analysis can then proceed in a manner similar to the original procedure. The maximum capacity is now 106, as shown in Figure 7-8(b), instead of the 112 shown in Figure 7-7(e).

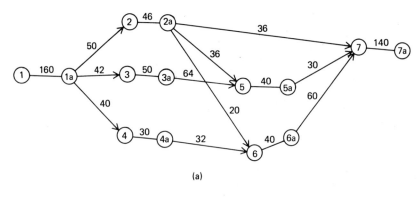

(a)

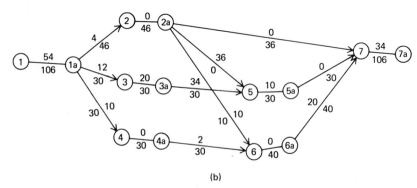

(b)

Figure 7-8 (a) Network with artificial links to simulate node capacities. (b) Solution to (a).

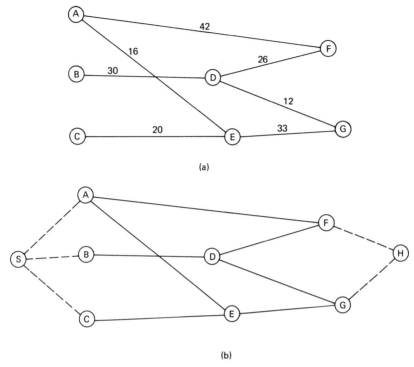

Figure 7-9 (a) Network with multiple inputs and outputs. (b) Modification of (a) with imaginary source and sink.

Multiple Inputs and Outputs

Networks with multiple inputs and/or outputs can be evaluated by a similar procedure. Consider the network in Figure 7-9(a); the flow capacities are shown for each link. The sources are A, B, and C, and the sinks are F and G. The first step is to alter the network by adding a single source and single sink, tied into the others by links of unlimited capacity, as in Figure 7-9(b). The network analysis then continues in the same manner as previously discussed.

SCHEDULING APPLICATIONS: PERT AND CPM

The network applications considered so far have dealt with problems in which the actual physical layout of a system was in the form of a network. The examples were transportation and communications layouts. Another category of network applications consists of problems which do not concern actual networks but which can be approached by laying them out with network models. CPM (critical path method) or PERT (program evaluation and review technique) provides a method for formulation of some types of scheduling problems. A PERT or CPM network is a schematic model used to depict a group of activities and events necessary to complete a project. To begin with, the activities making up the project are defined, along with any required sequence or prerequisites and the expected time to complete each activity. The network presents a considerable amount of information in a compact form. It shows all of the activities required to complete the project and their sequential relationships. It also helps to identify which tasks are critical in terms of meeting the overall schedule, and it aids the decision maker in allocating resources and controlling the project.

The probabilistic approaches to PERT as it was originally developed are covered briefly later in this chapter; current applications frequently deal with the expected activity time on a deterministic basis only. Although the CPM approach differs from the PERT approach in a few respects, the concepts are similar. Therefore a generalized PERT approach will be utilized here so as to maintain a continuous flow in the presentation. The discussion will bring in the important concepts of both types of network scheduling, rather than emphasizing the differences between PERT and CPM methods as they were originally developed.

Applicability of PERT

The value gained from the use of network scheduling techniques depends to a great extent upon selection of correct areas for application. The following types of projects would be suitable for application of network concepts:

1. Projects that are carried out only one time, such as large-scale projects, building construction, research and development programs, product planning, maintenance, and start-up activities in a factory. Network analysis is especially valuable for projects whose completion time is important, such as fulfilling a contract with a penalty clause.

2. Projects whose planning and scheduling must be done together in order to represent properly the requirements and interdependencies. Although the sequence of activities is important, in general many activities can be carried out independently of others.

3. Projects, consisting of well-defined tasks and events, in which the completion of all tasks and events completes the overall project. In this case, a single starting point and a single finish point can be identified.

4. Projects for which there is little or no past experience and many uncertainties are involved.

Advantages of PERT

There are several advantages to be gained from the use of a network to depict a project.

1. The preparation of the network helps the manager to think through the project systematically, making sure that the sequence requirements are adequate and necessary. It also forces the manager to prepare time estimates for individual portions of the total project; this in turn helps him or her to identify possible improvements in these portions or improvements in the relationship of the portions to the whole project. Any constraints found to be unnecessary can be removed to speed up project completion.

2. The network provides a compact summary of the project plan in a form suitable for review by the various departments or persons involved. The network diagram serves as a means of compiling ideas from all of the parties concerned and of identifying possible problems and sources of delay without lengthy coordination meetings.

3. Analysis of the network will reveal the critical path, which is the series of activities in the network that takes the longest time. This longest-time path represents the minimum time in which the project can be completed, since all paths in the network must be completed in order to finish the whole project. When it is necessary to shorten the project completion time, the network solution will identify those activities which, if shortened, could contribute to a reduction in total completion time. It will also identify those activities for which extra effort would not be beneficial; extra time can be taken for some of these without lengthening the total project time.

4. Since the network will be helpful in the identification of related tasks and their time-sequence relationships, responsibilities can be better assigned and resources used to greater advantage.

5. The network analysis will identify the earliest possible starting date and latest allowable completion date for each activity.

6. The completed network can be used as a control to monitor progress of the project as the actual work is accomplished. As problems occur, the network can be used in determining possible alternative solutions.

An Example of Network Scheduling by PERT

A company has decided to replace a piece of equipment used for production in the plant. Table 7-1 lists all of the major activities necessary to complete the changeover to the new equipment. Each activity making up the project is described and assigned a letter symbol, and the expected time to complete

Table 7-1 List of activities making up a project

Activity	Description	Expected time (days)	Immediate predecessors
A	Prepare specifications	8	None
B	Secure bids and award contracts	5	A
C	Remove existing equipment	2	A
D	Reschedule production work	3	B
E	Prepare foundations	3	C
F	Make electrical modifications	3	D, E
G	Make plumbing modifications	2	D, E
H	Paint	4	E
I	Purchase and wait for delivery of equipment	4	B
J	Assemble equipment	4	I
K	Install equipment	3	J, F, G
L	Train operators	4	B
M	Check out equipment	2	K, L
N	Reschedule production	1	M
	Restart production (final event)	0	N

the activity is given. In addition, the immediate predecessors for each activity are specified—those tasks that must be completed before the activity can begin. For example, activity F, electrical modifications, will take three days, but cannot begin until activities D and E are both completed. A table such as this must be formulated by the analyst before the drawing of the network. The identification of activities that must be performed sequentially, as well as those that can be carried out concurrently, follows from the preparation of the table.

Preparation of the PERT Network   The PERT network is made up of a set of activities or tasks that comprise the project, together with events that identify the start or end of an activity. Events are represented by circles. Events do not consume any time, since typically they consist of starting or ending an activity. Activities, on the other hand, are the time-consuming tasks making up the project; they are represented by directional lines or arrows indicating flow from the start to the end of the task.

Figure 7-10 shows the symbols individually and as used together. Activity A could be the task of ordering materials, and event 1 could be defined as "start project" or "start ordering materials." Event 2 might be either "complete ordering materials" or "start activity B." In Figure 7-10, the sequence illustrates the situation in which activity B can start only after activity A has been completed.

Now we can convert the project information in Table 7-1 into a PERT network. This is done by starting at the initial activity or activities, those

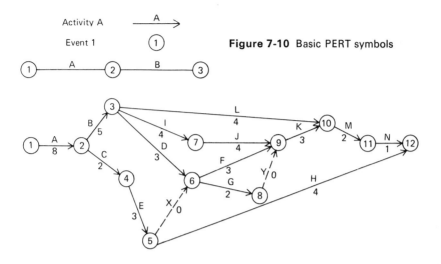

Figure 7-10 Basic PERT symbols

Figure 7-11 PERT network for project in Table 7-1

that have no predecessors. In this case there is only one activity without a predecessor. It is represented by a line drawn from the initial or start event (circle), as in Figure 7-11. The event circles can be numbered. Event 1 could be called "start project" or "start specifications," and event 2 could be referred to as "complete specifications." An event circle represents the completion of one or more activities and also the start of one or more other activities. Sometimes activity A is referred to as activity 1-2; it is desirable that the numbers be established so that any activity can be represented by two numbers, the first of which is smaller than the second. This is often important when utilizing a computer program to solve a network. By following through Table 7-1 and drawing the arrows from the circles completing the predecessor activities, we prepare Figure 7-11, which represents the completed project network. However, there are some other significant factors pertaining to the drawing of the network.

Network Restrictions A correctly constructed PERT diagram should be noncyclical. An incorrect, cyclical condition is shown in Figure 7-12. The cycle implies that C and D must precede E and that C must also follow E, which is an impossible condition. This is easy to notice in a small network; however, it is not always easy to notice in a large network diagram. Checking to assure that the end event is numbered higher than the start event for each activity will assure that there are no cycles in the network.

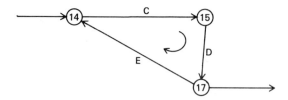

Figure 7-12 A closed loop or cycle is not permitted in a PERT network.

Sometimes it is necessary to insert a *dummy activity* in a network in order to describe the constraints properly. Activities or events in the network should reflect all prerequisite task requirements but should not include requirements beyond those stated, since this will place unnecessary constraints on the ability to meet the schedule. Figure 7-13 represents tasks D, E, F, G, and H from Figure 7-11, in both the incorrect and the correct manner. Activities F, G, and H as stated in Table 7-1 must all be preceded by E; however, only F and G must also be preceded by activity D. Therefore Figure 7-13(a) would not be correct, since it imposes the additional requirement that D be completed before H can start. It would be undesirable to impose this additional constraint, since it would delay the start of task H if E were completed before D. This problem is handled by inserting the dummy activity X, as shown in Figure 7-13(b). The diagram now correctly reflects the constraints, since E must precede F, G, and H but D need not be completed before H can start. The dummy activity is assigned zero time and is represented by a dotted line. Since it is allocated zero performance time, it will not affect the total project schedule. Figure 7-13(b) corresponds to the equivalent portion of the total network in Figure 7-11.

Sometimes dummy activities are also utilized to provide a distinct definition of each activity by a starting and ending event. This method of

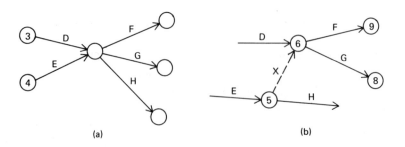

Figure 7-13 (a) Incorrect representation. (b) Correct representation using a dummy activity.

Figure 7-14 (a) Two activities with same starting and ending events. (b) Use of a dummy activity to facilitate description of activities by event numbers.

identification is necessary for some computer programs. In Figure 7-14, activities F and G start and end with the same event. Figure 7-14(a) is proper; however, activity F and activity G would both be described by 6-9. Figure 7-14(b) uses a dummy activity to provide an alternative representation, so that activity F is represented by 6-9 and activity G is represented by 6-8. The dummy activity again is assigned zero time and the total network time and activity sequences are not affected.

The Critical Path The identification of the critical path is one of the most important results of PERT network analysis. The critical path, the series of activities in the network that will take the longest time, governs the span of time for the entire project. The sum of the activity times along the critical path is the shortest possible completion time for the entire project. There are several paths through any network, and the time to complete any path can be determined by adding the times of the activities along the path. Many activities are on more than one path. For example, activity B in Figure 7-11 appears on path A-B-L-M-N, A-B-D-G-Y-K-M-N, and two other paths. Activity A is contained in all paths. One way to determine the critical path would be to enumerate all paths in the network and select the longest one. This is done for Figure 7-11 in the following table.

Path	Total time (*days*)
A-B-L-M-N	20
A-B-I-J-K-M-N	27
A-B-D-F-K-M-N	25
A-B-D-G-Y-K-M-N	24
A-C-E-X-F-K-M-N	22
A-C-E-X-G-Y-K-M-N	21
A-C-E-H	17

The critical path is A-B-I-J-K-M-N, with a time span of 27 days, the longest of any path shown. This means that the project cannot be completed in less than 27 days, unless a means is found to shorten an activity along the critical path or to change the precedence requirements. If any activity along the critical path were shortened by one day, then the total project would also be shortened by one day. Shortening an activity which is not on the critical path, such as activity H, would not improve the total project time. Activity H is thus considered to have slack time, since it could actually consume some extra time without affecting the time for the total project.

It is apparent, then, that any effort to cut the total project completion time should concentrate first on those activities along the critical path. Suppose, however, that an analysis showed that, by adding more personnel, activity I could be cut to 2 days and activity J could be cut to 3 days, reducing the critical path A-B-I-J-K-M-N from 27 to 24 days. Although this reduces the original critical path by 3 days, it only reduces the total project time by 2 days, because the path A-B-D-F-K-M-N, which takes 25 days, now becomes the critical path. The reduction of time in the critical path is beneficial to the total project only up to the point at which another path replaces the original as the critical path.

In the relatively simple network of the example given, it was relatively easy to enumerate all of the paths and select the critical one. However, in a more complex network, this enumeration process might be very time-consuming; networks for real projects often contain hundreds of activities. A quicker and more systematic method to identify the critical path is to utilize the concepts developed in Chapter 6. This involves starting at either the initial event or the last event in the network. We will start at the last event and work back toward the beginning. In Figure 7-15 (the same project network as in Figure 7-11), the number in parentheses after each event circle represents the time needed to complete the project from that event circle. The numbers are obtained by starting at the final event and working backwards, adding each activity time in turn, and entering the total after the event circle. Wherever there are two activities leaving the right side of an event circle, the longest time is used in subsequent calculations. For example, the 12 at the event circle preceding activity D is calculated by adding the 3 for activity D to the 9 required to reach the end through activity F; we use the 9 of F rather than the 8 of G because the 9 is larger. Similarly, the 5 for activity B is added to the 14, the largest of the three values from L, I, and D, to obtain the value of 19. Thus, the time of 27 appearing next to the start event circle is the critical path time, or longest path time through the whole network.

The critical path now can be easily identified by starting at the initial event and, at each event circle, branching to the path with the largest

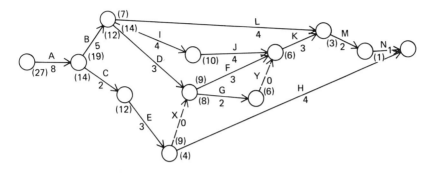

Figure 7-15 Solution for the critical path

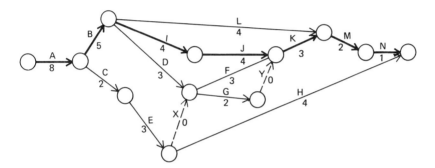

Figure 7-16 The critical path

number. Thus, at the second event circle, the path along activity B is selected, because the 19 is larger than the 14. This procedure identifies the critical path A-B-I-J-K-M-N, shown in Figure 7-16 as a heavy line.

Start and Finish Time Boundaries The identification of boundaries for the start and finish times are very useful in scheduling and in monitoring progress of the project. The objective of this discussion is to identify in a project the earliest and latest times that activities in the project can start or finish without affecting the overall schedule. The following list defines the terms and the constraints involved. The first two items depend upon other activities that must be completed prior to the activity in question, whereas the second two items depend upon activities that must follow the one in question.

1. EARLIEST START TIME (EST) The earliest time that an activity can start, calculated on the basis of the other activities that must be completed first.

2. EARLIEST FINISH TIME (EFT) EST plus the activity time.

3. LATEST START TIME (LST) The latest time that an activity can start without delay of the entire project.

4. LATEST FINISH TIME (LFT) The latest time that an activity can finish without delay of the entire project (LST plus the activity time).

The latest start time is available from our solution for the critical path. The value next to each node in Figure 7-15 is the minimum time required from that node to the finish of the project. Since the shortest total project time (along the critical path) is 27 days, subtracting each time-to-the-end from 27 days will yield a latest start time for each activity, measured from the beginning. This LST is shown in Figure 7-17 as the second of the two numbers under the activity letter. The first of the two numbers is the EST, or earliest time that each activity can start. This is obtained by beginning at the first event in the network and adding the time for each activity in turn. The EST for activity D is governed by those other activities that must be completed before D can start. Wherever two or more activities lead into a single event circle, the ESTs of the activities diverging from that event circle are calculated from the largest EFT (EST plus activity time) coming into that circle. Figure 7-17 shows the EST and LST for each activity in the project network. As an example, using Figure 7-15, the earliest and latest start and finish times for activity L are calculated as follows:

$$EST(\text{Activity L}) = A + B = 8 + 5 = 13,$$
$$EFT(\text{Activity L}) = EST + L = 13 + 4 = 17,$$
$$LST(\text{Activity L}) = \text{Critical path time} - N - M - L$$
$$= 27 - 1 - 2 - 4 = 27 - 7 = 20,$$
$$LFT(\text{Activity L}) = LST + L = 20 + 4 = 24.$$

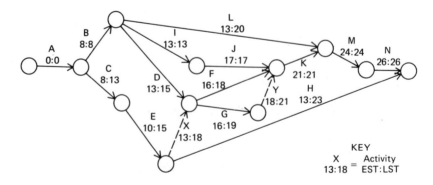

Figure 7-17 Project network showing earliest start time (EST) and latest start time (LST) for each activity

It can be noticed that along the critical path the earliest start times (ESTs) and latest start times (LSTs) are the same.

The span of time over which each activity can be performed is defined as the *maximum available time (MAT)* and is calculated as follows:

$$MAT = LFT - EST$$
$$= 24 - 13 = 11.$$

The *slack time* is the extra time available to perform an activity—the time in excess of the expected time. It is calculated as follows:

$$Slack = LFT - EST - t_e$$
$$= 24 - 13 - 4 = 7.$$

Table 7-2 summarizes all of the values for each activity. Those activities with zero slack are on the critical path.

Uncertainty Factors in PERT
The analysis so far has involved deterministic calculations and has not brought in probabilistic concepts or factors of uncertainty. Each activity has been represented by a fixed expected time; in real problems, however, there may be difficulties in directly determining the expected activity times. For any activity A, with an expected completion time of 8 days, the question can be asked, "What is the probability of completing the task in 7 days, or in 10 days?" PERT or CPM methodology provides a means of bringing factors of uncertainty into the analysis. A task with an expected completion time of 8 days might, on occasion, take 4 days and at other

Table 7-2 Values (in days) for each activity

Activity	Expected time	EST	EFT	LST	LFT	MAT	Slack
A	8	0	8	0	8	8	0
B	5	8	13	8	13	5	0
C	2	8	10	13	15	7	5
D	3	13	16	15	18	5	2
E	3	10	13	15	18	8	5
F	3	16	19	18	21	5	2
G	2	16	18	19	21	5	3
H	4	13	17	23	27	14	10
I	4	13	17	13	17	4	0
J	4	17	21	17	21	4	0
K	3	21	24	21	24	3	0
L	4	13	17	20	24	11	7
M	2	24	26	24	26	2	0
N	1	26	27	26	27	1	0

times take as many as 16 days, depending upon factors of uncertainty such as weather, strikes, or normal variations that are difficult to predict exactly. When the risks become apparent, it may be necessary to reallocate the available resources among the activities. If weather can substantially affect the time on one activity, it may be desirable to allocate more personnel to the task when the weather is good in order to alleviate the chance of a long delay caused by bad weather.

Factors of uncertainty can be taken into account by considering three possible values for each activity time before arriving at the expected time to use in the analysis. The three possible values are:

1. OPTIMISTIC TIME (t_o) The shortest possible time required to complete the activity when all goes well. On a probability basis, there might be only one chance in a hundred of completing the task in a time shorter than this.

2. PESSIMISTIC TIME (t_p) The longest possible time required for an activity, assuming that problems of an unusual nature arise. As a general rule, there would be one chance in a hundred that the activity would take more time than this.

3. MOST LIKELY TIME (t_m) An estimate of the time required for an activity, allowing for typical interruptions and problems.

Since PERT networks are particularly applicable to one-time projects, which have not been carried out previously, there are usually many unknowns and uncertainties. The task of arriving at a valid expected time is often made easier by starting with the three time estimates. When the three estimates have been made, the expected time is then computed by taking a weighted average of the three values. The equation used to compute this weighted average is:

$$t_e \text{ (Expected time)} = \frac{t_o + 4t_m + t_p}{6}.$$

The calculations are based on the assumption of a random variable ranging from t_o to t_p and following a beta distribution, as shown in Figure 7-18. The t_e will then be the mean of the beta distribution.

The *variance* σ^2—the square of the standard deviation—can be determined for each activity as follows:

$$\sigma^2 = \left(\frac{t_p - t_o}{6}\right)^2.$$

The expected time for the whole project is the sum of the expected times along the critical path. The variance for the whole project is calculated by

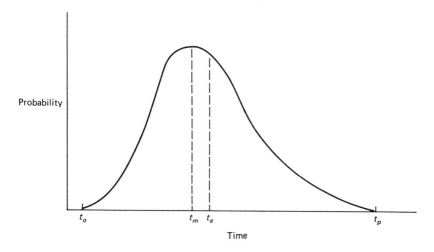

Figure 7-18 Beta distribution of activity times

taking the sum of the variances along the critical path. For the project we have used as an example, it would be:

$$\sigma^2_{\text{project}} = \sigma_A{}^2 + \sigma_B{}^2 + \sigma_I{}^2 + \sigma_J{}^2 + \sigma_K{}^2 + \sigma_M{}^2 + \sigma_N{}^2.$$

The probability of meeting a scheduled completion date can be determined by:

$$\frac{\text{Scheduled time—Earliest expected time}}{\substack{\text{Standard deviation of sum of activity} \\ \text{times (along critical path)}}} = \text{Area under normal curve.}$$

To see how this is used, assume that the "area under the normal curve" calculated by the formula came out to be .4. Then, from a table of normal curve probabilities, we find that the probability of meeting the scheduled date is .6554. Probability values below .3 indicate that the schedule cannot reasonably be met with the given resources. If the scheduled time equals the sum of the expected times along the critical path, the probability of completing the project on schedule is .5. Probability values higher than .7 are an indication that the resources allocated to the project may be too high.

As an example, consider activity A from Table 7-1. In the table the expected time for activity A is given as 8 days. Assume instead that the person scheduling the project obtained the following information for activity A:

$$t_o = 6 \text{ days,}$$
$$t_p = 16 \text{ days,}$$
$$t_m = 8 \text{ days.}$$

The expected time would then be calculated as follows:

$$t_e = \frac{t_o + 4t_m + t_p}{6} = \frac{6 + 4(8) + 16}{6} = 9.0.$$

The variance for activity A would be:

$$\sigma^2 = \left(\frac{t_p - t_o}{6}\right)^2 = \left(\frac{16 - 6}{6}\right)^2 = 2.78.$$

The expected time and variance for any of the other activities could also have been calculated in this manner. The value for the expected time obtained here would be used in finding the critical path, the EST, and the other values discussed earlier.

Control

The discussion so far has illustrated the use of PERT as a tool for planning and analysis. The network representation of a project is also useful as a control—that is, for monitoring the project as the work progresses. As events in the network are accomplished, the actual completion date can be entered in each event circle alongside the scheduled completion time. This is especially important for events along the critical path, where delay in an activity would jeopardize the project schedule. Variance from the expected completion time is then evident. The actual completion times can also be compared to the latest possible completion times, to determine the effect on the overall project. This comparison will highlight the need for reallocation of resources or other action to compensate for schedule slippages.

Resource Allocation

PERT activities actually involve work-load assignments, and the analysis often relates to the availability of certain skills to accomplish the task. In some cases, the available people may have the skills to handle more than one of the activities making up the project. The PERT network can be useful in determining the assignment of personnel or equipment so as to reduce either the total time needed or the total costs. In cases of unforeseen problems, resources on noncritical tasks might be temporarily transferred to activities on the critical path, as long as there is sufficient slack in the noncritical path.

Cost Versus Time It is apparent that the time span of any activity is usually dependent upon the amount of resources allocated to it. Activities can therefore be shortened with an associated increase in cost. The project manager can determine the additional costs for activities performed on a crash basis, and thus find the costs for shortening the total project time. The additional, or incremental, costs for activities on the critical path would be examined first, since shortening of activities not on the critical path would have no immediate benefit. Each activity on the critical path would be examined to determine the added cost per unit of time saved. If a project were to be shortened, the initial crash efforts would concentrate on the activity with the lowest incremental cost per unit of time saved.

Once an activity had been selected for crashing, or for allocation of additional funds to secure reduction in time, the network would be revised to incorporate the new time. If further compression of total project time were needed, the process would be repeated. This repetition would continue until the time for the critical path was reduced to the desired goal. This procedure reduces the total time to the desired goal with the minimum cost increment.

Conversion to a Bar Chart   A PERT chart can be converted into a bar chart to aid the manager in monitoring the schedule and in identifying improvements in resource allocation. The PERT chart in Figure 7-17 showed the EST and LST for each activity. These data are converted into a bar chart in Figure 7-19. The procedure is as follows.

1. Draw bars for all activities on the critical path, where the EST and LST are identical.

2. Draw in a dotted line showing the range over which each other activity make take place. For example, activity C can start anywhere from day 8 (EST) to day 13 (LST) and extend for two days.

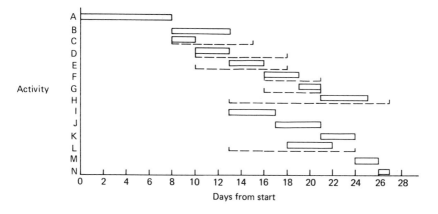

Figure 7-19 Bar chart equivalent to PERT diagram of Figures 7-11 and 7-17

3. The bar for each activity not on the critical path can then be placed anywhere along the dotted line. In some cases, the activity might be split into two parts.

In making the determination of where to place the bar, several factors can be considered.

1. Starting the activity early would reduce the chance that a problem or delay would affect the whole project schedule. Thus, an early start would tend to compensate for possible uncertainties.

2. Starting at the LST would delay the outlay of cash for labor and materials as long as possible, thus avoiding carrying costs of work in progress.

3. The resources could be allocated so as to make the best use of available personnel and equipment. If the same person could handle D and E, they could be scheduled as in Figure 7-19.

This trade-off procedure can continue until a good schedule is ready. The resulting bar chart or Gantt chart is frequently used as a control in factory scheduling, since the bars can be filled in to show status as the work proceeds. The PERT and bar charts can be utilized together in problem solving as unforeseen situations arise.

PROBLEMS

1. The following represents a map of towns and roads with the distances between towns shown.

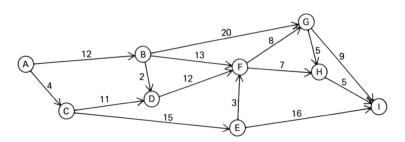

Determine the shortest route from A to I.

2. There are six drilling operations with distances between them as shown in the map. A set of roads is to be built so that a truck can get from any location to any other location. Considering that the cost of road construction is proportional to distance, determine the tree of minimum cost.

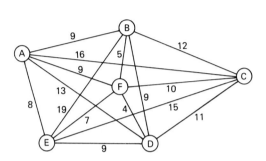

3. Pipeline capacities in gallons per minute between various stations are shown in the following map. Determine the maximum flow capacity from 1 to 8, considering flow only in the directions of the arrows.

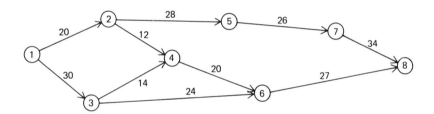

4. In problem 3, how would the network flow capacity from 1 to 8 be changed if flow were permitted in either direction?

5. In problem 3, with oriented flow, assume that all station (node) capacities are 50 gallons per minute except for stations 4, 5, and 6, which have capacities of 25 gallons per minute. How does this affect the network capacity?

6. There are two sources, 1 and 2, as shown in the following map. What is the maximum combined flow capacity from 1 and 2 to 7?

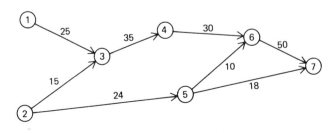

7. Construct a PERT network for the following project, and determine the critical path.

Activity	Time	Immediate predecessors
A	4	None
B	1	None
C	1	A
D	1	B
E	6	B
F	8	E
G	2	F
H	4	E
I	1	H
J	5	G, I
K	5	C, D
L	7	K

8. In problem 7, determine the earliest possible start time and latest possible start time for each activity. Plot them in the form of a bar chart.

9. Assume that you are letting a contract for widening a street. Draw a PERT diagram for the activities from the start of preparation of specifications until contractor go-ahead. Determine the critical path and the shortest time to complete the set of tasks.

Task	Description	Expected time (working days)	Immediate predecessors
A	Prepare specifications for job	5	None
B	Notify property owners	2	None
C	Select prospective bidders	4	None
D	Contact prospective bidders	4	C
E	Send out requests for bid	3	A, D
F	Hold a bid conference	2	E
G	Secure property owners' approval	14	B
H	Wait for bidders to prepare bids	10	F
I	Receive bids	2	H
J	Evaluate bids	5	I
K	Prepare final job schedule	2	G, J
L	Arrange details with water company	4	G, J
M	Notify selected bidders	1	K
N	Negotiate and sign contract	2	L, M
	Go-ahead for contractor	0	N

10. For problem 9, prepare a table showing the earliest start time, earliest finish time, latest start time, latest finish time, and slack time for each activity.

11. Construct a PERT diagram for the following information, and determine the critical path.

Activity	t_o	t_m	t_p	Immediate predecessors
A	1	2	4	None
B	2	4	6	A
C	2	6	10	A
D	6	8	10	B
E	4	6	8	C
F	6	10	14	C
G	8	10	12	D, E
H	12	14	16	F
I	4	8	12	G, H
J	10	12	16	G, H
K	2	4	6	I
L	6	10	14	J

12. For problem 11, assume that the schedule allows 40 days to complete the whole project, and calculate the probability of completion by the scheduled date.

13. For problem 11, the contractor wants to quote a scheduled completion date that would give him a 90 percent chance of attainment. How many days should he allow in his schedule?

SUPPLEMENTARY READINGS

Busaker, R. G., and T. L. Saaty. *Finite Graphs and Networks*. McGraw-Hill, New York, 1965.

Ford, L. R., and D. R. Fulkerson. *Flows in Networks*. Princeton University Press, Princeton, N.J., 1962.

Harary, Frank. *Graph Theory*. Addison-Wesley, Reading, Mass., 1969.

Kaufmann, A. *Graphs, Dynamic Programming, and Finite Games*. Academic Press, New York, 1967.

Kaufmann, A., and G. Desbazeille. *The Critical Path Method*. Gordon and Breach, New York, 1969.

Kruskal, J. B. "On the Shortest Spanning Subtree of a Graph." *Proceedings of the American Mathematical Society*, 1956.

Levin, R., and C. A. Kirkpatrick. *Planning and Control with PERT/CPM.* McGraw-Hill, New York, 1966.

Maxwell, L. M., and M. B. Reed. *The Theory of Graphs.* Pergamon Press, New York, 1971.

Schaffer, L. R., J. B. Ritter, and W. L. Meyer. *Critical Path Method.* McGraw-Hill, New York, 1965.

Weist, J. D., and F. Levy. *A Management Guide to PERT/CPM.* Prentice-Hall, Englewood Cliffs, N.J., 1969.

8/Game
Theory

DECISION making under conditions of uncertainty was examined in Chapter 4. Probability models and Bayesian decision theory were applied to a variety of problems. This chapter discusses two special cases of decision theory under uncertainty. The first is a situation in which there are two players or firms playing against each other in an aggressive manner. This differs from strict games against nature, in which nature should be considered as a nonhostile opponent.

The second is decision making under conditions of "total ignorance," when there is insufficient information to speculate intelligently on the probabilities of states of nature. In situations of this sort, it is impossible or not meaningful to assign probabilities, and the formal concepts of expected value do not apply. (We will discuss later how some decision strategies, specifically the Laplace philosophy, allow for specification of states of nature as equally probable when no information is given to indicate otherwise. This criterion will be called the criterion of insufficient reason.)

TWO-PERSON, ZERO-SUM GAMES

Two-person, zero-sum games are a special case of decision making in which the following conditions apply.

1. There are two players, and each has a finite set of strategies available to him.

2. Each of the two players or firms, A and B, knows the alternative actions available to him and to his opponent and the outcome or payoff for any possible combination of these actions.

3. The two decision makers have conflicting goals. If player A is interested in maximizing his gains and/or minimizing his losses, then player B is interested in maximizing *his* gains and/or minimizing *his* losses. A's gain is B's loss and vice versa.

4. Each player has a preference order for the plays (that is, a best move), and this preference order is known by his opponent. In other words, each opponent will play using a prescribed decision rule, and all available decision rules are known by the other player. Given this known set of decision rules, each player will move assuming that the opponent will select *his* optimum move.

5. The players each have only one move or strategy, and the moves are taken concurrently or in such a way that each player does not know the particular move selected by the other player, although he does know the rules available to the other player.

6. In game theory, each player is assumed to try to do the best that he can. It is further assumed that he has the decision-making capabilities to determine his best play or strategy at any point in the game.

A business situation that closely parallels this kind of game is the collective bargaining of a labor union and management. There are in general two sides, labor and management, which have conflicting goals, and each side is trying to do the best it can. Both have sets of plays, and within each set there are certain preferences. Neither side wants to commit itself completely at one time, but each knows fairly well the preferences of the other.

More generally, the situation can be shown in equation form as follows, where the Greek letters α and β represent the alternative actions available to the respective participants, A and B, and S_1 and S_2 represent the sets of options for A and B.

$$S_1 = \{\alpha_1, \alpha_2, ..., \alpha_n\},$$
$$S_2 = \{\beta_1, \beta_2, ..., \beta_m\}.$$

For example, in the labor-management bargaining, labor could be viewed as player A and management as player B. The various α strategies are potential strategies that labor can choose, such as seeking an hourly wage increase only, seeking an hourly wage increase plus a hospitalization plan, seeking changes in the seniority structure, and so forth. The entire set of α strategies is called S_1. The various β strategies are those of management,

Table 8-1 Payoffs for player A in a
two-person, zero-sum game

Player A \ Player B	β_1	β_2
α_1	10	-3
α_2	9	2

such as offering nothing, suggesting a wage decrease, offering a lower wage increase than demanded, offering the hospitalization only, and so forth. The entire set of α strategies is called S_2.

All possible strategies are known by each participant in the game, and these strategies form an $m \times n$ matrix of payoffs (or losses). For example, Table 8-1 is written in terms of payoffs to player A. Thus, an $\alpha_1 \beta_1$ combination of actions (which in the bargaining example may mean that each side attempts to settle on a wage hike of some sort) will yield a payoff of 10 from B to A, while $\alpha_1 \beta_2$ would result in a loss of 3 by A and a gain of 3 by B. In a zero-sum game such as this, the losses of one player are the gains of the other.

STRICTLY DETERMINED GAMES

Decision Rules

Table 8-2 shows some assumed payoffs to player A for various α and β strategy combinations. As stated previously, each participant knows the strategies available to himself, those available to his opponent, and the payoffs. In terms of strictly determined games in general, player A could assume that the worst is always going to happen to him; as a result, he would select the strategy that yielded the largest minimum payoff. This decision criterion turns out to be the best possible one, because it is assumed

Table 8-2 Payoffs for player A in a strictly determined game

Player A \ Player B	β_1	β_2	β_3	Row minimum
α_1	10	8	11	8
α_2	4	2	0	0
Column maximum	10	8	11	

that opponent B has the capability of determining his own best action, which in turn creates the worst situation for A. In this case, A would select strategy α_1. He would be following the strategy of maximizing his minimum gain, called the *maximin* strategy. Conversely, player B would be interested in minimizing his losses. As a result, if he also assumed the worst was going to happen (that is, that A would make the optimum plays), he would select the strategy yielding the smallest maximum payoff, β_2, which is a *minimax* strategy. If each player did not follow the correct strategy, the other player would be able to burden him with a needless loss. This would be non-rational decision making.

Dominating Strategies

Upon further examination of Table 8-2, we see that, regardless of player B's reaction, player A is better off playing strategy α_1 than α_2, because for each $\alpha_1\beta_j$ combination the payoff is higher than for the matching $\alpha_2\beta_j$; in other words, each payoff in the first row is larger than the corresponding payoff in the second row. Strategy α_1 then *dominates* α_2 for player A. For player B, who is interested in minimizing his losses, strategy β_2 dominates strategy β_1; however, β_2 does not dominate β_3, nor does β_3 dominate β_1. It is never in the best interest of a player to select a dominated strategy, because he would always be better off playing some other strategy. It follows, then, that each player will strike dominated strategies from the matrix.

Equilibrium Point

In the games we have been discussing, there exists a maximin strategy for player A which guarantees him at least P, and a minimax strategy for player B which guarantees that player A gets only payoff P. This results in an *equilibrium*, or *saddle point*. In the 3×3 payoff matrix of Table 8-3, player A's maximin strategy α_2 coincides with player B's minimax strategy

Table 8-3 Payoffs for player A, with the equilibrium point circled

Player A \ Player B	β_1	β_2	β_3	Row minimum
α_1	−3	4	−1	−3
α_2	(2)	5	3	2
α_3	1	−7	10	−7
Column maximum	2	5	10	

β_1 at the circled value. If one player deviates from the strategy represented by this equilibrium, he will be subjecting himself to needless loss. For example, if player B chooses his minimax or best strategy β_1 and player A deviates from his maximin strategy by playing α_1, A's payoff will decrease from 2 to -3. When competitive situations are in a state of disequilibrium, they always gravitate toward the equilibrium pair of strategies. Games that have this equilibrium point are said to be *strictly determined*.

GAMES NOT STRICTLY DETERMINED

A two-person, zero-sum game is not always resolved by an equilibrium point. For example, in the matrix of Table 8-4, there is no single element that is both the minimum of a row and the maximum of a column. A player's blind usage of a minimax or maximin strategy, in this case, could lead to unnecessary losses inflicted by the opposing player. For example, if player A selected his maximum-security strategy α_2, he would at least obtain his payoff of 4. Player B, following the minimax rule, would select β_1. But because there is no equilibrium point and because of the complete payoff information available to each player, if player A suspects player B is going to employ β_1 he will realize that he is better off taking α_1 rather than α_2. However, player B, if he has the foresight to predict player A's approach, will recognize that he is better off playing β_2, with which the loss is 3 rather than 6. We can see by the circling of all four values that the cyclical reasoning process will lead to situations in which either A or B is luring the other into a wrong decision.

We know that each player or firm would want to protect its position by concealing the intended strategy. To avoid being lured into making the wrong decision, a player must therefore employ a random process to select his strategy on each particular play. The player first, however, will need to

Table 8-4 Payoffs for player A in a game that is not strictly determined

Player A \ Player B	β_1	β_2	Row minimum
α_1	⑥	③	3
α_2	④	⑧	4
Column maximum	6	8	

know how to alternate between the choices in order to achieve his best overall payoff. In other words, a relative frequency for playing each alternative must be determined.

Choosing α_1 with a certain frequency or probability and α_2 with a certain probability is called a *mixed strategy*; it differs from the *pure strategy* of always making one choice or the other. In a pure strategy, the probability of selecting the particular action is 1.0.

Selecting Mixed Strategies

To solve for the proper mix of strategies, probabilities similar to the indifference probabilities introduced in Chapter 4 are employed. For player A, let p stand for the probability of selecting strategy α_1 and $1-p$ for the probability of selecting α_2. Then if B selects β_1, player A's expected gain (EG) is:

$$EG|\beta_1 = 6p + 4(1-p).$$

If B selects β_2, player A's expected gain is:

$$EG|\beta_2 = 3p + 8(1-p).$$

Equating the two expected values results in the optimum mixed-strategy probabilities for player A. Intuitively, we can say that this mixed strategy is optimum because A becomes indifferent to which strategy B selects. He is in effect independent of B if he employs his optimum mixed strategy. More theoretically, we should note that the independence is in the statistical sense; it is a long-run phenomenon, existing over a number of trials, and it does not necessarily pertain to a single trial.

Equating $EG|\beta_1$ and $EG|\beta_2$ and solving for the probabilities, we find that

$$6p + 4(1-p) = 3p + 8(1-p),$$
$$2p + 4 = -5p + 8,$$
$$7p = 4,$$
$$p = 4/7,$$
$$(1-p) = 3/7.$$

In Figure 8-1, the line R_1 was drawn by substituting $p=0$ and $p=1$, respectively, into the equation for $EG|\beta_2$. When $p=0$, the term $3p+8(1-p)$ takes the value of 8; when $p=1$, the value is 3. For the line R_2, the values are obtained in the same manner using the term $6p+4(1-p)$ from the equation for $EG|\beta_1$; the values are 4 and 6. The lines represent the expected gains for player A, given the strategy selected by B. Following the maximin strategy, player A will employ a mixed strategy using the

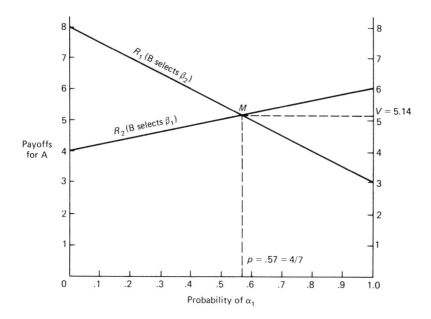

Figure 8-1 Graphic solution of mixed strategy probabilities for player A

probability of selecting α_1 shown at point M on the graph. This probability of .57 or 4/7 is the same that we calculated using the equations. If A selects a p less than 4/7 and player B reacts as expected (remember that each player has complete information about the decision rules of the game), the payoff can be read from line R_2. When p is greater than 4/7, the payoff can be read from R_1. In both cases the strategy is nonoptimum.

Value of the Game

By inserting the values of p and $1-p$ back into the equation for $EG \mid \beta_1$, we obtain the equilibrium payoff, which is also called the *value of the game*:

$$6(p) + 4(1-p) = 6(4/7) + 4(3/7) = 36/7 = 5.14.$$

This value is shown at point V in Figure 8-1. We could obtain the same value by substituting into the equation for $EG \mid \beta_2$. Note that by playing the mixed strategy player A is assured a long-run payoff of 5.14, while if he employed a pure strategy of selecting either α_1 or α_2 his guaranteed payoff would be smaller. With a pure strategy of α_1, for example, the assured long-run payoff is only 3; this outcome is actually unlikely, because it represents the combination of A's minimin gain strategy and B's maximax loss strategy, which represents irrational behavior.

The optimum strategy for player B can be calculated in the same manner.

Let q stand for the probability of selecting β_1, $1-q$ for the probability of selecting β_2, and EL for the expected loss.

$$\text{EL}|\alpha_1 = \text{EL}|\alpha_2,$$
$$6q + 3(1-q) = 4q + 8(1-q),$$
$$3q + 3 = -4q + 8,$$
$$q = 5/7,$$
$$1 - q = 2/7.$$

When we substitute the values of q and $1-q$ into the equation for $\text{EL}|\alpha_1$, the value of the game is determined to be:

$$6(5/7) + 3(2/7) = 36/7 = 5.14.$$

We can now see that the value of the game for player A has been equated to the value for player B, and the result is an equilibrium solution. Note also that the long-run loss incurred when player B uses the strategy represented by these probabilities is less than would be expected if B played any pure strategy.

Applying Mixed Strategies

In order to apply the mixed strategy correctly and remove any tendency toward bias, a player should randomly select an action for each play, allowing the frequency of each choice to be dictated by the mixed-strategy solution. For example, if the optimum mixed strategy is to employ α_1 20 percent of the time and α_2 80 percent of the time, the player could make use of a random-number table to select the strategy to employ on a particular trial. Choosing from two-digit numbers between 00 and 99, the player would employ α_1 when a number came up from 00 to 19, and α_2 when the number was from 20 to 99.

$2 \times n$ GAMES

A $2 \times n$ game exists when there are two players, one with two strategies and the other with more than two strategies. Although there are several alternative ways of solving a $2 \times n$ game, graphic solution is often the easiest. In the game shown in Table 8-5, we could solve for the appropriate mixed strategy in a manner similar to that for a 2×2 payoff matrix. If B uses β_1, A's payoff is:

$$1p + 4(1-p) = 4 - 3p.$$

Table 8-5 Payoffs for player A in a 2×3 game

Player B / Player A	β_1	β_2	β_3
α_1	1	4	5
α_2	4	3	1

If B uses β_2, A's payoff is:

$$4p + 3(1-p) = 3 + p.$$

And for β_3, A's payoff is:

$$5p + 1(1-p) = 1 + 4p.$$

We can see from Figure 8-2 that player B would not want to play β_2, because a mixed strategy involving β_1 and β_3 would give a minimax solution. Eliminating β_2 as a feasible alternative, the probability that A should play α_1 can be obtained as before by finding the p that will satisfy

$$4 - 3p = 1 + 4p.$$

Therefore,

$$3 = 7p,$$
$$p = 3/7.$$

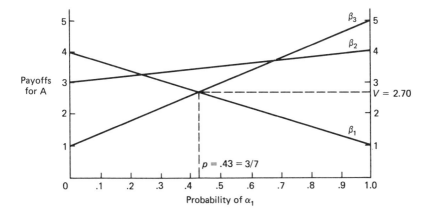

Payoffs for A

$p = .43 = 3/7$

Probability of α_1

$V = 2.70$

Figure 8-2 Mixed strategy probabilities for player A in a 2×3 game

Solving for the probabilities for player B, we see that

$$1q + 5(1-q) = 5 - 4q,$$
$$4q + 1(1-q) = 1 + 3q,$$
$$5 - 4q = 1 + 3q,$$
$$7q = 4,$$
$$q = 4/7.$$

The appropriate mixed strategies for B are $\{4/7, 0, 3/7\}$. For A they are $\{3/7, 4/7\}$. The value of the game for A can then be shown to be:

$$(3/7)[1q + 5(1-q)] + (4/7)[4q + 1(1-q)] = 2.70.$$

For B the value is

$$(4/7)[1p + 4(1-p)] + (0)[4p + 3(1-p)] + (3/7)[5p + 1(1-p)] = 2.70.$$

Now we can consider a generalized graphic solution to $2 \times n$ zero-sum games. In Figure 8-3 there are n straight lines, each representing a separate pure strategy by player A. The convex set $\{OPQRS\}$ represents the feasible solutions to the game, with the minimax solution lying along the range between the highest points, Q and R. This suggests that the optimum $p(\alpha_1)$ ranges from p_1 to p_2. Under different conditions there may be a single apex of the convex set that represents the single optimum frequency for α_1.

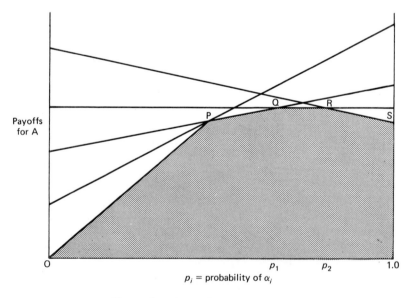

Figure 8-3 Generalized $2 \times n$ solution

MATRIX SOLUTIONS

When dealing with 2×2 games, we can make use of matrix algebra to solve for the appropriate mixed-strategy probabilities and the value of the game. Generally, if the payoff matrix is designated by Z, we can calculate the appropriate mixed-strategy probabilities as follows:

$$\text{A's probabilities} = \frac{[1 \quad 1] \times Z_{\text{adj}}}{[1 \quad 1] \times Z_{\text{adj}} \times \begin{bmatrix} 1 \\ 1 \end{bmatrix}},$$

$$\text{B's probabilities} = \frac{[1 \quad 1] \times Z_{\text{cof}}}{[1 \quad 1] \times Z_{\text{adj}} \times \begin{bmatrix} 1 \\ 1 \end{bmatrix}}.$$

The value of the game can be found from

$$[p(\alpha_1) \quad p(\alpha_2)] \times Z \times \begin{bmatrix} p(\beta_1) \\ p(\beta_2) \end{bmatrix}.$$

For instance, in a previous example, we had a 2×2 payoff matrix:

$$\begin{array}{cc} & \begin{array}{cc} \beta_1 & \beta_2 \end{array} \\ \begin{array}{c} \alpha_1 \\ \alpha_2 \end{array} & \begin{bmatrix} 6 & 3 \\ 4 & 8 \end{bmatrix}. \end{array}$$

Using the matrix approach, we could determine player A's optimum strategies as follows:

$$\frac{[1 \quad 1] \times \begin{bmatrix} 8 & -3 \\ -4 & 6 \end{bmatrix}}{[1 \quad 1] \times \begin{bmatrix} 8 & -3 \\ -4 & 6 \end{bmatrix} \times \begin{bmatrix} 1 \\ 1 \end{bmatrix}} = \frac{[4 \quad 3]}{[4 \quad 3] \times \begin{bmatrix} 1 \\ 1 \end{bmatrix}} = \frac{[4 \quad 3]}{[7]},$$

$p(\alpha_1) = 4/7 = $ optimum mixed-strategy probability for α_1,
$p(\alpha_2) = 3/7 = $ optimum mixed-strategy probability for α_2.

To find player B's strategies, we solve

$$\frac{[1 \quad 1] \times \begin{bmatrix} 8 & -4 \\ -3 & 6 \end{bmatrix}}{[1 \quad 1] \times \begin{bmatrix} 8 & -3 \\ -4 & 6 \end{bmatrix} \times \begin{bmatrix} 1 \\ 1 \end{bmatrix}},$$

which can be reduced to

$$\frac{[5 \quad 2]}{[4 \quad 3] \times \begin{bmatrix} 1 \\ 1 \end{bmatrix}} = \frac{[5 \quad 2]}{[7]}.$$

Then

$$p(\beta_1) = 5/7,$$
$$p(\beta_2) = 2/7.$$

Using these probabilities to solve for the value of the game, we find that

$$V = [4/7 \quad 3/7] \times \begin{bmatrix} 6 & 3 \\ 4 & 8 \end{bmatrix} \times \begin{bmatrix} 5/7 \\ 2/7 \end{bmatrix} = [36/7 \quad 36/7] \times \begin{bmatrix} 5/7 \\ 2/7 \end{bmatrix}$$

$$= 36/7 = 5.14.$$

These results correspond exactly to those obtained previously.

LIMITATIONS OF TWO-PERSON GAMES

Games of the sort we have discussed so far, pitting one player against another, have fewer direct business applications than other topics covered in this book. The application of two-person, zero-sum games to a business situation can have some serious limitations. Most business decisions are not made in situations of total knowledge and under zero-sum conditions. Although game theory has been extended to cover cooperative, variable-sum, and n-person games, the solution algorithms are highly arbitrary at best. The limitations of the concepts we have discussed derive from some facts of the real world that can be summed up as follows.

1. Game theory implies a sequence of turns or plays, while in actual practice strategies take the form of long-term activities on the part of both parties.

2. Usually there are more than two parties with decision-making capabilities; the additional parties could be other competitors, customers, or regulatory agencies. Because of the possibilities of coalitions, such as in price fixing, it is difficult to extend game theory to more than two participants. Explicit and/or implicit agreements made between parties in selecting alternative strategies generally are not within the rules of a game.

3. Establishing valid payoff values is often difficult, and frequently the values used are gross estimates.

4. Usually the parties involved do not have information at hand as to their opponents' alternative strategies and the value of the outcomes. In a real situation, the zero-sum concept also cannot be assumed. Competitor strategies or market growth can bring more customers into the picture and vary the payoff values.

These limitations should not inhibit the study of two-person game theory, because there are some positive contributions that come from it. Study of the processes involved in gaming enhances a manager's analytical capabilities and helps an executive learn to cope with situations involving competition. Most important, the theory of two-person games shows that adherence to a standard practice of maximization can prove destructive to a firm in a highly competitive market. In our examples, we saw that if competitor B can count on the opposition's choosing a standard maximization decision rule, then B can make decisions that are to his benefit and to A's disadvantage. This points out the merit in the more conservative maximin-minimax approach to making decisions.

Further, the concept of a mixed strategy makes sense from an entrepreneur's point of view. In the area of advertising, for example, the firm often wants its actions to be unpredictable to its competitor and will often make unexpected placements of advertisements in magazines or on television. One of the major concerns of the advertiser is prediction of what the competitor is going to do. Because of incomplete information, this prediction is usually very difficult. However, if one or the other firm adheres to a standard decision rule, its competitive position is potentially endangered. These principles apply to any situation in which there is a conflict of interest, including labor-management disagreements, political questions, and war. In general, then, two-person game theory provides useful insights into human behavior in competitive situations.

GAMES AGAINST NATURE

Under the category of games against nature, the procedures are divided according to the objective sought. The question, "What are we trying to achieve?" should first be answered so that the proper strategy can be selected.

Maximin Criterion

In games against nature in which the decision maker has no information about the probabilities of occurrence of different states of nature, it is insufficient simply to take a weighted average of the conditional payoffs, as we did with Bayesian procedures, because the missing probabilities are the necessary weighting factors. There are several decision criteria for the manager to choose from.

If the maximin criterion is chosen, the decision maker is attempting to maximize his minimum possible gain, by selecting the alternative course of action for which the minimum payoff is highest. In other words, as we saw in two-person games, this process finds a strategy where the worst possible outcome is better than the worst possible outcome for any other strategy. An application of this criterion to a game against nature is illustrated in Table 8-6. A firm is considering marketing its canned aerosol product with a new fragrance, lemon, but it has no information on the probabilities of market reactions S_1 and S_2. The manager feels that the two alternative strategies are to market the product with the new fragrance and to continue marketing the product in its present form. Using the maximin criterion, the decision maker would choose action A_2, since it leads to the largest minimum payoff, -1.

But remember that this situation differs from a two-person game because there really are not two opponents. It should be quickly seen that in a game against nature the maximin criterion is extremely pessimistic; as a matter of fact, it is often called the criterion of pessimism. With the pessimistic approach, the magnitudes of the payoffs other than those at the minimum are ignored. This criterion can be effective only when nature is considered to be extremely hostile and when each action by the firm will be met by a counterbalancing reaction by nature. Note that this makes the assumption of total ignorance somewhat questionable; specification of the intent of nature implies some knowledge. This situation actually involves the attitudes of a decision maker, and there are other, sometimes more satisfactory, methods of dealing with these attitudes, such as utility theory.

Minimax Regret Criterion

For the minimax regret criterion, the payoff matrix is reformulated to reflect the difference between the best payoff in a situation and the payoff(s)

Table 8-6 Payoffs for marketing of aerosol, showing the values used for the maximin criterion

Firm's strategies \ Market reactions	S_1 (New fragrance preferred)	S_2 (Old fragrance preferred)	Row minimum
A_1 (Market new fragrance)	8	-4	-4
A_2 (Keep same fragrance)	-1	3	-1

Table 8-7 Regrets corresponding to the payoffs in Table 8-6

Market reactions Firm's strategies	S_1 (New fragrance preferred)	S_2 (Old fragrance preferred)	Maximum regret
A_1 (Market new fragrance) A_2 (Keep same fragrance)	0 9	7 0	7 9

other than the best. In Table 8-7, the manager has listed what the monetary regrets would be, given an improper selection of an alternative course of action. The objective is to select that strategy yielding the smallest maximum regret, which in this case would be A_1.

The value of 9 in the matrix was derived from taking the difference between the favored payoff under S_1, which is 8, and the inferior payoff, which is -1. The value of 7 was calculated in the same way. The regret for having made the right decision is, of course, 0.

Note that with a minimax regret criterion the decision would be made to select A_1, while A_2 was selected with the maximin criterion. In both cases, the firm is regarded as conservative, and nature is somewhat tenuously assumed to be capable of reacting hostilely to the strategy selected.

Laplace Criterion, or the Criterion of Insufficient Reason
The Laplace criterion assumes that in decisions under uncertainty, when the probabilities of future states of nature are unknown, the probabilities should be assumed to be equal. Generally, then,

$$EG(A_i) = R_1(1/n) + R_2(1/n),$$

where EG refers to expected gain, R_1 is the payoff of strategy A_i given state of nature S_1, R_2 is the gain from strategy A_i given state of nature S_2, and n is the number of possible states of nature. Therefore,

$$EG(A_1) = 8(1/2) + -4(1/2) = 2,$$
$$EG(A_2) = -1(1/2) + 3(1/2) = 1.$$

Action A_1 would be selected.

In using this criterion, it is assumed that all states of nature are equally likely to occur. Because the criterion is used under conditions of total ignorance regarding the probabilities, the assumption that the probabilities are equal seems somewhat untenable; however, strictly speaking, this criterion assumes a nondominant environment, which is, in fact, synonymous with total uncertainty.

Maximax Criterion

As the maximin and minimax regret criteria are said to be pessimistic, the maximax criterion could just as easily be called the criterion of optimism. The decision maker, using maximax, selects the strategy that has the maximum payoff regardless of the other entries in the matrix—in other words, the maximum of the maximums. In examining Table 8-6, we can see that strategy A_1 would be selected, because the payoff of 8 is the highest in the matrix. According to the maximax criterion, strategy A_1 dominates strategy A_2. Use of this principle is similar to decision making in which an alternative course of action is eliminated because the decision maker feels it is inferior to another alternative.

Hurwicz Criterion

Hurwicz suggested using a weighted average of the maximum and minimum payoffs to select the desired strategy. A coefficient of optimism, α, which can take on any value between 0 and 1, inclusive, is used as the weighting factor. This α reflects how optimistic the decision maker is about the maximum payoff. The α is multiplied by the maximum payoff of each strategy, and $1-\alpha$ is multiplied by the minimum payoff of each strategy. The products are then summed and the strategy with the highest sum is selected.

In our example, if the decision maker specified an α of .65, the weighted sum or expected gain for each strategy would be:

$$EG(A_1) = .65(8) + .35(-4) = 5.2 - 1.4 = 3.8,$$
$$EG(A_2) = .35(1) + .65(3) = .35 + 1.95 = 2.3.$$

Strategy A_1 would be selected. The weighting factors reflect the decision maker's subjective opinion about the probabilities of the outcomes.

Conclusions About Decision Criteria

The minimax regret, Laplace, maximax, and Hurwicz criteria resulted in the selection of action A_1, while the maximin criterion led to the selection of A_2. The fact that the criteria resulted in different conclusions is not unusual and in no sense provides support for selecting one model over another. It is clear that the decision maker is attempting to optimize under each of the models, but the results will often vary depending upon the criterion selected.

Each criterion discussed here may fit particular situations, but there is no generally accepted criterion under the circumstances of total ignorance. A viable alternative is to attempt to find information regarding the possibilities of occurrence of particular states of nature. The initial specification that there are states of nature implies that the decision maker has assigned at least a nonzero probability to their occurrence.

The decision maker who starts with these decision models will be progressively encouraged to move away from the extreme of, for example, the Laplace criterion. These models are fundamentally weak decision tools, because they use only a small portion of the total data that is on hand or can be obtained. The decision maker may move first to zero-sum, two-person games and then to other procedures such as Bayesian ones that allow for incorporation of additional information.

PROBLEMS

1. The managers of gas station A are considering awarding monetary prizes to customers who receive certain numbers on cards that they are given after purchases of gasoline. Station B, across the street, may lose some money until its managers can come up with a strategy of their own. The following matrix shows the payoffs for A.

Station A \ Station B	β_1 (Do nothing)	β_2 (Lower price)
α_1 (Introduce card game and lower price)	6	1
α_2 (Lower price)	3	2

   (a) What is the appropriate strategy for each station, according to minimax and maximin decision rules?

   (b) Is there an equilibrium or saddle point in this game?

   (c) If your answer to (b) is yes, where is the saddle point? If no, why not?

   (d) Are any of the strategies dominated by other strategies?

2. In problem 1, assume that the payoff matrix for the two stations is as follows.

Station A \ Station B	β_1	β_2
α_1	3	5
α_2	4	1

   (a) What type of strategy should be employed by stations A and B?

   (b) Why would strict adherence to a particular pure strategy prove non-optimum for either of the stations?

(c) In what specific frequencies should α_1, α_2, β_1, β_2 be employed? Use graphic methods or algebra to find the answer.

(d) What is the value of the game?

3. (a) Use matrix algebra to solve for the appropriate strategies in problem 2. Do your results correspond to those found in 2(c)? Why or why not?

(b) Use matrix methods to solve for the value of the game. Do your results correspond to those in 2(d)? Why or why not?

4. The Marker Company, makers of railroad signal equipment, has a limited line of products that it sells to railroads. The managers of Marker believe that they need to diversify the product line so that they can sell to other industries as well as railroads. Each course of action (α) given below represents a particular diversification strategy, and the Ss are states of nature whose probabilities are not known.

	S_1	S_2	S_3
α_1	4	5	2
α_2	10	-5	4
α_3	6	6	3

(a) Is there a dominant strategy for Marker? What is meant by a dominant strategy?

(b) What strategy would be selected under the following decision rules? (1) Maximin (2) Minimax regret (3) Maximax (4) Laplace.

(c) Can you select a solution that is most appropriate in this case?

(d) Under what conditions would each of the four decision criteria be most appropriate? Do these criteria describe any common decision situations? Which ones?

(e) How would the decision rules used in a two-person game differ from those in (b) above?

5. Mr. Neville, an assistant to Ruby Marker, the president of Marker Company, has made a strong case that additional information can and should be collected. After analysis of the situation in problem 4, Mr. Neville has modified the data to reflect the following subjective probabilities:

$$P(S_1) = .70,$$
$$P(S_2) = .20,$$
$$P(S_3) = .10.$$

(a) According to expected monetary value and Bayesian procedures, which action would be optimum?

(b) How does this solution differ from those in problem 4(b)? What accounts for this difference?

(c) What are the advantages of using the Bayesian approach and EMV? What are the drawbacks?

6. Set up a problem in which a technical, quantitative approach to solution would be impractical.

7. The 3N Company, makers of industrial adhesives, is attempting to get a reading on the promotional literature it is using compared to that used by its main competitor, Stickum, Inc. The 3N managers have asked their sales-people to indicate on a four-point scale (excellent, good, fair, poor) how the three promotional approaches do compared to the three approaches Stickum uses. After compilation of the data, the average rankings given to the combinations are as follows.

3N \ Stickum	β_1	β_2	β_3
α_1	Excellent	Poor	Excellent
α_2	Excellent	Poor	Good
α_3	Fair	Fair	Good

(a) What would you advise 3N to do?
(b) Assuming that Stickum and 3N will employ their strategies without collusion, what do you feel Stickum will do?
(c) What implication does your result in (b) have for 3N?

8. In a labor-and-management bargaining situation the two parties each have two possible positions.

   Labor
   α_1 Seek wage increases
   α_2 Seek improvements in the hospitalization program

   Management
   β_1 Allow some wage increases
   β_2 Offer only a cost-of-living raise

The payoffs for labor are shown in the following table.

Labor \ Management	β_1	β_2
α_1	25	2
α_2	10	14

(a) Assuming that the final pact is concluded by negotiation between the parties, does this negotiation meet the assumptions of a two-person, zero-sum game? Why or why not?

(b) Assuming that the conditions of the game do meet the assumptions of a two-person, zero-sum game: (1) Is there a dominant strategy for labor? If so, what is it? (2) Is there a dominant strategy for management? If so, what is it? (3) Is there a saddle point (equilibrium point) in the game? If so, what is its value? (4) Are mixed strategies needed? If so, what are they? What does a mixed strategy mean in this situation? (5) What is the value of the game?

SUPPLEMENTARY READINGS

Bierman, H., C. P. Bonini, and W. H. Hausman. *Quantitative Analysis for Business Decisions*, 4th ed. Irwin, Homewood, Ill., 1973.

Burger, E. *Introduction to the Theory of Games*. Prentice-Hall, Englewood Cliffs, N.J., 1963.

Dresher, M. *Games of Strategy, Theory, and Applications*. Prentice-Hall, Englewood Cliffs, N.J., 1961.

Glicksman, A. M. *An Introduction to Linear Programming and the Theory of Games*. Wiley, New York, 1963.

Kemeny, J. G., A. Schleifer, J. L. Snell, and G. L. Thompson. *Finite Mathematics with Business Applications*. Prentice-Hall, Englewood Cliffs, N.J., 1962.

Levin, R. I., and R. B. Desjardins. *Theory of Games and Strategies*. International, Scranton, Pa., 1970.

Luce, R. D., and H. Raiffa. *Games and Decisions*. Wiley, New York, 1957.

McKinsey, J. C. C. *Introduction to the Theory of Games*. McGraw-Hill, New York, 1952.

Vajda, S. *An Introduction to Linear Programming and the Theory of Games*. Wiley, New York, 1960.

Williams, J. D. *The Complete Strategyst*, rev. ed. McGraw-Hill, New York, 1966.

9/Inventory Concepts

INVENTORY and its control command the attention of top management in many different types of firms. A large proportion of a manufacturing company's current assets is often represented by inventory. A retail store or wholesale establishment is actually just an inventory of merchandise.

There are several different types of inventories. Manufacturing plants have inventories of raw materials, purchased parts, partially completed items (work in process), finished products, and spare parts. Banks and insurance companies have inventories of forms, advertising literature, and so on. Retail and wholesale establishments are essentially large inventories. Techniques can be developed that will apply to all types of inventories, although not always in the same way. Since there can be considerable cost savings with an improved inventory-management system, the techniques merit the attention of management.

Consider a firm that has an inventory value of half a million dollars. If the firm did not hold the inventory, the money could be invested elsewhere at an interest rate of at least 8 percent and earn at least $40,000 per year. Often a company must borrow money to maintain its inventory, or use capital that could be used for other company purposes. In addition to this capital cost, there are costs for storage, insurance, taxes, damage, and so on; costs of carrying inventory typically run from 10 to 35 percent of the inventory value. On the other hand, there are many benefits from carrying inventories.

BENEFITS OF INVENTORIES

Inventories satisfy several important needs in an enterprise. These needs can be divided into the following categories.

1. PROTECTION AGAINST VARIATIONS IN DEMAND Forecasts attempt to predict demand over future periods; however, uncertainty and variation in demand bring about the need for inventories to meet a range of contingencies.

2. ABILITY TO TAKE ADVANTAGE OF ECONOMIC ORDER SIZES AND PRICE DISCOUNTS The costs of holding inventories can be traded off against the advantages of larger orders and resulting price discounts.

3. FLEXIBILITY IN PRODUCTION SCHEDULING A higher level of finished-product inventory relieves pressures on the production department to fill rush orders, and permits the factory to manufacture in efficient lot sizes. Products with high setup costs can be produced in larger lots to offset these costs.

4. DECOUPLING OF OPERATIONS Inventory use makes possible continuous, year-round production even though the product demand may be seasonal. Finished goods can be stored during slack seasons, thus avoiding layoffs and other disadvantages of intermittent operations. Also, operations feeding into assembly lines can produce at the most efficient rates without the necessity of working at a slower pace to match the pace of the assembly line.

5. PROTECTION AGAINST UNFORESEEN DELIVERY DELAYS A supplier may not meet his delivery schedule, and it is very costly to have to shut down an assembly line because of a shortage of parts. Inventory can guard against reasonable variations in delivery time, rejections of defective material, or other unexpected occurrences.

COSTS ASSOCIATED WITH INVENTORIES

A variety of costs is associated with the management of inventory. The costs described here will be dealt with in greater depth in subsequent discussions. Some of these costs increase when inventory level increases, while others occur when inventory level is too low.

Carrying (Holding) Costs
Carrying costs are those costs incurred simply because the inventory is held. These costs include:

1. CAPITAL COST The interest that could have been earned elsewhere if the money were not tied up in inventory.
2. INSURANCE Premiums to insure the inventory.
3. TAXES Taxes on inventory value levied by some communities.
4. OBSOLESCENCE The accumulation of items in the inventory that are no longer usable.
5. DETERIORATION The loss from items like batteries that deteriorate with shelf life.
6. STORAGE SPACE The rent paid, or the value of the space if used for purposes other than inventory.
7. OPERATION OF STORAGE DEPARTMENT Costs for personnel, heat, light, record keeping, and so forth.

Carrying costs for inventory are usually expressed as an annual percentage, similar to an interest rate, and they commonly vary from 10 to 35 percent. These percentages can mean a substantial cost to a company. The percentage usually relates to inventory value at the average inventory level, although the level actually will vary considerably for each item. Storage costs are sometimes related to the maximum inventory size, since a certain amount of space must be set aside for each type of item even though the actual inventory level may be depleted at any particular time. In subsequent considerations here, when only a single figure represents all carrying costs, the percentage will be related to the average inventory level.

Ordering Costs

Ordering costs include all costs that occur each time an order is placed to bring material into the inventory. They include costs of writing the requisition, communication to a supplier, equipment setup, shipping, and inspection. They may apply to material purchased outside or to parts ordered from elsewhere in the same facility. Ordering costs are expressed as a cost per order.

Shortage Costs

Shortage costs result from being out of stock when the items are needed. If an assembly line must be shut down because of the lack of a part, the attendant costs are defined as shortage costs. If a customer order is lost because the item wanted is not in inventory, this lost sale is considered a shortage cost. If a customer is lost because of frequent inability to fill his or her orders, this loss is considered a shortage cost. The value of equipment that is out of use because of the lack of a spare part ordinarily carried in inventory is also classified as a shortage cost. Shortage costs are not as easy to measure or quantify as the other types of costs.

DECISIONS IN INVENTORY MANAGEMENT

There are many decisions involved in inventory management, but the three basic ones are:

1. The amount to order at one time.

2. When to place the order.

3. How much protection to provide against stockouts.

Arriving at these decisions involves the trade-off of certain factors against others. Costs of carrying inventory, such as capital cost, obsolescence, insurance, and taxes, influence the company management to say "Keep the inventory small." At the same time there are pressures to make them say "Keep the inventory large." Salespeople want to be able to fill customers' orders. Production managers do not want to endure production-line shutdowns caused by a lack of parts. Figure 9-1 considers this dilemma from a trade-off point of view, showing that there is some point at which the total cost is at a minimum.

The decision about the quantity to order at one time affects the average level of inventory carried. The cost of carrying the inventory, which increases with order size, is traded off against the costs of frequent orders or setups, which decrease with larger order sizes. The trade-off picture is provided in Figure 9-2.

Inventory decision making then becomes a problem of trading off one advantage against another, or one disadvantage against another. Since all of the factors involved cannot reasonably be considered simultaneously,

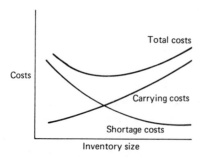

Figure 9-1 Trade-off of carrying costs and shortage costs

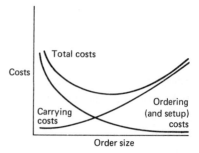

Figure 9-2 Trade-off of carrying costs and ordering costs

the best approach is to consider them systematically. In some real situations, all of the various considerations and uncertainties may apply, while in other situations some of the uncertainties can be reduced or eliminated.

AVERAGE INVENTORY

Carrying costs are normally based upon the average inventory level. Insurance premiums, for example, would be calculated from the average value of the inventory, although an actual loss might be higher or lower.

If one order were placed per year and the use rate were steady, the inventory level could be portrayed as in the left-hand part of Figure 9-3, and the average level would be one-half of the maximum level. If smaller orders of half the quantity were placed every six months, as shown in the right-hand part of Figure 9-3, then the peaks would be lower and the average would be half of the lower peak. In each case, the total quantity ordered per year would be the same. If the yearly use rate were not steady, as in Figure 9-4, the average level could be found by taking an average of points

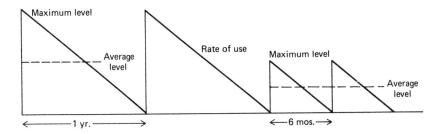

Figure 9-3 Inventory level for one-year and six-month ordering cycles

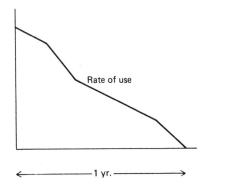

Figure 9-4 Inventory level with varying use rate

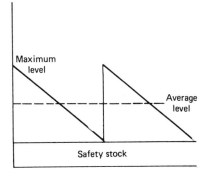

Figure 9-5 Inventory level with safety stock

selected periodically. For example, if we selected the points at monthly intervals, the twelve mid-month levels could be summed and divided by twelve to obtain an average level.

Often a firm will maintain a safety stock to be utilized only where unexpected demands occur. In this case, the inventory including safety stock would be portrayed by Figure 9-5, and the average inventory would be the safety stock plus one-half of the order size. Often a safety stock is rotated to avoid deterioration, but the average inventory would still be calculated as the safety-stock level plus one-half of the order quantity.

ECONOMIC ORDERING QUANTITY (EOQ)

The first of the three basic inventory-management decisions is determining the quantity to order at one time, which in turn affects the level of inventory carried and the ordering frequency. To make this determination, management must trade off the costs of carrying a larger inventory against the costs of more frequent orders. If larger quantities are ordered at one time, the average inventory is larger and thus the carrying costs are greater. On the other hand, smaller quantities per order result in more orders and higher ordering costs per year. As illustrated in Figure 9-2, there will be some point at which the sum of these two categories of cost will be at a minimum. This economic ordering quantity, or minimum-cost order size, is expressed as EOQ, or just Q in formulas. The other known factors for a particular business situation are as follows.

R = the yearly requirement or usage for the product, usually derived from marketing forecasts and production plans.

C = the carrying cost expressed as a percentage of inventory value per year.

V = the value of an individual item—normally the price paid for it.

P = the ordering cost, expressed as cost per order.

t = the interval between receipts of material *or* between orders.

Q and t are shown in Figure 9-6.

The carrying cost for a year is the average inventory value times the percentage cost per year (C). Since the average inventory value is

$$\frac{\text{Peak inventory (or order size)}}{2} \times V,$$

the carrying cost per year becomes:

$$\frac{Q}{2} \times V \times C = \frac{QVC}{2}.$$

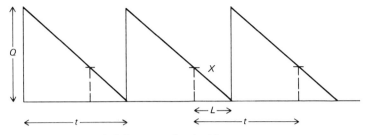

Figure 9-6 Inventory level with constant use rate

The ordering cost is the number of orders per year times the cost per order:

$$\frac{R}{Q} \times P = \frac{RP}{Q} .$$

It can be observed that:

1. $V \times C$ is the cost of carrying one item in inventory for one year.
2. The annual dollar value of the product per year is $R \times V$.
3. The orders per year equal R/Q.

From Figure 9-2 it can be seen that the minimum total cost occurs when ordering costs equal carrying costs. Equating the expressions for these two values results in:

$$\frac{QVC}{2} = \frac{RP}{Q} ,$$

$$Q^2 = \frac{2RP}{VC} ,$$

$$Q = \sqrt{\frac{2RP}{VC}} .$$

This Q then represents the quantity to order at one time to achieve the best cost trade-off between carrying costs and ordering costs for the ideal case in which use rate is constant.

As an example, consider the Timeco Company, which makes 36,000 clocks per year of a specific style. Cases are ordered from an outside supplier, and the ordering cost is $50 per order. Cases are purchased at $.50 each, and inventory carrying costs are 20 percent. The economic ordering quantity Q would be:

$$Q = \sqrt{\frac{2RP}{VC}} ,$$

$$= \sqrt{\frac{2(36,000)(50)}{(.50)(.20)}} = \sqrt{36,000,000}$$

$$= 6,000 \text{ cases.}$$

The total costs per year can then be calculated as follows:

$$\text{Ordering costs} = \frac{RP}{Q} = \frac{(36,000)(50)}{6,000} = \$300.$$

$$\text{Carrying costs} = \frac{QVC}{2} = \frac{(6,000)(.50)(.20)}{2} = \$300.$$

As shown earlier, the carrying and ordering costs are equal at the economic ordering quantity; the total costs are the sum of these two, or $600 at the EOQ.

Alternate Derivation of EOQ
The economic ordering quantity can also be determined from calculus by letting total costs (T) equal ordering costs plus carrying costs, or:

$$T = \frac{RP}{Q} + \frac{QVC}{2}.$$

At the point where T is at a minimum, the slope of the total cost curve, or the derivative of T with respect to Q, will be zero:

$$\frac{dT}{dQ} = -\frac{RP}{Q^2} + \frac{VC}{2} = 0,$$

$$Q^2 = \frac{2RP}{VC},$$

$$Q = \sqrt{\frac{2RP}{VC}}.$$

This is the same formula as that previously determined by algebra.

Our calculations of minimum-cost order quantities have been based on cost per order and carrying-cost percentages, which are often only rough estimates. It can be shown, however, that the determination of the economic ordering quantity is not highly sensitive to these estimated factors. Frequently, the value of Q comes out as a fraction or an odd number; it would, of course, be rounded off. A further analysis of such sensitivity is given by Magee and Boodman.[1]

Storage Costs and EOQ
Storage costs are frequently separated from the holding or carrying costs. This separation is made because storage costs are often more closely related

[1] J. F. Magee and D. M. Boodman, *Production Planning and Inventory Control*, McGraw-Hill. New York, 1967, pp. 371–372.

to the size of the maximum inventory than to the size of the average inventory. In typical situations, it is necessary to set aside and hold storage space of sufficient size to handle the largest possible amount of stock. The total cost would then be the ordering costs plus the carrying costs plus the storage costs, or:

$$\frac{RP}{Q} + \frac{QVC}{2} + QK.$$

The last term, consisting of the maximum inventory level (Q) times the storage cost per unit (K), has been added to the equation developed earlier. The economic ordering quantity would then be:

$$Q = \sqrt{\frac{2RP}{VC+2K}}.$$

Storage cost is expressed as a cost per unit; it is more closely related to size, shape, and other factors than to value.

LEAD TIME AND REORDER POINT

Lead time is the lapse of time from placement of an order until the material is received. In Figure 9-6 the lead time is identified as L; the reorder point, or the amount in inventory at the time of the reorder, is identified as X. In dealing with inventories, it is customary to make calculations using working days rather than calendar days. If n were the number of working days per year, which would typically be from 200 to 250, then the daily usage of an item would be R/n items per day. Each order of Q items would last $Q/(R/n)$ or Qn/R days. This is equivalent to the time between orders with a steady rate of use. The reorder point X, or number of items in inventory when the reorder is placed, would then be the daily use times the lead time L:

$$X = \frac{R}{n} \times L.$$

GRADUAL REPLACEMENT

Our derivation of the EOQ has assumed that inventory is replenished by the receipt of an order all at one time. This is typical of orders received by a firm from an outside supplier. But if a particular part used on a factory assembly line were made in another area of the same factory, it would be possible to use the parts on the assembly line as the lot of parts was produced. Usually, in this situation, the parts are produced at a faster rate than they are used on the assembly line. The inventory, as shown in Figure 9-7, builds up at first; the rate of increase is less than the rate of manufacture, since some of the parts are used directly and do not go into inventory. Upon completion of the parts order, the inventory is depleted at a steady rate until the order is completely used. The cycle then repeats, as illustrated in the figure.

The quantity ordered is still identified as Q. The inventory will not, however, reach a level of Q because the items are used as they are produced. Consider that the rate of the part's manufacture is m and the rate of its use on the assembly line is u. The inventory increases for the period t_1 and then decreases at a steady rate for the period t_2. The maximum inventory level of Z is calculated as follows:

$$Q = mt_1 = u(t_1 + t_2),$$

$$Z = t_1(m-u) = \frac{Q}{m}(m-u)$$

$$= Q(1-u/m).$$

The average inventory over a period of one or more cycles would be $Z/2$. Then the carrying cost over a year would be:

$$\frac{Z}{2} \times V \times C = \frac{QVC}{2}(1-u/m).$$

The ordering cost is the same as for the previous model:

$$\frac{RP}{Q}.$$

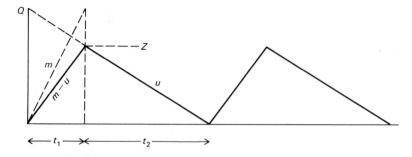

Figure 9-7 Model for replacement of inventory concurrent with use of inventory

Equating the ordering cost to the carrying cost results in:

$$\frac{RP}{Q} = \frac{QVC}{2}(1-u/m),$$

$$Q^2 = \frac{2RP}{VC(1-u/m)},$$

$$Q = \sqrt{\frac{2RP}{VC(1-u/m)}}.$$

This formula for economic ordering quantity is similar to the one calculated earlier, except for the addition of $(1-u/m)$ to the denominator. The term u/m is the ratio of part-use rate to part-manufacture rate.

As an example, consider the previous Timeco Company problem, but now assume that the company decides to make its own cases. The price and other factors are the same:

$$R = 36,000 \text{ cases per year,}$$
$$P = \$50 \text{ per order,}$$
$$C = 20 \text{ percent per year,}$$
$$V = \$.50 \text{ per unit.}$$

The assembly line produces clocks at a rate of 36,000 per year, or 3,000 per month. The cases, however, are manufactured at the rate of 9,000 per month. The minimum-cost order size is then as follows:

$$Q = \sqrt{\frac{2RP}{VC(1-u/m)}}$$

$$= \sqrt{\frac{2(36,000)(50)}{(.50)(.20)(1-3,000/9,000)}} = \sqrt{\frac{2(36,000)(50)}{(.50)(.20)(.67)}}$$

$$= \sqrt{53,730,000} = 7,330.$$

This result is larger than the ordering quantity of 6,000 for the prior example, in which the entire order came into stock at one time. This is logical, since the effect of the change has been to reduce the average inventory level and thus the resulting annual carrying costs. Thierauf and Grosse give formulas for production-run quantities when the costs of setup are related to two or more similar products.[2]

---

[2] Robert J. Thierauf and Richard A. Grosse, *Decision Making Through Operations Research*, Wiley, New York, 1970, pp. 214–216.

PRICE DISCOUNTS

The methods described previously show how to trade off the ordering cost against the carrying cost to determine the economic ordering quantity. But there are still other factors, which may influence the decision maker to change the order size. These factors will be considered one at a time, since attempting to consider them simultaneously results in very complex algebra.

To examine the effects of price discounts available on purchase orders for large quantities, assume that the Conco Company uses 12,000 switches per year, supplied at a price of $3.00 per item. Carrying costs are 16 percent of the value of the average inventory, and ordering costs are $20 per order. The economic order quantity is then:

$$Q = \sqrt{\frac{2RP}{VC}} = \sqrt{\frac{2(12,000)(20)}{(3.00)(.16)}} = 1,000.$$

The supplier offers discounts for increased order sizes as follows.

Order size	Price per item
Less than 2,000	$3.00
2,000 or over	2.92
4,000 or over	2.90

The problem then is to determine if it is advantageous to increase the order size above the EOQ of 1,000 and take a price discount. The problem is evaluated by calculating the total cost of material, ordering, and carrying at the minimum-cost order size within each price-discount range. In this example, the break points for the discount rates are 2,000 and 4,000. If the calculated EOQ is below the break point for a discount rate, the best point to take that discount will be at the lowest quantity at which the discount can be obtained. From Figure 9-2 it can be seen that the total cost of ordering and carrying increases as the order size moves away from the EOQ point. Therefore, within each price-discount range, costs will be lowest at the least quantity at which the discount is available, unless the calculated EOQ for the range falls above this minimum value.

To solve the problem, the total stocking cost for a year is calculated at the economic ordering quantity and at each potentially more advantageous point. The EOQ at $2.92 would be:

$$Q = \sqrt{\frac{2(12,000)(20)}{(2.92)(.16)}} = 1,014.$$

The EOQ at $2.90 would be:

$$Q = \sqrt{\frac{2(12,000)(20)}{(2.90)(.16)}} = 1,017.$$

Table 9-1 Calculation of costs per year for Conco switches

Costs \ Order size	1,000	2,000	4,000
Ordering costs (RP/Q)	$ 240	$ 120	$ 60
Carrying costs (QVC/2)	240	480	960
Material costs (RV)	36,000	35,040	34,800
Total annual stocking cost	$36,480	$35,640	$35,820

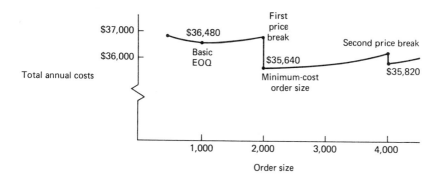

Figure 9-8 Price breaks and total annual costs for Conco switches

These quantities are very close to the original EOQ at the $3.00 price, showing that EOQ is not very sensitive to these small price changes. Since the EOQs are below the break points for the price discounts, the optimum point to take each discount is at the minimum quantity at which it is available. The points to evaluate are 2,000 and 4,000 units. The costs involved are calculated in Table 9-1 for the original EOQ (1,000) and for the other two points. The total annual stocking costs are graphed in Figure 9-8. In this case, ordering in quantities of 2,000 to take advantage of the discount would save $840 per year over the basic EOQ at the $3.00 price. The total annual stocking cost is lower at 2,000 than at either other order size; therefore 2,000 is the optimum order.

SAFETY STOCKS

Two of the three basic inventory-management decisions have been dealt with. The amount to order at one time was handled by economic ordering quantity concepts, modified by price-discount considerations. The ordering frequency was derived from this EOQ concept. The third area for decision, which concerns protection against stockouts, is approached through the consideration of safety stocks, sometimes called buffer stocks.

A safety stock is defined as the inventory level maintained at all times for unexpected events. Although items from the safety stock are often used, their use is not planned. When a safety stock is carried, the inventory is portrayed by Figure 9-9. The maximum inventory is now $Q + S$, where S is the safety stock. The minimum inventory is S under planned circumstances, and the average inventory is $Q/2 + S$. The formula for calculation of the economic ordering quantity remains unchanged, since the cost of carrying the safety stock is a constant.

Safety stocks are carried to protect against unexpected variations of two types: variation in the lead time and variation in the use or demand. In Figure 9-9 an increase in the use rate after the reorder point would necessitate depleting the safety stock to point S_1. (We can assume for now that any increase in the use rate prior to the reorder point would be detected by monitoring of the inventory level; the safety stock needs to provide protection only during the lead time.) A delay in delivery, making the actual ordering time longer than the planned lead time, would necessitate dipping into the safety stock to the point S_2. An increase in use rate combined with a delay in delivery would result in depleting the safety stock to point S_3.

The amount of safety stock to be carried depends upon the risk that the firm is willing to take that a stockout will occur. The risk in any instance depends upon the probabilities of different degrees of variation in use rate and delivery time.

First consider protection against variation in use rate. If the firm is willing to take a 2 percent chance that a stockout will occur, then a use rate can be projected that will not be exceeded more than 2 percent of the time. In Figure 9-9 projection of such a rate results in safety stock requirement S_1.

The amount of protection needed against longer-than-ordinary delivery time can be calculated by ascertaining the lead time that will not be exceeded

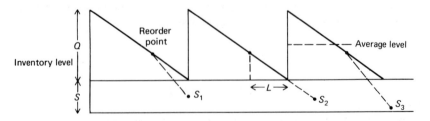

Figure 9-9 Inventory model with safety stock

more than a certain percentage of the time (say, 3 percent). In Figure 9-9 projection of the normal use-rate line to allow for this lead time shows the safety stock level S_2 required to guard against delays in delivery.

If an increase in use rate occurred at the same time as a delay in delivery, the situation would be that of the last cycle of Figure 9-9. If the risks were the same as before, the probability would be $.02 \times .03 = .0006$ that the combined variation would result in a shortage as great as S_3. Determination of safety stock size depends on the trade-off of risks and costs of stock-outs against the costs of carrying safety stock and the possibilities of replenishment by backordering or special orders. We will have more to say about this following our discussion of reordering systems.

REORDERING SYSTEMS

Inventory-control systems require some means of monitoring to determine when it is necessary to place a reorder to replenish the stock. The control systems are usually placed in one of two categories, depending upon how the monitoring takes place. One method is to monitor the inventory level and to place a reorder when the level falls below the reorder point. The monitoring can consist either of actually observing the stock or of checking the inventory records. In the latter case, records must be kept of replenishments and withdrawals to show the current inventory level at any time. The second method provides for monitoring at established time intervals. At set intervals, the stock is observed to determine how many items should be ordered, if any.

Although in actual practice inventory-control systems may vary from these concepts, the two basic systems will be discussed here to establish the merits of each.

Reordering Based on Inventory Level

The system of allowing the inventory level to determine the time of reordering is also defined in the literature as a fixed-order-quantity system, perpetual-reordering system, fixed-quantity–variable-cycle method, or fixed-order-size model. When monitoring of the inventory level shows that the reorder point has been reached, a new order is placed for quantity Q. Since the inventory level is always at the same point when the new order is placed, the order quantity is the same each time. Hence the frequent use of "fixed order quantity" to identify the system.

When there is an increase in the use rate, the time at which the reorder is placed occurs earlier than normal. Since monitoring of the inventory level detects the increased use rate, the safety stock needs to serve as a safeguard for the increased rate of use only from the reorder time to the delivery date. The safety stock, however, must also protect against unfavorable variation in delivery time. This method is often used for high-value or critical inventory items for which close control is important.

Reordering Based on Time Intervals

The type of system based on time intervals is sometimes referred to as a fixed-order-interval reordering system, a fixed-cycle–variable-quantity method, or a periodic system. At fixed intervals, the inventory level is observed and an order is placed to replenish the inventory to the original level. In this system, because of possible variation in use rate, the reorder quantity may be larger or smaller than the calculated EOQ. Since the inventory level is not observed until the end of the fixed interval, the safety stock must provide protection against use-rate variation during the entire period, as well as against delivery-time variation. This means that a larger safety stock is needed under a time-interval monitoring system.

One primary advantage of time-interval or periodic reordering is the elimination of the need for keeping extensive records of inventory level. This type of system would be favorable to firms having a large number of types of items in inventory, especially if they were low-value items. Another advantage of the periodic approach is that it can permit the supplier to plan ahead. If the supplier knows that he will receive an order for a particular item every ninety days, he can forecast his production, even though the exact size of the order will not be learned until later.

In the ideal model, with no variation in use rate and certain lead time, the two reordering systems will provide the same results. It is the realities of uncertainty that bring about the advantages and disadvantages of each reordering method.

BACKORDERING VERSUS SAFETY STOCKS

A company buys and uses approximately 300 electronic controls per year for replacing worn-out controls in customers' equipment. Ordering and test-setup costs are $300 per order, price per unit is $240, and carrying costs are 30 percent of the average inventory value per year. The economic ordering quantity from the supplier is then:

$$Q = \sqrt{\frac{2RP}{VC}} = \sqrt{\frac{2(300)(300)}{(240)(.30)}} = 50.$$

Since the use rate varies considerably from time to time, reorders are placed when the inventory level reaches a certain amount. If there are 25 working days per month, the average use rate is one per day. The lead time is 10 working days. Single items can be specially ordered from the supplier in limited quantity at a total cost of $255, including delivery costs for one-day service. The company will place these special orders, since it is committed by warranty to supply the parts within one day for vital pieces of equipment in its customers' factories. The company wishes to determine the optimum safety stock, if any, to carry. Since the customers' needs can be met by the one-day special order, the decision will be based on cost considerations.

Because the use rate averages one unit per day, the lead time of 10 working days establishes a reorder point of 10 items. If a safety stock is kept, the inventory level at the reorder point is 10 units above the safety stock level. Safety stock is carried to protect against variation in both lead time and demand rate. Historical data have provided the frequencies shown in Table 9-2.

The costs of carrying safety stock are calculated as follows:

For 1 unit $240 × .30   = $72 per year, or $6 per month.
For 2 units $240 × 2 × .30 = $144 per year, or $12 per month.
For 3 units $240 × 3 × .30 = $216 per year, or $18 per month.

Table 9-3 shows the costs that occur per month under various safety stock policies and possible shortage conditions. As an example, for safety stock policy 1 (1 item in safety stock) and shortage condition 3, the total cost is

Table 9-2 Variation in delivery time and use rate

Actual delivery time (days)	Frequency (percentage of time)
10 or fewer	60
11	20
12	20
	100

Use in 10-day period (items)	Frequency (percentage of time)
10 or fewer	50
11	20
12	20
13	10
	100

Table 9-3 Combined monthly costs of safety stock and special orders for various safety stock policies and shortage conditions

Safety stock policy	Actual shortage condition			
	0	1	2	3
0	$ 0	$15	$30	$45
1	6	6	21	36
2	12	12	12	27
3	18	18	18	18

the sum of the cost of carrying 1 item in safety stock for a month and the cost of specially ordering 2 items:

$$\$6 + 2(\$15) = \$36.$$

Using values from Table 9-3, the costs resulting from the different safety stock policies can be evaluated. For each policy, the total cost is

Probability of shortage of 0 × cost if shortage is 0
+ probability of shortage of 1 × cost if shortage is 1

and so on, until all of the possible shortage conditions have been accounted for. First we will evaluate the four safety stock sizes (policies) considering protection against use-rate variation only:

Policy 0: Total cost = .50(0) + .20(15) + .20(30) + .10(45)
= 3 + 6 + 4.5 = $13.50 per month.
Policy 1: Total cost = .50(6) + .20(6) + .20(21) + .10(36)
= 3 + 1.2 + 4.2 + 3.6 = $12.00 per month.
Policy 2: Total cost = .50(12) + .20(12) + .20(12) + .10(27)
= 6 + 2.4 + 2.4 + 2.7 = $13.50 per month.
Policy 3: Total cost = .50(18) + .20(18) + .20(18) + .10(18)·
= 9 + 3.6 + 3.6 + 1.8 = $18.00 per month.

The lowest total cost is $12.00 per month, for policy 1. Therefore the best policy is to carry a safety stock of 1 item, if protection is needed against use-rate variation only.

If the safety stock were designed for protection against delivery delays, the calculations would be performed in a similar manner. The more practical case, however, considers both use-rate variations and delivery delays. Table 9-4 shows the approximate shortage conditions during the delivery period for various combinations of delivery times and demands during the delivery period. Shown in parentheses are the probabilities of these simultaneous occurrences. For example, consider the use of 13 items

Table 9-4 Approximate shortage conditions and probabilities for various combinations of use rate and delivery time

Use in 10-day period (items) / Actual delivery time (days)	10	11	12	13
10	0 (.30)	1 (.12)	2 (.12)	3 (.06)
11	1 (.10)	2 (.04)	3 (.04)	4 (.02)
12	2 (.10)	3 (.04)	4 (.04)	5 (.02)

in the 10-day period and an actual delivery time of 11 days. The probability of this occurrence is $(0.10)(0.20) = .02$, as shown in the table. The shortage would be very close to 4 (3 due to use and 1 delivery).

The total cost for each safety stock can then be calculated by adding the cost of carrying the safety stock for one month to the sum of the probabilities of each shortage condition times the special order costs if that condition arises. For instance, consider policy 1. The cost to carry 1 item of safety stock is $6.00. There will be no need to place a special order for the three cases in Table 9-4 where the shortage is given as 0 or 1. In the three cases where the shortage is 2, the probabilities of .10, .04, and .12 are added and multiplied by 15 ($255 − $240), which is the extra cost of each specially ordered item. In this case there is one such item. To complete the total cost, the process is continued for shortages of 3, 4, and 5.

Policy 0

$$
\begin{aligned}
\text{Carrying cost} &= \$\ 0.00 \\
(.30)0 &= \quad 0.00 \\
(.10+.12)15 &= \quad 3.30 \\
(.10+.04+.12)30 &= \quad 7.80 \\
(.04+.04+.06)45 &= \quad 6.30 \\
(.04+.02)60 &= \quad 3.60 \\
(.02)75 &= \quad \underline{1.50} \\
&\quad\ \ \$22.50 \text{ per month}
\end{aligned}
$$

Policy 1

$$
\begin{aligned}
\text{Carrying cost} &= \$\ 6.00 \\
(.30+.10+.12)0 &= \quad 0.00 \\
(.10+.04+.12)15 &= \quad 3.90 \\
(.04+.04+.06)30 &= \quad 4.20 \\
(.04+.02)45 &= \quad 2.70 \\
(.02)60 &= \quad \underline{1.20} \\
&\quad\ \ \$18.00 \text{ per month}
\end{aligned}
$$

Policy 2

Carrying cost = $12.00

(.78)0 =   0.00
(.14)15 =   2.10
(.06)30 =   1.80
(.02)45 =   .90

$16.80 per month

Policy 3

Carrying cost = $18.00

(.92)0 =   0.00
(.06)15 =   .90
(.02)30 =   .60

$19.50 per month

Policy 4

Carrying cost = $24.00

(.98)0 =   0.00
(.02)15 =   .30

$24.30 per month

Policy 5

Carrying cost = $30.00

(1.0)0 =   0.00

$30.00 per month

The cost for policy 2 (a safety stock of 2 items) is less than any of the others, when the safety stock is considered as protection against variations both in use rate and delivery time.

SUMMARY OF INVENTORY CONCEPTS

Management of inventories involves decisions about the quantity to order at one time, when to reorder, and how much stock to carry to protect against uncertainties. We have formulated models for ideal situations, recognizing that real-life situations vary from the ideal. Variations from the ideal can be handled by a number of alternative methods that can be adapted to particular situations.

Ordering quantities are based on the trade-off between the costs of carrying inventories and the costs of frequent orders or setups. Reorder points or intervals are based on use rates and order sizes. The amount of stock to carry to protect against heavier-than-expected use or longer-than-expected delivery time is determined by the trade-off between the costs of carrying the stock and the costs or penalties resulting from a stockout.

Figures for deriving inventory decisions come from demand forecasts and cost estimates. Although these figures may be in error, the inventory calculations are not highly sensitive to the errors. These figures also have other uses in the firm.

LIST OF SYMBOLS

C = carrying cost expressed as a percentage per year.
K = storage cost per item of inventory.
L = lead time.
m = rate of manufacture.
P = ordering cost per order, including setup costs.
Q = quantity added to inventory at one time to minimize total costs (also referred to as EOQ).
R = yearly requirement for an item.
S = safety stock maintained for unexpected demands.
T = total costs (ordering and carrying).
u = rate of use or demand.
V = value of one item.
X = reorder point.

PROBLEMS

1. The James Electric Company purchases 32,000 transformers each year at a cost of $10 each. The ordering costs are $30 per order and the carrying costs are $3 per unit per year. Determine the minimum-cost order quantity, the annual carrying costs and ordering costs, and the number of orders per year.

2. The Airco Company manufactures air conditioners. It produces the compressor in its machine shop at a cost of $50 per unit. Carrying costs are 16 percent per year, and a year's requirement is 20,000 units. There are 250 working days per year, and the assembly operates continually. The machine shop producing the compressor can produce 160 units per day. The costs of ordering and setup are $100 per order. Determine the minimum-cost lot size for producing compressors and the number of orders per year.

3. The Airco Company in problem 2 can purchase the compressors from an outside firm if its factory load becomes too heavy. The cost is still $50 per unit, and the lead time is 4 working days. A safety stock of 200 units is planned. What are the minimum-cost order quantity and the reorder point? The ordering and carrying costs are the same as in problem 2.

4. A retail store estimates demand for an item at 4,000 per year. Each item costs the retail store $10. Ordering costs are $40 per order, and carrying costs are 10 percent per year. Determine the economic ordering quantity and the total costs of ordering and carrying. If the actual demand turned out to be 4,800 rather than 4,000, what would be the percentage error in total costs caused by the poor estimate?

5. The forecasted need is 8,000 units, with carrying costs of 25 percent and ordering costs of $100. The price is $10 per unit. If the order size is equal to 700 or more, the price is reduced to $9. What quantity should be ordered?

6. A company stocks a spare part for a machine it sells. The expected demand for next year is 600 items. The purchase cost from a supplier is $20 per item, and the ordering costs are $12 per order. The carrying costs are 20 percent. The following price discounts are offered by the supplier.

Order size	Discount
100–199	3%
200 or over	6%

In what quantity should the order be placed?

7. In problem 6, suppose that the demand were 2,400 per year and the discount schedule were as follows.

Order size	Discount
100–199	2%
200 or over	5%

Determine the minimum-cost order quantity.

8. The following information is provided:

> Annual use is 24,000 units.
> Ordering costs are $120 per order.
> Carrying costs are 20 percent.
> Price of each item is $20.
> Lead time is 10 days.
> There are 240 working days per year.

Determine the EOQ and orders per year. In the past two years, the use rate has gone as high as 140 units per day. For a reordering system based on the inventory level, what safety stock is required to protect against this higher use rate? What would be the reorder point at this safety stock level? What would be the carrying costs for a year?

9. In problem 8, if a periodic reordering system were used, what safety stock would be required?

10. In problem 8, assume a constant use rate with no variation. What safety stock is required to protect against a possible delivery delay of three days?

11. In problem 8, with a reordering system based on the inventory level, what safety stock is required to protect against both a use rate of 140 units per day and a delivery delay of three days? What are the annual carrying costs for this situation?

12. The Ronth Company wants to use one machine to produce three different products required on the assembly line at the same facility. The following information is provided.

	Product A	*Product B*	*Product C*
Yearly requirements	10,000	5,000	20,000
Production rate per year	50,000	50,000	50,000
Carrying costs per unit per year	$1.00	$4.00	$2.00
Setup time (at $10 per hr.)	4 hrs.	1 hr.	3 hrs.

Determine the EOQ for each product. Can the yearly requirements be produced on one machine?

SUPPLEMENTARY READINGS

Bierman, H., C. P. Bonini, and W. H. Hausman. *Quantitative Analysis for Business Decisions*, 4th ed. Irwin, Homewood, Ill., 1973, chapters 10–12.

Buffa, E. S., and W. H. Taubert. *Production-Inventory Systems: Planning and Control*. Irwin, Homewood, Ill., 1972.

Chase, Richard B., and Nicholas J. Aquilano. *Production and Operations Management*. Irwin, Homewood, Ill., 1973, chapters 8–9.

Hadley, G., and T. M. Whitin. *Analysis of Inventory Systems*. Prentice-Hall, Englewood Cliffs, N.J., 1963.

Magee, J. F., and D. M. Boodman. *Production Planning and Inventory Control*. McGraw-Hill, New York, 1967.

Shore, Barry. *Operations Management*. McGraw-Hill, New York, 1973, chapter 14.

Starr, M. K., and D. W. Miller. *Inventory Control: Theory and Practice*. Prentice-Hall, Englewood Cliffs, N.J., 1962.

Stockton, R. *Basic Inventory Systems: Concepts and Analysis*. Allyn and Bacon, Boston, 1965.

Taha, Hamdy A. *Operations Research*. Macmillan, New York, 1971, chapter 13.

Thierauf, Robert J., and Richard A. Grosse. *Decision Making Through Operations Research*. Wiley, New York, 1970, chapter 7, pp. 183–221.

Wagner, H. *Principles of Management Science*. Prentice-Hall, Englewood Cliffs, N.J., 1975, chapter 14.

10/Linear Programming Formulation

LINEAR programming is a technique for solving certain types of resource-allocation problems. The resource to be allocated can be dollars, time, material, equipment, storage space, or labor, and the technique can be applied to many different areas of an organization. In a typical application, certain resources are available in limited quantities, and the problem is to allocate these resources among competing alternative activities so that some objective is achieved. The activities are called *decision variables*, and the value of each variable represents the level at which the activity is performed. If the variables are the products a company is capable of producing, then their values indicate production levels. The objective is some function of the decision variables, usually a profit contribution, revenue, amount of time, cash flow, or cost. Optimizing the *objective function* implies finding the values of the decision variables that either maximize profit or minimize cost.

As implied by the word *linear*, the relationships among the variables must be capable of representation by linear equations. For example, in order to double the output of a product, the quantity of resources to be used in the product must be doubled (this situation is sometimes referred to as constant return to scale). In the same manner, the per-unit cost or profit of a product must be the same regardless of the production or sales levels (this situation is often referred to as constant return to scale in a purely competitive market). Both of these situations involve linear relationships. The assumptions of linearity are usually valid for a limited range of values of the decision variables. A further requirement for a linear programming problem is that the decision variables be independent. The profit or cost for each item must not depend upon the sales volumes or production levels of other products, and the resource requirements of a product must not depend upon the production levels of the other products. When these requirements are met, the objective function and the relationships between the variables and the resources (constraints) can be represented as linear equations or linear inequalities. Linear programming techniques involve finding the solution to a set of equations that maximizes or minimizes the objective function.

The primary objectives of this chapter are to:

1. Examine some of the applications of linear programming and demonstrate when a decision maker will benefit from the use of it.

2. Give the reader experience in converting the facts of a problem to the linear programming format, so that a solution can be obtained by one of the available computer programs.

3. Give the reader an intuitive feel for the linear programming solution process, by examining graphic methods for solving simple linear programming problems.

TYPICAL APPLICATIONS

Typical linear programming problems involve determination of the optimum use of a set of limited resources for competing demands. The following are some common areas of application.

1. A factory produces several different products. Two alternative products are being considered in order to take up the available production time in four areas of the shop. The problem is to determine which product, or which combination of the products, will provide the greatest profit. This problem is concerned with the product mix that makes the best use of the limited time in the shop.

2. Certain raw materials or inputs are available in limited quantities to a processing plant. The plant produces several end products. Each end product yields a certain profit and utilizes certain quantities of the inputs. The objective is to allocate the available inputs to the various products so as to provide the maximum profit.

3. A manufacturing company has five plants in different cities and seven warehouses at various locations. Each warehouse needs a certain quantity of product, and each factory has a defined capacity. There is also an established cost for transporting the product from each factory to each warehouse. The objective is to allocate the factory outputs to the warehouses so as to minimize the total transportation costs, while fulfilling all the needs.

4. A company must allocate the funds in its advertising budget among the various media. The variables are the different media under consideration. In addition to the overall budget restriction, there are constraints on the use of each of the media, based upon considerations of economy or company policy. The objective may be to maximize some measure of product exposure to consumers.

Problems in the real world involve many variables and constraints and require solution methods more sophisticated than those presented in this chapter. The simplex technique, discussed in Chapter 11, is an algebraic method for solving large problems of this type, and several variations of it are available in a variety of computer programs. The graphic method presented in this chapter is applicable only to small problems, but it provides insights into the solution procedure for larger problems.

A PRODUCTION-ALLOCATION PROBLEM

A company makes lawn mowers and bicycles. Each product passes through the three departments in the plant: machine shop, stamping, and assembly. Painting, packing, and other tasks are involved, but in this problem it is assumed that for these jobs there is sufficient time available to meet potential needs. The marginal profit (sales price less variable costs) is $8 per bicycle and $10 for each mower. Assume that the manufacturer can sell all of each product produced and that the marginal profits per unit are constant for all combinations of bicycles and mowers that do not exceed the production constraints. The man-hours available per week in each department are as follows.

Machine shop	200 hours
Stamping	180 hours
Assembly	108 hours

The *technological coefficients* representing the time requirements for units of each product in each shop are given in Table 10-1.

Table 10-1 Time requirements (in hours) for bicycles and mowers

	Machine shop	Stamping	Assembly
Bicycle	5	3	4.0
Mower	4	6	2.5

Mathematical Formulation

The problem is to determine the most profitable number of bicycles and mowers to produce under the constraints of available man-hours in the three shops. Let X_1 be the decision variable for the number of bicycles to produce, and let X_2 be the corresponding decision variable for mowers. For example, $X_1 = 3$ represents the decision to produce 3 bicycles per week. The objective of this problem is to

$$\text{Maximize:} \quad X_o = 8X_1 + 10X_2,$$

where 8 and 10 are the respective marginal profits (in dollars) and X_o, the objective function, is the total profit.

Since the time available in each shop does not have to be completely used, the constraints may be represented as less-than-or-equal-to inequalities. The machine shop constraint is:

$$5X_1 + 4X_2 \leq 200.$$

The coefficients of X_1 and X_2 mean that 5 hours of machine shop time are used to produce each bicycle and 4 hours to produce each mower. Also note that the left-hand side of the constraint represents the number of hours of machine shop time used to produce a particular combination of bicycles and mowers. The constraint explicitly states that the values of X_1 and X_2 are restricted to those combinations which do not use more machine shop time than is available (200 hours). The technological coefficients are also called *substitution ratios* between the resources and the products: 5 hours of machine shop time can be substituted for each bicycle and 4 hours for each mower. Constraint equations for stamping and assembly are formulated in a similar manner:

$$3X_1 + 6X_2 \leq 180 \quad \text{(stamping)},$$
$$4X_1 + 2.5X_2 \leq 108 \quad \text{(assembly)}.$$

Since negative quantities of bicycles and mowers have no meaning in this problem, the values of the decision variables must be nonnegative. These additional constraints are expressed as:

$$X_1 \geq 0,$$
$$X_2 \geq 0.$$

In sum, the problem is expressed in standard linear programming form as:

$$\text{Maximize:} \quad X_o = 8X_1 + 10X_2,$$

subject to

$$5X_1 + 4X_2 \leq 200,$$
$$3X_1 + 6X_2 \leq 180,$$
$$4X_1 + 2.5X_2 \leq 108,$$
$$X_1 \geq 0,$$
$$X_2 \geq 0.$$

General Mathematical Representation

For the general problem, there are n decision variables, such as production levels, written as X_j ($j = 1, ..., n$), and m constraints, such as production capacities. The variable X_o represents the value of the objective function,

$$X_o = c_1 X_1 + c_2 X_2 + \cdots + c_n X_n,$$

where each c_j is the contribution (profit or cost) to the objective of the variable X_j. A typical constraint is:

$$a_{i1} X_1 + a_{i2} X_2 + \cdots + a_{in} X_n \leq b_i,$$

where b_i represents the amount of a resource available (or other restriction) and the a_{ij} values are the technological or substitution coefficients of the variables. Each a_{ij} represents the number of units of the resource b_i in one unit of the variable X_j. Therefore the b_i units of the resource are sufficient for b_i/a_{ij} units of X_j. The less-than-or-equal-to inequality indicates that the sum of the values of the variables times the amounts used per unit of the variables cannot exceed the available amount, b_i. Constraints may be restrictions other than resource availabilities, so the a_{ij} values could be negative or zero as well as positive. The constraints may also be represented as equalities ($=$) or greater-than-or-equal-to inequalities ($\geq$). An additional constraint for linear programming problems is that the decision variables be nonnegative: $X_i \geq 0$ ($i = 1, ..., n$). An activity cannot be performed at a negative level.

The standard form of a maximizing problem involving less-than-or-equal-to constraints on resources is:

$$\text{Maximize:} \quad X_o = c_1 X_1 + c_2 X_2 + \cdots + c_n X_n,$$

subject to

$$a_{11} X_1 + a_{12} X_2 + \cdots + a_{1n} X_n \leq b_1,$$
$$a_{21} X_1 + a_{22} X_2 + \cdots + a_{2n} X_n \leq b_2,$$
$$\vdots$$
$$a_{m1} X_1 + a_{m2} X_2 + \cdots + a_{mn} X_n \leq b_m,$$

and

$$X_i \geq 0.$$

Graphic Illustration

The constraints and objective functions of problems with two variables can be represented graphically. While real business problems usually have more than two variables and must be solved using algebraic methods, the graphic approach provides useful insights into the structure of the problem.

In Figure 10-1 the number of bicycles in the production-allocation problem is represented by values on the X axis, while the number of mowers is represented by values on the Y axis. The nonnegativity constraints restrict the feasible values of X_1 and X_2 to the quadrant shown, where all values of X_1 and X_2 are either positive or zero. Consider the constraint for the machine shop:

$$5X_1 + 4X_2 \leq 200.$$

This constraint is graphed using the limiting (equality) condition and solving for the X_1 and X_2 intercepts. Substituting $X_1 = 0$ into the equation and solving for X_2 yields $X_2 = 50$. Likewise, $X_1 = 40$ if $X_2 = 0$. The line connecting these points represents the combinations of numbers of bicycles and mowers that use exactly 200 hours of machine shop time. Points below the line represent combinations of values for X_1 and X_2 that use less than 200 hours, since any point below the line can be reached from a point on the line by reducing the value of X_1 and/or X_2. The shaded area of Figure 10-1 contains the combinations of values of X_1 and X_2 that satisfy the

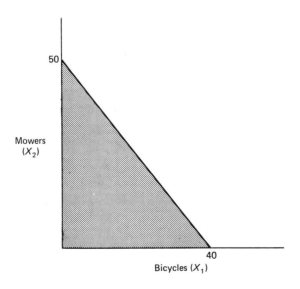

Figure 10-1 Graph of machine shop constraint in the bicycle-mower problem

machine shop constraint as well as the nonnegativity requirements. However, we also have to consider the stamping and assembly operations.

The intercepts for the stamping constraint are found as follows:

$$\text{When} \quad X_1 = 0, \quad X_2 = 30.$$
$$\text{When} \quad X_1 = 60, \quad X_2 = 0.$$

The intercepts for the assembly constraint are calculated in the same way:

$$\text{When} \quad X_1 = 0, \quad X_2 = 43.2.$$
$$\text{When} \quad X_1 = 27, \quad X_2 = 0.$$

The shaded area in Figure 10-2 is the *solutions space* or set of feasible solutions; it represents the pairs of values for X_1 and X_2 that satisfy, simultaneously, the nonnegativity conditions and the machine shop, stamping, and assembly constraints. Note the fractional value for the X_2 intercept of the assembly constraint. It may seem odd to have a value of 43.2 mowers. But this value is an acceptable solution, since it is not unreasonable to allow goods in the process of manufacture to be carried over into the following week. Many problems permit fractional solutions. Also note that the machine shop constraint no longer forms a boundary

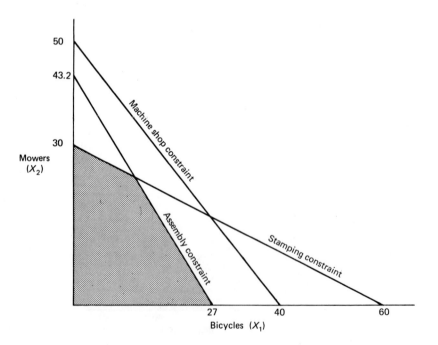

Figure 10-2 Graph of all three constraints in the bicycle-mower problem

for the region of feasible solutions. Such a redundant constraint has implications for the efficiency of the simplex method.

Optimum Solution

The problem is to find the pair of values of X_1 and X_2 in the shaded region of Figure 10-2 that maximizes profit. The objective function

$$X_o = 8X_1 + 10X_2$$

is really a family of equations for the different values of X_o (profit). All isoprofit (equal-profit) lines have the same slope, and each one represents the combination of values of X_1 and X_2 yielding a particular profit. Consider the point $X_1 = 20$, $X_2 = 0$ in Figure 10-3. The profit of this solution is $160 ($8 \times 20 + 10 \times 0$). The line A in Figure 10-3 is the graph of the equation

$$160 = 8X_1 + 10X_2$$

and represents all combinations of X_1 and X_2 that yield a profit of $160. For example, the X_2 intercept is at $X_1 = 0$, $X_2 = 16$, values that lead to a profit of $160. The objective is to find the pair of values of X_1 and X_2 in the solutions space that belongs to the isoprofit line with the greatest value of X_o.

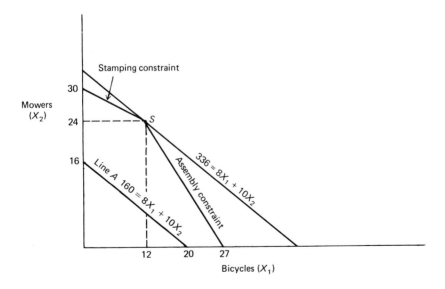

Figure 10-3 Optimum solution (S) of the bicycle-mower problem

Intuitively, we judge that this point must be at the boundary of the feasible region. Consider that every point in the feasible region above A can be reached from a point on A by increasing X_1 and/or X_2. Since A yields profit of $160, and the coefficients of X_1 and X_2 in the objective function are positive, every point above the line must yield more than $160 profit. The optimum solution to the problem must be a point in the feasible region located in such a position that no part of the feasible region is above the isoprofit line passing through that point. The only points that could satisfy this condition are the corner points of the feasible region. Considering the slope of the line A, we see that isoprofit lines passing through the intercepts of the stamping and assembly constraints would be below other points in the feasible region. The point S ($X_1 = 12$, $X_2 = 24$) in Figure 10-3 is the only point in the feasible region that is on an isoprofit line above all other points of the feasible region. This solution means that the company should manufacture 12 bicycles and 24 mowers; the associated profit is $336 ($8 \times 12 + 10 \times 24$). Usually, the optimum solution is a corner point, but it may be any point along an edge if the objective function has the same slope as a constraint that borders the feasible region. When this situation occurs, there is an infinite number of solutions—all the points along that particular boundary of the feasible region.

The algebraic solution methods for a maximizing problem involve an examination, sequentially, of the corner points of the solutions space until one is found yielding a higher value of the objective than any of the others. This particular point then represents the optimum solution.

Other Considerations

Finding the optimum solution to the original problem is only one feature of linear programming. A more important use of programming is to determine the effect on the optimum solution of changes in the parameters of the problem. Linear programming analysis provides clues as to how changes in the process or the constraints might result in a new problem with a different optimum solution. In many problems, the objective-function coefficients, the technological coefficients, and even the resource availabilities are estimates or are otherwise subject to change.

For instance, what if an increase in costs changed the profit margins? Since the objective function does not affect the solutions space, changes in the slope of the profit line can be easily evaluated on the graph. In Figure 10-3, as long as the slope of the objective function is between the slopes of the stamping and assembly constraints, the original solution ($X_1 = 12$, $X_2 = 24$) is still the optimum. If the slope of the objective function is less than the slope of the stamping constraint or greater than the slope of the assembly constraint, then the optimum solution is at a different corner point. Suppose that the profit margin of X_2 were fixed at $10. If the profit margin of X_1 were $5, the objective function would have the same slope as the stamping constraint, since the ratio of the coefficients would be the same: $5/10 = 3/6$. A reduction below $5 for X_1 would change the optimum solution to $X_1 = 0$ and $X_2 = 30$. Likewise, if the profit margin for X_1 were $16, the objective-function slope would equal the slope of the assembly constraint $(16/10 = 4/2.5)$; any profit margin above $16 for X_1, with X_2 held at $10, would change the solution to $X_1 = 27$ and $X_2 = 0$. In a similar way, fixing the profit of X_1 at $8 yields a minimum of $5 $(8/5 = 4/2.5)$ and a maximum of $16 $(8/16 = 3/6)$ for X_2; only between these values will the original solution be valid.

A change in capacity is somewhat more difficult to evaluate graphically. Consider increasing the hours available in the assembly department by hiring an additional employee. As capacity is increased, the assembly constraint moves away from the origin, staying parallel to its original position in Figure 10-3; this alters the solutions space. If the profit margins remain the same, the optimum solution will be at the new intersection of the stamping and assembly constraints. The value of increased capacity can be evaluated by comparing the profit obtained from the new solution to the profit of the original solution. In another situation, there may be an extra salaried employee available for assignment. He or she could be assigned to either assembly, stamping, or the machine shop. Which assignment would contribute the greatest amount of profit?

For larger problems, the effect of such changes in the parameters is not easily evaluated using geometric methods. However, the same principles are employed in the algebraic techniques of sensitivity analysis, covered in Chapter 12.

Procedures similar to those we have discussed are used in the formulation of all linear programming problems. The only major variations occur when objective functions are to be minimized rather than maximized, and when constraints are either strict equalities or greater-than-or-equal-to inequalities rather than the less-than-or-equal-to inequalities of the bicycle-mower problem.

A BLENDING PROBLEM

The objective of the bicycle-mower problem was to maximize profit. Now let us consider a problem for which the objective is to minimize costs.

Chemical analysis has shown that a particular farm requires that fertilizer

Table 10-2 Amounts of ingredients available in two fertilizers (in units per ton)

	Type of Fertilizer		
Ingredient	Type 1 ($36 per ton)	Type 2 ($32 per ton)	Minimum needed
Nitrogen	6	2	5
Phosphorus	3	4	4

with at least 5 units of nitrogen and 4 units of phosphorus be applied to each acre in production. Two commercial fertilizers are available, type 1 and type 2, which contain these ingredients in the amounts shown in Table 10-2. The farmer's problem is to determine what proportions of 1 and 2 to use in order to have a mixture that provides the required amounts of nitrogen and phosphorus at the minimum cost. The objective function becomes:

$$\text{Minimize:} \quad X_o = 36X_1 + 32X_2,$$

where X_1 and X_2 represent the numbers of tons of types 1 and 2 needed to make a mixture with the required ingredients. Since the requirements for nitrogen and phosphorus are minimums, the constraints are of the greater-than-or-equal-to type; they can be expressed as:

$$6X_1 + 2X_2 \geq 5 \quad \text{(nitrogen),}$$
$$3X_1 + 4X_2 \geq 4 \quad \text{(phosphorus).}$$

In addition, there are the nonnegativity constraints:

$$X_1 \geq 0,$$
$$X_2 \geq 0.$$

The constraint for nitrogen states that the number of tons of X_1 times 6 units per ton plus the number of tons of X_2 times 2 units per ton must yield at least 5 units of nitrogen. The constraint for phosphorus has a similar meaning.

Figure 10-4 contains the two constraint lines plotted from the limiting (equality) conditions. The solutions space, the area above and to the right of both constraints, is shaded in the figure. The cost lines can be drawn in the same way as the profit lines for the bicycle-mower problem, and the optimum solution again is at a corner of the feasible region. Since the coefficients are positive, reducing X_1 and/or X_2 reduces the cost. Because the objective is to minimize costs, no part of the solutions space should be *below* the cost line that passes through the optimum solution. Line A in Figure 10-4 represents the cost line that meets this condition; it passes

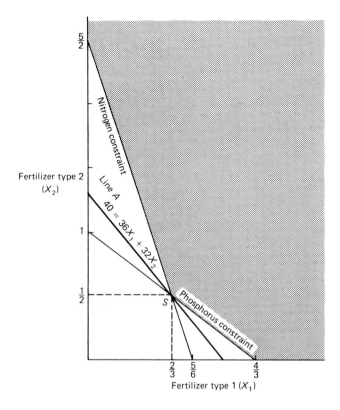

Figure 10-4 Optimum solution (S) for the fertilizer-blending problem

through point S, the optimum solution. The solution then is $X_1 = \frac{2}{3}$ ton and $X_2 = \frac{1}{2}$ ton. The minimum cost is $\frac{2}{3} \times 36 + \frac{1}{2} \times 32$, or \$40. This solution means that $1\frac{1}{6}(\frac{2}{3} + \frac{1}{2})$ ton of the mixture used on each acre provides the required units of nitrogen and phosphorus at a minimum cost of \$40 per acre.

PROBLEM VARIATIONS

For the wide variety of problems that can be solved by linear programming, problem formulation is an art in which success depends upon the insight of the user. While it is impractical to cover all existing applications, a few examples are presented to illustrate possible variations.

Variable Resources
Suppose that in the bicycle-mower problem additional capacity can be obtained for the assembly department at a premium of \$.75 per hour, and

additional capacity for the stamping department at a premium of $1 per hour. These premiums are above the regular labor rates, which are included in the profit margins of bicycles and mowers. If X_3 represents additional hours in stamping and X_4 additional hours of assembly time, then the constraints are

$$3X_1 + 6X_2 \le 180 + X_3,$$
$$4X_1 + 2.5X_2 \le 108 + X_4,$$

or

$$3X_1 + 6X_2 - X_3 \le 180,$$
$$4X_1 + 2.5X_2 - X_4 \le 108.$$

The machine shop constraint remains unchanged. Since the coefficients of X_3 and X_4 are negative, larger values of X_1 and X_2 are permitted and the solutions space may be expanded. Of course, in the objective function,

$$\text{Maximize:} \quad X_o = 8X_1 + 10X_2 - 1.0X_3 - .75X_4,$$

X_3 and X_4 are included as negative quantities, since positive values of X_3 and X_4 increase costs (decrease profits). But this decrease in profits may be offset by the increases permitted in X_1 and X_2.

Nonresource Constraints
Suppose that in the bicycle-mower problem an additional restriction is placed upon the utilization of the machine shop time. In the machine shop the total number of man-hours spent on bicycles cannot be more than 40 percent of the man-hours spent on mowers. Since the number of hours to be spent on mowers is undetermined, the constraint must be stated with X_1 and X_2 unknown. From the machine shop constraint, we know that $5X_1$ is the total time spent on bicycles, while $4X_2$ is the total time spent on mowers. The new constraint is

$$5X_1 \le .4(4X_2),$$

or

$$5X_1 - 1.6X_2 \le 0.$$

Calculation of Technological Coefficients
The technological coefficients, or a_{ij} values, tell us the units of resource b_i applied to each unit of variable X_j. Suppose that 54 tons of an ore are available for use in two alloys, 1 and 2. Each ton of the ore produces $\frac{1}{3}$ of a ton of alloy 1 or $\frac{1}{2}$ of a ton of alloy 2. Using the reciprocals of these values, we can write the constraint as

$$3X_1 + 2X_2 \le 54,$$

since 3 tons of the ore are in each ton of alloy 1 and 2 tons of the ore in each ton of alloy 2.

More Than Two Decision Variables

The data in Table 10-3 reveal the relationships between products A and B and workers C and D. The technological coefficients are the number of hours each laborer requires to produce one unit of each product. For example, worker C can make a unit of A in 4 hours or a unit of B in 3 hours. Assume that worker C has 48 hours available while worker D can work 36 hours, and that at least 13 units of A and 7 units of B are needed. Also assume that each unit is made by a single worker. While more involved than the preceding problems, this problem can be formulated using four variables: X_1 is the units of A made by C, X_2 is the units of B made by C, X_3 is the units of A made by D, and X_4 is the units of B made by D. The objective function is:

$$\text{Maximize:} \quad X_o = 22X_1 + 34X_2 + 22.5X_3 + 32.5X_4,$$

where the profit margin of X_1 is the selling price ($30) less the labor costs ($8 = 2×4). The profit margins of the other variables are computed similarly. The constraints are

$$
\begin{aligned}
4X_1 + 3X_2 &\leq 48 \quad \text{(time of worker C)}, \\
5X_3 + 5X_4 &\leq 36 \quad \text{(time of worker D)}, \\
X_1 + X_3 &\geq 13 \quad \text{(amount of A)}, \\
X_2 + X_4 &\geq 7 \quad \text{(amount of B)},
\end{aligned}
$$

plus the nonnegativity constraints

$$
\begin{aligned}
X_1 &\geq 0, \\
X_2 &\geq 0, \\
X_3 &\geq 0, \\
X_4 &\geq 0.
\end{aligned}
$$

Table 10-3 Product-worker technological values

Worker / Product	A	B	Labor costs
C	4 hrs.	3 hrs.	$2/hr.
D	5 hrs.	5 hrs.	$1.50/hr.
Selling price less material costs	$30/unit	$40/unit	

Since this problem involves more than two decision variables, an algebraic method, such as the simplex algorithm, is necessary to find the optimum solution.

REMARKS ON LINEAR PROGRAMMING

While problem recognition and formulation are important and sometimes difficult parts of any linear programming application, finding the optimum solution and performing the sensitivity analysis are the real objectives. The simplex method, covered in Chapter 11, provides an efficient solution procedure for the more complex problems with several variables. Even though computer programs using the simplex method are readily available, an understanding of the simplex technique enables a decision maker to obtain the maximum benefit from the linear programming application. This understanding is also needed to perform a sensitivity analysis, tracing the effects of changes in the parameters of a problem. Sensitivity analysis is explained in Chapter 12. Many times the observations resulting from it are of greater value than obtaining the optimum solution to the original problem.

PROBLEMS

1. A company produces two products, A and B. The contribution for product A is $10 and for product B $6. The hours required to produce one unit of each product at each of two factories are shown in the following table.

Product \ Factory	#210	#310
A	12	4
B	4	8

There are 60 hours available at factory #210 and 40 hours at factory #310. Determine the optimum product mix and the resulting maximum contribution.

2. Solve the following problem graphically.

$$\text{Maximize:} \quad C = 6X_1 + 7X_2,$$

under the constraints

$$2X_1 + X_2 \le 8,$$
$$2X_1 + 3X_2 \le 12,$$
$$X_1 \ge 0,$$
$$X_2 \ge 0.$$

3. A company makes three products, A, B, and C, each of which is produced from three main elements, E_1, E_2, and E_3. Each product also contains low-cost elements readily available. The products are packed in 100-pound bags. The contribution for a bag of A is $3, for a bag of B $5, and for a bag of C $4. Each product utilizes the number of pounds of each element shown.

Product \ Element	E_1	E_2	E_3
A	2	0	3
B	3	2	2
C	0	5	4

There are the following limits on the amounts of the elements available.

E_1	800 lbs.
E_2	1,000 lbs.
E_3	1,500 lbs.

How would you determine how much of each product should be produced to maximize contribution? Set up the problem but do not solve it.

4. A company produces four products, P_1, P_2, P_3, and P_4. Each unit requires machine shop time and assembly time as well as materials purchased from outside the plant. Product P_1, which utilizes 2 hours of machine shop time and 1 hour of assembly time, requires purchased materials costing $10. Each unit of product P_2 uses 1 hour of machine shop time, 3 hours of assembly time, and $5 worth of purchased materials. Product P_3 takes 2.5 hours of machine shop time, 2.5 hours of assembly time, and $2 worth of purchased material. P_4 uses $12 of purchased material, 5 hours of machine shop time, and no assembly time. The profits from each product are as follows.

P_1	$40 per unit
P_2	$24 per unit
P_3	$36 per unit
P_4	$23 per unit

The available time is 240 hours per week in the machine shop and 320 hours per week in assembly. The company has decided to limit expenditures for purchased material to $2,000 per month.

The marketing department has indicated that weekly demand for each product will not exceed the following.

Product	Maximum demand
P_1	40
P_2	no limit
P_3	32
P_4	no limit

The marketing managers have contracted to supply a customer with 20 units of P_4 per week.

Set up the equations in linear programming form. The objective is to maximize profit.

5. A sand and gravel company operates two pits that produce different mixtures of sand and gravel. After the output is washed, it is separated into three grades. A construction company has a contract with the sand and gravel company to take 120 tons of the fine, 80 tons of the medium, and 240 tons of the coarse grade per week. It costs the sand and gravel company $20 per hour to operate one pit and $25 per hour for the other pit. In an 8-hour operation, the first pit produces 20 tons of fine, 20 tons of medium, and 120 tons of coarse. The second pit produces 60 tons of fine, 20 tons of medium, and 40 tons of coarse.

For how many hours should each pit be operated to meet the requirements most economically?

6. A customer of the Ajay Company requires 1,000 pounds of a dry chemical mixture consisting of three component elements, A, B, and C. The cost of the elements per pound is $2 for A, $3 for B, and $4 for C.

The mixture must contain at least 200 pounds of A. It cannot contain more than 450 pounds of B, and it must contain at least 100 pounds of C. Formulate the constraints and the objective function of this problem.

7. Solve the following problem graphically.

$$\text{Maximize: } \text{Profit} = 30X + 30Y,$$

subject to

$$3X + Y \leq 30{,}000,$$
$$Y \leq 12{,}000,$$
$$X \leq 8{,}000.$$

SUPPLEMENTARY READINGS

Bierman, H., C. P. Bonini, and W. H. Hausman. *Quantitative Analysis for Business Decisions*, 4th ed. Irwin, Homewood, Ill., 1973.

Charnes, A., and W. W. Cooper. *Management Models and Industrial Applications of Linear Programming*. Wiley, New York, 1961.

Hadley, G. *Linear Programming*. Addison-Wesley, Reading, Mass., 1962.

Levin, R. I., and R. P. Lamone. *Linear Programming for Management Decisions*. Irwin, Homewood, Ill., 1969.

Llewellyn, R. W. *Linear Programming*. Holt, Rinehart and Winston, New York, 1964.

Stockton, R. S. *Introduction to Linear Programming*. Irwin, Homewood, Ill., 1971.

Thompson, G. E. *Linear Programming*. Macmillan, New York, 1971.

Wagner, H. *Principles of Management Science*. Prentice-Hall, Englewood Cliffs, N.J., 1975, chapters 2–5.

11/The Simplex Algorithm

FINDING the solution to real-life linear programming problems requires the use of an efficient procedure or algorithm. An algorithm is a set of systematic instructions that produces the optimum solution, if there is one. The simplex algorithm consists of a set of iterative steps—a few rules applied repeatedly until the solution is reached. As a result of the simplicity and efficiency of the algorithm, most computer programs use the simplex method to solve linear programming problems.

Even though an analyst relies entirely upon computer programs to solve linear programming problems, a thorough understanding of the simplex method will allow him or her to derive the maximum benefit from the solutions and data provided by computers. Knowledge of the procedural details and sensitivity analysis process will enable the analyst to formulate and solve a problem efficiently, and to evaluate the impact of problem variations upon the optimum solution.

COMPUTATIONAL DETAILS

Chapter 10 demonstrated that the optimum solution to a linear programming problem occurs at one or more of the corner points of the solutions space. Each of the corner points of the solutions space represents a different solution to a system of simultaneous linear equations (the constraints of the problem). The simplex method is an algebraic procedure for systematically examining these solutions to determine which corner point represents the optimum. The simplex method is easiest to master if it is studied in parts. Once the computational details of finding the solutions are understood, the purpose of each step in the algorithm becomes more meaningful, and a basis is established for sensitivity analysis, described in Chapter 12.

Problem Structure

The computational steps involve generating one solution from another, or going from one corner point to another. This procedure uses operations similar to those for solving simultaneous equations. The details of problem structure and the algorithm are presented first in the context of a maximizing problem. Minimizing problems require minor changes in the algorithm and the initial structure.

Since the standard form of linear programming problems usually involves inequalities, while the algebraic method is based upon linear equalities, it is necessary to introduce additional variables to convert the constraints into equalities. The nonnegativity conditions (all $X_i \geq 0$), established to control the iterative procedure (solutions with negative values are not examined), are not converted to equalities with the other constraints. The additional decision variables are called *slack variables* for less-than-or-equal-to constraints and *surplus (negative-slack) variables* for greater-than-or-equal-to constraints. Constraints originally stated as equalities do not require slack or surplus variables. In a particular solution, the value of each slack or surplus variable is the amount by which the corresponding constraint is not satisfied, or the amount required to convert the inequality to an equality. Thus, a slack variable represents the unused resources and a surplus variable represents the excess over the minimum requirements for a solution.

In the bicycle-mower problem of Chapter 10, the objective function and constraints were:

$$\text{Maximize:} \quad X_o = 8X_1 + 10X_2,$$

subject to

$$5X_1 + 4X_2 \leq 200 \quad \text{(machine shop)},$$
$$3X_1 + 6X_2 \leq 180 \quad \text{(stamping)},$$
$$4X_1 + 2.5X_2 \leq 108 \quad \text{(assembly)},$$

and

$$X_i \geq 0.$$

Inclusion of the slack variable, X_3, converts the machine shop constraint to

$$5X_1 + 4X_2 + X_3 = 200.$$

In a solution, the value of X_3 represents unused man-hours in the machine shop.

Slack variables X_4 and X_5 are similarly defined for the stamping and assembly constraints. Since the value of a solution is measured in terms of the values of the real variables (X_1 and X_2), the slack (and surplus) variables have zero coefficients in the objective function. The bicycle-mower problem is restated as:

$$\text{Maximize:}\quad X_o = 8X_1 + 10X_2,$$

subject to

$$
\begin{aligned}
5X_1 + 4X_2 + X_3 \quad\quad\quad &= 200, \\
3X_1 + 6X_2 \quad\quad + X_4 \quad\; &= 180, \\
4X_1 + 2.5X_2 \quad\quad\quad + X_5 &= 108,
\end{aligned}
$$

and

$$X_i \geq 0.$$

Problem Solution

In general, a linear programming problem involves more variables than equations, a condition that results in an infinite number of solutions. In other words, the feasible solutions space bounded by the constraints contains an infinite number of points. Each point represents a set of values for the decision and slack (or surplus) variables that satisfies the equations. Only the solutions representing the corner points need to be examined. These corner points are called *basic feasible solutions* and have a very precise definition. In a linear programming problem with n variables, including slack and surplus variables, and m equations ($n > m$), assigning values of zero to $n - m$ of the variables and solving the m equations in terms of the remaining m variables produces a basic solution. In a system of m linear equations with m unknowns, if a solution exists it must be unique. A basic feasible solution requires that the values of all variables satisfy the nonnegative condition. In the bicycle-mower problem, setting the values of two of the variables at zero and solving the three equations in terms of the other three unknowns yields a basic solution. Once a basic feasible solution is found, the nonnegativity constraint can be used to assure that other basic solutions calculated will also be feasible.

For the bicycle-mower problem, including the slack variables produces an initial basic feasible solution: If $X_1 = 0$ and $X_2 = 0$, then $X_3 = 200$, $X_4 = 180$, and $X_5 = 108$. To find other basic feasible solutions, the information contained in the substitution ratios or technological coefficients is exploited. These coefficients represent the amount by which each solution variable must change for any increase in a nonsolution variable (X_1 or X_2 in this case), if the resulting solution is to satisfy the equations. For instance, if the value of X_2 is increased from 0 to 1, X_3, the solution variable in the first equation, must decrease by 4 (hours), X_4 must decrease by 6 in the second equation, and X_5 must decrease by 2.5 in the third equation. The explanation of these changes is that each mower requires 4 hours of machining, 6 hours of stamping, and 2.5 hours of assembly.

But the solution $X_2 = 1$, $X_3 = 196$, $X_4 = 174$, and $X_5 = 105.5$ is not a basic solution, since only one of the five variables (X_1) has a value equal to zero. If X_2 is to be made positive, one of the current solution variables (X_3, X_4, or X_5) must be reduced to zero in order to produce a basic solution. To determine which variable is eliminated from the solution, divide the right-hand values by the substitution ratios: $200/4 = 50$, $180/6 = 30$, and $108/2.5 = 43.2$. The minimum of these ratios, 30, indicates that X_4 is to be eliminated; that is, as the value of X_2 is increased from 0, the available hours of stamping time are exhausted before the hours available in the machine shop or assembly department.

This minimum-ratio computation serves two purposes: The nonnegativity condition is maintained by determining the maximum amount of X_2 to introduce, and the variables in the next solution are determined (X_2, X_3, and X_5). The ratio is computed for positive technological coefficients only. If the coefficient in one equation is negative, then an increase in the corresponding variable must be offset by an *increase* in the solution variable of that equation. And if the substitution coefficient in one equation is zero, increasing the value of the variable does not change the value of the equation's solution variable.

The matrix row procedures of Chapter 3 are used to find the basic solution involving X_2, X_3, and X_5 from the initial solution involving X_3, X_4, and X_5. This initial solution was obtained from the original constraint equations of the bicycle-mower problem, which are:

$$5X_1 + 4X_2 + X_3 \qquad\qquad = 200,$$
$$3X_1 + 6X_2 \qquad + X_4 \qquad = 180,$$
$$4X_1 + 2.5X_2 \qquad\qquad + X_5 = 108.$$

The steps of the iteration procedure are as follows.

1. Divide the coefficients and the right-hand side of the second equation by 6—the technological coefficient of X_2 yielding the minimum ratio. This divisor is called the *pivot element*.

$$(3X_1 + 6X_2 + X_4 = 180)/6$$

yields

$$.5X_1 + X_2 + .1667X_4 = 30.$$

2. Eliminate X_2 from the first equation by adding to the coefficients and to the right-hand side of the first equation -4 times the corresponding entries of the equation resulting from step 1.

$$
\begin{array}{rrrl}
5X_1 + 4X_2 + X_3 & & = & 200 \\
-4(.5X_1 + X_2 & + .1667X_4 & = & 30) \\
\hline
3X_1 & + X_3 - .6667X_4 & = & 80
\end{array}
$$

3. Eliminate X_2 from the third equation by adding to its coefficients and to its right-hand side -2.5 times the corresponding entries of the equation obtained in step 1.

$$
\begin{array}{rrrl}
4X_1 + 2.5X_2 & + X_5 & = & 108 \\
-2.5(.5X_1 + X_2 + .1667X_4 & & = & 30) \\
\hline
2.75X_1 & - .4167X_4 + X_5 & = & 33
\end{array}
$$

These operations merely solve the original system of equations (with a solution involving X_3, X_4, and X_5) for a solution involving X_2, X_3, and X_5. The resulting system of equations is:

$$
\begin{array}{llll}
3X_1 & + X_3 - .6667X_4 & = 80 & \text{(step 2)}, \\
.5X_1 + X_2 & + .1667X_4 & = 30 & \text{(step 1)}, \\
2.75X_1 & - .4167X_4 + X_5 & = 33 & \text{(step 3)}.
\end{array}
$$

The basic feasible solution is $X_1 = 0$, $X_2 = 30$, $X_3 = 80$, $X_4 = 0$, and $X_5 = 33$. The system of equations resulting from each iteration of these steps is different and, if graphed, produces different lines; however, the equations are altered in such a manner that the same set of values provides solutions to all the equations in each system.

From the basic feasible solution involving (positive values of) X_2, X_3, and X_5, we can produce another solution. The new solution will introduce either X_1 or X_4, which currently have values of zero. If X_4 is selected, the operations will produce the same solution represented by the original constraints of the problem. Therefore, consider X_1 as the incoming variable. Beginning with the solution $X_1 = 0$, $X_2 = 30$, $X_3 = 80$, $X_4 = 0$, and $X_5 = 33$, we will increase the value of X_1. From the substitution ratios, we see that, if X_1 is increased from 0 to 1, X_3 decreases by 3, X_2 decreases by .5, and X_5 decreases by 2.75. What do these changes actually mean? Note that the current basic solution requires all of the available time in the stamping department ($X_4 = 0$). From the original constraints,

$$
\begin{array}{llll}
5X_1 + 4X_2 + X_3 & & = & 200, \\
3X_1 + 6X_2 & + X_4 & = & 180, \\
4X_1 + 2.5X_2 & + X_5 & = & 108,
\end{array}
$$

we know that each unit of X_1 requires 3 hours of stamping while each unit of X_2 requires 6 hours of stamping. Thus, if X_1 is increased by 1 unit (1 bicycle), a reduction of X_2 (the number of mowers) by .5 (3/6) unit is necessary to provide the required amount of assembly time.

Returning to the set of equations derived from our first series of steps, we calculate the ratios of the right-hand values to the technological coefficients, resulting in 26.7, 60, and 12 for the first, second, and third equations, respectively; the minimum ratio is 12, corresponding to the third equation. The details of the iteration are as follows.

1. Divide the right-hand side and the coefficients of the third equation by 2.75.

$$(2.75X_1 - .4167X_4 + X_5 = 33)/2.75$$

yields

$$X_1 - .1515X_4 + .3636X_5 = 12.$$

2. Add to the coefficients and to the right-hand side of the first equation -3 times the corresponding values in the equation found in step 1.

$$
\begin{array}{r}
3X_1 + X_3 - .6667X_4 \qquad\qquad = 80 \\
-3(X_1 \qquad - .1515X_4 + .3636X_5 = 12) \\
\hline
X_3 - .2121X_4 - 1.0909X_5 = 44
\end{array}
$$

3. Add to the right-hand side and to the coefficients of the second equation $-.5$ times the values in the equation resulting from step 1.

$$
\begin{array}{r}
.5X_1 + X_2 + .1667X_4 \qquad\qquad = 30 \\
-.5(X_1 \qquad - .1515X_4 + .3636X_5 = 12) \\
\hline
X_2 + .2424X_4 + .1818X_5 = 24
\end{array}
$$

These computations produce the new system of equations:

$$
\begin{array}{rl}
X_3 - .2121X_4 - 1.0909X_5 = 44 & \text{(step 2),} \\
X_2 \quad + .2424X_4 - .1818X_5 = 24 & \text{(step 3),} \\
X_1 \quad - .1515X_4 + .3636X_5 = 12 & \text{(step 1).}
\end{array}
$$

This solution involves decisions to produce 12 bicycles ($X_1 = 12$) and 24 mowers ($X_2 = 24$). Also, there are 44 unused man-hours of machine shop time ($X_3 = 44$).

The details of the computational steps involve using matrix row procedures to introduce one variable into the solution and remove another. The rules of the simplex algorithm govern the selection of the incoming variable as well as of the variable to remove from the solution.

THE SIMPLEX ALGORITHM: MAXIMIZING

A decision rule, used to determine which of many basic feasible solutions to examine, provides the essence of the simplex algorithm. This rule is based upon the obvious requirement that the next solution be better, as measured by the objective function, than the current solution. Thus, the objective function is used to determine which of the basic solutions to examine next.

The computations involved in selecting the incoming variables are simplified if the objective function is rearranged and included with the other equations in the system to be solved. For the bicycle-mower problem, we rearrange the objective function as

$$X_o - 8X_1 - 10X_2 = 0,$$

and use this equation as the first in the system of equations. The result is

$$
\begin{aligned}
X_o - 8X_1 - 10X_2 &= 0, \\
5X_1 + 4X_2 + X_3 &= 200, \\
3X_1 + 6X_2 \phantom{{}+X_4} + X_4 &= 180, \\
4X_1 + 2.5X_2 \phantom{{}+X_5} + X_5 &= 108,
\end{aligned}
$$

yielding the solution $X_3 = 200$, $X_4 = 180$, and $X_5 = 108$. The value of this solution is $X_o = 0$, since no bicycles ($X_1 = 0$) and no mowers ($X_2 = 0$) are produced.

The traditional presentation of the simplex method, in tabular form, is illustrated in Tables 11-1 through 11-3. Table 11-1 contains the right-hand sides and the coefficients of the variables in the initial system of equations. Each subsequent table contains only the coefficients and right-hand sides of the equations resulting from a particular iteration. The first row in each tableau contains the objective-function coefficients of the variables. In the first row of Table 11-1, the signs of the coefficients of X_1 and X_2 are changed, so it is necessary to reverse their meaning. The coefficient of each variable represents the *increase* in the objective function (the value of X_o) *per unit*

Table 11-1 Initial tableau for the bicycle-mower problem

X_o	X_1	$\downarrow$ X_2	X_3	X_4	X_5	Solution value	Incoming-variable ratio
1	−8	−10				0	
	5	4	1			200	200/4 = 50
	3	⑥		1		180	180/6 = 30
	4	2.5			1	108	108/2.5 = 43.2

of the variable if it is selected as the incoming variable for the next solution. After several iterations, some of these coefficients may be positive. The positive values would indicate the *decrease* in X_o if the corresponding variable were introduced into the solution. By definition, the objective-function coefficients of the solution variables are zero. In this problem, if either X_1 or X_2 is increased to a positive level, the resulting solution yields a higher profit than the current solution.

The decision rule of the simplex method dictates selecting as the incoming variable the one resulting in the largest *per-unit* increase in the value of the solution. Applying this rule, we select X_2 as the incoming variable, since 10 is larger than 8. (The arrow pointing to the X_2 column in Table 11-1 identifies the incoming variable.) At the right side of Table 11-1 the ratios of the solution values to the technological coefficients of X_2 are shown. Since 30 is the minimum ratio, the value 6 (circled) in column X_2 is the pivot element.

The details of the iteration are the same as those used earlier for changing the solution containing X_3, X_4, and X_5 to the solution with X_2, X_3, and X_5. The only additional step involves eliminating the coefficient of X_2 from the first row (objective function). When X_2 is introduced into the solution, the effect upon profit (the value of X_o) must be determined. But first the numbers in the third row (pivot equation) are divided by 6, resulting in the following.

						Solution
X_o	X_1	X_2	X_3	X_4	X_5	value
	.5	1		.1667		30

Note that these values make up the third row of Table 11-2 (the second tableau). Now the -10 in the first row of Table 11-1 is eliminated by adding to the numbers of that row 10 times the values in the transformed third row.

							Solution
	X_o	X_1	X_2	X_3	X_4	X_5	value
	1	-8	-10				0
10(		.5	1		.1667		30)
	1	-3			1.6667		300

The results of this operation and of the remainder of the iteration are shown in the second tableau, Table 11-2. The new solution is $X_2 = 30$, $X_3 = 80$, and $X_5 = 33$. Since X_2 is the only real variable and each unit of X_2 contributes $10 to profit, the value of this solution (X_o) is $300. At each stage the right-hand side of the first equation is the objective-function value of the solution.

Table 11-2 Second tableau for the bicycle-mower problem

X_o	X_1 ↓	X_2	X_3	X_4	X_5	Solution value	Incoming-variable ratio
1	−3			1.6667		300	
	3		1	−.6667		80	$80/3 = 26.67$
	.5	1		.1667		30	$30/.5 = 60$
	(2.75)			−.4167	1	33	$33/2.75 = 12$

After each iteration is performed, the values in the first row of the tableau indicate the net change (increase if negative and decrease if positive) that will occur in the value of the solution per unit of the variable if the variable is increased from its current level. After the first iteration, the objective-function coefficient of X_1 is −3. The value of X_o increases by $3 with every increase of one unit of X_1. This value is checked by using the coefficients from the original objective-function equation $(X_o − 8X_1 − 10X_2 = 0)$ and the substitution ratios of the current solution (3, .5, and 2.75 for the second through the fourth rows of the X_1 column). If X_1 is increased, each additional unit contributes $8. But each unit increase in X_1 causes X_3 (the solution variable of the second row) to decrease by 3 units, X_2 (the solution variable of the third row) to decrease by .5 units, and X_5 (the solution variable of the fourth row) to decrease by 2.75 units. Since X_2 is the only solution variable with a nonzero coefficient in the original objective-function equation, the net change for increasing X_1 is the gain from increasing X_1 minus the loss for decreasing X_2, or $8 − .5($10) = 3.

When we perform the iteration on the objective function as well as on the rest of the system of equations, a glance at each solution determines which nonsolution variable to introduce with the next iteration. In this case it is X_1. In Table 11-2 the ratios used to determine the pivot element in the X_1 column indicate that the fourth row is the pivot equation. The steps of the iteration for converting Table 11-2 to Table 11-3 are the same as before. The −3 is eliminated from the first row of Table 11-2 by adding to the values of that row 3 times the numbers in the transformed pivot equation (the fourth row of Table 11-3).

	X_o	X_1	X_2	X_3	X_4	X_5	Solution value
	1	−3			1.6667		300
3(		1			−.1515	.3636	12)
	1				1.2122	1.0908	336

Table 11-3 Optimum solution for the bicycle-mower problem

X_o	X_1	X_2	X_3	X_4	X_5	Solution value
1				1.2122	1.0909	336
			1	−.2121	−1.0909	44
		1		.2424	−.1818	24
	1			−.1515	.3636	12

The result of the complete iteration is the tableau of Table 11-3. The solution $X_1 = 12$, $X_2 = 24$, $X_3 = 44$, $X_4 = 0$, $X_5 = 0$ has a value of $336.

At this stage the coefficients of the nonsolution variables (1.2122 and 1.0908) in the objective function are *positive*. Thus, introducing either X_4 or X_5 will *reduce* the value of X_o. The optimum solution has been found. Generalizing the steps involved in this problem produces the simplex algorithm. The steps of the algorithm are:

1. Select as the incoming variable the one with the largest negative coefficient in the first row. If all the coefficients are nonnegative, the optimum solution has been found.

2. Compute the ratios of the right-hand-side values to the technological coefficients of the incoming variable. Ratios are not computed for zero or negative technological coefficients, or for the first row (the objective function).

3. Select as the pivot element the technological coefficient that produced the smallest ratio.

4. Perform the pivoting operation. Divide the pivot element into the coefficients and the right-hand-side of the corresponding equation. Eliminate the coefficient of the incoming variable from the other equations by subtracting from these equations the appropriate multiples of the equation that contains the pivot element.

5. Repeat this procedure starting with step 1.

Some additional, minor details are involved in special cases that may be encountered in some problems. Here we can note three special cases.

First, if in step 2 of the algorithm *all* of the technological coefficients for an incoming variable are nonpositive, then the problem is stated so that the objective function is unbounded—the values of the decision variables may be made arbitrarily larger.

Second, if in the optimum solution a nonsolution variable has a zero coefficient in the objective function, then an alternate optimum solution exists. In fact, infinitely many optimum solutions exist. In the two-variable problems of Chapter 10, this situation would occur if the objective function had the same slope as a constraint bordering the solutions space.

Third, if at the iteration one of the right-hand-side values is zero, the solution is degenerate—*more* than $n-m$ variables have zero values. A degenerate solution could cause the iterations to cycle, to produce repeatedly the same sets of solutions. Computer programs contain steps to avoid the problem of cycling if degeneracy occurs. As a practical matter, no real problem has been reported in which cycling occurs.

The simplex algorithm must be altered slightly if a problem involves minimizing the objective function or if some of the constraints are equalities or greater-than-or-equal-to inequalities.

THE SIMPLEX ALGORITHM: MINIMIZING

Linear programming problems with an objective function to be minimized generally require surplus variables as well as an alteration of the objective function. The constraints and objective function of the fertilizer-blending problem of Chapter 10 are:

$$\text{Minimize:} \quad X_o = 36X_1 + 32X_2,$$

subject to

$$6X_1 + 2X_2 \geq 5 \quad \text{(nitrogen requirement)},$$
$$3X_1 + 4X_2 \geq 4 \quad \text{(phosphorus requirement)},$$

and

$$X_i \geq 0.$$

Problem Structure

Including the surplus variable X_3 in the nitrogen constraint yields

$$6X_1 + 2X_2 - X_3 = 5.$$

The nonnegativity condition requires that the coefficient of X_3 be negative; otherwise the *value* of X_3 would have to be negative in order to satisfy the greater-than-or-equal-to inequality of the condition. And practical considerations of the solution method require that the nonnegativity condition apply to all variables. In a solution, the value of X_3 will represent the amount by which the mix of fertilizers X_1 and X_2 exceeds the minimum requirement of 5 units of nitrogen. The surplus variable X_4 for phosphorus is defined in the same manner, resulting in a restatement of the blending problem as:

$$\text{Minimize:} \quad X_o = 36X_1 + 32X_2,$$

subject to

$$6X_1 + 2X_2 - X_3 \qquad = 5,$$
$$3X_1 + 4X_2 \qquad - X_4 = 4,$$

and

$$X_i \geq 0.$$

Objective Functions

Linear programming problems with the objective of minimizing costs require additional formulation procedures to obtain the solution. Instead of altering the rules of the algorithm from maximizing to minimizing, the objective function is altered so that the maximizing algorithm actually minimizes. This change is accomplished by reversing the signs of the coefficients of the variables in the objective function. Thus, in the problem,

$$\text{Minimize:} \quad X_o = 36X_1 + 32X_2$$

is equivalent to

$$\text{Maximize:} \quad X_o = -36X_1 - 32X_2,$$

which is rearranged for inclusion with the constraints as

$$\text{Maximize:} \quad X_o + 36X_1 + 32X_2 = 0.$$

The justification for this alteration is apparent when we observe, for example, that the minimum of the numbers 3, 8, 4, 10, 15, 2, and 9 is the maximum of the numbers -3, -8, -4, -10, -15, -2, and -9 with its sign reversed. The reversing procedure seems unnecessary for hand computation, but computer programs are designed to minimize or to maximize but not to do both. The decision maker must alter the objective function of one or the other type of problem in order to use the program.

A more serious computational difficulty exists in minimizing, as well as in some maximizing, problems. In the bicycle-mower problem, all constraints are of the less-than-or-equal-to type. Including slack variables produces an initial basic feasible solution. Since there are no minimum utilization levels of the resources in such a problem, the initial values of the slack variables indicating a zero production level represent a feasible solution. But if a problem, such as the blending problem, contains constraints that are either strict equalities or greater-than-or-equal-to inequalities, an initial feasible solution does not exist. Computer programs handle such problems in a variety of ways. One approach involves performing iterations under the direction of an artificial objective function, until a feasible solution is found. The remaining iterations are then controlled by the real objective function. If a feasible solution does not exist, the iterations terminate while under the direction of the artificial objective function.

This artificial objective function is constructed by defining a new variable, X_{n+1}, using only the equality and greater-than-or-equal-to inequality constraints. In the blending problem, both constraints are used to construct the artificial objective function, which is

$$\text{Maximize:} \quad X_5 = 9X_1 + 6X_2 - X_3 - X_4 - 9,$$

rearranged as

$$\text{Maximize:} \quad X_5 - 9X_1 - 6X_2 + X_3 + X_4 = -9.$$

The right-hand side, -9, is the negative of the sum of the right-hand sides of the two constraints. The coefficients of the variables in the rearranged form of this objective function are the negatives of the sums of the coefficients of the variables in the two constraints.

Iterations

As iterations are performed under the direction of this artificial objective function, the variables are brought into the solution and eliminated from this objective function, as well as from the appropriate constraints and from the real objective function. During the process the value of X_5, originally -9, increases. As soon as all the real and surplus variables are eliminated from the artificial objective function, the value of X_5 is zero if the resulting solution is feasible, and negative if no feasible solution exists. The altered blending problem is:

$$\text{Maximize:} \quad X_5 \qquad - 9X_1 - 6X_2 + X_3 + X_4 = -9,$$
$$X_o + 36X_1 + 32X_2 \qquad\qquad = 0,$$

subject to

$$6X_1 + 2X_2 - X_3 \qquad = 5,$$
$$3X_1 + 4X_2 \qquad - X_4 = 4,$$

and

$$X_i \geq 0.$$

Table 11-4 Initial tableau for the fertilizer-blending problem

	X_5	X_o	↓ X_1	X_2	X_3	X_4	Solution value	Incoming-variable ratio
Artificial objective	1		-9	-6	1	1	-9	
Real objective		1	36	32			0	
			⑥	2	-1		5	$5/6 = .8333$
			3	4		-1	4	$4/3 = 1.3333$

Table 11-4 is the initial tableau for this blending problem. Applying the usual simplex rules, we select X_1 (indicated by the arrow) as the incoming variable; it has the largest negative coefficient in the artificial objective function. The ratios of the solution values to the technological coefficients indicate that the coefficient 6 in the third row of the X_1 column is the pivot element. The steps of the iteration are:

1. Divide the coefficients of the third row (the first constraint) by 6 to produce the following.

X_5	X_o	X_1	X_2	X_3	X_4	Solution value
		1	.3333	−.1667		.8333

This becomes the third row of Table 11-5.

2. Add to the first row 9 times the row obtained in step 1.

	X_5	X_o	X_1	X_2	X_3	X_4	Solution value
	1		−9	−6	1	1	−9
9(			1	.3333	−.1667		.8333)
	1			−3	−.5	1	−1.5

This becomes the first row of Table 11-5.

3. Add to the second row −36 times the row obtained in step 1.

	X_5	X_o	X_1	X_2	X_3	X_4	Solution value
		1	36	32			0
−36(			1	.3333	−.1667		.8333)
		1		20	6		30

This yields the second row in Table 11-5.

4. Add to the values in the fourth row −3 times the row obtained in the step 1.

	X_5	X_o	X_1	X_2	X_3	X_4	Solution value
			3	4		−1	4
−3(			1	.3333	−.1667		.8333)
			3		.5	−1	1.5

This becomes the fourth row in Table 11-5.

Table 11-5   Second tableau for the fertilizer-blending problem

	X_5	X_o	X_1	$\downarrow$ X_2	X_3	X_4	Solution value	Incoming-variable ratio
Artificial objective	1			-3	$-.5$	1	-1.5	
Real objective		1		20	6		30	
			1	.3333	$-.1667$		.8333	.8333/.3333 = 2.5
				③	.5	-1	1.5	1.5/3 = .5

At this stage X_2 is selected as the incoming variable. The ratio computations indicate that the fourth row of this tableau is the pivot equation. The steps of the iteration are:

1. Divide the values of the fourth row by 3 (the pivot element) to produce the following.

X_5	X_o	X_1	X_2	X_3	X_4	Solution value
			1	.1667	$-.3333$	.5

This becomes the fourth row in Table 11-6.

2. Add to the values of the first row 3 times the row obtained in step 1.

	X_5	X_o	X_1	X_2	X_3	X_4	Solution value
	1			-3	$-.5$	1	-1.5
3(				1	.1667	.3333	.5)
	1						0

This yields the first row in Table 11-6.

3. Add to the numbers in the second row -20 times the row obtained in step 1.

	X_5	X_o	X_1	X_2	X_3	X_4	Solution value
		1		20	6		30
$-20($				1	.1667	.3333	.5)
		1			2.6667	6.6667	40

This becomes the second row in Table 11-6.

Table 11-6 Optimum solution for the fertilizer-blending problem

	X_5	X_o	X_1	X_2	X_3	X_4	Solution value
Artificial objective	1						0
Real objective		1			2.6667	6.6667	40
			1		−.2222	.1111	.6667
				1	.1667	−.3333	.5

4. Add to the values in the third row −.3333 times the row obtained in step 1.

	X_5	X_o	X_1	X_2	X_3	X_4	Solution value
			1	.3333	−.1667		.8333
−.3333(				1	.1667	.3333	.5)
				1	−.2222	.1111	.6667

This yields the third row of Table 11-6.

In Table 11-6 the value of X_5 is zero, indicating that the solution is feasible. Also, the coefficients in the real objective function are nonnegative, showing that this solution is the optimum. The solution $X_1 = .6667$ ton and $X_2 = .5$ ton corresponds to a cost of $40 per acre. If this solution were not optimum, the artificial objective function would be eliminated from the tableau, and the iterations would continue using the real objective function.

CONCLUSION

The simplex algorithm provides a systematic procedure for solving linear programming problems. Its iterative characteristics are ideally suited for computer application of the technique. The decision rule for selecting the incoming variable is relatively efficient and easily employed. Experience indicates that most problems are solved within $2m$ iterations, where m is the number of constraints. For very large problems, more efficient algorithms exist, which are based upon modifications of the decision rules controlling the iterations.

The main advantage of the simplex algorithm is the information contained in the system of equations representing the optimum solution. The sensitivity of the solution to changes in the parameters of the problem is determined by performing simple calculations upon this set of equations.

PROBLEMS

1. Use the simplex method to solve problem 3 of Chapter 10.

2. Use the simplex algorithm, with the artificial objective function, to solve problem 4 of Chapter 10.

3. Solve problem 5 in Chapter 10 using the simplex method.

4. Solve problem 6 in Chapter 10 using the simplex method.

5. In Chapter 10, on page 215, the problem of determining the optimum mixture of products A and B made by workers C and D is formulated using four decision variables. As a result of the minimum production constraints on A and B, this problem does not have an initial basic feasible solution. Formulate the artificial objective function of this problem.

6. Use the simplex algorithm to find the optimum solution in problem 5.

12/Sensitivity Analysis

THE COMPLETE application of the linear programming technique involves a sensitivity analysis of the optimum solution. The analysis indicates the effect upon the optimum solution of changes in the parameters of the problem, namely of the objective-function coefficients, c_j's, and the resource limits, b_i's. In addition to revealing the sensitivity of the solution to changes in the parameters, the analysis provides insights into the economic problem of resource allocation. In many instances the parameters are deterministic equivalents of stochastic (probabilistic) variables, and the analysis discloses the stability of the solution. The sensitivity analysis involves the *ceteris paribus* condition: changes in one parameter are examined, holding all others fixed. This one-dimensional type of analysis can be extended to handle simultaneous changes in the parameters, but the procedure is more complicated and the results are less revealing.

Geometrically, sensitivity analysis determines limits on changes, in both the slope of the objective function and the positions from the origin of the constraints, that result in the same set of solution variables as the original optimum solution. For real problems this analysis is performed algebraically rather than graphically as in Chapter 10. Sensitivity analysis is best examined in the context of a sample problem.

A SAMPLE PROBLEM

The technological coefficients, profits, and resource limits listed in Table 12-1 are for an allocations problem with the objective of maximizing profits. The five decision variables, X_1 through X_5, represent the quantities

Table 12-1 Technological values for resource-allocation problem

Decision variable Resource	X_1	X_2	X_3	X_4	X_5	Resource limit
Raw material A (lbs.)	2.0	2.5	1.2	.75	.9	4,995
Raw material B (lbs.)	.9	—	1.8	2.0	1.5	2,520
Shop C (hrs.)	.1	.2	.4	.2	.4	54.75
Shop D (hrs.)	.4	.3	.3	—	.4	59.60
Profit per unit	$6	$17	$20	$9	$4	

of five different products that the company can manufacture. In addition to the restrictions indicated in the table, contractual obligations require the production of at least as many units of X_2 as X_4, with a safety stock of at least 80 units of X_2. This additional restriction is expressed as

$$X_2 \geq X_4 + 80$$

or

$$X_2 - X_4 \geq 80.$$

In standard form this problem is stated as

$$\text{Maximize:} \quad X_o = 6X_1 + 17X_2 + 20X_3 + 9X_4 + 4X_5,$$

subject to

$$2X_1 + 2.5X_2 + 1.2X_3 + .75X_4 + .9X_5 \leq 4,995,$$
$$.9X_1 \qquad\quad + 1.8X_3 + 2X_4 + 1.5X_5 \leq 2,520,$$
$$.1X_1 + .2X_2 + .4X_3 + .2X_4 + .4X_5 \leq 54.75,$$
$$.4X_1 + .3X_2 + .3X_3 \qquad\quad + .4X_5 \leq 59.60,$$
$$X_2 \qquad\qquad - X_4 \qquad\qquad \geq 80,$$

and all

$$X_i \geq 0,$$

or with slack and surplus variables as

$$X_o - 6X_1 - 17X_2 - 20X_3 - 9X_4 - 4X_5 = 0,$$
$$2X_1 + 2.5X_2 + 1.2X_3 + .75X_4 + .9X_5 + X_6 = 4,995,$$
$$.9X_1 + 1.8X_3 + 2X_4 + 1.5X_5 + X_7 = 2,520,$$
$$.1X_1 + .2X_2 + .4X_3 + .2X_4 + .4X_5 + X_8 = 54.75,$$
$$.4X_1 + .3X_2 + .3X_3 + .4X_5 + X_9 = 59.60,$$
$$X_2 - X_4 - X_{10} = 80,$$

and all

$$X_i \geq 0.$$

For linear programming problems that do not have an initial basic feasible solution, an artificial objective function is constructed from the equality and greater-than-or-equal-to inequality constraints. The current problem contains only one constraint of this type—the relationship between X_2 and X_4. Table 12-2 is the initial tableau of the problem. In the artificial objective function (X_{11}), the coefficients of the variables are the negatives of the sums of the coefficients of the variables in the equality and greater-than-or-equal-to inequality constraints. And the right-hand side of the function is the negative of the sum of the right-hand sides of these constraints.

Using this artificial objective function to control the iterations, we select X_2 as the incoming variable, since it has the largest negative coefficient in the first row. The ratios of the solution values to the technological coefficients of X_2 indicate that the last constraint is the pivot equation.

Performing the iteration produces the solution in Table 12-3. In the artificial objective function the coefficients of the variables X_1 through X_{10} are zero. And since the value of X_{11} is also zero, this solution is feasible. This solution ($X_2 = 80$, $X_6 = 4,795$, $X_7 = 2,520$, $X_8 = 38.75$, and $X_9 = 35.60$), producing a profit of $1,360 ($X_o = 1,360$), is not optimum, since there are decision variables with negative coefficients in the real objective function.

At this point the artificial objective function is dropped from the tableau and the iterations continue under the direction of the real objective function. Using this objective function, we select X_4 as the incoming variable (X_4 yields a higher per-unit profit, $26, than any other decision variable at this stage). The ratio computations indicate that the pivot element is the .4 in the X_4 column.

Completing the iteration produces the solution of Table 12-4. Since the coefficients of the decision variables in the objective function are positive or zero, this solution is the optimum. The values of the decision variables indicate that 198.6667 units of the product corresponding to X_2 and 75.0833 units of the product corresponding to X_4 should be produced to yield the maximum profit of $4,053.0833. Also 4,442.0208 pounds of A (X_6) and 2,369.8333 pounds of B (X_7) are unused, while the available times in shops C and D are completely used ($X_8 = 0$, $X_9 = 0$). This final tableau contains all the information necessary to perform the sensitivity analysis.

Table 12-2   Initial tableau for the resource-allocation problem

	X_{11}	X_o	X_1	$\downarrow$ X_2	X_3	X_4	X_5
Artificial objective	1			−1		1	
Real objective		1	−6	−17	−20	−9	−4
			2	2.5	1.2	.75	.9
			.9		1.8	2	1.5
			.1	.2	.4	.2	.4
			.4	.3	.3		.4
				①		−1	

Table 12-3   Second tableau for the resource-allocation problem

	X_{11}	X_o	X_1	X_2	X_3	$\downarrow$ X_4	X_5
Artificial objective	1						
Real objective		1	−6		−20	−26	−4
			2		1.2	3.25	.9
			.9		1.8	2	1.5
			.1		.4	④	.4
			.4		.3	.3	.4
				1		−1	

Table 12-4   Optimum solution for the resource-allocation problem

	X_o	X_1	X_2	X_3	X_4	X_5
Real objective	1	9.1667		6		24.6667
		−.7083		−2.05		−2.9333
		2.5667		−.2		.1667
		−.8333		1	1	.6667
		2.1667				.6667
		1.3333	1	1		1.3333

X_6	X_7	X_8	X_9	X_{10}	Solution value (b_i)	Incoming-variable ratio
				1	−80	
					0	
1					4,995	4,995/2.5 = 1,998
	1				2,520	—
		1			54.75	54.75/.2 = 273.75
			1		59.60	59.60/.3 = 198.67
				−1	80	80/1 = 80

X_6	X_7	X_8	X_9	X_{10}	Solution value (b_i)	Incoming-variable ratio
					0	
				−17	1,360	
1				2.5	4,795	4,795/3.25 = 1,475.4
	1				2,520	2,520/2 = 1,260
		1		.2	38.75	38.75/.4 = 96.875
			1	.3	35.60	35.60/.3 = 118.67
				−1	80	—

X_6	X_7	X_8	X_9	X_{10}	Solution value (b_i)
		45	26.6667		4,053.0833
1		−3.75	−5.8333		4,442.0208
	1	−10	6.6667		2,369.8333
		5	−3.3333		75.0833
		−5	6.6667	1	43.5833
			3.3333		198.6667

SENSITIVITY PROCEDURES

The end result of the sensitivity analysis is a set of values (maximums and minimums) for the per-unit profits, c_j's, of the decision variables and for the resource limits, b_i's. This set of values indicates the range over which the solution (X_2 and X_4 nonnegative and X_1, X_3, and X_5 zero) remains optimum.

Objective Function

Instead of re-solving the problem with different values for the c_j's to see which sets produce the same solution as in Table 12-4, we use algebraic relationships among the values in the optimum solution to determine systematically the range over which the c_j's may vary before the solution changes. The range is determined for the c_j's of X_1, X_2, X_3, X_4, and X_5 (the c_j's of the slack and surplus variables are fixed at zero). The analysis requires a determination of the limits for each variable's c_j which produces, for the solution of Table 12-4, an objective function with nonnegative coefficients. The calculations are made simpler if we recall that the transformed objective function at any iteration can be obtained from the technological coefficients or substitution ratios at that iteration and the original c_j values.

For example, Table 12-5 contains the substitution ratios of X_5, from Table 12-4, as well as the original c_j's of the solution variables. Recall that the coefficients of X_5 in the second through the sixth rows of Table 12-4 are the substitution ratios between X_5 and the solution variables for the corresponding equations. In particular, the -2.9333 ratio between X_5 and X_6 indicates that X_6 increases by 2.9333 units if X_5 increases by one unit, while the .1667 ratio indicates that X_7 decreases by .1667 unit if X_5 increases by one unit. And the ratio between X_5 and X_o indicates that the profit decreases by \$24.6667 for every unit increase in X_5. This decrease in profit resulting from the introduction of X_5 can be calculated using the original c_j's and the substitution ratios as follows.

Table 12-5 Substitution ratios for X_5

Row in Table 12-4	Substitution ratio	Variable involved	Original c_j
First	24.6667	X_o	—
Second	-2.9333	X_6	0
Third	.1667	X_7	0
Fourth	.6667	X_4	9
Fifth	.6667	X_{10}	0
Sixth	1.3333	X_2	17

$$
\begin{aligned}
\text{Profit from increasing } X_5 \text{ one unit} &= &&= -4 \\
\text{Profit from increasing } X_6 &= 2.9333(0) &&= 0 \\
\text{Profit from reducing } X_7 &= -.1667(0) &&= 0 \\
\text{Profit from reducing } X_4 &= -.6667(-9) &&= 6 \\
\text{Profit from reducing } X_{10} &= -.6667(0) &&= 0 \\
\text{Profit from reducing } X_2 &= -1.3333(-17) &&= \underline{22.6667} \\
& && \quad\;\; 24.6667
\end{aligned}
$$

Note that for this calculation the signs of the substitution ratios from Table 12-5 have been changed, since in Table 12-5 a negative ratio indicates an increase while a positive ratio indicates a decrease in the corresponding solution variable.

Treating one of the c_j's in this calculation as an unknown, we can determine a limit (maximum or minimum) of the per-unit profit of the corresponding variable. Assume that c_5 is the unknown. The same calculation produces $c_5 + 28.6667$ instead of 24.6667 $(-4 + 28.6667)$. As long as $c_5 + 28.6667$ is nonnegative, the original solution (Table 12-4) is optimum. The limit on c_5 is determined from

$$c_5 + 28.6667 \geq 0,$$

or

$$c_5 \geq -28.6667.$$

Then, as long as the per-unit profit of X_5 does not exceed \$28.6667, the original optimum solution remains optimum. (Recall that the signs of the original per-unit profits were changed for inclusion of the objective function in the tableau.) Two observations can be made at this point. First, the c_j of each nonsolution variable is included in the calculation of the objective-function coefficient of that variable only. And since the objective is to maximize profit, there are no minimums to the ranges of the c_j's of the nonsolution variables. These variables will enter the solution only if they become more (rather than less) profitable. Second, the c_j's of the solution variables are included in the calculation of the objective-function coefficients for several nonsolution variables. For example, X_4 is the solution variable of the fourth row in Table 12-4. The c_4 value is included in the calculation of the objective-function coefficients of X_1, X_3, X_5, X_8, and X_9, since the substitution ratios between X_4 and these variables are nonzero. The solution variable X_2 is on the sixth row of the tableau. The c_2 value is included in the calculation of the objective-function coefficients of X_1, X_3, X_5, and X_9.

Table 12-4 is condensed to Table 12-6 for the sensitivity analysis of the objective function. The second, third, and fifth rows of Table 12-4 are

Table 12-6 Condensation of Table 12-4 for sensitivity analysis

Row in Table 12-4		Nonsolution variable				
		X_1	X_3	X_5	X_8	X_9
Fourth (X_4)	-9	.8333	-1	$-.6667$	-5	3.3333
Sixth (X_2)	-17	-1.3333	-1	-1.3333	0	-3.3333
	c_j	-6	-20	-4	0	0
First (X_o)		9.1667	6	24.6667	45	26.6667

eliminated, since the objective-function coefficients of the corresponding variables (slacks X_6 and X_7 and surplus X_{10}) are fixed at zero. However, columns for the slack variables X_8 and X_9 are included, since their objective-function coefficients must be nonnegative in Table 12-4 for that solution to remain optimum. Also, the signs of the substitution ratios from Table 12-4 are reversed for Table 12-6 in order to reflect their proper interpretation. Multiplying the substitution ratios of each row by $c_4 = -9$ or $c_2 = -17$ and adding the results to the c_j's of the nonsolution variables produces the objective-function coefficients (the X_o row).

Table 12-6 provides a framework for the sensitivity analysis. For instance, repeating the calculations that we used for c_5, but treating c_1 and c_3 as the unknowns, we produce the results in Table 12-7. The nonsolution variables, X_8 and X_9, are not included, since their coefficients are fixed at zero. Then the maximums on the per-unit profits are \$15.1667 for X_1, \$26 for X_3, and \$28.6667 for X_5. Note that these maximums are the sums of the original c_j's for these variables and their coefficients in the objective function of the optimum solution. Or

$$\text{for } X_1, \quad 15.1667 = 6 + 9.1667,$$
$$\text{for } X_3, \quad 26 = 20 + 6,$$
$$\text{for } X_5, \quad 28.6667 = 4 + 24.6667.$$

Table 12-7 Sensitivity to changes in nonsolution variables

X_1	X_3	X_5
.8333 (-9)	$-1(-9)$	$-.6667(-9)$
$-1.3333(-17)$	$-1(-17)$	$-1.3333(-17)$
c_1	c_3	c_5
$c_1 + 15.1667 \geq 0$	$c_3 + 26 \geq 0$	$c_5 + 28.6667 \geq 0$
or	or	or
$c_1 \geq -15.1667$	$c_3 \geq -26$	$c_5 \geq -28.6667$

Table 12-8 Sensitivity to changes in X_4

X_1	X_3	X_5	X_8	X_9
$.8333c_4$	$-1c_4$	$-.6667c_4$	$-5c_4$	$3.3333c_4$
$-1.3333(-17)$	$-1(-17)$	$-1.3333(-17)$	$0(-17)$	$-3.3333(-17)$
-6	-20	-4	0	0
$33c_4 + 16.6667 \geq 0$	$-c_4 - 3 \geq 0$	$-.6667c_4 + 18.6667 \geq 0$	$-5c_4 \geq 0$	$3.3333c_4 + 56.6667 \geq 0$
$c_4 \geq -20$	$c_4 \leq -3$ (max.)	$c_4 \leq 28$	$c_4 \leq 0$	$c_4 \geq -17$ (min.)

Performing similar calculations, but treating c_4 as the unknown, we produce the results in Table 12-8. Since both greater-than-or-equal-to and less-than-or-equal-to inequalities are present, c_4 has both a maximum and a minimum. The maximum is -3, the smallest of the less-than-or-equal-to inequalities, while the minimum is -17, the larger of the greater-than-or-equal-to inequalities. These values translate to a minimum per-unit profit of $3 for X_4 and a maximum per-unit profit of $17, since the sign of the original c_4 was changed for inclusion in the initial tableau.

Alternatively, this range on c_4 can be computed from the X_o row and the X_4 row in Table 12-6. The calculations are summarized in Table 12-9, where positive substitution ratios in the X_4 row determine upper bounds while negative coefficients determine lower bounds. The ratio of the values in the X_o row to the values in the X_4 row plus the original c_4 value determines the bounds on the per-unit profit of X_4. The largest lower bound (minimum) is $3 while the smaller upper bound (maximum) is $17.

Letting c_2 be unknown produces the results in Table 12-10 for the sensitivity range of X_2. Since the relationships are all less-than-or-equal-to inequalities, there is a maximum but no minimum for the value of c_2. The smallest of the maximums is -11, so the limit on the per-unit profit of X_2 is a *minimum* limit of $11 (the sign of c_2 was reversed for Table 12-2).

The alternative calculations for this limit are illustrated in Table 12-11. All the limits are lower bounds, since the substitution ratios are all negative. The minimum value of profit for X_2 (the largest of the lower bounds) is $11.

Sensitivity analysis for the objective function of a maximizing problem can be summarized as follows.

1. The maximum increase in the c_j of a nonsolution variable is the objective-function coefficient of the variable in the final solution. This value is the decrease in profit for a one-unit increase in the nonsolution variable. If the profit of the variable were increased by more than this amount, then the total profit would increase rather than decrease when the nonsolution variable was introduced.

Table 12-9 Limits for c_4

Bound	Row in Table 12-6 X_o	X_4	$(X_o$ row/ X_4 row$)$ + profit of X_4 = limit			
Upper	9.1667	.8333	11 +	9	=	20
Lower	6	−1	−6 +	9	=	3 (largest lower)
Lower	24.6667	−.6667	−37 +	9	=	−28
Lower	45	−5	−9 +	9	=	0
Upper	26.6667	3.3333	8 +	9	=	17 (smaller upper)

Table 12-10 Sensitivity to changes in X_2

X_1	X_3	X_5	X_8	X_9
.8333 (−9)	−1(−9)	−.6667(−9)	−5(−9)	3.3333(−9)
−1.3333c_2	−1c_2	−1.3333c_2	0c_2	−3.3333c_2
−6.0	−20	−4	0	0
−13.5 − 1.3333c_2 ≥ 0	−11 − c_2 ≥ 0	2 − 1.3333c_2 ≥ 0	—	−30 − 3.3333c_2 ≥ 0
c_2 ≤ −10.125	c_2 ≤ −11 (max)	c_2 ≤ 1.5	—	c_2 ≤ −9

Table 12-11 Limits for c_2

Bound	Row in Table 12-6 X_o	X_2	$(X_o$ row/X_2 row$)$ + profit of X_2 = limit		
Lower	9.1667	−1.3333	−6.875 +	17	= 10.125
Lower	6	−1	−6 +	17	= 11 (largest)
Lower	24.6667	−1.3333	−18.5 +	17	= −1.5
—	45	0	—	—	—
Lower	26.6667	−3.3333	−8 +	17	= 9

2. Using the equation in the final solution containing a solution variable, divide the *negatives* of all (nonzero) substitution ratios into the objective-function coefficients of the associated nonsolution variables. The set of quotients will in general contain both positive and negative values. The smallest positive quotient plus the c_j value represents the maximum (smallest upper bound) of the solution variable's c_j. The least negative quotient (the one with the smallest absolute value) plus the c_j value is the minimum c_j of the solution variable.

The results of our sensitivity analysis on the objective function are summarized in Table 12-12. It should be remembered that the maximum and/or minimum profits represent the range over which each c_j may vary without affecting the optimum solution—but only if the remaining c_j's are fixed at their original values.

Table 12-12 Permissible variations in profits

Variable \ Profits	Minimum	Maximum
X_1	—	$15.1667
X_2	$11	—
X_3	—	26
X_4	3	17
X_5	—	28.6667

To apply the sensitivity procedure to the objective function of a minimizing problem (solved with a maximizing algorithm after alteration of the objective function), we modify the rules as follows, to allow for the change in the signs of the c_j's.

1. The maximum *decrease* in the c_j of a nonsolution variable is the objective-function coefficient of the variable in the final solution.

2. Using the equation in the final solution containing a solution variable, divide all (nonzero) substitution ratios into the objective-function coefficients of the associated nonsolution variables. The smallest positive quotient is the maximum allowable increase in the solution variable's c_j, and the least negative quotient (the one with the smallest absolute value) is the maximum allowable decrease.

Resource Limitations

The sensitivity analysis of the b_i values on the right-hand side (RHS) determines, under the *ceteris paribus* condition, the range over which each resource limit can vary before the set of variables in the optimum solution changes. Of course, any change in resources changes the values of the solution variables and, possibly, the value of the objective function, but there is a range of values of the resources over which the *variables* in the optimum solution remain the same.

Consider again the original problem, complete with slack variables and objective functions. If e_4 represents a change in the hours available in shop C, then Table 12-13 is the initial tableau of the problem. When we apply the simplex algorithm to this expanded problem, the RHS at each stage will involve the quantity e_4. However, the objective-function co-efficients and substitution ratios are not affected by e_4. The optimum solution is contained in Table 12-14. Note that the coefficients of e_4 in the RHS are the same, row for row, as the coefficients of X_8 in this optimum solution. The reason is that, in the expanded problem as shown in Table 12-13, e_4 and X_8, the slack variable for shop C, are represented in exactly

Table 12-13 Initial tableau for the sensitivity to shop C time

X_{11}	X_o	X_1	X_2	X_3	X_4	X_5	X_6	X_7	X_8	X_9	X_{10}	Solution value (b_i)
1			−1		1						1	−80
	1	−6	−17	−20	−9	−4						0
		2	2.5	1.2	.75	.9	1					4,995
		.9		1.8	2	1.5		1				2,520
		.1	.2	.4	.2	.4			1			54.75 + e_4
		.4	.3	.3		.4				1		59.60
			1		−1						−1	80

Table 12-14 Optimum solution for the sensitivity to shop C time

X_o	X_1	X_2	X_3	X_4	X_5	X_6	X_7	X_8	X_9	X_{10}	Solution value (b_i)
1	9.1667		6		24.6667			45	26.6667		4,053.0833 + 45e_4
	−.7083		−2.05		−2.9333	1		−3.75	−5.8333		4,442.0208 − 3.75e_4
	2.5667		−.2		.1667		1	−10	6.6667		2,369.8333 − 10e_4
	−.8333		1	1	.6667			5	−3.3333		75.0833 + 5e_4
	2.1667				.6667			−5	6.6667	1	43.5833 − 5e_4
	1.3333	1	1		1.3333				3.3333		198.6667

the same way. And since the row and column operations of the iteration procedure are applied uniformly to all variables, the coefficients of e_4 and X_8 will be identical in each equation of every solution, including the optimum solution.

The RHS of the tableau in Table 12-14 is used to determine the limits for the range of available hours in shop C for the set of solution variables in the original optimum solution. Note the value of X_o. The value 4,053.0833 + 45e_4 indicates that every additional hour of time in shop C will increase profit by $45. This $45 is the coefficient of the slack variable (in the optimum solution) for the time in shop C. In general, *a slack variable's coefficient in the objective function of the optimum solution is its marginal contribution*, which applies to increments of the resource over its limiting range. This limiting range is determined by finding the values of e_4 that keep the RHS nonnegative.

These calculations are illustrated in Table 12-15. The limiting range for e_4 is from the largest lower bound (− 15.0167) to the smallest upper bound (8.7167). Since there were 54.75 hours available in shop C originally, the optimum solution involves X_2, X_4, X_6, X_7, and X_{10} for any number of hours in shop C from 39.7333 (54.75 − 15.0167) to 63.4667 (54.75 + 8.7167). Thus, over the range of 39.7333 hours to 63.4667 hours in shop C, each additional hour, allocated optimally, contributes $45 to the profit of the solution.

Table 12-15 Sensitivity to shop C time

Row in Table 12-14	RHS	Range of e_4 Lower bound	Upper bound
Second	$4,442.0208 - 3.75e_4 \geq 0$		$e_4 \leq 1,184.5$
Third	$2,369.8333 - 10e_4 \geq 0$		$e_4 \leq 236.9833$
Fourth	$75.0833 + 5e_4 \geq 0$	$-15.0167 \leq e_4$	
Fifth	$43.5833 - 5e_4 \geq 0$		$e_4 \leq 8.7167$

If this same procedure is used to determine the range of hours in shop D, the RHS of the optimum solution is illustrated in Table 12-16. The coefficients of e_5 are the same as the coefficients of X_9, the slack variable for shop D. The range of e_5 is calculated in Table 12-17. The minimum for e_5 is -6.5375, and its maximum is 22.525. Since 59.60 hours were originally available for shop D, the current solution variables remain optimum for the range of hours in shop D from 53.0625 ($59.60 - 6.5375$) to 82.125 ($59.60 + 22.525$). And the marginal value of each hour in shop D is \$26.6667.

The optimum solution to the original problem does not require all of the available raw material A or raw material B. Since in Table 12-4 there are 4,442.0208 (X_6) pounds of A left over, A's original availability can be reduced to 552.9792 ($4,995 - 4,442.0208$) without affecting the optimum

Table 12-16 RHS for variable time in shop D

Row in Table 12-14	RHS
First	$4,053.0833 + 26.6667e_5$
Second	$4,442.0208 - 5.8333e_5$
Third	$2,369.8333 + 6.6667e_5$
Fourth	$75.0833 - 3.3333e_5$
Fifth	$43.5833 + 6.6667e_5$
Sixth	$198.6667 + 3.3333e_5$

Table 12-17 Sensitivity to shop D time

Row in Table 12-14	RHS	Range of e_5 Lower bound	Upper bound
Second	$4,442.0208 - 5.8333e_5 \geq 0$		$e_5 \leq 75.775$
Third	$2,369.8333 + 6.6667e_5 \geq 0$	$-355.475 \leq e_5$	
Fourth	$75.0833 - 3.3333e_5 \geq 0$		$e_5 \leq 22.525$
Fifth	$43.5833 + 6.6667e_5 \geq 0$	$-6.5375 \leq e_5$	
Sixth	$198.6667 + 3.3333e_5 \geq 0$	$-59.6 \leq e_5$	

solution. And since X_6 does not appear in the objective-function equation of the final solution, changing the amount of A available for allocation does not affect the profit of the optimum solution. Likewise, raw material B can be reduced to 150.1667 (2,520 − 2,369.8333) without affecting either the optimum solution or its profit.

CONCLUSION

In many practical applications of linear programming, the original optimum solution has limited value. The constraints and the objective function are based upon estimates of technological and profit relationships. The sensitivity analysis reveals the solution's stability if these estimates were to be changed. In addition, the analysis yields insights into the economic implications of optimum resource allocation. Rarely in a linear programming problem are the parameters fixed values. More commonly prices and costs, c_j's, fluctuate over time, as do the resource limits, b_i's. The procedures of this chapter may be used to examine the extent to which the optimum mix of products is affected by these changing economic conditions.

PROBLEMS

1. The linear programming problem,

$$\text{Maximize:} \quad X_o = 27X_1 + 13X_2 + 35X_3 + 45X_4 + 19X_5,$$

subject to

$$25X_1 + 36.4X_2 + 42X_3 + 23X_4 + 4X_5 + X_6 = 5{,}240,$$
$$12.4X_1 + 21.8X_2 + 36X_3 + 9.4X_4 + 12.3X_5 + X_7 = 7{,}560,$$
$$1X_1 - 1X_2 - 1X_3 - 1X_4 - X_8 = 7,$$
$$25.3X_1 + 17.9X_2 + 8.7X_3 + 10.3X_4 + 9.5X_5 - X_9 = 550,$$

and

$$X_i \geq 0,$$

where X_6 and X_7 are slack variables and X_8 and X_9 are surplus variables, has an optimum solution represented in the following tableau:

Row	X_o	X_1	X_2	X_3	X_4	X_5	X_6
First	1		59.93	60.785			.9368
Second			6.2734	26.8913			.4586
Third			.6023	1.7142		1	−.0433
Fourth		1	.229	.253			.0244
Fifth			1.229	1.253	1		.0244

Row	X_7	X_8	X_9	b
First	1.2401	11.7969		14,201.1578
Second	.6232	− 6.1066	1	6,607.4184
Third	.0954	.0998		493.4352
Fourth	− .0079	− .4875		71.4012
Fifth	− .0079	.5125		64.4012

For each variable determine the range of the objective-function coefficient which leaves this optimum solution unchanged.

2. A metal fabricating company must make a decision on the product mix during the coming month. The four products being considered require raw material (ore) plus casting and finishing. The technological relationships are represented in the following table.

Resources \ Products (1,000-lb. units)	A	B	C	D	Available resource
Ore	1 ton	5	3	2	500 tons
Casting	7 hrs.	3	3	4	400 man-hours
Finishing	4 hrs.	—	1	9	800 man-hours
Profit per 1,000 lbs.	16	28	25	10	
Decision variable	X_1	X_2	X_3	X_4	

The linear programming formulation of this problem is to

$$\text{Maximize:} \quad X_o = 16X_1 + 28X_2 + 25X_3 + 10X_4,$$

subject to

$$X_1 + 5X_2 + 3X_3 + 2X_4 + X_5 \qquad\qquad = 500,$$
$$7X_1 + 3X_2 + 3X_3 + 4X_4 \qquad + X_6 \qquad = 400,$$
$$4X_1 \qquad + X_3 + 9X_4 \qquad\qquad + X_7 = 800,$$

and

$$X_i \geq 0,$$

where X_5, X_6, and X_7 are slack variables. The final tableau of the simplex method yields:

X_o	X_1	X_2	X_3	X_4	X_5	X_6	X_7	b
1	33.3333			20.3333	1.5	6.8333		3,483.3333
	− 3	1		− 1	.5	− .5		50
	5.3333		1	2.3333	− .5	.8333		83.3333
	− 1.3333			6.6667	.5	− .8333	1	716.6667

(a) Determine the maximum and/or minimum value of the profit for each product which leaves this optimum solution unchanged.
(b) If additional ore were available at $1.30 per ton, could the profit be increased?
(c) If 80 additional tons of ore were available at $1.20 per ton, how much would be purchased?
(d) If the next 100 tons, over and above the 80 tons in part (c), cost $1.45 per ton, what is the *total* amount of extra ore that should be purchased?
(e) If the man-hours available in the finishing department could be transferred to the casting department, how much should be transferred?

3. The manager of a large discount store is planning next month's purchases for a new department. There are four products which must be purchased in case lots. The following table includes the costs per case, storage space requirements, and the inventory processing time. In addition to these restrictions, the number of cases of product 2 must not exceed one-half of the number of cases of product 4.

	Product				*Available resource*
	A	*B*	*C*	*D*	
Cost	$35 per case	20	50	5	$2,300
Storage space	73 cu. ft.	12	45	25	1,500 cu. ft.
Processing time	55 minutes	40	80	45	5,670 minutes
Marginal profit	$90	40	75	20	

The linear programming formulation is to

$$\text{Maximize:} \quad X_o = 90X_1 + 40X_2 + 75X_3 + 20X_4,$$

subject to

$$
\begin{aligned}
35X_1 + 20X_2 + 50X_3 + 5X_4 + X_5 &= 2{,}300, \\
73X_1 + 12X_2 + 45X_3 + 25X_4 + X_6 &= 1{,}500, \\
55X_1 + 40X_2 + 80X_3 + 45X_4 + X_7 &= 5{,}670, \\
X_2 - .5X_4 + X_8 &= \phantom{0{,}00}0,
\end{aligned}
$$

and

$$X_i \geq 0,$$

where X_5, X_6, X_7, and X_8 are slack variables. The tableau of the optimum solution is:

Row	X_o	X_1	X_2	X_3	X_4	X_5
First	1	31.6667			11.6667	
Second		-46.1111			-19.4444	1
Third		1.6222		1	.6889	
Fourth		-74.7778			9.8889	
Fifth			1		-.5	

Row	X_6	X_7	X_8	b
First	1.6667		20	2,500
Second	-1.1111		-6.6667	633.3333
Third	.0222		-.2667	33.3333
Fourth	-1.7778	1	-18.6667	3,003.3333
Fifth			1	

(a) Determine the maximum and/or minimum marginal profits of the products that do not change this solution.

(b) Suppose that the manager could use part of the $2,300 in working capital to lease more storage space, how much more space should be leased if it cost $1.20 per cubic foot for the duration of the planning period?

4. A livestock feed manufacturer is attempting to determine the least cost mix of six basic ingredients of cattle feed, satisfying four nutritional requirements. The relationships are given in the following table:

Ingredients (in tons) / Nutritional requirements	1	2	3	4	5	6	Minimum requirements
A	50 lbs.	75	43	22	70	55	3,870 lbs.
B	83 units	20	59	32	68	20	4,320 units
C	40 lbs.	17	33	37	45	47	7,740 lbs.
D	37 oz.	—	15	49	—	24	2,530 oz.
Cost per ton	$70	38	52	105	65	80	
Decision variables	X_1	X_2	X_3	X_4	X_5	X_6	

The linear programming formulation of this problem is to

Minimize: $X_o = 70X_1 + 38X_2 + 52X_3 + 105X_4 + 65X_5 + 80X_6,$

subject to

$$50X_1 + 75X_2 + 43X_3 + 22X_4 + 70X_5 + 55X_6 - X_7 \qquad\qquad\qquad = 3{,}870,$$
$$83X_1 + 20X_2 + 59X_3 + 32X_4 + 68X_5 + 20X_6 \qquad - X_8 \qquad\qquad = 4{,}320,$$
$$40X_1 + 17X_2 + 33X_3 + 37X_4 + 45X_5 + 47X_6 \qquad\qquad - X_9 \qquad = 7{,}740,$$
$$37X_1 \qquad\quad + 15X_3 + 49X_4 \qquad\quad + 24X_6 \qquad\qquad\qquad - X_{10} = 2{,}530,$$

and

$$X_i \geq 0,$$

where X_7, X_8, X_9, and X_{10} are surplus variables. The final tableau of the simplex method is as follows.

Row	X_o	X_1	X_2	X_3	X_4	X_5	X_6
First	1	1.5333	13.4444		37.4		5.1778
Second		−.92	.3778		−1.5733	1	−.1289
Third		−8.3333	−48.5556		8.3333		4.7778
Fourth		−.0267	5.6889		53.7467		65.6356
Fifth		2.4667		1	3.2667		1.6

Row	X_7	X_8	X_9	X_{10}	b
First			1.4444	.2889	−11,910.8888
Second			−.0222	.0489	48.3111
Third	1		−1.5556	.5556	6,764.4444
Fourth		1	−1.5111	−.6089	8,916.4889
Fifth				−.0667	168.6667

Determine the maximum and/or minimum cost of the ingredients which does not change this solution.

13/Transportation and Logistics Applications

TRANSPORTATION and logistics problems are generally stated in a mathematical programming framework. While these distribution problems, meeting the linearity assumptions, can be solved with the simplex method, their special structure allows solution by a less complicated and more efficient algorithm. This simplified algorithm was developed for problems involving the least cost necessary to distribute a product available at several locations to a number of different destinations. But a large class of single-resource-allocation problems can be considered in the framework of a transportation problem.

In the typical transportation problem, there is a single type of resource (product) available at different locations (sources). The alternative uses (destinations) of the resource have fixed demands that may be satisfied by various combinations of allocations from the sources. The merit of a feasible solution (a schedule satisfying the demands of the destinations and not violating the capacities of the sources) is evaluated as a function (transportation cost) of the amount allocated from each source to each destination. The transportation algorithm is easier to understand if a sample problem and the general formulation are presented first. With the sample problem we will develop a general procedure for constructing an initial basic feasible solution. As in the general linear programming problem, the optimum solution will always be a basic feasible solution—the number of positive-valued decision variables does not exceed the number of constraints. Then we will discuss an iterative scheme for discovering a

255

better (and eventually the optimum) solution. Once the algorithm is complete, short cuts and other computational refinements will be explained. Finally, we will discuss a technique for resolving problems presented by a degenerate solution.

PROBLEM STRUCTURE

Table 13-1 shows the available units of a product at four sources (factories) and the demands for the product at four destinations (warehouses). While there are no constraints on either the number of sources or the number of destinations, note that the total demand is equal to the total supply. If a problem involves a total supply exceeding the total demand, a fictitious destination is established with the requirement necessary to equalize total supply and total demand. Likewise, if total demand exceeds the available supply, a fictitious source is set up with the capacity necessary to equalize supply and demand.

The matrix of Figure 13-1 is the framework for the algorithm. Each cell of the matrix represents a shipping route (decision variable) from a source, listed at the left end of the row, to a destination, listed at the top of the column. The entries at the bottoms of the columns are the requirements of the destinations, while the numbers at the ends of the rows are the availabilities at the sources. The circled entries in each cell are the incremental costs for the supply shipped over the route. These costs could include manufacturing and selling expenses as well as the per-unit transportation costs for shipments over the route. The objective of the problem is to find the shipping schedule (values of the decision variables) that satisfies the capacities of the sources and the requirements of the destinations and costs the least.

To establish the general form of the problem, let r_i $(i = 1, ..., m)$ be the available units at source i and a_j $(j = 1, ..., n)$ be the requirement of destination j. Then $\sum r_i = \sum a_j$, including possible dummy sources or

Table 13-1 Demands and capacities for the transportation problem

Destination	Demand (units)	Source	Capacity (units)
1	22	1	24
2	28	2	18
3	17	3	12
4	23	4	36
	90		90

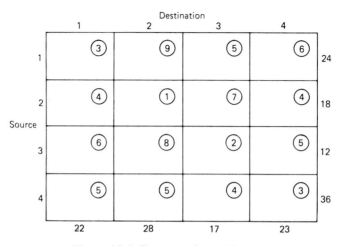

Figure 13-1 Transportation matrix

destinations. Let X_{ij} represent an amount shipped along the route from source i to destination j, while c_{ij} is the incremental cost along this route. In a feasible solution, the variable must satisfy the nonnegativity requirement $(X_{ij} \geq 0)$. The objective of the problem is to find values of the X_{ij} variables that minimize

$$\sum_{\text{(over all cells)}} c_{ij} X_{ij}$$

subject to the supply restriction

$$\sum_{\text{(over row } i)} X_{ij} = r_i$$

for every row, and the demand requirement

$$\sum_{\text{(over column } j)} X_{ij} = a_j$$

for every column.

Because of the special structure of the constraints (every X_{ij} has a unit coefficient), the matrix of Figure 13-1 provides the framework for the solution of the problem. The initial solution and the iterations are handled in the matrix without manipulating the constraints and the objective function as in the simplex method. A feasible solution is a set of X_{ij} values satisfying the constraints and nonnegativity requirement. In the general linear programming problem, a basic solution contains as many solution variables as there are constraints. The transportation problem has $n+m$ constraints, but because total supply is equal to total demand, only

$n+m-1$ of these constraints are independent. *Any* of the constraints can be found using a linear combination of the other $n+m-1$ constraints. And in a basic feasible solution, no more than $n+m-1$ of the X_{ij}'s are positive; the remaining ones equal zero.

INITIAL SOLUTION

The first step of the algorithm is to find an initial basic feasible solution. While any set of X_{ij} values satisfying the constraints could serve as an initial solution, it is desirable that the initial solution be close to the optimum solution, so that fewer iterations will be required to find the optimum. A procedure that gives a very good initial allocation involves selecting the X_{ij}'s of the basic solution in the order of increase of the c_{ij}'s. As we find the value for each X_{ij}, the row and column requirements are decreased; then the procedure is repeated on the reduced problem.

In the matrix of Figure 13-1, the minimum c_{ij} is c_{22}, which is 1. The value of X_{22} is set equal to the minimum of r_2 and a_2, which is 18. If X_{22} is larger than 18, some X_{ij} on row 2 must be negative (violating the non-negativity constraint) for the row requirement to be satisfied. Figure 13-2 shows the reduced problem with $X_{22} = 18$. The c_{ij}'s of the second row are eliminated, since the row requirement is met with $X_{22} = 18$. The lowest c_{ij} of the reduced problem is c_{33}, which is 2. The allocation $X_{33} = 12$ yields the matrix of Figure 13-3. At this stage there is a tie between c_{11} and c_{44} for the lowest cost. But since these two costs involve different rows and different columns, the allocations $X_{11} = 22$ and $X_{44} = 23$ may be made independently. If these costs were in the same row (or column), an arbitrary choice could be made in lieu of a more elaborate tie-breaking procedure. Repeating the process produces the initial allocation illustrated in Figure 13-4. This allocation represents a basic feasible solution, since $n+m-1 = 4+4-1 = 7$ and there are 7 positive-valued solution variables. The cost of this shipping schedule is $255 ($22 \times 3 + 2 \times 9 + 18 \times 1 + 12 \times 2 + 8 \times 5 + 5 \times 4 + 23 \times 3)$. For small problems this initial solution may be the optimum, or at least very close to it. But a procedure for checking optimality leads directly to the iteration scheme of the transportation method.

ITERATION PROCEDURE

The iteration procedure for the transportation problem uses rules identical to those of the simplex method, but the iterations are easier to perform. The empty cells of Figure 13-4 represent nonsolution variables; X_{32}, for

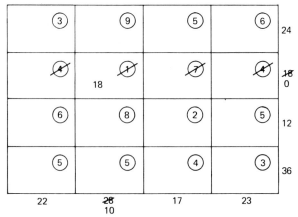

Figure 13-2 First solution variable

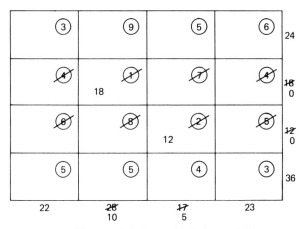

Figure 13-3 Second solution variable

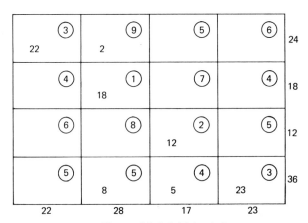

Figure 13-4 Initial solution

example, is 0. If such a variable is brought into the solution (made positive), the other solution variables must be adjusted to maintain the row and column restrictions; at least one of the other solution variables must be removed (set equal to zero), to maintain a basic solution.

Examining this adjustment procedure reveals a means of evaluating the proposed solution. Let d represent an unspecified positive value for X_{32}. In Figure 13-5 the effect of setting X_{32} at d is shown. The value X_{33} must be reduced to $12-d$ to maintain the requirement of row 3. Likewise, X_{43} must be increased to $5+d$ and X_{42} must be reduced to $8-d$ to maintain the requirements of columns 3 and 2, respectively. Changes in the other solution variables are unnecessary. This same idea can be employed for every empty cell of Figure 13-4, but sometimes more than three solution variables are involved (try the procedure for X_{31}). By tracing the readjustments necessary, we can evaluate the cost of each proposed new solution before the iteration is actually performed. For example, when we increase X_{32}, the *net* per-unit (for X_{32}) change in the cost of the solution is $c_{32}-c_{33}+c_{43}-c_{42}$; the plusses and minuses correspond to the increases and decreases in the X_{ij}'s. If X_{32} is increased, the net cost change is $5 = 8-2+4-5$ per unit, an increase in the total cost.

Each boxed number in a cell of Figure 13-6 represents the net cost change (increase if positive, decrease if negative) of increasing the corresponding solution variable. These cost changes, calculated using the same readjustment procedure as for X_{32}, are listed in Table 13-2. At this stage increasing either X_{13} or X_{14} reduces total cost. The variable X_{13} is chosen, since the per-unit cost saving is greater (recall the similar rule of the simplex method). The maximum amount that X_{13} can be increased (to reduce to total cost as much as possible) depends upon the changes in the other solution variables. X_{12} will change to $2-d$, X_{42} to $8+d$, and X_{43} to $5-d$. If X_{13} is made larger than 2, then X_{12} will be negative. Thus, the maximum amount a nonsolution variable can be increased is the minimum value of all the

Table 13-2 Net per-unit cost changes for nonsolution variables

Row	Column	Cost adjustment	Net cost changes
1	3	$c_{13}-c_{12}+c_{42}-c_{43}$	$5-9+5-4 = -3$
1	4	$c_{14}-c_{12}+c_{42}-c_{44}$	$6-9+5-3 = -1$
2	1	$c_{21}-c_{11}+c_{12}-c_{22}$	$4-3+9-1 = 9$
2	3	$c_{23}-c_{22}+c_{42}-c_{43}$	$7-1+5-4 = 7$
2	4	$c_{24}-c_{22}+c_{42}-c_{44}$	$4-1+5-3 = 5$
3	1	$c_{31}-c_{11}+c_{12}-c_{42}+c_{43}-c_{33}$	$6-3+9-5+4-2 = 9$
3	2	$c_{32}-c_{33}+c_{43}-c_{42}$	$8-2+4-5 = 5$
3	4	$c_{34}-c_{33}+c_{43}-c_{44}$	$5-2+4-3 = 4$
4	1	$c_{41}-c_{11}+c_{12}-c_{42}$	$5-3+9-5 = 6$

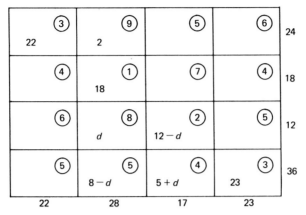

Figure 13-5 Evaluation of X_{32}

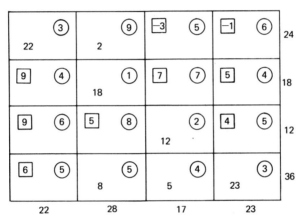

Figure 13-6 Evaluation of nonsolution variables

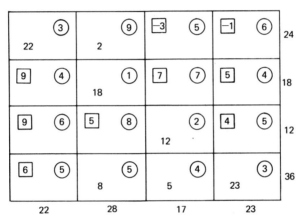

Figure 13-7 Optimum solution

solution variables that must be reduced (recall the minimum-ratio rule of the simplex method). Performing the iteration with the maximum value for X_{13} produces the solution in Figure 13-7, with a cost of $249 ($255 - 3 \times 2$).

Again the boxed entries of the cells of Figure 13-7 are the cost changes for the nonsolution variables. Since these values all indicate increased costs, the solution of Figure 13-7 is the minimum-cost shipping schedule. This algorithm works for any linear transportation problem.

In some problems the objective function may involve maximizing profit rather than minimizing cost. Instead of changing the rules used in the algorithm, it is easier to subtract all c_{ij} values (incremental profits) from an arbitrary number larger than any of the c_{ij} values. The resulting numbers may be used as opportunity costs in the application of the minimizing algorithm. The optimum solution, the one that minimizes these opportunity costs, is also the profit-maximizing solution.

COMPUTATIONAL SHORT CUTS

Regardless of the type of problem, there are computational short cuts that increase the efficiency of the method. We will discuss a simpler computation of the net cost changes and an initial allocation technique that frequently yields solutions closer to the optimum than the minimum-cost procedure illustrated in Figures 13-2 through 13-4.

Net Cost Changes
We do not need to trace the cost changes resulting from adjustments in the values of the solution variables. In every basic solution a set of row values

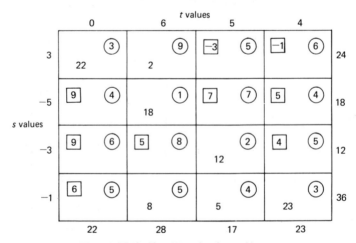

Figure 13-8 Simple evaluation scheme

and column values can be determined so that the c_{ij} of every solution variable (each cell with an allocation) is equal to the sum of the corresponding row and column values. The nonsolution variables can be directly evaluated using these row and column values.

Let s_i represent the row i value and t_j the column j value. Figure 13-8 is the same initial solution presented in Figure 13-4. The s_i and t_j values, shown along the left and top margins, are determined by arbitrarily setting t_1 at 0. (Any t_j or s_i value may be chosen arbitrarily.) When $t_1 = 0$, s_1 must be 3 (X_{11} is a solution variable and $c_{11} = 3$). And since $s_1 = 3$, $t_2 = 6$ ($s_1 + t_2 = 3 + 6 = 9 = c_{12}$). When $t_2 = 6$, $s_2 = -5$ and $s_4 = -1$. If $s_4 = -1$, then $t_3 = 5$ and $t_4 = 4$. Finally, if $t_3 = 5$, then $s_3 = -3$. The net per-unit cost change of each nonsolution variable is $c_{ij} - (s_i + t_j)$. Thus, the boxed values in Figure 13-6 could be computed as follows:

$$
\begin{aligned}
c_{13} - (s_1 + t_3) &= 5 - (3 + 5) = -3, \\
c_{14} - (s_1 + t_4) &= 6 - (3 + 4) = -1, \\
c_{21} - (s_2 + t_1) &= 4 - (-5 + 0) = 9, \\
c_{23} - (s_2 + t_3) &= 7 - (-5 + 5) = 7, \\
c_{24} - (s_2 + t_4) &= 4 - (-5 + 4) = 5, \\
c_{31} - (s_3 + t_1) &= 6 - (-3 + 0) = 9, \\
c_{32} - (s_3 + t_2) &= 8 - (-3 + 6) = 5, \\
c_{34} - (s_3 + t_4) &= 5 - (-3 + 4) = 4, \\
c_{41} - (s_4 + t_1) &= 5 - (-1 + 0) = 6.
\end{aligned}
$$

Using Figure 13-7, we can see that setting t_1 at 0 a second time produces the following set of s_i and t_j values: $t_1 = 0$, $t_2 = 3$, $t_3 = 2$, $t_4 = 1$, $s_1 = 3$, $s_2 = -2$, $s_3 = 0$, and $s_4 = 2$. And corresponding calculations produce the same net cost changes illustrated in Figure 13-7.

Vogel Approximation Method

The Vogel approximation method (VAM) is a procedure for generating an initial solution to the transportation problem that is very close to the optimum solution. The method involves the calculation of penalty costs for each row and column. These penalties represent the *additional* per-unit cost of *not* allocating all of the row or column requirement to the solution variable with the minimum c_{ij} in the row or column. Each penalty is computed by subtracting the smallest c_{ij} from the second-smallest c_{ij} in the same row or column.

Once the penalties are determined, the first allocation is made to the row or column with the largest penalty. In the selected row or column the cell with the smallest c_{ij} is chosen as the solution variable. Its value is set at the

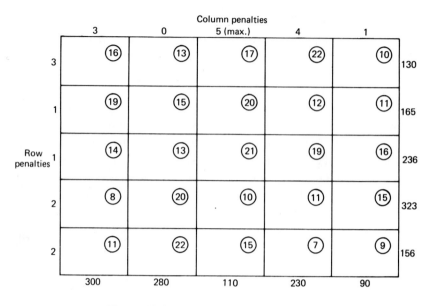

Figure 13-9 VAM row and column penalties

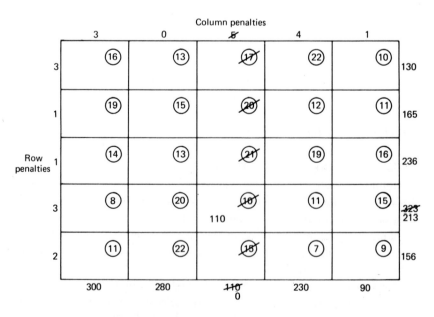

Figure 13-10 Recalculated row penalties

minimum of the corresponding row and column requirements; in this way the requirements are reduced. The penalties must now be determined for the reduced problem. If the value of the solution variable satisfies a row requirement, then the penalty for that row is eliminated and all column penalties must be recomputed. And if a column requirement is satisfied, the penalty for that column is deleted and the row penalties must be redetermined.

Figure 13-9 contains the supplies and demands of five sources and five destinations (right and bottom margins). The incremental costs are the circled values in the cells of the matrix, and the row and column penalties are listed along the left and top margins. The maximum penalty of 5 indicates that the first allocation should be in column 3. The solution variable is X_{43}, since $c_{43} = 10$ is smaller than any other c_{ij} in column 3. Set the value of X_{43} at 110. Then the supply for row 4 is adjusted to 213, the penalty for column 3 is eliminated, and the new penalties are 3, 1, 1, 3, and 2 for rows 1 through 5, respectively. Since the column requirement has been eliminated, none of the cells in column 3 can be used in the penalty calculations of the rows. Figure 13-10 shows the recalculated row penalties with the c_{ij} values of column 3 eliminated. With the new set of penalties, column 4 is selected, and X_{54}, the new solution variable, is set at 156. Since the row 5 supply is now eliminated, the column penalties must be recomputed using the costs in rows 1 to 4. Figure 13-11, on page 266, contains the results of this recalculation. This process is continued until the initial basic feasible solution in Figure 13-12 is obtained. While the effort involved in using VAM is greater than for the minimum-c_{ij} method, the initial solution is usually closer to the optimum.

With VAM, a slight complication arises if ties exist for the largest penalty. In this case either an arbitrary choice can be made or a more involved secondary-penalty scheme can be used. Rarely will the more complicated procedure make a significant reduction in the number of iterations necessary to reach the optimum solution. A much more important computational problem exists if a solution is degenerate.

DEGENERACY

In the simplex method, a degenerate solution can lead to cycling and a possible breakdown of the algorithm. For transportation problems a degenerate solution has similar implications. A degenerate feasible solution, having fewer than $n+m-1$ positive solution variables (the remaining solution variables are at the zero level), can occur in either of

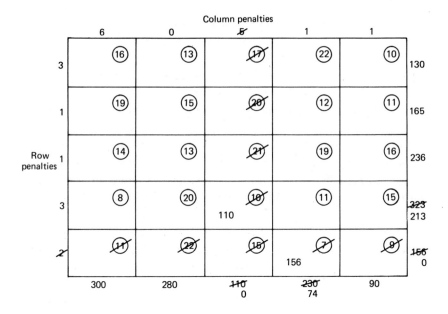

Figure 13-11 Recalculated column penalties

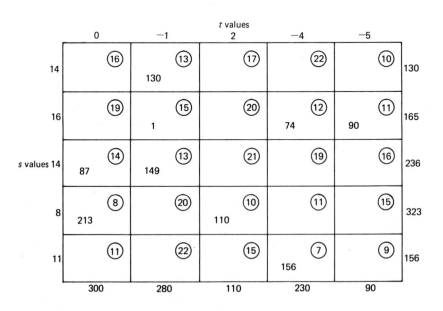

Figure 13-12 VAM initial solution

two ways. When we constructed the initial solutions of Figure 13-4 and Figure 13-12, all but the last solution variable satisfied either a row or a column requirement, but not both. Thus, each of these initial solutions had exactly $n+m-1$ positive solution variables. If, as we made the initial allocations, any but the last solution variable had satisfied both a row and a column requirement simultaneously (the requirements at that stage would have had to be equal), then the initial solution would have been degenerate. This possibility exists if the sum of *fewer* than m of the row requirements is equal to the sum of *fewer* than n of the column requirements.

Under this circumstance, even if the initial solution is not degenerate, it is possible for an iteration to produce a degenerate solution. If, in adjusting the values of the solution variables to bring an X_{ij} into the solution, we come across a tie for the smallest value between two or more solution variables that must be reduced, then one variable is brought into the solution and two or more are removed.

The matrix in Figure 13-13 contains an intermediate (nonoptimum) solution to a transportation problem involving four sources and three destinations. The net cost changes of the nonsolution variables indicate that X_{41} should be brought into the solution. With the d entries tracing the sequence of adjustments in the solution variables, X_{13} and X_{42}, of the variables to be reduced, are tied for the minimum value. In the next solution, shown in Figure 13-14, $X_{41} = 10$, $X_{42} = 0$, and $X_{13} = 0$. A direct consequence of this (or any other) degenerate solution is that the net cost changes for some of the nonsolution variables cannot immediately be evaluated. To determine the t_j and s_i values, set t_1 at 0. Then $s_2 = 2$, $s_3 = 9$, $s_4 = 3$, and $t_3 = -2$. Now, s_1 and t_2 cannot be determined. If any

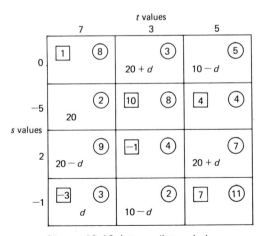

Figure 13-13 Intermediate solution

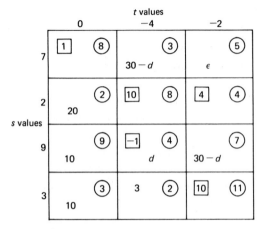

Figure 13-14 Degenerate solution

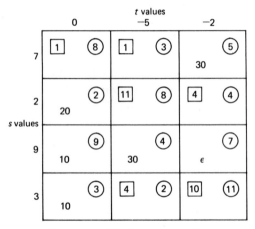

Figure 13-15 Optimum solution

one of the nonsolution variables in row 1 or column 2 had a positive value, the sequence of t and s values could be completed. To resolve degeneracy, let ε stand for an arbitrarily small (but positive) value and place it in any of these cells. In this case, the cell for row 1, column 3 is chosen. If $X_{13} = \varepsilon$, then $s_1 = 7$ and $t_2 = -4$. The resulting evaluation indicates that X_{32} should be brought into the solution. When we adjust the values of the solution variables, X_{12} and X_{33} are eliminated and both X_{32} and X_{13} are brought into the solution. Now the ε value is no longer needed for X_{13}. The new solution, illustrated in Figure 13-15, is still degenerate. By placing the ε value in the cell of row 3, column 3, we can determine the t and s values shown along the margins. The evaluations indicate that the degenerate solution of Figure 13-15 (with ε equal to 0) is the optimum.

The choice of the cell in which to place the ε value can be made arbitrarily, so long as the sequence of t and s values can be completed. For example, if X_{22} is given the value of ε in Figure 13-12, we can verify that the optimum solution of Figure 13-15 is produced in two iterations, one of which involves shifting the ε value from X_{22} to X_{32}.

CONCLUSION

The solutions to distribution problems are found more efficiently with the transportation method than with the simplex algorithm. Both VAM and the minimum-c_{ij} technique produce initial solutions very close to the optimum. The special structure of the constraints (unit coefficients for the X_{ij}'s) allows us to use a less complicated iteration procedure.

PROBLEMS

1. At three factories a company has available a total of 2,000 cases of dog food that must be shipped to five warehouses. The demands of the warehouses, the supplies available at the different factories, and the transportation costs per case are given in the following matrix.

Factory / Warehouse	1	2	3	Demand
1	.50	.65	.54	320
2	.48	.55	.60	470
3	.72	.60	.58	440
4	.53	.51	.57	350
5	.45	.49	.59	420
Supply	900	500	600	2,000

Use the minimum-c_{ij} method for the initial solution and find the least-cost distribution schedule.

2. A company has four jobs to be completed and five machines available that can do part or all of the work on any of the jobs. Because of differences in machines and jobs, the cost per hour varies from one job to another for each machine. These costs, together with the number of hours required for each job and the hours available for each machine, are given in the following matrix.

Machine \ Job	A	B	C	D	Hours available
1	20	25	30	25	10
2	15	24	17	25	5
3	17	28	18	20	5
4	21	23	19	24	7
5	19	20	23	27	8
Hours required	10	15	10	5	

(a) Make whatever alterations in the problem are necessary and find the least-cost assignment of machine hours to jobs.

(b) Suppose that a contract requires that job B be completed. Alter the problem and find the least-cost solution. How much more costly is this solution than the one in which job B did not have to be completed?

3. As part of an overall plant-layout study, a company is evaluating the locations of four parts bins serving six machines. The capacities and demands given in the following matrix are for a frequently used part. The transportation "costs" are the distances between the various bins and the various machines. The criterion used to evaluate this layout is the minimum total distance for the distribution of parts to machines.

Machine \ Bin	1	2	3	4	Parts required
1	10	20	25	40	500
2	10	25	15	35	600
3	20	10	25	20	400
4	15	15	10	25	500
5	25	10	10	15	300
6	35	15	15	5	700
Parts available	750	750	750	750	3,000

(a) Find the best distribution schedule for this layout.

(b) How much could this layout be improved if the availabilities were 750, 650, 900, and 700 for bins 1 through 4, respectively?

4. A company is to subcontract work on four assemblies. The five subcontractors have agreed to submit a bid price on each assembly type and a limit on the total number of assemblies (in any combination) for which they are willing to contract. These bids, the contract limits, and the requirements for assemblies are given in the following matrix.

Assembly \ Subcontractor	A	B	C	D	E	Assemblies required
1	3.45	3.80	3.00	3.10	3.70	500
2	3.40	3.10	3.50	3.10	3.20	300
3	3.35	3.50	3.50	3.20	3.40	300
4	3.60	3.00	3.40	3.30	3.90	400
Contract limits	250	280	330	360	380	

What is the least costly schedule of contracts to be awarded?

5. A decision is to be made about how to distribute a product available at four factories to five markets. The following table lists the availabilities and demands and the *profit* per unit for the distribution from each plant to each market. These profits take into account the sale price in each market, the variable costs in each factory, and the transportation costs from each factory to each market.

Market \ Factory	1	2	3	4	Requirement
1	5	6	3	8	420
2	7	8	5	4	490
3	3	6	7	5	510
4	4	9	2	7	530
5	4	7	5	3	550
Availability	700	500	800	1,000	

(a) Find the most profitable distribution.
(b) If the limited storage space at factory 4 required that all 1,000 units be shipped to a market, what would the most profitable distribution be?
(c) In comparing the answers to parts (a) and (b), what would you conclude about the value of storage space at factory 4?

SUPPLEMENTARY READINGS

Bierman, H., C. P. Bonini, and W. H. Hausman. *Quantitative Analysis for Business Decisions.* Irwin, Homewood, Ill., 1973.

Hadley, G. *Linear Programming.* Addison-Wesley, Reading, Mass., 1962.

Levin, R. I., and C. A. Kirkpatrick. *Quantitative Approaches to Management.* McGraw-Hill, New York, 1975.

Llewellyn, R. W. *Linear Programming.* Holt, Rinehart and Winston, New York, 1964.

Thompson, G. E. *Linear Programming.* Macmillan, New York, 1971.

Wagner, H. *Principles of Management Science.* Prentice-Hall, Englewood Cliffs, N.J., 1975.

14/Queuing Models

WAITING lines at bank windows, grocery stores, storerooms, and toll booths are common occurrences to which queuing concepts can be applied. Customers waiting for a TV repair service to come to their homes to repair their TV sets are involved in a type of queuing in which a physical waiting line does not exist. A variety of problems involving queues or waiting lines can be handled by techniques that are quite simple to apply.

Decisions in waiting-line problems involve the trade-off of two kinds of costs. The increased costs of providing faster service must be traded off against the costs of creating a longer waiting line. Sometimes the costs of waiting in line are easily discernible, as when employees paid by the hour must wait in line to obtain needed tools or materials. When customers must wait in line to purchase a commodity or service, the costs of a longer line are less tangible; they relate to the possible decision by the customer not to enter the waiting line or to go elsewhere in the future. Even a short wait for service at a restaurant or service station can be quite annoying. Sometimes small improvements in the method of service result in substantial reductions in waiting lines.

As an example, consider a queuing situation in which there are 40 machinists earning $6 per hour in a factory machine shop served by a tool crib whose one attendant is paid $4 per hour. Waiting lines or queues of varied lengths have been observed at the tool crib at various times throughout the day. Management raises a logical question as to the economic feasibility of hiring an additional crib attendant to reduce the time lost by machinists waiting in line. This question may be very valid even though the attendant may presently be idle at some times. Here the two costs are easily defined, and both are paid by the factory management; however, quite often the costs are not so readily defined. Consider the case of a supermarket. The value of the customers' time is not so tangible, but it may be reflected in future business. How many check-out counters are required to provide a reasonable waiting time?

Organizations want to provide good customer service, but improved service involves increased costs that may affect the company's competitive position by forcing it to raise prices. The cost of providing improved service must be weighed against the cost of not providing the service. Queuing or waiting-line models attempt to trade off the costs and establish the optimum decision. Often there are more than two alternatives to evaluate. For example, faster but more expensive check-out equipment can often considerably reduce waiting times.

THE STRUCTURE OF A QUEUING SYSTEM

A queuing system consists of the waiting line and the service facility for which the elements in the line are waiting. Other important factors are the rate and manner in which elements arrive at the waiting line and the priorities, if any, for entering the service facility from the waiting line. These essentials of a queuing system are illustrated in Figure 14-1.

An arriving unit is defined as the smallest entity that is handled by the system at one time. Care must be taken in defining the unit. A man standing in a theater ticket line with his family of four would be a single unit, since the family would be served as a unit at the counter and the service time would be closer to that of a single-ticket purchase than to that of four single-ticket purchases. Arrivals could also be in batches: groups might arrive at the theater ticket line together, but each person would purchase his or her own ticket. Some basic waiting-line structures are shown in Figure 14-2.

The arrivals that form the waiting line come from a source. This source can be finite or infinite. If there are 20 mechanics in an automotive servicing facility, the source of persons who may line up at the parts counter is finite.

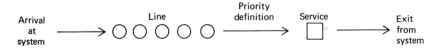

Figure 14-1 Simple queuing structure

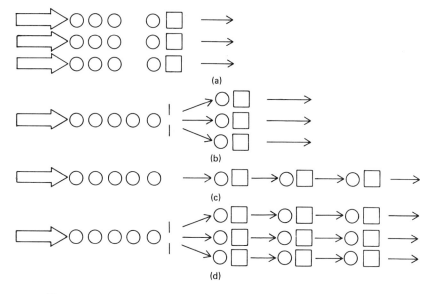

Figure 14-2 Some basic waiting-line structures. (a) Three single channel–single phase cases. (b) A three-channel–single phase case. (c) A single channel–three-phase case. (d) A three-channel–three-phase case.

In actual practice, the size of the source population in relation to the servicing capacity is really more important than the absolute size of the source population. The finite case requires more involved mathematics, because the number of units in the queuing system affects the size of the population from which the arrivals come. Often the population from which the arrivals come is assumed to be infinite, even though it is really some large number, because this assumption simplifies the calculations and often provides answers that are sufficiently accurate. Each of the factors—arrivals, the waiting line, priority, and service—will be considered in detail in this chapter as the queuing formulas are developed.

THE DECISION-MAKING PROCESS

A variety of decisions or questions may face management in a queuing situation.

1. THE NUMBER OF SERVICE FACILITIES At a service point, such as a bank or a turnpike or bridge toll-collection booth, how many of the service facilities should be operated at a particular time? Should additional service facilities be constructed?

2. THE EFFICIENCY OF SERVICE FACILITIES Automated service, or higher-paid personnel, may be more efficient and reduce the waiting time.

3. THE STRUCTURE OF THE QUEUE In a bank, customers often select a line and then switch to a different line as the situation changes. A single line dispersing to several channels (or a take-a-number system) might be more fair to the customers.

4. CONTROLS ON THE ARRIVALS OR ARRIVAL RATES Price changes may cause changes in arrival rates at ticket counters. The pattern of arrivals can be controlled to some extent by the servicing facility with the common practice, for instance, of changing the ticket price after 5:00 P.M. Signs may direct customers to certain facilities for quick service, as in a supermarket.

5. NUMBER OF SERVERS COMPRISING A SERVICE FACILITY The size of the maintenance crew sent on service calls can be weighed against other factors.

The decision-making process usually involves a trade-off of the increased cost of improved service against the savings or added revenue brought about by the improved service. In the tool-crib problem, the cost of adding servers at $4 per hour would be compared to the cost of making $6-per-hour machinists wait in line. In the ticket-line or supermarket situation, the cost of additional servers would be compared to customer inconvenience, or potential loss of customers.

ARRIVALS

The arrival process involves the rate and manner in which the units arrive at the waiting line. It can be considered in either of two ways. One approach would be to measure the intervals between arrivals; the other would be to pick a time interval and describe the arrivals and their spacing within that time frame. Studies have shown that in many real situations the arrival rates follow a Poisson distribution, while the time between service completions follows the negative exponential distribution. This is commonly called the Poisson arrival–exponential service model; it has been found to be sufficiently realistic for evaluation of many practical situations.

Only in unusual circumstances do the units arrive at an even rate, with an equal time between arrivals. Items generated by a machine or an automatically controlled process would leave the machine and arrive at the

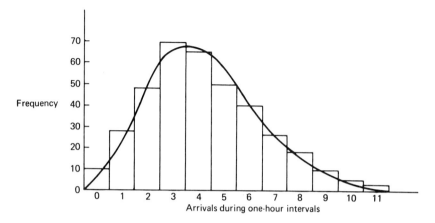

Figure 14-3 A Poisson distribution of arrivals

next point at a constant rate. A receptionist for a doctor's office may attempt to give arrivals a constant rate by scheduling appointments.

Arrivals can also be categorized as controllable or uncontrollable. Changing ticket prices for different periods of the day can control the arrival rate. In some cases, such as arrivals at passenger boarding areas for commercial airlines, the units or passengers can always be expected to arrive at the service facilities in concentrated periods before flights.

The ability of the arriving unit to decide not to enter the waiting line can also affect the system's characteristics. A motorist arriving at a toll booth on a turnpike will have to wait in line, but a person may avoid a line at a filling station by going instead to a nearby station or waiting until later. Deciding not to enter the line is called *balking*. Entering the queue but later departing before being served is called *reneging*.

As we mentioned, in many real-world situations the arrival rates can be described reasonably well by a Poisson distribution. Studies have tended to validate the usefulness of the Poisson, although frequently other distributions conform more closely to the actual rates. The assumption of Poisson arrivals is convenient for the mathematical analysis of the model. The resulting equations can be readily solved. Figure 14-3 shows a typical group of data with a well-fitting Poisson distribution. A Poisson distribution describes a situation with random arrivals in which any unit arrives independently of other arrivals and independently of the existing waiting line. The Poisson distribution implies that an arrival can occur at any time and that its probability is the same regardless of what has occurred previously and regardless of how long the waiting line is. The probabilities of the various numbers of arrivals in a time period form the Poisson distribution. The concept can be associated with a variety of real situations.

The times between successive events can also be tabulated into a distribution, which takes the form of an exponential distribution. The Poisson distribution for arrivals per unit time and the exponential distribution for times between arrivals furnish two alternative ways to describe the same process. It might be said of a particular system that the arrival rate is Poisson with an average of 20 per hour, or that the time between arrivals is exponential with an average of $\frac{1}{20}$ hour, or 5 minutes.

THE QUEUE

The two basic characteristics of queues or waiting lines are the length of the line and the number of lines. A theater ticket line can have almost infinite potential length, as may the line at a toll booth for a bridge. In other words, the source of arrivals is very large. Actually the term *infinite* is more related to the capacity of the system than to the prospect that the line may grow to an infinite length. In other words, if the source from which the arrivals come is large relative to the typical number of units in the system, the characteristics of the queuing system are similar to those of a system whose source is very large.

A line can have limited capacity because of restrictions on physical space. A legal restriction may prohibit a car-wash line from extending into the street. Such a restriction would complicate the formulas normally available for solution of waiting-line problems. The arriving unit that is denied entry to the line may seek service elsewhere or attempt to enter the line again at a later time.

The most simple queuing system has one single-file line. Figure 14-1 and Figures 14-2(b), (c), and (d) show systems with single lines. Multiple-line systems can take on a variety of forms. Figure 14-2(a) is one example; others will be examined as formulas are developed.

SERVICE PRIORITY

The priority with which units in the waiting line are admitted to service, sometimes referred to as the queue discipline, affects the system's characteristics and formulas. Basic queuing concepts assume a first in–first out (FIFO) priority; units are served in the order in which they enter the line. The concepts also assume that a unit will not leave the waiting line. In any real application, any priority, reservation, or other factor differentiating between the importance of the units in line or changing the sequence of service must be considered in developing and using queuing formulas.

THE SERVICE FACILITY

The service facility performs the function for which the queue is forming. The structure of the service facility can be changed, and the changes can be very influential in achieving improvements in the queuing system's efficiency.

Service facilities can be classified in terms of channels and phases. The number of channels is the number of parallel paths or the number of service units available for simultaneous servicing. The phases are the sequential steps in a service series. By these definitions, Figure 14-1 shows a single channel–single phase system. Figure 14-2 shows some other queuing configurations involving both multiple-phase and multiple-channel structures. Tellers' windows in a bank are examples of a multichannel–single phase structure if there is a single line as in Figure 14-2(b). In the more usual situation at a bank, shown by Figure 14-2(a), each window has its own line and there are independent queuing systems.

The ability of a service facility to provide service can be expressed in terms of service times or service rates. There are some real-life situations in which the service time is constant; usually these involve mechanically paced operations, as in an automatic car wash. The time from hookup to release of the car is fixed. In most situations, however, the service time is not constant. Times to serve a customer at a bank window or grocery check-out counter will vary from customer to customer. The average time to purchase tickets at a theater window is much smaller, but the time will also vary from customer to customer, depending upon the amount of change and the questions to be answered.

As we remarked earlier, statistical analyses have demonstrated that the distribution of service times in many real-world situations follows the negative exponential distribution; the service rates follow a Poisson distribution. With these distributions, it can be shown that the probability of the occurrence of either an arrival or a service completion during a specific time interval does not depend on the time of occurrence of the immediately preceding event. The Greek letter mu (μ) is generally used throughout the literature to represent the average service rate or expected number of completions for a period. The mean service time is then $1/\mu$. It has become common practice to discuss a service in terms of a rate, and most formulas utilize the symbol μ as a rate. Although the negative

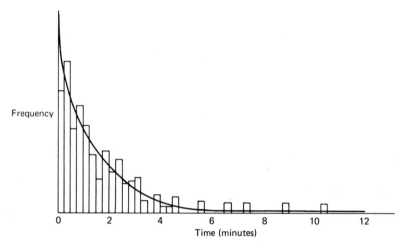

Figure 14-4 Negative exponential distribution for tool-crib service time

exponential is the most widely used, other distributions such as the Erlang and the hyperexponential have been shown to be more representative in particular cases. Figure 14-4 shows the shape of a typical negative exponential curve matched to some actual tool-crib service times collected by one of the authors.

When the assumption of Poisson and negative exponential distributions can be shown to be reasonably valid, the resulting formulas describing the waiting-line characteristics turn out to be quite simple. Knowledge of the mean service rate and mean arrival rate makes it possible to determine a considerable number of parameters describing the waiting line. For the Poisson distribution, the standard deviation is the square root of the mean; for the negative exponential distribution, the standard deviation is equal to the mean. When the arrival rates and service rates do not fit these distributions, the formulas become more complex. Simulation is often the only feasible approach when the distributions do not match the elementary cases defined.

QUEUING SYMBOLS

The following symbols, employed in the queuing formulas of this chapter, are used fairly consistently in the queuing literature.

λ = mean rate of arrival (average number of arrivals per unit of time, based on the Poisson distribution unless otherwise specified).

μ = mean service rate (average number of units served per unit of time). This is the rate that could be attained if the service facility were always busy. The service rate is also assumed to be randomly distributed according to the Poisson curve. If there is more than one channel, this is the rate for one service channel.

S = average (or expected) number of units in the system (waiting in the queue and being served).

L_q = average (or expected) number of units in the queue or waiting line.

T = expected time in the system (waiting time and service time).

W_q = expected waiting time in the queue.

ρ = utilization factor = λ/μ.

n = number of units in the system.

P_n = probability of n units in the system at time t.

P_0 = probability of no units in the system at time t (or the proportion of the time that service facility is idle).

N = number of service channels.

M = population size of the source from which arrivals come (when it is considered to be finite).

ASSUMPTIONS FOR MODELS AND FORMULAS

For the queuing model and formulas described in this chapter, the following assumptions will be made, since these assumptions apply to a majority of real-life problems. When these assumptions are not appropriate, it is necessary to use much more complicated mathematics.

1. POISSON ARRIVAL DISTRIBUTION The use of the Poisson distribution implies that an arrival can occur at any time t and that the probability of this occurrence is not affected by what has occurred previously or by the length of the waiting line.

2. EXPONENTIAL SERVICE DISTRIBUTION It can be observed from Figure 14-4 that long service times sometimes occur, but there is a high probability that a service time will be shorter than the average.

3. INFINITE SOURCE OF ARRIVING UNITS Although real situations do not have infinite sources of arriving units, this assumption is fairly valid when the source of potential arriving units is large—especially when units, after servicing, rejoin the source.

4. RATE OF SERVICE GREATER THAN RATE OF ARRIVAL If the rate of arrival were greater than the rate of service, the queue would increase indefinitely and queuing concepts would not apply.

5. NO LIMIT ON QUEUE LENGTH This assumption is usually valid.

6. FIRST IN–FIRST OUT (FIFO) SERVICE Units retain their position in line, with the result that they are served in the order in which they entered the line.

7. UNITS, ONCE IN THE QUEUE, DO NOT LEAVE It is assumed that there is no reneging.

8. ARRIVING UNITS ENTER THE QUEUE It is assumed that each unit that arrives enters the queue and does not balk.

SINGLE CHANNEL–SINGLE PHASE EQUATIONS

The following equations apply to the simplest queuing model, illustrated in Figure 14-1. The derivation of these equations is shown in the appendix to this chapter.

The expected number in the system is:

$$S = \frac{\lambda}{\mu - \lambda}.$$

The expected number in the waiting line is:

$$L_q = \frac{\lambda^2}{\mu(\mu - \lambda)} = S - \frac{\lambda}{\mu}.$$

The expected time in the system is:

$$T = \frac{1}{\mu - \lambda}.$$

The expected time in the waiting line is:

$$W_q = \frac{\lambda}{\mu(\mu - \lambda)}.$$

The utilization factor, or the probability of a busy system, is:

$$\rho = \frac{\lambda}{\mu}.$$

Since $\mu > \lambda$,

$$0 \leq \rho < 1.$$

The probability of n units in the system is:

$$P_n = \left(1 - \frac{\lambda}{\mu}\right)\left(\frac{\lambda}{\mu}\right)^n.$$

The probability of an idle system (no units in the line or being served) is:

$$P_0 = \left(1 - \frac{\lambda}{\mu}\right)\left(\frac{\lambda}{\mu}\right)^0 = 1 - \frac{\lambda}{\mu} = 1 - \rho.$$

Some Sample Calculations

EXAMPLE 1

Data have been accumulated at a baking facility regarding the waiting time for delivery trucks to be loaded. The data show that the average arrival rate for trucks at the loading dock is 2 per hour. The average time to load a truck, using 3 loaders, is 20 minutes, so the service rate is 3 trucks per hour.

The expected number of trucks in the system is:

$$S = \frac{\lambda}{\mu - \lambda} = \frac{2}{3-2} = 2 \text{ trucks.}$$

The expected number of trucks waiting to be served is:

$$L_q = \frac{\lambda^2}{\mu(\mu - \lambda)} = \frac{4}{3(3-2)} = 1.33 \text{ trucks.}$$

The expected time that a truck is in the system (including waiting and loading) is:

$$T = \frac{1}{\mu - \lambda} = \frac{1}{3-2} = 1 \text{ hour.}$$

The expected time in the waiting line is:

$$W_q = \frac{\lambda}{\mu(\mu - \lambda)} = \frac{2}{3(3-2)} = .667 \text{ hour.}$$

The probability that a truck has to wait for service is:

$$\rho = \frac{\lambda}{\mu} = \frac{2}{3} = .667.$$

The probability of no units in the system (an idle system) is:

$$P_0 = 1 - \frac{\lambda}{\mu} = 1 - \frac{2}{3} = .333.$$

EXAMPLE 2

In example 1, management is considering hiring another loader at $5 per hour to reduce the loading time. Drivers are paid $4 per hour, and truck utilization is valued at $3 per hour. Should the additional loader be hired if an increase in the service rate to 4 trucks per hour would result?

In example 1 there is an average of 2 trucks in the system, with an expected waiting time of 1 hour per truck. This costs the company

$$2 \text{ trucks} \times \$(4+3) \text{ per hour} = \$14 \text{ per hour.}$$

If the additional loader were hired, the loading time would be proportionately smaller; it would be 15 minutes, and μ would equal 4. Then

$$T = \frac{1}{\mu - \lambda} = \frac{1}{4-2} = \tfrac{1}{2} \text{ hour,}$$

$$S = \frac{\lambda}{\mu - \lambda} = \frac{2}{4-2} = 1 \text{ truck.}$$

The new cost would be:

$$1 \text{ truck} \times \$(4+3) + \$5 \text{ (new loader)} = \$12.$$

There would be a net saving of $2 per hour if the new loader were hired.

EXAMPLE 3

A heating company provides 24-hour home heating repair service in the customer's home. The repair service can handle customer calls at the rate of 10 per day. Calls come in at the rate of 8 per day. Both rates follow the Poisson distribution.

The expected number of customers waiting for service is:

$$L_q = \frac{\lambda^2}{\mu(\mu-\lambda)} = \frac{(8)^2}{10(10-8)} = \frac{64}{20} = 3.2 \text{ customers.}$$

The average waiting time is:

$$W_q = \frac{\lambda}{\mu(\mu-\lambda)} = \frac{8}{10(10-8)} = \frac{8}{20} = .4 \text{ day.}$$

The proportion of the time that the service is idle is:

$$P_0 = 1 - \frac{\lambda}{\mu} = 1 - \frac{8}{10} = .20 \text{ (or 20 percent of the time).}$$

The probability that one customer is in the system (one being serviced and none waiting) is:

$$P_1 = \left(\frac{\lambda}{\mu}\right)^n \left(1 - \frac{\lambda}{\mu}\right) = (.80)^1 (1-.80) = .16.$$

The probability that someone is waiting because the service is busy is:

$$P_{2 \text{ or more}} = 1 - P_1 - P_0 = 1 - .16 - .20 = .64.$$

Service Rate for Minimum Total Cost

The total cost of a queuing system is the sum of the cost of service and the cost of waiting. The mean waiting cost is the product of waiting cost per unit per period (C_w) times the mean number in the system:

$$\text{Waiting cost} = C_w S = \frac{C_w \lambda}{\mu-\lambda}.$$

The mean service cost per period is the cost of servicing one unit (C_s) times the mean service rate per period:

$$\text{Service cost} = C_s \mu.$$

Therefore, if total cost is represented by C_T,

$$C_T = \frac{C_w \lambda}{\mu-\lambda} + C_s \mu.$$

Differentiating total cost with respect to μ, and equating the result to zero, we find that

$$\frac{dC_T}{d\mu} = -C_w \lambda (\mu - \lambda)^{-2} + C_s = 0,$$

$$(\mu - \lambda)^2 = \frac{\lambda C_w}{C_s},$$

$$\mu - \lambda = \sqrt{\frac{\lambda C_w}{C_s}},$$

$$\mu = \lambda \pm \sqrt{\frac{\lambda C_w}{C_s}}.$$

The minus sign is dropped, since the service rate must exceed the arrival rate in a queuing solution.

As an example, assume 25 arrivals per hour. The cost of servicing one unit is $4, and the cost of waiting is $5 per unit. Then the service rate that yields the lowest total cost is:

$$\mu = 25 + \sqrt{\frac{25(5)}{4}}$$

$$= 25 + 5.6 = 30.6 \text{ units per hour.}$$

The optimum total cost will occur when the mean service rate is around 30 per hour.

MULTICHANNEL–SINGLE PHASE EQUATIONS

The following equations apply to the system illustrated in Figure 14-2(b), where N is the number of parallel channels and μ is the service rate of a single channel. These equations can be reduced to those for the single channel case by letting N equal 1 and simplifying.

The probability of no units in the system is:

$$P_0 = \frac{1}{\displaystyle\sum_{n=0}^{N-1} \frac{1}{n!}\left(\frac{\lambda}{\mu}\right)^n + \frac{1}{N!}\left(\frac{\lambda}{\mu}\right)^N \left(\frac{N\mu}{N\mu - \lambda}\right)}.$$

The expected number in the waiting line is:

$$L_q = \frac{(\lambda/\mu)^{N+1}}{(N-1)!\left(N - \frac{\lambda}{\mu}\right)^2} \times P_0.$$

The expected number in the system is:

$$S = L_q + \frac{\lambda}{\mu}.$$

The expected time in the system is:

$$T = \frac{S}{\lambda}.$$

The expected time in the waiting line is:

$$W_q = \frac{L_q}{\lambda}.$$

As an example, imagine that the bakery facility from example 1 on page 283 is planning to expand its facilities so that the new average arrival rate will be 4 trucks per hour. Two alternatives are available, each of which will result in the same service cost:

> Alternative 1 one loading dock with an average service time of 10 minutes;
> Alternative 2 two loading docks with an average service time of 20 minutes each.

Which will provide the best service? Each truck and driver costs the company $7 per hour.

For alternative 1,

$$T = \frac{1}{\mu - \lambda} = \frac{1}{6 - 4} = \tfrac{1}{2} \text{ hour,}$$

$$S = \frac{\lambda}{\mu - \lambda} = \frac{4}{6 - 4} = 2 \text{ trucks,}$$

Waiting cost $= 2$ trucks $\times$ \$7 per hour $=$ \$14 per hour.

For alternative 2,

$$P_0 = \cfrac{1}{1 + \dfrac{\lambda}{\mu} + \dfrac{1}{2}\left(\dfrac{\lambda}{\mu}\right)^2 \left(\dfrac{2\mu}{2\mu - \lambda}\right)}$$

$$= \cfrac{1}{1 + \dfrac{4}{3} + \dfrac{1}{2}\left(\dfrac{4}{3}\right)^2 \left(\dfrac{8}{8 - 3}\right)} = \cfrac{1}{1 + 1.33 + 1.42}$$

$$= \frac{1}{3.75} = .267,$$

$$L_q = \frac{(\lambda/\mu)^{N+1}}{(N-1)!\left(N-\dfrac{\lambda}{\mu}\right)^2} \times P_0 = \frac{(4/3)^3}{\left(2-\dfrac{4}{3}\right)^2} \times .267$$

$$= \frac{2.37}{.45} \times .267 = 1.40,$$

$$S = L_q + \frac{\lambda}{\mu} = 1.4 + \frac{4}{3} = 1.73 \text{ trucks,}$$

Waiting cost = 1.73 trucks × \$7 per hour = \$12.11.

The two-channel system is \$1.89 per hour cheaper than the one-channel system in terms of cost of waiting.

CONSTANT SERVICE RATE

The following equations would apply to a single channel system if the service time were fixed and the arrivals followed the Poisson distribution:

$$L_q = \frac{\lambda^2}{2\mu(\mu-\lambda)},$$

$$S = \frac{\lambda(2\mu-\lambda)}{2\mu(\mu-\lambda)} = L_q + \frac{\lambda}{\mu},$$

$$T = \frac{\lambda + 2(\mu-\lambda)}{2\mu(\mu-\lambda)} = W_1 + \frac{1}{\mu},$$

$$W_q = \frac{\lambda}{2\mu(\mu-\lambda)}.$$

Imagine a car wash that requires 4 minutes to handle a car from hookup to release. Cars arrive according to a Poisson distribution at a mean rate of 12 per hour. The expected number in the waiting line is:

$$L_q = \frac{\lambda^2}{2\mu(\mu-\lambda)} = \frac{(12)^2}{2(15)(15-12)} = \frac{144}{90} = 1.6 \text{ cars.}$$

The expected time in the waiting line is:

$$W_q = \frac{\lambda}{2\mu(\mu-\lambda)} = \frac{12}{2(15)(15-12)} = \frac{12}{90} = .133 \text{ hour (or 8 minutes).}$$

If the service time had been exponential, the waiting time would have been:

$$W_q = \frac{\lambda}{\mu(\mu-\lambda)} = \frac{12}{15(15-12)} = \frac{12}{45} = .266 \text{ hour (or 16 minutes).}$$

Thus, the constant service time results in a waiting line of half the length.

FINITE POPULATION–SINGLE CHANNEL SYSTEM

In some situations the number of potential users is limited. The previous equations assumed an infinite population of potential arrivals; however, if an arrival or a service completion will affect the probability of future arrivals, the equations are different. As a general rule, if the source population from which arrivals come is less than 30, the equations given in this section should be used. Consider the case of a mechanic who services 6 trucks. The mean time between repairs is 8 hours, and it forms an exponential distribution. The mean repair time is 1.5 hours. This problem would be solved by the following equations. The symbols are the same as used previously, with the addition of M, the size of the population of potential arrivals. If there are S customers in the system, then there are $M - S$ left as potential arrivals.

$$P_0 = \frac{1}{\sum_{n=0}^{n=M} \frac{M!}{(M-n)!} \left(\frac{\lambda}{\mu}\right)^n},$$

$$P_n = \frac{M!}{(M-n)!} \left(\frac{\lambda}{\mu}\right)^n P_0,$$

$$S = M - \frac{\mu}{\lambda}(1 - P_0),$$

$$L_q = M - \frac{\lambda+\mu}{\lambda}(1 - P_0).$$

The finite population–multichannel system is discussed by Hillier and Lieberman and by Shamblin and Stevens.*

ESTIMATING PARAMETERS

In a real problem to be evaluated by a queuing model, it is necessary to estimate the arrival rate λ and the service rate μ. In addition, it may be necessary to verify the shape of the arrival and service distributions.

The mean arrival rate can be estimated by counting arrivals for a period of time. Dividing the number of arrivals by the time yields the arrival rate λ. Arrivals occur instantaneously; for services, which take time, the counting is slightly different. If a period of time is selected and a count taken of the number of services completed, a difficulty can arise: A service

* F. S. Hillier and G. J. Lieberman, *Introduction to Operations Research*, Holden-Day, San Francisco, 1974, chapters 9–10; and J. E. Shamblin and G. T. Stevens, Jr., *Operations Research*, McGraw-Hill, New York, 1974, chapter 8.

may be only partially completed at the end of the time period. Therefore, a better approach to estimating μ, the average service time, would be to pick a certain number of items and measure the time taken to complete service for them. As in any sampling process, more observations provide closer estimates, and confidence intervals for the estimates can be determined.

To obtain a picture of the arrival distribution, the decision maker can record and plot times between arrivals as in Figure 14-3. The service distribution is formed by recording each elapsed time for accomplishing a service and plotting as in Figure 14-4. If the shapes are considered to be sufficiently close to the Poisson and exponential distributions, the values of λ and μ provide the parameters needed to solve the queuing equations. Standard statistical tests can be utilized to test the fit of the data to the assumed distribution.

APPENDIX: DERIVATION OF QUEUING EQUATIONS

In this appendix we will derive the basic queuing equations for the single channel–single phase system with Poisson arrivals and exponential service. We will find an equation to evaluate the probability that there will be n units in the system at time t or at $t+\Delta t$. In the derivation, the $(\Delta t)^2$ terms will be neglected. The following symbols will be used.

λ = mean arrival rate.

μ = mean service rate.

n = number of units in system.

$P_n(t)$ = probability of n units in system at time t.

$\lambda(\Delta t)$ = probability that there is an arrival between t and $(t+\Delta t)$.

$1 - \lambda(\Delta t)$ = probability that there are no arrivals between t and $(t+\Delta t)$ (higher-order terms are neglected).

$\mu(\Delta t)$ = probability of a departure (a service completed) between t and $(t+\Delta t)$.

$1 - \mu(\Delta t)$ = probability of no departures between t and $(t+\Delta t)$.

There are three ways in which the system can reach state n at $(t+\Delta t)$.

1. There are n units in the system at t, and no arrivals or departures occur. Therefore there are still n units at $(t+\Delta t)$. The probability of this is:

$$P(\text{a}) = P_n(t)(1-\lambda \Delta t)(1-\mu \Delta t).$$

2. There will be n units in the system at $(t+\Delta t)$ if there are $n+1$ units at t, with no arrivals and one departure. The probability of this is:

$$P(\text{b}) = P_{n+1}(t)(1-\lambda \Delta t)\mu \Delta t.$$

3. There will also be n units in the system at $(t+\Delta t)$ if there are $n-1$ units at t, with one arrival and no departures. The probability of this is:

$$P(c) = P_{n-1}(t)(\lambda \Delta t)(1-\mu \Delta t).$$

Since the events are mutually exclusive, the probability of n units at $(t+\Delta t)$ will be the sum of these three probabilities:

$$
\begin{aligned}
P_n(t+\Delta t) &= P(a) + P(b) + P(c) \\
&= P_n(t)(1-\lambda \Delta t)(1-\mu \Delta t) + P_{n+1}(t)(1-\lambda \Delta t)\mu \Delta t \\
&\qquad + P_{n-1}(t)(\lambda \Delta t)(1-\mu \Delta t) \\
&= P_n(t)(1-\lambda \Delta t-\mu \Delta t) + P_{n+1}(t)(\mu \Delta t) + P_{n-1}(t)(\lambda \Delta t).
\end{aligned}
$$

At this point, all of the higher-order $(\Delta t)^2$ terms, which are small, have been omitted. Continuing to simplify, we find that

$$P_n(t+\Delta t) = P_n(t) - P_n(t)(\lambda \Delta t+\mu \Delta t) + P_{n+1}(t)\mu \Delta t + P_{n-1}(t)(\lambda \Delta t).$$

Then we subtract $P_n(t)$ from both sides of the equation and divide by Δt:

$$\frac{P_n(t+\Delta t) - P_n(t)}{\Delta t} = -P_n(t)(\lambda+\mu) + \mu P_{n+1}(t) + \lambda P_{n-1}(t).$$

Letting Δt approach zero, we have

$$\frac{dP_n(t)}{dt} = -(\lambda+\mu) P_n(t) + \mu P_{n+1}(t) + \lambda P_{n-1}(t).$$

In the steady-state condition,

$$\frac{dP_n(t)}{dt} = 0.$$

Setting the expression equal to zero and solving for $P_n(t)$, we find that

$$P_n(t) = \frac{\mu}{\lambda+\mu} P_{n+1}(t) + \frac{\lambda}{\lambda+\mu} P_{n-1}(t),$$

where n is positive and not zero, since a departure is possible.

Now consider the situation in which the system has zero units at $(t+\Delta t)$; this can come about in two ways:

1. There are zero units in the system at time t and no arrivals in Δt.

2. There is one unit in the system at time t, with no arrivals and one departure in Δt.

Therefore

$$
\begin{aligned}
P_0(t+\Delta t) &= P(d) + P(e) \\
&= P_0(t)(1-\lambda \Delta t) + P_1(t)(1-\lambda \Delta t)\mu \Delta t.
\end{aligned}
$$

Neglecting $(\Delta t)^2$ terms gives us

$$P_0(t+\Delta t) = P_0(t)(1-\lambda\,\Delta t) + P_1(t)\mu\,\Delta t.$$

We solve as before:

$$\frac{P_0(t+\Delta t) - P_0(t)}{\Delta t} = -\lambda P_0(t) + \mu P_1(t) = 0,$$

$$P_1(t) = \frac{\lambda}{\mu} P_0(t),$$

$$P_0(t) = \frac{\mu}{\lambda} P_1(t).$$

Returning to the previous equation for $P_n(t)$,

$$P_n(t) = \frac{\mu}{\lambda+\mu} P_{n+1}(t) + \frac{\lambda}{\lambda+\mu} P_{n-1}(t),$$

we let $n = 1$:

$$P_1(t) = \frac{\mu}{\lambda+\mu} P_2(t) + \frac{\lambda}{\lambda+\mu} P_0(t).$$

We substitute the previous expression for $P_0(t)$ to obtain

$$P_1(t) = \frac{\mu}{\lambda+\mu} P_2(t) + \frac{\lambda}{\lambda+\mu} \cdot \frac{\mu}{\lambda} P_1(t).$$

In the steady-state condition, the state is independent of time, so the (t) can be dropped. Then

$$P_1 = \frac{\mu}{\lambda+\mu} P_2 + \frac{\mu}{\lambda+\mu} P_1,$$

$$P_1\left(1 - \frac{\mu}{\lambda+\mu}\right) = \frac{\mu}{\lambda+\mu} P_2,$$

$$P_2 = \frac{\lambda}{\mu} P_1 = \left(\frac{\lambda}{\mu}\right)^2 P_0.$$

In the same manner,

$$P_3 = \left(\frac{\lambda}{\mu}\right) P_2 = \left(\frac{\lambda}{\mu}\right)^3 P_0,$$

$$P_4 = \frac{\lambda}{\mu} P_3 = \left(\frac{\lambda}{\mu}\right)^4 P_0,$$

$$P_n = \left(\frac{\lambda}{\mu}\right)^n P_0.$$

The sum of the probabilities is one, so

$$\sum_{n=0}^{\infty} P_n = 1.$$

This means that

$$\sum_{n=0}^{\infty} \left(\frac{\lambda}{\mu}\right)^n P_0 = P_0 \sum_{n=0}^{\infty} \left(\frac{\lambda}{\mu}\right)^n = 1.$$

Since, for queuing theory,

$$\frac{\lambda}{\mu} < 1 \quad \text{and} \quad \sum_{n=0}^{\infty} a^n = \frac{1}{1-a},$$

we see that

$$P_0 \left(\frac{1}{1 - \frac{\lambda}{\mu}}\right) = 1,$$

$$P_0 = 1 - \frac{\lambda}{\mu},$$

and

$$P_n = \left(\frac{\lambda}{\mu}\right)^n \left(1 - \frac{\lambda}{\mu}\right).$$

Solving for the expected number in the system gives us

$$S = \sum_{n=0}^{\infty} n P_n = \sum_{n=0}^{\infty} n \left(\frac{\lambda}{\mu}\right)^n \left(1 - \frac{\lambda}{\mu}\right),$$

$$= \left(1 - \frac{\lambda}{\mu}\right) \sum_{n=0}^{\infty} n \left(\frac{\lambda}{\mu}\right)^n$$

$$= \left(1 - \frac{\lambda}{\mu}\right) \frac{\lambda/\mu}{(1 - \lambda/\mu)^2}$$

$$= \frac{\lambda}{\mu - \lambda}.$$

Then the expected time in the system, T, is determined as follows, since there are λ arrivals per unit of time and each is expected to wait T.

$$\lambda T = S,$$

$$T = \frac{S}{\lambda} = \frac{1}{\lambda}\left(\frac{\lambda}{\mu - \lambda}\right) = \frac{1}{\mu - \lambda}.$$

The expected time in the queue is then the time in the system minus the time in service:

$$W_q = T - \frac{1}{\mu}$$

$$= \frac{1}{\mu - \lambda} - \frac{1}{\mu} = \frac{\lambda}{\mu(\mu - \lambda)} \, .$$

The expected number in the queue is the arrival rate times the mean waiting time:

$$L_q = \lambda W_q = \frac{\lambda^2}{\mu(\mu - \lambda)} \, .$$

These formulas provide the pertinent information about the system in terms of arrival and service rates.

PROBLEMS

1. A system has Poisson arrivals and exponential service times. The average arrival rate is 4 per hour, and the average service time is 10 minutes. Determine these parameters:

   (a) average number in the system.
   (b) average time in the system.
   (c) expected line length.
   (d) expected time in line.
   (e) probability of 0, 1, 2, or 3 customers in the system.
   (f) probability of 2 or more customers in the system.

2. Customers arrive every 4 minutes, on the average, and the service time is 2.5 minutes. What percentage of the time is the service facility idle?

3. A drive-in bank window has an average of 15 customers per hour. The average service time is 3 minutes. Assuming a Poisson arrival–exponential service situation, determine:

   (a) the probability that a customer will have no wait.
   (b) the probability of one customer in the system.
   (c) the probability of one or more customers in the system.
   (d) the probability of a queue.
   (e) the average waiting time in the queue.
   (f) the average waiting time in the system.
   (g) the average number of customers in the system.

4. A plant storeroom operates 24 hours per day. Maintenance people arrive at an average of 4 per hour to get parts needed to repair equipment. The average service time is 12 minutes. What is the expected lost time in a 24-hour period

for the maintenance people who must wait? If their wages are $4 per hour, what is the cost of waiting?

5. In problem 4, the addition of a storeroom assistant at $3 per hour is under consideration. This would improve the service rate to 6 per hour. Should the change be made?

6. A registration office with a single service window experienced an arrival rate of 25 applicants per hour (Poisson) and an average service time of 2 minutes (exponential).

   (a) What were the average waiting time and average waiting-line length?
   (b) During the license-renewal period, the arrival rate increased to 100 per hour, but the service time decreased to 45 seconds. How did these changes affect the line length and waiting time?

7. A large warehouse has over 200 fork lifts and other equipment for handling materials. Because of the continuous use, breakdowns have been occurring at an average of 3 per hour, following a Poisson distribution. Each maintenance person is paid $4 per hour, and downtime costs the company $25 per hour, since cargo trucks are often delayed. The company has a mobile repair unit, so only one crew can be used. One maintenance person can service an average of 5 units per hour; a crew of two can service 7 per hour; and a crew of three can service 8 per hour. What is the crew size that minimizes costs?

8. A post-office window serves customers at an average rate of 4 per minute. Customers arrive at an average rate of 3 per minute.

   (a) How long does an average customer wait in line?
   (b) What is the average number of customers present, including the one being served?
   (c) What percentage of the time is the clerk at the window idle?
   (d) What is the probability that three or more people will be at the window at a particular time?

9. In problem 8, if there were a fixed service time of 15 seconds, how would this affect the waiting time and line length?

10. A bank drive-in window serves customers at a rate of one every 3 minutes. Customers arrive at a rate of 24 per hour. What are the average waiting-line length and waiting time? If the service rate were improved to 24 per hour, how would this affect the answers?

11. A company is considering two alternative maintenance services. Either service will charge by the hour. Service A charges $10 per hour, and its average service time is 2 hours per machine. Service B charges $15 per hour, and its service rate is .7 machines per hour. Machine breakdonws average 12 in a 40-hour work period. Downtime costs are $12 per hour per machine. Which service should be selected? Both services will have a full-time representative at the company.

12. In problem 11, what would be the cost if service A charged only for the actual working time of its representative?

13. A company is building an addition to its manufacturing facility. Management desires an analysis of how to handle machine breakdowns for the combined new and old facilities. The rate is predicted to be 6 breakdowns per 8-hour shift, with a Poisson distribution. Service times are exponentially distributed. Two alternatives are under consideration for handling the maintenance.

    (a) Expand the present maintenance facility so that it can handle 11 breakdowns per 8-hour shift.

    (b) Build a new maintenance facility in the new area; the capacity of each facility would be 6 units per 8-hour shift. The combined maintenance operations would form a two-channel system.

    If the cost of the two alternatives is equal, which will provide the better service in terms of time out of service (T) for the equipment? What other factors should be considered?

SUPPLEMENTARY READINGS

Beckmann, Petr. *Introduction to Elementary Queuing Theory and Telephone Traffic*. Golden Press, Boulder, Colo., 1968.

Cox, D. R., and W. L. Smith. *Queues*. Wiley, New York, 1961.

Hillier, F. S., and G. J. Lieberman. *Introduction to Operations Research*. Holden-Day, San Francisco, 1974, chapters 9–10.

Lee, A. *Applied Queuing Theory*. Macmillan, Toronto, 1966.

Panico, J. A. *Queuing Theory*. Prentice-Hall, Englewood Cliffs, N.J., 1969.

Saaty, Thomas L. *Elements of Queuing Theory*. McGraw-Hill, New York, 1961, chapter 14.

Shamblin, J. E., and G. T. Stevens, Jr. *Operations Research*. McGraw-Hill, New York, 1974, chapter 8.

Taha, Hamdy A. *Operations Research*. Macmillan, New York, 1971, chapter 14.

Thierauf, Robert J., and Richard A. Grosse. *Decision Making Through Operations Research*. Wiley, New York, 1970, chapter 14.

Wagner, H. *Principles of Management Science*. Prentice-Hall, Englewood Cliffs, N.J., 1975, chapter 15.

15/Markov Analysis

MARKOV analysis is a technique for evaluating the current state and trends of a variable in order to predict future states or conditions. Currently, the primary applications involve market share or brand switching; however, Markov processes can also be used for other categories of problems.

Problems suitable for Markov analysis, or for what are frequently called Markov processes or chains, have certain characteristics. First, the variable moves from one state or condition to another state or condition, and the probability of the next event in a successive sequence of trials depends only upon the present state, not upon any prior event. Second, there is a finite set of possible states, and the probabilities of going to those various states from any given state are measurable and remain constant over time.

Markov processes are also classified by order. The case where the next event depends only on the prior state is called first order. A second-order analysis assumes that actions in the coming period depend upon events in the prior two periods. In a similar manner, a third-order process assumes that actions in the coming period depend upon the prior three periods. Studies have shown the first-order process to be reliable for most practical problems, so higher-order processes will not be considered in this text.

In a Markov process, there are as many possible states as possible outcomes, and as each set of outcomes occurs the process is said to have incremented one step. In many applications, a step is a time period, but the steps need not progress with time. The term n is used to increment the steps; if the present state is $n = 0$, then the next possible outcome is represented as $n = 1$, the one after that is $n = 2$, and so forth. A work assignment problem can be used to illustrate a simple Markov process.

A WORK-ASSIGNMENT EXAMPLE

A computer is operated continuously, around the clock, with three crews of personnel. For administrative purposes, the work is divided into four-hour shifts. At the beginning of each four-hour shift, the computer is either operating or is down for repair service. If the computer is down, the crew is assigned other work for that four-hour period. Assume that data have been collected that show a relationship between the state of the computer (either operating or down) at the beginning of a shift and the state of the computer at the start of the previous shift. These data are given in Table 15-1.

If the computer is operating at the start of a shift, the probability that it will be operating at the start of the following shift is .8, and the probability that it will be down is .2. If the computer is down at the start of a period, the probability that it will be operating at the start of the next shift is .7, and the probability that it will be down is .3. We will identify the computer's two possible states as state 1 (being in operation) and state 2 (being down for service). As Table 15-2 shows, regardless of the state of the computer at the start of any period, there are only two possible states at

Table 15-1 States of a computer for two consecutive shifts

State at start of shift	Number of observations	Times operating at start of next shift	Times not in service at start of next shift
Operating	100	80	20
Not in service	100	70	30

Table 15-2 Probability relationships between computer states for two consecutive shifts

To \ From	Operating (state 1)	Not in service (state 2)
Operating (state 1)	.8	.7
Not in service (state 2)	.2	.3
	1.0	1.0

the beginning of the following period, so the sum of the probabilities in any column of the table is 1.0.

Tree Representation

The status of the computer can be represented by probability trees, as shown in Figures 15-1 and 15-2. These trees are identical in structure to those developed in Chapter 2. The number in any circle represents the state at the beginning of a shift, and the beginning of shift 1 is considered the present state. The trees can then be evaluated to determine the probability that the system will be in any particular state at any particular time, given the initial state for shift 1.

If the computer is in state 1 (operating) at the start of shift 1, the probability that it is in state 1 at the start of shift 3 is:

$$P(\text{State 1; shift 3} \mid \text{state 1; shift 1}) = .8(.8) + .2(.7)$$
$$= .64 + .14 = .78,$$

where the left-hand side of the formula is read, "Probability of being in state 1 at shift 3, given state 1 at shift 1."

For the fourth shift,

$$P(\text{State 1; shift 4} \mid \text{state 1; shift 1}) = .8(.8)(.8) + .8(.2)(.7) + .2(.7)(.8)$$
$$+ .2(.3)(.7)$$
$$= .512 + .112 + .112 + .042$$
$$= .778.$$

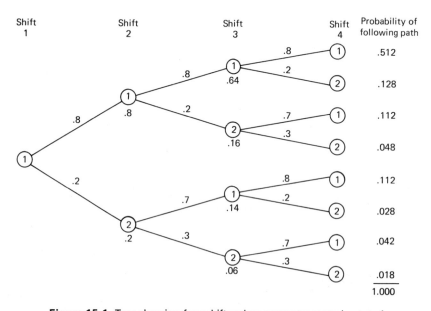

Figure 15-1 Tree showing four shifts when computer starts in state 1

This represents the probability of being in state 1 at shift 4, given state 1 at shift 1. In a like manner, the probability of being in state 2 at shift 4, given state 1 at shift 1, would be:

$$P(\text{State } 2; \text{ shift } 4 \,|\, \text{state } 1; \text{ shift } 1) = 1 - .778 = .222,$$

or calculated differently,

$$P(\text{State } 2; \text{ shift } 4 \,|\, \text{state } 1; \text{ shift } 1) = .8(.8)(.2) + .8(.2)(.3) + .2(.7)(.2)$$
$$+ .2(.3)(.3)$$
$$= .128 + .048 + .028 + .018$$
$$= .222.$$

It can be observed from the tree that the probability of the computer's being in state 1 at shift 4, given state 1 at shift 1, would be:

$$P(\text{State } 1; \text{ shift } 4 \,|\, \text{state } 1; \text{ shift } 1) = .8P(\text{State } 1; \text{ shift } 3 \,|\, \text{state } 1; \text{ shift } 1)$$
$$+ .7P(\text{State } 2; \text{ shift } 3 \,|\, \text{state } 1; \text{ shift } 1)$$
$$= .8(.78) + .7(.22) = .624 + .154$$
$$= .778,$$

or in general,

$$P(\text{State } 1; \text{ shift } n+1 \,|\, \text{state } 1; \text{ shift } 1) = .8P(\text{State } 1; \text{ shift } n \,|\, \text{state } 1; \text{ shift } 1)$$
$$+ .7P(\text{State } 2; \text{ shift } n \,|\, \text{state } 1; \text{ shift } 1).$$

Utilizing this formula to review the previous calculations, we can evaluate the probabilities of being in state 1 at various shifts (given state 1 initially) as follows:

$$P(\text{State } 1; \text{ shift } 2 \,|\, \text{state } 1; \text{ shift } 1) = .8(1) = .8,$$

$$P(\text{State } 1; \text{ shift } 3 \,|\, \text{state } 1; \text{ shift } 1) = .8(.8) + .7(.2)$$
$$= .64 + .14 = .78,$$

$$P(\text{State } 1; \text{ shift } 4 \,|\, \text{state } 1; \text{ shift } 1) = .8(.78) + .7(.22)$$
$$= .624 + .154 = .778,$$

$$P(\text{State } 1; \text{ shift } 5 \,|\, \text{state } 1; \text{ shift } 1) = .8(.778) + .7(1-.778)$$
$$= .6224 + .1554 = .7778,$$

$$P(\text{State } 1; \text{ shift } 6 \,|\, \text{state } 1; \text{ shift } 1) = .8(.7778) + .7(.2222)$$
$$= .62224 + .15554 = .77778.$$

If the computer is in state 1 at the initial shift, the probability that it is in state 1 at a subsequent shift tends toward 7/9 as the number of shifts increases.

State 2 as the Initial State

In a like manner, the probability can be calculated for the computer's being in state 1 at any future shift, given that it was in state 2 at shift 1. This

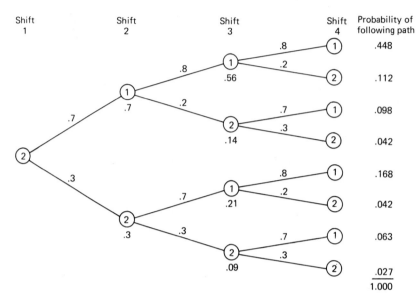

Figure 15-2 Tree showing four shifts when computer starts in state 2

situation is represented by Figure 15-2. The general formula is:

$$P(\text{State 1}; \text{shift } n+1 \,|\, \text{state 2}; \text{shift 1}) = .7P(\text{State 2}; \text{shift } n \,|\, \text{state 2}; \text{shift 1})$$
$$+ .8P(\text{State 1}; \text{shift } n \,|\, \text{state 2}; \text{shift 1}).$$

The probabilities of being in state 1 at various shifts (given state 2 initially) are:

$$P(\text{State 1}; \text{shift 2} \,|\, \text{state 2}; \text{shift 1}) = .7(1) = .7,$$

$$P(\text{State 1}; \text{shift 3} \,|\, \text{state 2}; \text{shift 1}) = .7(.3) + .8(.7)$$
$$= .21 + .56 = .77,$$

$$P(\text{State 1}; \text{shift 4} \,|\, \text{state 2}; \text{shift 1}) = .7(.09 + .14) + .8(.21 + .56)$$
$$= .7(.23) + .8(.77)$$
$$= .161 + .616 = .777,$$

$$P(\text{State 1}; \text{shift 5} \,|\, \text{state 2}; \text{shift 1}) = .7(1 - .777) + .8(.777)$$
$$= .1561 + .6216 = .7777,$$

$$P(\text{State 1}; \text{shift 6} \,|\, \text{state 2}; \text{shift 1}) = .7(1 - .7777) + .8(.7777)$$
$$= .15561 + .62216 = .77777.$$

These figures show that the probability of the computer's being in state 1 at any shift, given that it was in state 2 initially, also tends toward 7/9 as the number of shifts increases.

Interpretation of Results

The calculations indicate that, regardless of the starting state, the probability of the computer's being in state 1 at the start of future shifts tends toward 7/9. For the Markov process, this probability of 7/9 is defined as the steady-state probability of being in state 1. By a similar line of analysis, the probability of being in state 2 can be shown to be 2/9. Logic also shows that if the computer is not in state 1 it will be in state 2; thus, the sum of the two mutually exclusive probabilities (7/9 and 2/9) is unity. Since the steady-state probability of 2/9 indicates that, over a long time period, the probability of the computer's being down at the start of a shift is 2/9, for 2/9 of the time the crew will be available for other assignments. It can also be concluded that, if this policy for crew assignment were followed and the probabilities retained the same values from period to period, the computer would be operating in about 7/9 of the shifts and out of operation in about 2/9 of the shifts. This type of information could help answer such questions as:

1. Will following this policy with this computer provide sufficient computing time to handle a given load?

2. How do the cost and available time for this policy compare with those for another policy—such as one of two-hour shifts, or of keeping the crew on standby rather than making reassignments?

3. How does the cost of this computer compare to that of another computer which provides equivalent or different in-service time?

STEADY-STATE FORMULA FOR TWO STATES

A formula for more efficient computation of a steady-state condition when there are two possible states can be developed. We consider that the system moves from state to state as time (or some other variable) goes from period to period. In the previous analysis we derived the equation,

$$P(\text{State 1}; \text{shift } n+1 \mid \text{state 1}; \text{shift 1}) = .8P(\text{State 1}; \text{shift } n \mid \text{state 1}; \text{shift 1})$$
$$+ .7P(\text{State 2}; \text{shift } n \mid \text{state 1}; \text{shift 1}),$$

where .8 was the probability of remaining in state 1 from one shift to the next and .7 was the probability of going from state 2 to state 1 from one shift to the next. These two values will now be labeled P_{11} and P_{21}, respectively, and *period* will be used instead of *shift* to generalize the relationship. Then

$$P(\text{State 1}; \text{period } n+1 \mid \text{state 1}; \text{period 1})$$
$$= P_{11} P(\text{State 1}; \text{period } n \mid \text{state 1}; \text{period 1})$$
$$+ P_{21} P(\text{State 2}; \text{period } n \mid \text{state 1}; \text{period 1}).$$

As the number of periods, n, increases and a steady state is approached, the probabilities become very similar from period to period. The probability at period n can be set equal to the probability at period $n+1$ if we assume that by that time a steady state will have been reached:

$$P(\text{State 1}; \text{period } n+1 \,|\, \text{state 1}; \text{period 1})$$
$$= P(\text{State 1}; \text{period } n \,|\, \text{state 1}; \text{period 1}).$$

Substituting into the prior equation, we find that

$$P(\text{State 1}; \text{period } n \,|\, \text{state 1}; \text{period 1})$$
$$= P_{11} P(\text{State 1}; \text{period } n \,|\, \text{state 1}; \text{period 1})$$
$$+ P_{21} P(\text{State 2}; \text{period } n \,|\, \text{state 1}; \text{period 1})$$
$$= P_{11} P(\text{State 1}; \text{period } n \,|\, \text{state 1}; \text{period 1})$$
$$+ P_{21} [1 - P(\text{State 1}; \text{period } n \,|\, \text{state 1}; \text{period 1})]$$
$$= \frac{P_{21}}{1 - P_{11} + P_{21}}.$$

Using the numbers from the prior example, we can calculate that

$$P(\text{State 1}; \text{period } n \,|\, \text{state 1}; \text{period 1}) = \frac{.7}{1 - .8 + .7} = \frac{7}{9}.$$

Also,

$$P(\text{State 1}; \text{period } n \,|\, \text{state 2}; \text{period 1}) = \frac{P_{21}}{1 - P_{11} + P_{21}} = \frac{7}{9}.$$

A similar approach will show that

$$P(\text{State 2}; \text{period } n \,|\, \text{state 2}; \text{period 1})$$
$$= P(\text{State 2}; \text{period } n \,|\, \text{state 1}; \text{period 1})$$
$$= \frac{P_{12}}{1 - P_{11} + P_{21}} = \frac{.2}{1 - .8 + .7} = \frac{2}{9}.$$

And also,

$$P(\text{State 2}; \text{period } n \,|\, \text{state 1}; \text{period 1}) = \frac{P_{12}}{1 - P_{11} + P_{21}} = \frac{2}{9}.$$

These formulas provide a direct approach to the steady-state condition by telling us the probability of transition from either state to the other.

THE TRANSITION-MATRIX APPROACH

The previous example considered two possible states or conditions. Markov processes are often applied to marketing problems that concern switching from one brand of a product to another brand. For example,

Table 15-3 Numbers of buyers for three brands of tractors

Brand	Period 1 buyers	Period 2 gains from A	B	C	Period 2 losses to A	B	C	Period 2 net buyers
A	60	0	10	10	0	18	18	44
B	50	18	0	10	10	0	15	53
C	40	18	15	0	10	10	0	53

farmers in a particular county may purchase any one of three brands of tractors. If the typical span of time between purchases is four years, this time is considered a period. Assume that the data shown in Table 15-3 have been collected.

The data from this table are converted to the following transition matrix, which shows transition probabilities.

$$\text{Brand purchased in a period}$$

$$\begin{array}{c} \text{Brand} \\ \text{purchased} \\ \text{in next} \\ \text{period} \end{array} \begin{array}{c} A \\ B \\ C \end{array} \begin{bmatrix} \dfrac{24}{60} = .40 & \dfrac{10}{50} = .20 & \dfrac{10}{40} = .25 \\[2ex] \dfrac{18}{60} = .30 & \dfrac{25}{50} = .50 & \dfrac{10}{40} = .25 \\[2ex] \dfrac{18}{60} = .30 & \dfrac{15}{50} = .30 & \dfrac{20}{40} = .50 \end{bmatrix}$$

This matrix is then simplified as follows.

$$\text{From}$$

$$\text{To} \begin{array}{c} A \\ B \\ C \end{array} \begin{bmatrix} .40 & .20 & .25 \\ .30 & .50 & .25 \\ .30 & .30 & .50 \end{bmatrix}$$

The numbers in the transition matrix can be interpreted in this way:

1. The first row shows that, in any period, brand A retains .40 of its customers and gains .20 of B's customers and .25 of C's customers.
2. The second row shows that, in one period, brand B gains .30 of A's customers, retains .50 of its own customers, and gains .25 of C's customers.
3. The third row shows that, in one period, C gains .30 of A's customers, gains .30 of B's customers, and retains .50 of its own.

It should be noted that the main diagonal of the matrix is really not dealing with "brand-switching" probabilities; the figures represent "brand-loyalty" probabilities. These can more aptly be called retention probabilities; the off-diagonal elements are the switching probabilities.

The reader should note that the calculations of probabilities in the transition matrix assume that the "from" states are along the top and the "to" states are along the left-hand side. This format is not very well standardized, and some articles and textbooks reverse the calculation procedure or the data. When the method described here is used, the data must be arranged with the "from" states along the top of the matrix. We can now continue with the matrix interpretation.

4. The first column is interpreted to mean that, in one period, A retains .40 of its own customers, loses .30 to B, and loses .30 to C.

5. The second column shows that, in one period, B loses .20 of its customers to A, retains .50 of its own, and loses .30 to C.

6. The third column shows that, in one period, C loses .25 of its customers to A, loses .25 to B, and retains .50 of its own.

The following is a generalized transition matrix.

$$
\begin{array}{c}
\text{From} \\
\begin{array}{ccc}
\text{A} & \text{B} & \text{C}
\end{array} \\
\text{To} \;
\begin{array}{c}
\text{A} \\
\text{B} \\
\text{C}
\end{array}
\begin{bmatrix}
P_{AA} & P_{BA} & P_{CA} \\
P_{AB} & P_{BB} & P_{CB} \\
P_{AC} & P_{BC} & P_{CC}
\end{bmatrix}
\end{array}
$$

This transition matrix can now be used to show the rate at which any of the three brands gains or loses market shares and to indicate whether a steady state will be reached in the future. The basic assumption in the use of Markov processes is that the customers shift from one brand to another in accordance with choices made in the past. In a first-order Markov process, the choice in a period depends only upon the outcomes of the prior period. A second-order Markov process assumes that choices for any brand depend upon choices made in the prior two periods. In the same manner, a third-order Markov process assumes that choices in a period depend upon choices in the prior three periods. Only the first-order Markov process is considered here, since it has proved to be a sufficiently reliable forecasting tool for future brand choices in marketing situations. Empirical tests have shown that first-order Markov processes are reliable enough to be preferred to zero-order models, which are not dependent upon past behavior.

The application of Markov chain models to brand switching also involves assumptions about the order of the switching process, its stationarity over the data period, and the likeness or homogeneity of transition matrices for

different consumers. *Stationarity* means that the brand-choice probabilities remain constant over the period of the analysis; they do not shift
from one purchase to the next. These assumptions appear reasonable in
many applications; however, in the long run, the probabilities are likely to
change as a result of marketing deals, new companies entering the field,
and the introduction or closing out of similar products.

A FIRST-ORDER MARKOV PROCESS

Suppose that the market shares in the previous example were .400 for
brand A, .333 for brand B, and .267 for brand C in a given period.
Management desires to predict the share in the next period, based on the
premise that customer shift from this period to the next will be based on the
current state only. This problem can be solved with a first-order Markov
process.

Calculations for Period 2

The expected shares for period 2 are obtained by multiplying the matrix
of transition probabilities by the matrix of market shares in the first period:

$$
\begin{array}{c}
\begin{array}{ccc} A & B & C \end{array} \\
\begin{array}{c} A \\ B \\ C \end{array}
\begin{bmatrix}
.40 & .20 & .25 \\
.30 & .50 & .25 \\
.30 & .30 & .50 \\
\hline
1.00 & 1.00 & 1.00
\end{bmatrix}
\end{array}
\times
\begin{bmatrix}
.400 \\
.333 \\
.267 \\
\hline
1.000
\end{bmatrix}
=
\begin{bmatrix}
.2934 \\
.3532 \\
.3534 \\
\hline
1.0000
\end{bmatrix}.
$$

Transition matrix   Period 1   Period 2
shares   expected shares

A's share in period 2 is obtained by multiplying the first row in the transition matrix by the period 1 shares column.

$$
\begin{aligned}
\text{Ability of A to retain} \times \text{A's share} &= .40 \times .400 = .1600 \\
\text{Ability of A to acquire} \times \text{B's share} &= .20 \times .333 = .0666 \\
\text{Ability of A to acquire} \times \text{C's share} &= .25 \times .267 = \underline{.0668} \\
\text{A's share in period 2} &= .2934
\end{aligned}
$$

B's share in period 2 is obtained by multiplying the second row by the period
1 shares column.

$$
\begin{aligned}
.30 \times .400 &= .1200 \\
.50 \times .333 &= .1665 \\
.25 \times .267 &= \underline{.0667} \\
\text{B's share in period 2} &= .3532
\end{aligned}
$$

C's share in period 2 is obtained by multiplying the third row by the period 1 shares column.

$$.30 \times .400 = .1200$$
$$.30 \times .333 = .0999$$
$$.50 \times .267 = .1335$$
$$\text{C's share in period 2} = \overline{.3534}$$

The market shares for the three brands for period 2 can then be summed as follows.

Brand	Share
A	.2934
B	.3532
C	.3534
	$\overline{1.0000}$

Calculations for Period 3

The market shares for period 3 can be determined by the same procedure. The transition matrix is multiplied by the brand shares for period 2:

$$
\begin{array}{c}
 & \begin{array}{ccc} A & B & C \end{array} \\
\begin{array}{c} A \\ B \\ C \end{array} &
\begin{bmatrix}
.40 & .20 & .25 \\
.30 & .50 & .25 \\
.30 & .30 & .50 \\
\hline
1.00 & 1.00 & 1.00
\end{bmatrix}
\end{array}
\times
\begin{bmatrix}
.2934 \\
.3532 \\
.3534 \\
\hline
1.0000
\end{bmatrix}
=
\begin{bmatrix}
.2763 \\
.3530 \\
.3707 \\
\hline
1.0000
\end{bmatrix}.
$$

Transition matrix	Period 2 expected shares	Period 3 expected shares

Calculations for Period 4

The brand shares for period 4 are calculated in the same way, by multiplying the transition matrix by the shares in period 3:

$$
\begin{array}{c}
 & \begin{array}{ccc} A & B & C \end{array} \\
\begin{array}{c} A \\ B \\ C \end{array} &
\begin{bmatrix}
.40 & .20 & .25 \\
.30 & .50 & .25 \\
.30 & .30 & .50 \\
\hline
1.00 & 1.00 & 1.00
\end{bmatrix}
\end{array}
\times
\begin{bmatrix}
.2763 \\
.3530 \\
.3707 \\
\hline
1.0000
\end{bmatrix}
=
\begin{bmatrix}
.2738 \\
.3520 \\
.3742 \\
\hline
1.0000
\end{bmatrix}.
$$

Transition matrix	Period 3 expected shares	Period 4 expected shares

It can be observed that from period to period the amount of change in brand shares diminishes, and they approach a steady-state condition. A more expedient method of calculating the steady-state condition will be shown later.

Alternate Method of Calculation for Period n

The determination of market shares for any period n could also have been made by raising the transition matrix to the power $n-1$ and multiplying by the original shares in period 1:

$$
\begin{array}{c} \\ A \\ B \\ C \end{array}
\begin{array}{ccc} A & B & C \\ \left[\begin{array}{ccc} .40 & .20 & .25 \\ .30 & .50 & .25 \\ .30 & .30 & .50 \end{array}\right]^{n-1} \end{array}
\times
\left[\begin{array}{c} .400 \\ .333 \\ .267 \end{array}\right]
=
\left[\begin{array}{c} \\ \\ \end{array}\right].
$$

Transition   Period 1   Period n
matrix   shares   expected
shares

The calculation for period 3 would then involve squaring the transition matrix:

$$
\left[\begin{array}{ccc} .40 & .20 & .25 \\ .30 & .50 & .25 \\ .30 & .30 & .50 \end{array}\right]
\times
\left[\begin{array}{ccc} .40 & .20 & .25 \\ .30 & .50 & .25 \\ .30 & .30 & .50 \end{array}\right]
=
\left[\begin{array}{ccc} .295 & .255 & .275 \\ .345 & .385 & .325 \\ .360 & .360 & .400 \end{array}\right].
$$

To see how this squaring is accomplished, examine the following sample calculations, which are like those of Chapter 3:

$$
\left[\begin{array}{ccc} .40 & .20 & .25 \end{array}\right]
\times
\left[\begin{array}{c} .40 \\ .30 \\ .30 \end{array}\right]
=
\left[\begin{array}{c} .295 \end{array}\right].
$$

Row 1   Column 1   Row 1, column 1

$$
\left[\begin{array}{ccc} .40 & .20 & .25 \end{array}\right]
\times
\left[\begin{array}{c} .20 \\ .50 \\ .30 \end{array}\right]
=
\left[\begin{array}{c} .255 \end{array}\right].
$$

Row 1   Column 2   Row 1, column 2

$$
\left[\begin{array}{ccc} .30 & .50 & .25 \end{array}\right]
\times
\left[\begin{array}{c} .25 \\ .25 \\ .50 \end{array}\right]
=
\left[\begin{array}{c} .325 \end{array}\right].
$$

Row 2   Column 3   Row 2, column 3

We are squaring the transition matrix because n is 3, and $n-1$ is 2.

The matrix of shares for period 3 is then the transition matrix, squared, times the shares in the first period:

$$
\begin{bmatrix} .40 & .20 & .25 \\ .30 & .50 & .25 \\ .30 & .30 & .50 \end{bmatrix}^2 \times \begin{bmatrix} .400 \\ .333 \\ .267 \end{bmatrix} = \begin{bmatrix} .295 & .255 & .275 \\ .345 & .385 & .325 \\ .360 & .360 & .400 \end{bmatrix} \times \begin{bmatrix} .400 \\ .333 \\ .267 \end{bmatrix}
$$

Transition matrix   Period 1   Transition matrix   Period 1
squared   shares   squared   shares

$$
= \begin{bmatrix} .2763 \\ .3530 \\ .3707 \end{bmatrix}.
$$

Period 3
expected
shares

This provides the same result as calculated for period 3 by the first method. Both methods may require time-consuming calculations; however, computer programs can be used to solve Markov-process problems.

STEADY-STATE CONDITIONS

In the problem we have been discussing, as the number of periods increases, the market shares of the competitors approach a steady state, or equilibrium. This will happen whenever two conditions are met:

1. The changes from period to period are constant. In other words, the transition matrix remains the same from one period to the next.

2. It is possible to go from one state to another state. This is often referred to as an *ergodic* property of the Markov chain. Some nonergodic situations will be described later.

The steady state will be the same, regardless of the starting conditions.

The steady-state or equilibrium condition can be determined by the use of matrix algebra and the solution of a set of simultaneous equations. The steady-state condition for the market-shares problem is shown by

$$
\begin{array}{ccc} & A & B & C \end{array}
$$

$$
\begin{array}{c} A \\ B \\ C \end{array} \begin{bmatrix} .40 & .20 & .25 \\ .30 & .50 & .25 \\ .30 & .30 & .50 \end{bmatrix} \times \begin{bmatrix} S_A \\ S_B \\ S_C \end{bmatrix} = \begin{bmatrix} S_A \\ S_B \\ S_C \end{bmatrix}.
$$

Transition matrix   Period   Period n
$n-1$ shares
shares

The shares in period $n-1$ are the same as the shares in period n, because a steady-state condition has been reached.

By multiplying the two matrices together and setting each value equal to the share in period n, we achieve the following set of equations. The final equation is based on the fact that the shares in any period must total unity.

$$.40S_A + .20S_B + .25S_C = S_A,$$
$$.30S_A + .50S_B + .25S_C = S_B,$$
$$.30S_A + .30S_B + .50S_C = S_C,$$
$$S_A + \quad S_B + \quad S_C = 1.0.$$

Collecting terms changes the set of equations to

$$-.60S_A + .20S_B + .25S_C = 0,$$
$$.30S_A - .50S_B + .25S_C = 0,$$
$$.30S_A + .30S_B - .50S_C = 0,$$
$$S_A + \quad S_B + \quad S_C = 1.0.$$

The values for the steady-state shares, S_A, S_B, and S_C, can then be found by solving these equations simultaneously. There are four equations and three unknowns; however, since there is some interrelationship in the first three equations, any two of the first three equations plus the last will provide the solution.

Subtracting the second equation from the first gives us the following result.

$$-.60S_A + .20S_B + .25S_C = 0$$
$$\underline{-(+.30S_A - .50S_B + .25S_C = 0)}$$
$$-.90S_A + .70S_B \qquad\quad = 0$$

In other words,

$$S_B = \frac{9}{7}S_A.$$

Using the same pair of original equations, we can multiply the first by 5 and the second by 2, and then subtract.

$$-3.00S_A + S_B + 1.25S_C = 0$$
$$\underline{-(\ .60S_A + S_B + \ .50S_C = 0)}$$
$$-2.40S_A \qquad\quad + 1.75S_C = 0$$

Rearranging this result gives us

$$S_C = \frac{240}{175}S_A.$$

We substitute these values into the last equation to solve for S_A:

$$S_A + \frac{9}{7}S_A + \frac{240}{175}S_A = 1,$$
$$S_A + 1.286S_A + 1.371S_A = 1,$$
$$3.657S_A = 1,$$
$$S_A = .2735.$$

Then

$$S_B = 1.286S_A = 1.286(.2735) = .3516,$$

and

$$S_C = 1.371S_A = 1.371(.2734) = .3749.$$

We can check the calculations by adding S_A, S_B, and S_C to see that their sum is 1.0.

Because the period-to-period transition probabilities remain the same, S_A, S_B, and S_C represent the equilibrium reached after a number of periods. The gains or losses from one period to the next start out large and gradually decrease. The changes in A's share of the market from period to period are plotted in Figure 15-3. The solid line is based on the assumption that A begins with 100 percent of the market, and the dashed line on the assumption that A begins with 40 percent. The same equilibrium points will be reached for a given transition matrix regardless of the initial shares. For example, assume that A starts out with 100 percent of the market. The shares for the second period would then be:

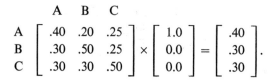

$$\begin{array}{c} \\ A \\ B \\ C \end{array} \begin{array}{ccc} A & B & C \\ \left[\begin{array}{ccc} .40 & .20 & .25 \\ .30 & .50 & .25 \\ .30 & .30 & .50 \end{array}\right] \end{array} \times \left[\begin{array}{c} 1.0 \\ 0.0 \\ 0.0 \end{array}\right] = \left[\begin{array}{c} .40 \\ .30 \\ .30 \end{array}\right].$$

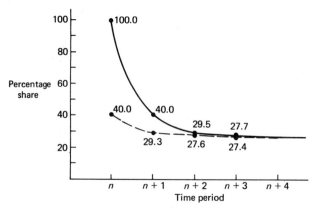

Figure 15-3 Share of market for brand A through several periods

The shares for the third period would be:

$$
\begin{bmatrix} .40 & .20 & .25 \\ .30 & .50 & .25 \\ .30 & .30 & .50 \end{bmatrix} \times \begin{bmatrix} .40 \\ .30 \\ .30 \end{bmatrix} = \begin{bmatrix} .295 \\ .345 \\ .360 \end{bmatrix}.
$$

And those for the fourth period would be:

$$
\begin{bmatrix} .40 & .20 & .25 \\ .30 & .50 & .25 \\ .30 & .30 & .50 \end{bmatrix} \times \begin{bmatrix} .295 \\ .345 \\ .360 \end{bmatrix} = \begin{bmatrix} .277 \\ .351 \\ .372 \end{bmatrix}.
$$

In this example, when A starts with a 100 percent market share, the shares change very rapidly in the second period and then approach the same equilibrium condition that we derived previously for an initial market share of 40 percent. That is why, when we solve the equations to obtain the steady-state condition, the original shares of the market do not enter the solution procedure.

After a steady-state solution is determined, the computations can be verified by multiplying the steady-state shares by the transition matrix. In our example, this would give:

$$
\begin{bmatrix} .40 & .20 & .25 \\ .30 & .50 & .25 \\ .30 & .30 & .50 \end{bmatrix} \times \begin{bmatrix} .2735 \\ .3516 \\ .3749 \end{bmatrix} = \begin{bmatrix} .2735 \\ .3516 \\ .3749 \end{bmatrix}.
$$

The shares obtained are identical to the shares in the prior period, proving that a steady state has been reached.

OTHER EQUILIBRIUM ANALYSES

A condition of equilibrium or a steady state will be reached if the system can move from one state to another and if the transition matrix remains the same. In the following case, A gains no customers but loses to B and C.

	A	B	C
A	.80	.00	.00
B	.15	.70	.20
C	.05	.30	.80

It is apparent that B and C will eventually take all of the customers from A. On the other hand, with the following transition matrix, A would lose no customers from period to period.

$$
\begin{array}{c}
\begin{array}{ccc} \text{A} & \text{B} & \text{C} \end{array} \\
\begin{array}{c} \text{A} \\ \text{B} \\ \text{C} \end{array}
\left[
\begin{array}{ccc}
1.0 & .08 & .10 \\
0.0 & .70 & .10 \\
0.0 & .12 & .80
\end{array}
\right]
\end{array}
$$

Eventually, in the steady state, A will gain all of the customers. This condition, in which one brand gains all of the customers, is sometimes referred to as a *sink*.

MARKETING-STRATEGY APPLICATIONS

The primary application of Markov processes is to marketing. As we have seen, the transition matrix, as determined from collected data, can be utilized to predict eventual market shares. The basic limitation is, of course, the assumption that the transition matrix is fixed from period to period. It can be expected that competitors will take actions to change the matrix values. The Markov approach is useful, however, to show the probable outcome if the present condition is projected into the future. It is especially applicable to short-term predicting, for which the period elapses before the competitors can react.

Take a matrix of the following form, in which the rows represent retention and gain and the columns show retention and loss.

$$
\begin{array}{c}
\begin{array}{ccc} \text{A} & \text{B} & \text{C} \end{array} \\
\begin{array}{c} \text{A} \\ \text{B} \\ \text{C} \end{array}
\left[
\begin{array}{ccc}
.40 & .10 & .20 \\
.40 & .50 & .30 \\
.20 & .40 & .50
\end{array}
\right]
\end{array}
$$

Calculation by the method described would show that the market shares would tend toward the equilibrium of $S_A = .20$, $S_B = .40$, and $S_C = .40$.

Under these circumstances, the producers of brand A would probably not be satisfied with the expected result. They might plan a price-discount campaign to retain their own customers—for example, by providing a coupon in each package that would give the customer a discount on the next purchase. Suppose that they determine that their campaign efforts would change the transition matrix to the following.

$$
\begin{array}{c}
\begin{array}{ccc} \text{A} & \text{B} & \text{C} \end{array} \\
\begin{array}{c} \text{A} \\ \text{B} \\ \text{C} \end{array}
\left[
\begin{array}{ccc}
.60 & .10 & .20 \\
.30 & .50 & .30 \\
.10 & .40 & .50
\end{array}
\right]
\end{array}
$$

This effort would cost $50,000 and would result in revised steady-state expected shares of $S_A = .245$, $S_B = .415$, and $S_C = .340$. Note that comparisons can be made between the two sets of equilibrium shares because they were calculated using separate transition matrices. The proposed policy would increase A's share of the market from .20 to .245. This strategy is to be compared to another marketing strategy, which would place more emphasis on gaining customers from B and C and less emphasis on retention. This second program would also cost $50,000, and the expected associated transition matrix would be:

$$
\begin{array}{c c c c}
 & A & B & C \\
A & \left[\begin{array}{c c c} .40 & .30 & .40 \\ .40 & .50 & .10 \\ .20 & .20 & .50 \end{array}\right]
\end{array}.
$$

In the resulting steady-state condition, $S_A = .375$, $S_B = .359$, and $S_C = .270$. Therefore the second strategy, which concentrates on acquisition of new customers, would appear to offer better results than the strategy of concentrating on retention of existing customers. If the costs of the two programs were not the same, it would be necessary to compare the expected shares to the relative costs of the strategies. This type of evaluation can be applied to other brand-share prediction problems.

In utilizing Markov models in market-share or other analyses, we must be careful to remember the assumptions made, since these become necessary conditions for successful application of the models. In summary, these assumptions are:

1. The probability of a transition, in first-order models, depends upon the current state and not upon prior periods.

2. Transition probabilities can be measured. For market-share applications, the firm may have to collect a set of household-purchase data over a period of time.

3. Transition probabilities remain stable over the period of application of the model. They do not change over time.

4. The probabilities are relatively homogeneous for all consumers; in other words, one group of consumers behaves like any other group.

5. When the problem concerns market shares, the consumers must purchase equal quantities each time they visit the market. We can see that the example of tractor purchases may be more amenable to Markov analysis than one dealing with hand soap or coffee.

6. Market conditions, including competitive strategies and market size, remain relatively constant.

PROBLEMS

1. Evaluate the following transition matrix, and determine the expected market share after one period if the initial shares are 10 percent for A, 40 percent for B, and 50 percent for C. Also determine the expected equilibrium condition.

From

		A	B	C
	A	.90	.05	.20
To	B	.10	.80	.20
	C	.00	.15	.60

2. A construction-crew foreman has kept records for a piece of earth-moving equipment, showing that if the item starts on one day the probability that it will start on the following day is .7. If it does not start on one day and a mechanic has to be called, the probability that it will start on the next day is .6. Assuming that it starts on day 1, draw a tree to show the probability of its starting on days 2, 3, and 4.

3. (a) For problem 2, determine the same probabilities by use of a transition matrix.
   (b) Calculate the steady-state probabilities if the machine starts on day 1.
   (c) Calculate the steady-state probabilities if the mechanic must be called on day 1.

4. The following represents a matrix of transition probabilities for three companies, A, B, and C. Determine the equilibrium market shares. Prove that the answer is correct.

From

		A	B	C
	A	.70	.30	.10
To	B	.10	.60	.20
	C	.20	.10	.70

5. Determine the equilibrium shares for the following transition matrix.

From

		A	B	C
	A	1.0	.20	.10
To	B	0.0	.70	.10
	C	0.0	.10	.80

6. Three competing companies, A, B, and C, came out with a new product in the same year, and in the first year of competition each company had an equal share of the market. During the first year, collected data showed the following.

Losses to

		A	B	C
	A	.80	.12	.08
Company	B	.20	.70	.10
	C	.05	.05	.90

If the total market size does not change, what are the market shares held at the beginning of the second year? If the buying pattern remains the same, what equilibrium condition can be predicted?

7. The Abar Taxi Company has the policy that cabs should return to the nearest stand if there is no assigned call. The company maintains three stands in the city—A, B, and C—and 24 cabs. Data show that cabs starting at each location return to other locations with the following probabilities.

Return to

		A	B	C
	A	.8	.2	.0
Start at	B	.2	.0	.8
	C	.2	.2	.6

Determine the expected number of cabs at each stand after a large number of calls.

8. A company factory consists of three buildings. A crew of 20 messsengers carry documents from one building to another and then wait at a station in the second building for the next assignment. The transition matrix for movement between buildings is as follows.

From

		X	Y	Z
	X	.20	.10	.50
To	Y	.50	.60	.00
	Z	.30	.30	.50

If there are about 200 messages per day, predict how the messengers will be distributed at the end of a day.

9. According to a construction company's policy, if it is raining at 7:30 A.M. work crews do not come in to work. Data have shown that if the crews come in to work on one day, the probability of acceptable weather on the next day is .7. If the crews do not come in to work on one day, the probability of acceptable weather on the next is .6. On what percentage of the days will the crews work? If a job were estimated to require 200 man-days, and a 4-man crew were used on a 5-day-per-week basis, what would be the expected time of completion in weeks?

SUPPLEMENTARY READINGS

Derman, C. *Finite State Markov Decision Processes.* Academic Press, New York, 1970.

Hillier, F. S., and G. J. Lieberman. *Introduction to Operations Research.* Holden-Day, San Francisco, 1974, chapter 12.

Howard, R. A. *Dynamic Programming and Markov Processes.* M.I.T. Press, Cambridge, Mass., 1960.

Kenney, John G., and J. Laurie Snell. *Finite Markov Chains.* Prentice-Hall, Englewood Cliffs, N.J., 1960.

Martin, J. J. *Bayesian Decision Problems and Markov Chains.* Wiley, New York, 1967.

16/Integer Programming

INTEGER programming is a special case of linear programming. In linear programming, the variables are permitted to take on fractional values—they are said to be continuous. Often, however, an optimum solution is necessary when some or all of the variables are integers. Suppose the solution to a linear programming problem indicates

> Hire 3.6 more people, *or*
> Buy 4.7 machines, *or*
> Build 1.4 additional loading docks.

The solution has not provided a usable answer, because it cannot be said that the optimum integer solution in any of the three cases would be the nearest integer value. One might suppose that the way to obtain the best integer solution would be to solve as if the variables were continuous and then round off. But if the optimum linear programming solution were to hire 3.6 people, and this and all other variables were required to take on integer values, the optimum solution would not necessarily be either 4 or 3. The rounded figure may not be optimum or feasible.

While some special classes of linear programming procedures, such as the transportation method, will yield integer solutions, there is no assurance that we will be able to identify the optimum integer value by the general linear programming approach.

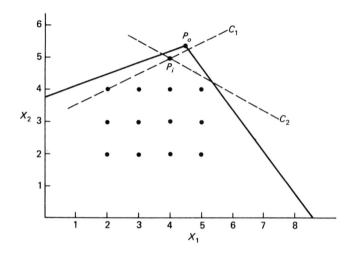

Figure 16-1 Secondary-constraint approach to an integer programming problem

Integer programming problems are classified as *pure* and *mixed*. In the former, integer solutions are required for all variables, while in mixed integer programming problems only some of the variables need to take on integer values.

There are many techniques for solving integer programming problems, but they fall into two basic categories. One of the basic approaches is the branch-and-bound technique. In this process, a finite but large possible number of integer solutions is established; the solutions are then sorted and reduced by upper and lower bounds until the possibilities are exhausted and the optimum solution is isolated. The second of the two basic approaches introduces secondary constraints, which narrow the feasible region around the integer solution points. The cutting-plane algorithm developed by R. E. Gomory is the best-known example of this approach.[*] In Figure 16-1 the constraints are shown. The optimum solution occurs at P_o, which is nonintegral for both variables. The secondary-constraint approach involves selecting additional constraints, C_1 and C_2, that force the nonintegral solution toward the optimum of the integer solutions, which are shown by the dots on the figure. In this case the optimum integer solution would be P_i.

* R. E. Gomory, "An Algorithm for Integer Solutions to Linear Programs," in *Recent Advances in Mathematical Programming*, ed. R. L. Graves and P. Wolfe, McGraw-Hill, New York, 1963.

THE BRANCH-AND-BOUND APPROACH

In many types of optimization problems that require integer solutions, the set of possible solutions consists of a finite number of items. It is, of course, possible to enumerate all of the combinations to find the one that provides the maximum or minimum value, depending upon the objective; but the branch-and-bound technique can be applied to many problems of this nature to obtain a solution more efficiently.

The branch-and-bound technique seeks a solution by a sequence of systematic steps. In the initial step, the total set of possible solutions is divided into smaller subsets. At the same time, upper or lower bounds are established for each subset in such a way that certain of the subjects can be discarded from the solutions under consideration. If the upper bound on all the values in a subset is lower than a presently available solution, when the objective is maximization, then there is no reason to examine the solutions in that subset further. When this approach is applied successfully, only a small portion of the total set of possible solutions needs to be specifically identified. In a minimization problem, the optimum solution would be shown to be smaller than any other examined solution and also smaller than any lower bound of the subsets that were not examined.

A Minimization Example

An assignment problem of the type discussed in Chapter 13 can now be examined and solved by the branch-and-bound technique. Consider a situation in which a company has four jobs to be done and four machines to do them. Any of the machines can perform any of the jobs, but because of the differences in the jobs and varied compatibilities with the machines, the times needed to perform any job are different for the various machines. Assume in this problem that the labor rates are the same for operators of all the machines, resulting in equal cost-per-hour figures. The objective is to minimize the total hours consumed to complete the four jobs; this will minimize the costs. (If the costs were different for the different machines, this factor could easily be brought into the problem.)

Table 16-1 is a time matrix for the four jobs on the four machines. Step 1 in the branch-and-bound technique is to establish the lower bound for all of the possible solutions. Since there are four machines and four jobs, each job must be assigned to a machine and all machines must be utilized. If there were a greater number of machines than jobs, a dummy job would be set in the matrix, and the machine assigned the dummy job in the solution would not be used. In this case there are 4! or 24 possible assignment arrangements—that is, 24 possible feasible solutions. The

Table 16-1 Matrix showing time (in hours) to complete each job with each machine

Job / Machine	R	S	T	U
A	56	48	64	52
B	76	40	60	64
C	64	32	80	68
D	80	60	52	56

lower bound of all solutions, LB, can be established by summing the lowest time elements in each column:

$$LB = 56 + 32 + 52 + 52 = 192.$$

It is obvious that this is not a feasible solution, since it assigns both jobs R and U to machine A; however, it does establish a limit that none of the solutions can possibly fall below. Therefore our answer will be at least 192 hours.

Step 2 is to make up four subsets—since any of the four machines can be assigned to any job—and to compute the lower bound for each of the subsets. As the steps progress, if a feasible solution can be identified as lower than the lower bound on another subset, then that whole subset can be discarded. If job R were assigned to machine A, there would be 3! or 6 feasible solutions. The lower bound of the feasible solutions for this situation is determined by taking the time of 56 hours to complete job R when it is assigned to machine A and adding the minimum time for each of the three remaining columns, excluding row A:

$$LB = 56 + (32 + 52 + 56) = 196.$$

Job R could be assigned to each other machine in turn in this same manner, resulting in the lower bounds in Table 16-2. Of the four lower bounds in step 1, the 196 is the lowest lower bound; it applies when job R is assigned to machine A. We can also note that three of the solutions are feasible, while the lowest, 196 hours, is not feasible. A feasible solution means here

Table 16-2 Lower bounds of subsets with fixed assignments to machine A

Subset	Calculation		Lower bound
R with A	$56 + (32 + 52 + 56)$	=	196 (not feasible)
R with B	$76 + (32 + 52 + 52)$	=	212 (feasible)
R with C	$64 + (40 + 52 + 52)$	=	208 (feasible)
R with D	$80 + (32 + 60 + 52)$	=	224 (feasible)

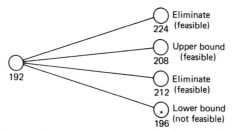

Figure 16-2 Branching diagram for steps 1 and 2

that one job is assigned to each machine. Since the time of 208 hours is the lowest of the feasible solutions, it now establishes an upper bound on the total time to perform the set of jobs. Thus, the answer will lie between 196 and 208. The solutions of 212 and 224 can be discarded as possible optimum solutions, since the known feasible solution of 208 is better. The information compiled thus far can be illustrated by the branching diagram in Figure 16-2.

The lower bound at the end of step 2, 196, is designated with an asterisk (*) in the figure, and job R is assigned to machine A while a search of this subset is made for a solution better than 208. As step 3, job S will be assigned to one of the three remaining machines, B, C, or D. When S is assigned to B, the lower bound for the subset is obtained by adding the times for R with A (56) and S with B (40) to the sum of the minimum times of the two remaining columns, excluding rows A and B:

$$LB = 56 + 40 + (52 + 56) = 204.$$

In a like manner, the other subsets are totaled to provide the results in Table 16-3. These results are presented in the expanded diagram of Figure 16-3. The lower bound at the completion of step 3 is now 196, again identified with an asterisk; this bound applies when R is assigned to A and S is assigned to C.

As the final step, step 4, job T is assigned to each of the two remaining machines. If the two previous assignments are made and T is assigned to B, the remaining lower bound will be:

$$LB = 56 + 32 + 60 + (56) = 204.$$

Table 16-3 Lower bounds of subsets in step 3

Subset	Calculation		Lower bound
(R with A) and (S with B)	56 + 40 + (52 + 56)	=	204 (not feasible)
(R with A) and (S with C)	56 + 32 + (52 + 56)	=	196 (not feasible)
(R with A) and (S with D)	56 + 60 + (60 + 64)	=	240 (not feasible)

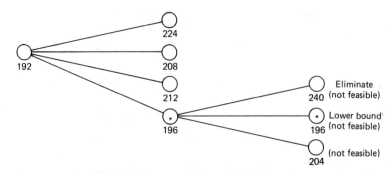

Figure 16-3 Branching diagram at completion of step 3

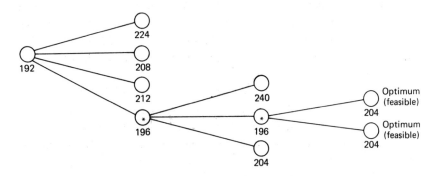

Figure 16-4 Final branching diagram

For the only other alternative, if T were assigned to D, the lower bound would be:

$$LB = 56 + 32 + 52 + (64) = 204.$$

Both of these are feasible solutions. These two solutions are also optimum, since they are equal to or below the lower bound of any unexplored subset. No further steps need be taken, and the final branching diagram is shown in Figure 16-4.

If neither of the values of the final step were below the lower bounds of all other subsets, it would be necessary to select the next lowest branch (in this case 204) for further subdividing in order to find the optimum solution. Although in this problem the procedure may seem trivial, with a larger number of possible feasible solutions the procedure could considerably shorten the time needed to identify the optimum solution.

Maximization Under Uncertainty

A simple maximization problem is handled using the same procedure as for the minimization problem, but the use of upper and lower bounds is

Table 16-4 Probability of successful development of each product by each engineer

Engineer	V $10M	W $10M	X $8M	Y $18M
A	.50	.40	.70	.20
B	.36	.44	.60	.30
C	.52	.60	.50	.28
D	.44	.64	.65	.32

reversed. The following example introduces a factor of uncertainty into the solution of a maximization problem.

A company wants to develop four products into manufacturable designs. Since there are four engineers available, one job must be assigned to each engineer. In Table 16-4, the company has assigned an expected profit value to each product assuming successful development of that product, along with a probability that each engineer can handle each product-development task. The matrix is converted into the conditional-profit matrix of Table 16-5 by multiplying each probability by the expected profit in millions of dollars.

The procedure from this point on is the same as for the simple minimization problem, except that the maximum will be sought. In step 1, the upper bound, UB, over all 24 feasible solutions is found by adding the maximum

Table 16-5 Expected profits in millions of dollars

Engineer	V	W	X	Y
A	5.0	4.0	5.6	3.6
B	3.6	4.4	4.8	5.4
C	5.2	6.0	4.0	5.0
D	4.4	6.4	5.2	5.8

Table 16-6 Upper bounds of subsets in step 2

Subset	Calculation		Upper bound
V with A	5.0 + (6.4 + 5.2 + 5.8)	=	22.4 (not feasible)
V with B	3.6 + (6.4 + 5.6 + 5.8)	=	21.4 (not feasible)
V with C	5.2 + (6.4 + 5.6 + 5.8)	=	23.0 (not feasible)
V with D	4.4 + (6.0 + 5.6 + 5.4)	=	21.4 (feasible)

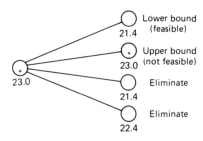

Figure 16-5 Branching diagram for steps 1 and 2

profits of the various columns without regard to feasibility:

$$\text{UB} = 5.2 + 6.4 + 5.6 + 5.8 = 23.0.$$

The same approach was used in the minimization problem except that the smallest values were selected. In step 2, the matrix is divided into subsets, and the upper bound is determined for each one, resulting in Table 16-6, shown on page 323. The equivalent branching diagram is shown in Figure 16-5. Step 3 is now begun, resulting in the calculations of Table 16-7, which is plotted in the branching diagram of Figure 16-6. The final dividing is performed on the upper-bound value of 22.6, which represents the assignment of product V to engineer C and product W to engineer D. If X is now assigned to A,

$$\text{UB} = 5.2 + 6.4 + 5.6 + (5.4) = 22.6.$$

Table 16-7 Upper bounds of subsets in step 3

Subset	Calculation		Upper bound
(V with C) and (W with A)	5.2 + 4.0 + (5.2+5.8)	=	20.2 (not feasible)
(V with C) and (W with B)	5.2 + 4.4 + (5.6+5.8)	=	21.0 (feasible)
(V with C) and (W with D)	5.2 + 6.4 + (5.6+5.4)	=	22.6 (feasible)

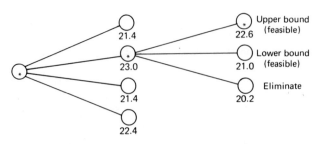

Figure 16-6 Branching diagram for step 3

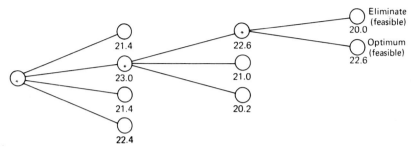

Figure 16-7 Final branching diagram

Table 16-8 Final assignments and expected profit

| Assignment | | Expected profit |
Product	Engineer	(millions)
V with C		$ 5.2
W with D		6.4
X with A		5.6
Y with B		5.4
		$22.6

If X is assigned to B,

$$\text{UB} = 5.2 + 6.4 + 4.8 + (3.6) = 20.0.$$

Both of these solutions are feasible, but the first is higher. Therefore the solution of 22.6, shown in the final branching diagram of Figure 16-7, is the optimum.

The answer, then, is to assign the products to the engineers as in Table 16-8, in order to achieve the optimum expected profit of $22,600,000.

Maximization of Probabilities

The previous problem involved uncertainties in the calculations, and the expected profits were summed to achieve the optimum solution. Next consider a problem in which elements of the same program or project are to be divided among different team members. A construction contractor has four crews, I, II, III, and IV, each of which can be assigned to any of four portions of a road-construction project that must be completed by a specified date. The date is critical, since a shopping center is scheduled to open then and a substantial penalty is provided in the contract if the date is not met. The total project consists of tasks A, B, C, and D. The contractor has considered the capabilities of each crew and has estimated the probabilities in Table 16-9 that the various crews can complete the various

Table 16-9 Probability that each crew can complete each task

Task Crew	A	B	C	D
I	.98	.95	.99	.97
II	.96	.95	.97	.96
III	.92	.90	.94	.98
IV	.87	.90	.92	.90

Table 16-10 Upper bounds of subsets in step 2

Subset	Calculation		Upper bound
A with I	.98 × (.95 × .97 × .98)	=	.8850 (not feasible)
A with II	.96 × (.95 × .99 × .98)	=	.8848 (not feasible)
A with III	.92 × (.95 × .99 × .97)	=	.8393 (not feasible)
A with IV	.87 × (.95 × .99 × .98)	=	.8019 (feasible)

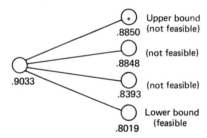

Figure 16-8 Branching diagram for steps 1 and 2

tasks by the required date. The contractor desires to maximize the probability that the total project will be completed by that date.

Step 1 is to find the upper bound for the probability of completing all tasks; it is the product of the largest probabilities in the various columns:

$$UB = .98 \times .95 \times .99 \times .98 = .9033.$$

The calculations and branching diagram for the step 2 subsets are shown in Table 16-10 and Figure 16-8. The procedure is the same as for the previous example, except that now we are multiplying probabilities instead of adding profits.

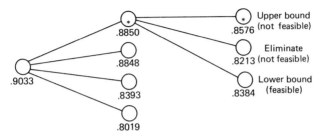

Figure 16-9 Branching diagram for step 3

Table 16-11 Upper bounds of subsets in step 3

Subset	Calculation		Upper bound
(A with I) and (B with II)	$.98 \times .95 \times (.94 \times .98)$	$=$	.8576 (not feasible)
(A with I) and (B with III)	$.98 \times .90 \times (.97 \times .96)$	$=$	.8213 (not feasible)
(A with I) and (B with IV)	$.98 \times .90 \times (.97 \times .98)$	$=$	.8384 (feasible)

This step reveals that the lower bound on the overall probability is .8019 and feasible; the upper bound is now .8850. In step 3, the diagram and calculations in Figure 16-9 and Table 16-11 are obtained. The branch with the upper bound of .8576 is explored next, in Table 16-12 and Figure 16-10. Since the .8394 is higher than .8384, it is not necessary to explore the

Table 16-12 Upper bounds of subsets in step 4

Subset	Calculation		Upper bound
(A with I) and (B with II) and (C with III)	$.98 \times .95 \times .94 \times (.90)$	$=$	.7876 (feasible)
(A with I) and (B with II) and (C with IV)	$.98 \times .95 \times .92 \times (.98)$	$=$	.8394 (feasible)

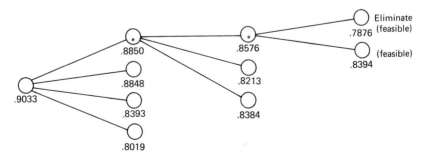

Figure 16-10 Branching diagram for step 4

Table 16-13 Upper bounds of subsets in step 3 (second phase)

Subset	Calculation		Upper bound
(A with II) and (B with I)	.96 × .95 × (.94 × .98)	=	.8401 (not feasible)
(A with II) and (B with III)	.96 × .90 × (.99 × .97)	=	.8297 (not feasible)
(A with II) and (B with IV)	.96 × .90 × (.99 × .98)	=	.8383 (feasible)

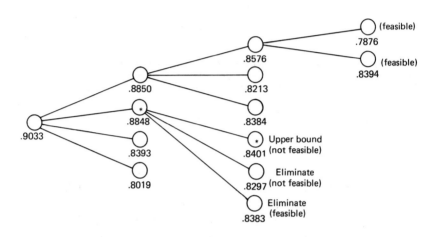

Figure 16-11 Branching diagram for step 3 (second phase)

paths from .8850 further; however, the upper bound of .8848 from step 2 is still greater than the best feasible solution of .8394, so it must be explored further. The value .8848 is investigated in Table 16-13 and Figure 16-11. This investigation concludes with .8394 still the highest feasible solution, but one higher upper bound remains: .8401. The .8401 is investigated next, in Table 16-14. Since none of its values is as high as the feasible solution of .8394, further investigation of this subset is abandoned. Since all feasible values are below the .8394 feasible solution, the .8394 is the optimum solution.

In this problem it was necessary to investigate so many alternatives that it would have been just as easy to enumerate all the alternative solutions;

Table 16-14 Upper bounds of subsets in step 4 (second phase)

Subset	Calculation		Upper bound
(A with II) and (B with I) and (C with III)	.96 × .95 × .94 × (.90)	=	.7715 (feasible)
(A with II) and (B with I) and (C with IV)	.96 × .95 × .92 × (.98)	=	.8223 (feasible)

Table 16-15 Variation of Table 16-1, when one machine is not able to handle one job

Job Machine	R	S	T	U
A	56	200	64	52
B	76	40	60	64
C	64	32	80	68
D	80	60	52	56

however, the problem illustrated the procedure to follow when the optimum solution is not found in the early steps of the process. Although the optimum probability is a decimal, it represents an integer solution, one that assigns whole tasks to whole crews.

Variations
In many real cases, the matrix may not be balanced; however, it can often still be adapted to the branch-and-bound technique. Assume that in the problem represented by Table 16-1 machine A is not able to perform job S. The matrix can still be solved by the branch-and-bound technique by placing a large number, such as 200, in the space previously occupied by the 48, as shown in Table 16-15. The 200 is large enough to force S away from A in the solution process. The problem is then solved in the same manner as before.

THE SECONDARY-CONSTRAINT APPROACH

With the secondary-constraint approach, we begin by obtaining an optimum solution to the linear programming problem without regard to the integer requirement. Additional constraints are then added to force an optimum integer solution. Consider the following problem:

$$\text{Maximize:} \quad X_o = 5X_1 + 4X_2,$$

subject to

$$2X_1 + 4X_2 \leq 32,$$
$$6X_1 + 3X_2 \leq 36.$$

The graphic solution in Figure 16-12 shows that the optimum solution is $X_1 = 2\frac{2}{3}$, $X_2 = 6\frac{2}{3}$. The area of feasible solutions is enclosed by the heavy lines in the figure. The value of the solution is:

$$X_o = 5(2\tfrac{2}{3}) + 4(6\tfrac{2}{3}) = 40.$$

If it were required that X_1 and X_2 both be integers, just dropping the fractions would produce $X_1 = 2$, $X_2 = 6$, with an X_o of 34. But from Figure 16-12, it can be seen that there are a number of other integer solutions, shown by the dots. All of these feasible integer solutions can now form a new feasible-solutions region. This region is bounded by the original constraints plus a new constraint that passes through the integer values:

$$X_1 + X_2 \le 9.$$

Viewing the isoprofit lines, we can see that a line parallel to the isoprofit lines and through the point $X_1 = 3$, $X_2 = 6$, would be farthest from the origin; this, therefore, is the optimum solution.

The secondary-constraint technique tries to identify the additional constraints that will force the solution to the optimum integer solution. In this case, with two variables, the graphic portrayal revealed the proper constraint; however, in more complex linear programming problems, the search for additional constraints can make use of the simplex algorithm.

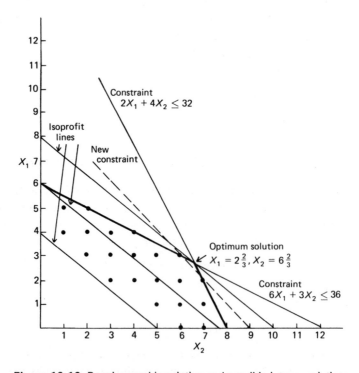

Figure 16-12 Regular graphic solution and possible integer solutions

As an illustration, the same problem can now be restated and solved by the simplex method described in Chapter 11. The problem is:

$$\text{Maximize:} \quad X_o = 5X_1 + 4X_2,$$

subject to

$$2X_1 + 4X_2 \le 32,$$
$$6X_1 + 3X_2 \le 36.$$

The resulting system of equations is:

$$
\begin{aligned}
X_o - 5X_1 - 4X_2 \qquad\qquad &= 0, \\
2X_1 + 4X_2 + X_3 \qquad\quad &= 32, \\
6X_1 + 3X_2 \qquad\quad + X_4 &= 36. \leftarrow
\end{aligned}
$$

In the objective-function equation, the largest negative value is -5, so X_1 is selected for elimination. Since $36/6$ is less than $32/2$, the value $6X_1$ is selected as the pivot. The result is:

$$
\begin{aligned}
X_o \quad -\tfrac{3}{2}X_2 \quad + \tfrac{5}{6}X_4 &= 30, \\
3X_2 + X_3 - \tfrac{1}{3}X_4 &= 20, \leftarrow \\
X_1 + \tfrac{1}{2}X_2 \quad + \tfrac{1}{6}X_4 &= 6.
\end{aligned}
$$

Now X_2 is selected for elimination and $3X_2$ is the pivot:

$$
\begin{aligned}
X_o \quad + \tfrac{1}{2}X_3 + \tfrac{2}{3}X_4 &= 40, \\
X_2 + \tfrac{1}{3}X_3 - \tfrac{1}{9}X_4 &= 6\tfrac{2}{3}, \\
X_1 \quad - \tfrac{1}{6}X_3 + \tfrac{1}{9}X_4 &= 2\tfrac{2}{3}.
\end{aligned}
$$

This provides the optimum solution: $X_1 = 2\tfrac{2}{3}$, $X_2 = 6\tfrac{2}{3}$, $X_o = 40$. A procedure will now be described to derive additional constraints. As each constraint is defined, a new simplex solution will be determined. The procedure is repeated until an integer solution is obtained.

1. The initial step in the approach is to select the constraint equation with the largest fractional part in the solution. In this case the $6\tfrac{2}{3}$ and $2\tfrac{2}{3}$ each have $\tfrac{2}{3}$ as the fraction. Therefore either can be taken; we will select the $6\tfrac{2}{3}$:

$$0X_1 + 1X_2 + \tfrac{1}{3}X_3 - \tfrac{1}{9}X_4 = 6\tfrac{2}{3}.$$

2. The next step is (a) to replace all of the coefficients in the constraint equation by the smallest nonnegative numbers that are congruent to the existing coefficients and (b) to set the result greater than or equal to

the fractional part of the right-hand side of the equation. Two numbers are congruent if their difference is an integer or zero. For example,

$4\frac{3}{4}$ is congruent to $\frac{3}{4}$, since the difference is an integer (4);

$-2\frac{2}{3}$ is congruent to $+\frac{1}{3}$, since when they are subtracted the result is -3;

$\frac{5}{6}$ is congruent to $\frac{5}{6}$, since the difference is zero.

The result is:

$$\tfrac{1}{3}X_3 + \tfrac{8}{9}X_4 \geq \tfrac{2}{3}.$$

3. Subtract a new slack variable, resulting in the equation to be added to the set. In this example the equation is:

$$\tfrac{1}{3}X_3 + \tfrac{8}{9}X_4 - X_5 = \tfrac{2}{3}.$$

This equation is now added to the simplex tableau, resulting in the following:

$$X_o \quad\quad +\tfrac{1}{2}X_3 + \tfrac{2}{3}X_4 \quad\quad = 40,$$
$$X_2 + \tfrac{1}{3}X_3 - \tfrac{1}{9}X_4 \quad\quad = 6\tfrac{2}{3},$$
$$X_1 \quad -\tfrac{1}{6}X_3 + \tfrac{1}{9}X_4 \quad\quad = 2\tfrac{2}{3},$$
$$\tfrac{1}{3}X_3 + \tfrac{8}{9}X_4 - X_5 = \tfrac{2}{3}.$$

4. At this point there are no negative coefficients in the objective-function equation, so we select the variable with the smallest positive coefficient, in this case X_3. The simplex procedure is then carried out to give:

$$X_o \quad\quad -\tfrac{2}{3}X_4 + \tfrac{3}{2}X_5 = 39,$$
$$X_2 \quad - X_4 + X_5 = 6,$$
$$X_1 \quad +\tfrac{5}{9}X_4 - \tfrac{1}{2}X_5 = 3,$$
$$X_3 + \tfrac{8}{3}X_4 - 3X_5 = 2.$$

This provides the optimum integer solution of $X_1 = 3$, $X_2 = 6$, and $X_o = 39$. We can verify the result with the original objective function:

$$X_o = 5(3) + 4(6) = 39.$$

If this step had not provided the integer solution, the equation with the largest fractional part in the right-hand column would have been selected to form the new constraint to be added to the set. The steps would then have been repeated.

PROBLEMS

1. The costs of performing each of four jobs on each of four machines are as follows.

Job Machine	A	B	C	D
I	$24	$32	$15	$31
II	18	19	26	35
III	20	28	30	25
IV	32	25	21	28

   If each job is to be performed by a different machine, make the assignments that will minimize the total cost. Use the branch-and-bound technique.

2. Four divisions of a company have made estimates on each of four contracts. The estimated profit that each division would make on each job is shown below in thousands of dollars.

Job Division	A	B	C	D
W	$42	$34	$40	$50
X	40	35	48	32
Y	38	40	29	39
Z	30	28	33	46

   Use the branch-and-bound approach to determine how to assign the jobs so as to maximize overall company profits.

3. Solve problem 2 with the assumption that division Z could not handle job C.

4. Determine the optimum solution and optimum integer solution of

$$\text{Maximize:} \quad X_o = X_1 + 4X_2,$$

   subject to

$$2X_1 + \ X_2 \le 5,$$
$$X_1 + 3X_2 \le 4.$$

5. Determine the optimum solution and optimum integer solution of

$$\text{Maximize:} \quad X_o = 30X_1 + 40X_2 + 20X_3,$$

subject to

$$2X_1 + 4X_2 + 3X_3 \leq 60,$$
$$2X_1 + X_2 + 2X_3 \leq 40,$$
$$2X_1 + 3X_2 + X_3 \leq 80.$$

6. Determine the optimum solution and optimum integer solution of

$$\text{Maximize:} \quad X_o = 2X_1 + 3X_2,$$

subject to

$$2X_1 + 2X_2 \leq 8,$$
$$4X_1 + 3X_2 \leq 10.$$

7. Determine the optimum solution and optimum integer solution of

$$\text{Minimize:} \quad X_o = X_1 - 2X_2,$$

subject to

$$6X_1 + 2X_2 \leq 9,$$
$$X_1 + 2X_2 \leq 4.$$

SUPPLEMENTARY READINGS

Beale, E. M. L. "Survey of Integer Programming." *Operations Research Quarterly*, 16 (June 1965), 219–228.

Forrest, J. J. H., J. P. Hirst, and J. A. Tomlin. "Practical Solution of Large Mixed Integer Programming Problems with Umpire." *Management Science*, 20 (January 1974), 736–773.

Gomory, R. E. "An Algorithm for Integer Solutions to Linear Programs." In *Recent Advances in Mathematical Programming*, edited by R. L. Graves and P. Wolfe. McGraw-Hill, New York, 1963.

Lawler, E. L., and D. E. Wood. "Branch and Bound Methods: A Survey." *Operations Research*, 14 (July–August 1966), 699–719.

17/Zero-One Programming

ZERO-ONE programming is a powerful technique for solving certain types of practical problems that are not readily solvable by the techniques described in the preceding chapters. Zero-one programming is another form of mathematical programming that searches for the best possible value of an objective function that satisfies a set of constraints. In linear programming, we ask *how much* of each variable, X_1, X_2, and so forth, to include; in zero-one programming, the solution shows *whether or not* to include each variable. In linear programming problems, each variable is free to take on any value within the constraint limits. Since the functions are continuous, each variable can assume an infinite number of values. In integer programming problems, the variables are limited to a finite number of integer values. In zero-one problems, the variable can take on only one of two values. Some typical areas in which the zero-one technique is of practical use are capital budgeting, maintenance, assignment, and dispatching.

A capital-budgeting problem may involve selecting equipment from among a number of alternatives. A piece of equipment is either selected or rejected. In a routing problem, a path is either chosen or not chosen. If several products are under consideration for development, a product is either selected or omitted. If a certain number of employees are available for assignment to a variety of jobs, an employee is either assigned to a job or not assigned to that job. In each of these problem situations, an alternative is either taken or not taken. The decision is a yes-no type of decision.

Since computer programs are available to solve zero-one programming problems, and solution by hand is not practical, this chapter will simply describe the techniques and concepts of zero-one programming, define the types or categories of problems to which the technique is applicable, and provide examples of how to set up the equation for a zero-one programming problem. A FORTRAN program for solving zero-one linear programming problems is given by McMillan and by Plane and Kochenberger.[1]

AN ASSIGNMENT PROBLEM

Assignment problems are frequently encountered. They are characterized by the requirement that a number of items be matched with an equal number of alternatives. Consider an example in which there are four workers available and four tasks to be completed. The different workers have different skills and wage rates. A cost has been determined for each worker-task combination, as shown in Table 17-1. Each employee is to be assigned exactly one task.

Variables with double subscripts will be used, since they make the formulation of the problem much easier. The first of the two subscripts refers to the row or worker and the second to the column or task. Thus, x_{23} refers to worker 2 performing task 3. We define x_{ij} as 1 if worker i is assigned to task j; otherwise, x_{ij} equals 0. The objective function can then be stated as:

$$\text{Minimize:} \quad x_o = 5x_{11} + 3x_{12} + 7x_{13} + 8x_{14} + 4x_{21} + 4x_{22}$$
$$+ 6x_{23} + 9x_{24} + 7x_{31} + 8x_{32} + 10x_{33} + 12x_{34}$$
$$+ 9x_{41} + 3x_{42} + 3x_{43} + 15x_{44}.$$

Table 17-1   Costs of task assignments

Worker \ Task	1	2	3	4
1	$5	$3	$ 7	$ 8
2	4	4	6	9
3	7	8	10	12
4	9	3	3	15

---

[1] Claude McMillan, Jr., *Mathematical Programming*, Wiley, New York, 1970, chapters 11–12, appendices C and H; and D. R. Plane and G. A. Kochenberger, *Operations Research for Managerial Decisions*, Irwin, Homewood, Ill., 1972, chapter 4, appendix A.

Since each x_{ij} will be either 1 or 0, this equation becomes merely the sum of the costs of the assignments made. The constraints require that each worker receive exactly one task:

$$x_{11} + x_{12} + x_{13} + x_{14} = 1,$$
$$x_{21} + x_{22} + x_{23} + x_{24} = 1,$$
$$x_{31} + x_{32} + x_{33} + x_{34} = 1,$$
$$x_{41} + x_{42} + x_{43} + x_{44} = 1.$$

The first equation represents the constraint that worker 1 receive just one task; the second represents the same constraint for worker 2; and so on. A group of additional constraints then provides that each task will be assigned to exactly one employee:

$$x_{11} + x_{21} + x_{31} + x_{41} = 1,$$
$$x_{12} + x_{22} + x_{32} + x_{42} = 1,$$
$$x_{13} + x_{23} + x_{33} + x_{43} = 1,$$
$$x_{14} + x_{24} + x_{34} + x_{44} = 1.$$

And, lastly, there is the usual zero-one constraint,

$$x_{ij} = 0 \text{ or } 1.$$

There are other types of problems for which this approach can be used, such as assigning shipments to vehicles, crews to airplanes, and jobs to machines. If there were more workers than tasks in this problem, a slack or dummy task could be added, and the associated cost would be the idle cost for an employee who is not assigned.

A KNAPSACK PROBLEM

Knapsack problems derive their name from the dilemma of the hiker or explorer who is going on an expedition and trying to decide which items to pack in a knapsack. A value is assigned to each item under consideration. The objective is to maximize the total value of the contents carried, given various weight, volume, and cost constraints. The technique for solving this type of problem has practical applications to capital-budgeting problems and to equipment design.

As an example of a knapsack problem, consider a cookware company that is designing a sales display case to be carried by the door-to-door salespeople. For each item of cookware, the following information is available: the item's expected sales for the coming year; its cost; and its weight. The company wishes to construct a display case that maximizes the total expected sales for the items selected. The display case is limited to 20 items, of whatever size (although some pots and pans are larger than others, the larger ones would allow smaller ones to fit inside). Each display case is also limited to $140 worth of items, and to no more than 48 pounds. There are three constraints, then—on quantity, cost, and weight.

Although the sales manager may say at this point, "Which items of cookware should the salespeople take?" the operations researcher may say, "How many of each item should be taken?" The researcher would then define x_i as the quantity of cookware item i to be carried, and x_i would be constrained to be either 0 or 1. This means that if x_i equals 1, item i is selected for the display case; if x_i equals 0, it is not selected. The problem, seen as a qualitative problem by the sales manager, is now formulated quantitatively. Additional symbols are defined:

$$s_i = \text{sales forecast for the coming year for item } i,$$
$$c_i = \text{cost of item } i,$$
$$w_i = \text{weight of item } i.$$

The objective is to maximize the total expected sales of the items selected:

$$\text{Maximize:} \quad x_o = s_1 x_1 + s_2 x_2 + s_3 x_3 + \cdots + s_n x_n,$$

or

$$\text{Maximize:} \quad x_o = \sum_{i=1}^{n} s_i x_i,$$

where there are n items of cookware under consideration. If item i is included, x_i has a value of 1, and s_i is included in the sum. If x_i is zero, the item is not included in the display case, and s_i does not enter into the value of x_o.

Next it is necessary to quantify the constraints. The weight limitation of 48 pounds can be expressed by setting the sum of the weights of all the items selected equal to or less than 48:

$$w_1 x_1 + w_2 x_2 + w_3 x_3 + \cdots + w_n x_n \leq 48,$$

or

$$\sum_{i=1}^{n} w_i x_i \leq 48.$$

Also, only 20 items of cookware can be taken. Since any differences in volume from item to item are being neglected here, the constraint can be specified as:

$$x_1 + x_2 + x_3 + \cdots + x_n \leq 20 \quad \text{or} \quad \sum_{i=1}^{n} x_i \leq 20.$$

The cost constraint, limiting the cost of items in the display case to $140, can be handled similarly:

$$\sum_{i=1}^{n} c_i x_i \leq 140.$$

As a final requirement, it is necessary to specify that

$$x_i = 0 \text{ or } 1.$$

The objective function and the constraints completely define the problem. As in linear programming, almost all real zero-one problems are solved by computer programs; this is actually the only possible way to solve the majority of them. There is no practical systematic procedure for solving zero-one programs by hand computation.

The cookware problem could be expanded to illustrate how some other constraints might be introduced. Suppose that there are six styles of frying pans in the company catalogue, but the company has decided that the display case will be limited to two frying pans. Further, suppose that the frying pans are represented by $i = 10$ through $i = 15$. The constraint can be formulated as:

$$x_{10} + x_{11} + x_{12} + x_{13} + x_{14} + x_{15} \leq 2,$$

or

$$\sum_{i=10}^{15} x_i \leq 2.$$

As an additional consideration, assume that certain items would not be selected unless certain other items were also included in the display case. For instance, assume that items 34 and 35 go with pan 30 and would not be included in the display case unless pan 30 were included. However, item 30 could be included without items 34 or 35, item 34 could be taken without 35, and item 35 could be taken without 34. A logical explanation might be that 34 and 35 were inserts to 30, such as in a double boiler whose basic pan could be used alone. This constraint could then be specified as:

$$x_{30} - x_{35} \geq 0$$

and

$$x_{30} - x_{34} \geq 0.$$

When x_{30} equals 0, item 30 is not taken. Also, x_{34} and x_{35} must be 0 (not taken) to satisfy the constraint. When $x_{30} = 1$, however, x_{34} can be 1 or 0 and x_{35} can be 1 or 0. In summary, the complete problem is represented as follows, where n is the number of alternative items being considered.

$$\text{Maximize:} \quad x_o = \sum_{i=1}^{n} s_i x_i \quad \text{(objective function)},$$

$$\sum_{i=1}^{n} x_i \le 20 \quad \text{(quantity constraint)},$$

$$\sum_{i=1}^{n} c_i x_i \le 140 \quad \text{(cost constraint)},$$

$$\sum_{i=1}^{n} w_i x_i \le 48 \quad \text{(weight constraint)},$$

$$\sum_{i=10}^{15} x_i \le 2 \quad \text{(frying-pan constraint)},$$

$$x_{30} - x_{34} \ge 0 \quad \text{(combination constraint)},$$

$$x_{30} - x_{35} \ge 0 \quad \text{(combination constraint)},$$

$$x_i = 0 \text{ or } 1 \quad \text{(zero-one constraint)}.$$

There are other types of knapsack problems. A common application of the technique, as we mentioned earlier, is to capital budgeting, in which projects to be funded must be selected from alternatives. Another practical problem involves determination of what to take on a space mission or a nuclear-submarine voyage. In the commercial area, a similar problem would be to determine what tools and spare parts to carry on a service van.

It might seem possible to solve a zero-one knapsack problem simply by listing or enumerating all possibilities; however, the number of possible combinations can become very large. If there were five different items for consideration, there would be 2^5 or 32 possible solutions; with 50 alternatives, the enumeration would become nearly impossible. Even with a computer, a problem with 100 alternatives is difficult to handle, and a more systematic approach becomes necessary. A computer program described by Plane and Kochenberger, which provides this systematic approach, has been used to solve problems with up to 40 alternatives.[2]

A TRAVELING-SALESMAN PROBLEM

Consider a salesman who must visit each of five cities. He is presently in one of the cities. Let d_{ij} equal the distance from city i to city j. Also let x_{ij}, equal to either 1 or 0, designate whether the salesman will go from city i directly to city j. The problem is illustrated by Figure 17-1.

---

[2] Plane and Kochenberger, appendix A.

Since the objective is to determine the route of minimum distance, the objective function is the sum of all the distances, each multiplied by the appropriate x_{ij}, where x_{ij} is either zero or one:

$$\text{Minimize:} \quad x_o = \sum_{i=1}^{5} \sum_{j=1}^{5} d_{ij} x_{ij}.$$

The following constraint states that the salesman must leave city 1 once and once only:

$$x_{11} + x_{12} + x_{13} + x_{14} + x_{15} = 1 \quad \text{or} \quad \sum_{j=1}^{5} x_{1j} = 1.$$

The salesman must also leave city 2 once and once only:

$$x_{21} + x_{22} + x_{23} + x_{24} + x_{25} = 1 \quad \text{or} \quad \sum_{j=1}^{5} x_{2j} = 1.$$

There are similar equations for each other city. And for every city, there is a constraint requiring the salesman to *enter* the city once and once only:

$$\sum_{i=1}^{5} x_{ij} = 1 \quad \text{for} \quad j = 1, 2, 3, 4.$$

Since, on any leg of the trip, the salesman must leave the city he is in, these constraints are added:

$$
\begin{aligned}
x_{11} &= 0, \\
x_{22} &= 0, \\
x_{33} &= 0, \\
x_{44} &= 0, \\
x_{55} &= 0.
\end{aligned}
$$

Finally, there are constraints to prevent a subtour solution, such as the one illustrated in Figure 17-2, which is a physically impossible solution. Some of the equations are redundant and can be omitted.

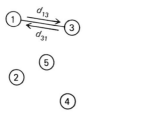

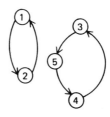

Figure 17-1 Layout of five cities

Figure 17-2 Example of sub-tour solution to be excluded

The fifth equation is made redundant by the third, the sixth by the second, and the eighth by the first.

$$x_{12} + x_{21} \leq 1,$$
$$x_{13} + x_{31} \leq 1,$$
$$x_{14} + x_{41} \leq 1,$$
$$x_{15} + x_{51} \leq 1,$$
$$x_{23} + x_{32} \leq 1,$$
$$x_{24} + x_{42} \leq 1,$$
$$x_{25} + x_{52} \leq 1,$$
$$x_{34} + x_{43} \leq 1,$$
$$x_{35} + x_{53} \leq 1,$$
$$x_{45} + x_{54} \leq 1.$$

When these redundant equations are discarded, we are left with all the constraints we need to define the problem completely.

ANOTHER ASSIGNMENT PROBLEM

Now we will consider an additional assignment problem, in which it becomes necessary to provide another type of constraint. The Apex Delivery Company has five deliveries to make and three available trucks; however, once a truck is loaded it will not return for the rest of the day. The data are shown in Table 17-2.

Let y_i equal 1 if truck i is used; otherwise it is 0. Let x_{ij} equal 1 if truck i carries the delivery for customer j; otherwise it is 0. Since the objective is to minimize total costs, the objective function becomes:

$$\text{Minimize:} \quad x_o = 6y_1 + 12y_2 + 10y_3.$$

The initial group of constraints requires that each customer have one and only one delivery:

$$x_{11} + x_{21} + x_{31} = 1,$$
$$x_{12} + x_{22} + x_{32} = 1,$$
$$x_{13} + x_{23} + x_{33} = 1,$$
$$x_{14} + x_{24} + x_{34} = 1,$$
$$x_{15} + x_{25} + x_{35} = 1.$$

Table 17-2 Demands of customers and characteristics of delivery trucks

Customer	Weight of goods (tons)	Truck	Cost per day	Capacity (tons)
1	1	1	$ 6	7
2	3	2	12	10
3	2	3	10	12
4	8			
5	4			

The second group of constraints provides that the weight capacity of each truck is not exceeded:

$$x_{11} + 3x_{12} + 2x_{13} + 8x_{14} + 4x_{15} \leq 7,$$
$$x_{21} + 3x_{22} + 2x_{23} + 8x_{24} + 4x_{25} \leq 10,$$
$$x_{31} + 3x_{32} + 2x_{33} + 8x_{34} + 4x_{35} \leq 12.$$

The next pair of constraints will cause y_1 to be 0 if truck 1 is not used, and y_1 to be 1 if truck 1 is used. The first is

$$x_{11} + x_{12} + x_{13} + x_{14} + x_{15} - y_1 \geq 0,$$

which states that y_1 cannot be 1 if all the x_{1j}'s are 0. The second,

$$x_{11} + x_{12} + x_{13} + x_{14} + x_{15} - 5y_1 \leq 0,$$

states that if any x_{1j} is 1, then y_1 must be 1 also. Each truck will require a similar pair of constraints; those for truck 2 will be:

$$x_{21} + x_{22} + x_{23} + x_{24} + x_{25} - y_2 \geq 0,$$
$$x_{21} + x_{22} + x_{23} + x_{24} + x_{25} - 5y_2 \leq 0.$$

Finally, the constraints for truck 3 will be:

$$x_{31} + x_{32} + x_{33} + x_{34} + x_{35} - y_3 \geq 0,$$
$$x_{31} + x_{32} + x_{33} + x_{34} + x_{35} - 5y_3 \leq 0.$$

This completes the set of equations for the problem.

As stated earlier, these simple illustrations can also be solved by enumeration or other means; however, they serve to illustrate a method that becomes useful for more complex problems with the same characteristics.

PROBLEMS

1. A company is considering four research and development projects for new products. The company wants to develop at least two of them. Project D cannot be selected without C; however, C can be selected without D. Each project requires the capital and the number of engineers shown in the following table. The present value of the expected profit for each project is also given.

Project	Capital needed $(\times 10^5)$	Engineers needed	Profit $(\times 10^6)$
A	$12	12	$12
B	3	21	15
C	15	3	9
D	15	6	6

The company has 21 engineers and $30 million available. Select the projects to maximize the return. Set up the equations, but do not solve.

2. A visitor leaving a country is limited to carrying 70 pounds on the plane. Other things already take up 25 pounds of this allocation. The following items are available.

Item	Value ($\times 10^3$)	Weight (lbs.)
1	$ 6.5	13
2	16.0	16
3	30.0	15
4	9.0	12
5	27.0	18

Set up the zero-one programming equations to maximize the value of the items taken.

3. Consider a traveling-salesman problem in which the costs of going from city i to city j are given in the following matrix.

City i \ City j	1	2	3	4
1	—	$ 9	$8	$6
2	$3	—	7	5
3	4	11	—	4
4	8	6	5	—

Determine the route with the minimum cost that allows the salesman to visit each city once and only once. Set up the equations, but do not solve.

4. Five projects are being considered for implementation over the next three years. The expected yearly expenditure in millions of dollars and the expected return above cost for each project are given in the accompanying table. The funds available are limited in each of the three years, and it is assumed that each project must be spread over the entire three-year period.

Project \ Expenditure	Year 1	Year 2	Year 3	Expected return
1	6	1	8	25
2	5	8	8	44
3	3	9	2	20
4	8	5	1	18
5	9	6	11	35
Funds available	29	27	30	

Treating this as a zero-one integer programming problem, set up the equations.

5. The following matrix shows the distances between cities. A traveling salesman is to visit each city once and only once, and the objective is to minimize the distance traveled. City 4 cannot be reached directly from city 1.

City i \ City j	1	2	3	4
1	—	4	15	—
2	21	—	9	6
3	15	6	—	12
4	9	3	5	—

Set up the equations, but do not solve.

6. Three trucks are to be unloaded at any of four available docks. Because of differences in loading equipment and cargoes, different unloading times in hours are associated with the various combinations, as shown in the following table.

Truck \ Dock	1	2	3	4
1	9	25	37	29
2	25	19	29	17
3	21	29	53	11

To which dock should each truck be assigned in order to minimize total unloading time? Set up the equations in zero-one form, but do not solve.

SUPPLEMENTARY READINGS

Conway, R. W., W. L. Maxwell, and L. W. Miller. *Theory of Scheduling.* Addison-Wesley, Reading, Mass., 1967.

Hillier, F. S., and G. J. Lieberman. *Introduction to Operations Research.* Holden-Day, San Francisco, 1974, chapter 17.

McMillan, Claude, Jr. *Mathematical Programming.* Wiley, New York, 1970, chapters 11–12, appendices C and H.

Plane, D. R., and G. A. Kochenberger. *Operations Research for Managerial Decisions.* Irwin, Homewood, Ill., 1972, chapter 4, appendix A.

Taha, Hamdy A. *Operations Research.* Macmillan, New York, 1971, chapter 10.

Wagner, H. *Principles of Management Science.* Prentice-Hall, Englewood Cliffs, N.J., 1975, chapter 11.

18/Simulation

SIMULATION models are abstract representations of real-world phenomena. They have to be sufficiently realistic to provide a dynamic representation of a real system; in other words, they must adequately replicate
a system's behavior over a span of time. Simulation should be viewed as
complementary to those techniques and models discussed previously in
this book, since it is most often needed in complex situations that cannot be
dealt with adequately by other decision-making techniques. It often
requires less restrictive assumptions than linear programming and Markov
analysis, for example, but its solutions often are less precise. Therefore
mathematical tools such as those discussed earlier are the first choice for
solving a problem, if they can be used efficiently; when the assumptions or
the complexity of a situation prohibit use of a standard mathematical
technique, simulation is often a valuable tool.

As an illustration of a situation to which simulation can be applied,
recall the discussion in Chapter 15 of equilibrium market shares under
stable market conditions. The assumption was made that competition,
market size, and quantity purchased remained constant. If the brand we
are selling can be classified as a repetitive-purchase, low-cost, household
product, such as hand soap, the "system" we are dealing with may be more
realistically depicted, as in Figure 18-1.

We can see even from a cursory examination of Figure 18-1 that the
system is much more involved than those examined in previous chapters.
The relationships among advertising, price discounts, inducements, and

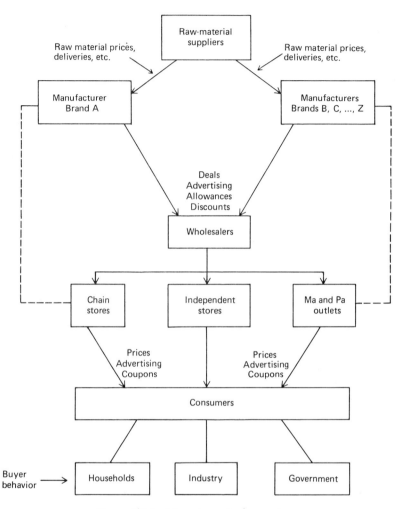

Figure 18-1 A brand-purchasing system

buyer behavior form a realistic marketing system that becomes difficult if not impossible to work with using standard methods. But subsystems or components of the system, such as advertising, lend themselves to simulations. This is not to imply that the entire system could not be simulated. There is a branch of simulation, called system simulation, that endeavors to simulate complex relationships such as those in Figure 18-1. However, simulations of a system as complex as this are exceedingly difficult to solve.

BASIC TERMINOLOGY

System The entire representation involved, including the entire set of symbols, equations, and parameters that is used to represent relationships among people, machines, materials, or other components, is called the system.

System Components The elements making up the system, such as airplanes, people, materials, and costs, are its components.

System Variables A component of the system that changes with time, such as the number of aircraft in a waiting line, or the number of muffler orders from a wholesaler, is a system variable.

System Parameters Components or attributes of the system that remain constant throughout the simulation are called parameters. These are assumed to be fixed. Examples are unit costs and profit rates.

System Relationships Functional statements that interconnect the system components and attributes are known as relationships. For example, the equation

Sales in a marketing system = Quantity demanded × Price

defines one relationship.

System States The values of the system variables at a static point in time determine the state of the system. For a single point in time, the system state is defined as the set of relationships among the variables of the system.

Endogenous Variables A variable that can be solved for within the system is called endogenous. For example, in an inventory simulation, stock levels would be determined within the system. Endogenous variables can be viewed as dependent or output variables of the system.

Exogenous Variables Variables that are independent inputs to the system are known as exogenous. These variables are assumed to have been set independently of the system being examined. They have an impact on the system, but the system has no impact on them. Controllable exogenous variables can be changed by the decision maker. Examples are how many people are employed, how many ball bearings are in stock, and how many delivery vans were purchased. (Remember that the system being modeled has no impact on these variables.) Uncontrollable exogenous variables are those on which the decision maker has no influence. Examples are changing currency-exchange rates, unemployment, and other economic conditions.

Typically, exogenous variables are handled in one of two ways in a simulation. First, they can be treated as preset by either the environment or the decision maker—in other words, as fixed inputs to the system. Second, they can be treated as probabilistic, if they are generated by a computer or some other random-process method. These probabilisitc exogenous variables can vary over the course of the simulation, as would economic conditions, for example.

Endogenous variables, unlike exogenous ones, are generated by the interaction of system variables as specified by the system relationships. Whether a variable is to be classified as endogenous or exogenous in a particular situation will depend upon the purposes of that simulation. For example, national unemployment may be considered to be an exogenous variable in the simulation of a small firm's marketing activities, but an endogenous variable in a simulation of the national economy.

Stochastic Models Stochastic models are ones in which at least one of the variables is a random variable and/or at least one system relationship is assumed to be probabilistic rather than exact.

Deterministic Models Models in which there is no random variable and all system relationships are assumed to be exact are deterministic models.

TYPES OF SIMULATION

A wide variety of classification schemes can be used to categorize simulation models, such as computer-noncomputer and mathematical-non-mathematical. But, typically, the models fall into four types: *Monte Carlo, system-simulation, heuristic*, and *game*.

Monte Carlo models deal with probabilistic processes and make use of random variables to explore the relationships within a system. Although Monte Carlo models can take many forms other than simulation, they are very applicable to stochastic simulations and, as will be shown later, are iterative in nature.

A system-simulation model takes the form of a complex reproduction of some operating system. Examples are market simulations and simulations of operating environments. These models differ from Monte Carlo ones in that (1) random samples drawn from the actual population are used rather than random-number generation, and (2) mathematical decision rules are used to arrive at a solution. However, as the mathematical complexity increases, the situation often lends itself more and more to Monte Carlo methods.

Heuristic models take the form of verbalized representations of management judgment. Frequently, computational routines are not available for finding the best solution and, as a result, management may utilize a heuristic approach. This approach involves rules of thumb, which help shorten the time necessary to make a decision. For example, the decision rule "advertise only in the five most widely read magazines" could be viewed as a rule of thumb in a decision situation. Heuristic models are not devoid of mathematics, since quantitative analysis can be used to test the decision rules. However, they are typically more verbal than other simulation approaches.

Game models are simulations that usually involve human participants. For example, there are many pencil-and-paper as well as computer games, involving decisions and resultant outcomes, that simulate business conditions. These are often used for executive and student training. There are also world-economy simulation games, war simulation games, and simulations of chess and poker.

MONTE CARLO MODELS

The Muffler Example

Consider the example discussed in Chapter 4, concerning the business firm that sells mufflers and is going to be faced with losses due to out-of-stock conditions. The entrepreneur may wish to simulate demands for the next 30 days. He may begin with the following outline.

System: Inventory and demand for mufflers

System components
1. Entrepreneur.
2. Mufflers.
3. Customers.

System variables
1. Number of mufflers in stock (exogenous, X_1).
2. Number of mufflers demanded (exogenous, X_2).
3. Loss of profit, which in this case occurs from out-of-stock conditions (endogenous, Y). Monthly profits are reduced when the mufflers are out of stock.

System parameters
1. Cost per muffler = C.
2. Loss of profit per muffler not sold = L = $5.

System relationships
1. $Y = (X_2 - X_1) \times L$.
2. If $X_1 > X_2$, $L = 0$.

Other conditions
1. When $X_1 > X_2$, there is no loss of profit for the day, but the profit from unsold mufflers is zero.
2. There is no carry-over of demand from one day to the next, because of the immediacy of each customer's need.
3. Because of current difficulties in getting mufflers, there is a fixed inventory level of 20 mufflers, replenished daily on a quota basis from a local supplier.

The probability table for the out-of-stock conditions, Table 18-1, is based on data the manager has collected over the past 100 days. If demand is an exogenous variable and is assumed to be random, we can simulate it through use of the random numbers in Table 18-2. We want to set random-number boundaries for each possible level of demand that reflect the relative frequency of occurrence of this demand in the past. For example, since the demand (X_2) of 22 occurred 5 percent of the time, we will allocate five numbers out of 100 total numbers to the simulated demand of 22. These five numbers are 00 through 04. On the other hand, for a relative frequency of .25, such as for a demand of 26 mufflers, we have to allocate 25 numbers, in this case 25 through 49. We can then select two-digit numbers from the random-number table and assign each to the appropriate

Table 18-1 Probabilities for muffler demands

Demand	Unfilled demand	Probability	Cumulative probability	Random numbers
≤ 20	0	.00	.00	—
21	1	.00	.00	—
22	2	.05	.05	00–04
23	3	.05	.10	05–09
24	4	.05	.15	10–14
25	5	.10	.25	15–24
26	6	.25	.50	25–49
27	7	.25	.75	50–74
28	8	.10	.85	75–84
29	9	.10	.95	85–94
30	10	.05	1.00	95–99
		1.00		

Table 18-2   Random numbers

10097	32533	76520	13586	34673	54876	80959	09117	39292	74745
37542	04805	64894	74296	24805	24037	20636	10402	00822	91685
08422	68953	19645	09303	23209	02560	15953	34764	35080	33608
99019	02529	09376	70715	38311	31165	88676	74397	04436	27659
12807	99970	80157	36147	64032	36653	98951	16877	12171	76833
66065	74717	34072	76850	36697	36170	65813	39885	11199	29170
31060	10805	45571	82406	35303	42614	86799	07439	23403	09732
85269	77602	02051	65692	68665	74818	73053	85247	18623	88579
63573	32135	05325	47048	90553	57548	28468	28709	83491	25624
73796	45753	03529	64778	35808	34282	60935	20344	35273	88435
98520	17767	14905	68607	22109	40558	60907	93433	50500	73998
11805	05431	39808	27732	50725	68248	29405	24201	52775	67851
83452	99634	06288	98083	13746	70078	18475	40610	68711	77817
88685	40200	86507	58401	36766	67951	90364	76493	29609	11062
99594	67348	87517	64969	91826	08926	93785	61368	23478	34113
65481	17674	17468	50950	58047	76974	73039	57186	40218	16544
80124	35635	17727	08015	45318	22374	21115	78253	14385	53763
74350	99817	77402	77214	43236	00210	45521	64237	96286	02655
69916	26803	66252	29148	36936	87203	76621	13990	94400	56418
09893	20505	14225	68514	46427	56788	96297	78822	54382	14598

Source: The RAND Corporation, *A Million Random Digits with 100,000 Normal Deviates*, Free Press, New York, 1955. Reprinted by permission of the publisher and author.

demand level. We choose 30 random numbers to provide us with the simulated demand conditions for the forthcoming 30 days.

The results are shown in Table 18-3. The random numbers were chosen from the left-hand column of Table 18-2—the first pair of digits in every row, then the second pair. (In this case, the upper-left-hand corner was assumed to be a random starting point. In practice, one should start from a random position.)

According to Table 18-3, during this period of hard-to-get materials, the entrepreneur is going to have an expected reduction in profit of $940 per month, with an average daily reduction of $31.33. It is interesting to note that this simulated estimate came very close to the expected daily loss of $32 that was calculated in Chapter 4.

The Cake Example
Monte Carlo simulation can also be used in a more dynamic decision situation, in which a firm wishes to test a decision rule. For example, a firm that sells cakes or any product with a limited shelf life may want to test whether a new decision rule is effective. Consider an instance of cake sales, like the one discussed in Chapter 4. The firm does not wish to sell day-old cakes and, as a result, those not sold on a given day are a total loss. The managers of the firm have a conflict over what particular decision rule

Table 18-3 Simulated profit losses for mufflers over a 30-day period

Day	Random number	Unfilled demand	Profit loss
1	10	4	$ 20
2	37	6	30
3	08	3	15
4	99	10	50
5	12	4	20
6	66	7	35
7	31	6	30
8	85	9	45
9	63	7	35
10	73	7	35
11	98	10	50
12	11	4	20
13	83	8	40
14	88	8	40
15	99	10	50
16	65	7	35
17	80	8	40
18	74	7	35
19	69	7	35
20	09	3	15
21	09	3	15
22	54	7	35
23	42	6	30
24	01	2	10
25	80	8	40
26	06	3	15
27	06	3	15
28	26	6	30
29	57	7	35
30	79	8	40
			$940

should be utilized for stocking cakes for the following day. After studying the past 100 days' information, manager A says that she has noticed a pronounced trend in the data: one day's demand appears to be linked to the demand of the day immediately preceeding it. The second manager (B) knows that the firm does very little to influence demand—there is no advertising—and she is convinced that demand is a random, exogenous variable. As a result, she says that the firm should stock each day the mean number of cakes sold over the last 100 days, or 27. More formally, the outline of the simulation would be as follows.

System: Inventory and demand for cakes

System components
1. Two managers.
2. Cakes.
3. Customers.

System variables
1. Number of cakes stocked.
    (a) $X_1 =$ quantity stocked under decision rule 1, which provides a stock on day t equal to the demand on day $t-1$ (exogenous).
    (b) $X_2 =$ constant stock of 27 (exogenous).
2. Number of cakes demanded (exogenous, X_3).
3. Profits.
    (a) $Y_1 =$ simulated profit under decision rule 1 (endogenous).
    (b) $Y_2 =$ simulated profit under decision rule 2 (endogenous).

System parameters
1. Profit per cake sold $= P = \$2$.
2. Cost per cake $= C = \$8$.
3. Loss per cake stocked but not sold $= L = \$8$.

System relationships
1. $Y_1 = (P \times X_3) - (L \times X_1)$.
2. $Y_2 = (P \times X_3) - (L \times X_2)$.
3. If $X_3 - X_1 \geq 0$, $L = 0$.
4. If $X_3 - X_2 \geq 0$, $L = 0$.

Other conditions
1. Cost of unfilled demand is zero.
2. The variable X_3 must be generated, while X_1 and X_2 will be set by decision rules.

Decision rules
1. For manager A,
$$X_{1,t} = X_{3,t-1}, \qquad X_{1,t+1} = X_{3,t}, \qquad \dots, \qquad X_{1,t+n} = X_{3,t+n-1},$$
where $t =$ present date.
2. For manager B,
$$X_{1,t} = \frac{\sum\limits_{t=1}^{n} X_t}{n} = \bar{X},$$
where $\bar{X} = 27$ from data of past 100 days.

The simulated demand conditions for this firm are shown in Table 18-4

Table 18-4 Demand frequencies for cakes

Demand	Frequency	Demand × frequency	Probability	Random numbers
25	10	250	.10	00–09
26	20	520	.20	10–29
27	20	540	.20	30–49
28	30	840	.30	50–79
29	10	290	.10	80–89
30	10	300	.10	90–99

Table 18-5 Simulated profits for cakes over a 24-day period

Day	Random number	Demand (X_3)	Stock, decision rule 1 (X_1)	Profit, decision rule 1 (Y_1)	Stock, decision rule 2 (X_2)	Profit, decision rule 2 (Y_2)
0	17	26	—	—	—	—
1	52	28	26	$ 52	27	$ 54
2	80	29	28	56	27	54
3	45	27	29	38	27	54
4	68	28	27	54	27	54
5	59	28	28	56	27	54
6	48	27	28	46	27	54
7	12	26	27	44	27	44
8	35	27	26	52	27	54
9	91	30	27	54	27	54
10	89	29	30	50	27	54
11	73	28	29	48	27	54
12	20	26	28	36	27	46
13	26	26	26	52	27	46
14	90	30	26	52	27	54
15	79	28	30	40	27	54
16	57	28	28	56	27	54
17	01	25	28	26	27	34
18	97	30	25	50	27	54
19	33	27	30	30	27	54
20	64	28	27	54	27	54
21	01	25	28	26	27	34
22	50	28	25	50	27	54
23	29	26	28	36	27	44
24	54	28	26	52	27	54
				$1,100		$1,220

and Table 18-5. The first three columns of Table 18-5 show the random numbers and estimated demands for the 24 working days of the upcoming month. To test the two decision rules, the demand for each day is matched against the stock as prescribed under the two seperate rules. The profit contributions are then calculated from the given parameters, relationships, and conditions. We can see from the result that the total profit from decision rule 1 is $1,100, while under decision rule 2 it is $1,220. These figures correspond to daily profits of $46.26 and $50.83, respectively. Therefore decision rule 2 would be followed.

Cautions

Two general cautions should be made at this point. First, the underlying demand condition was assumed to be a random variable, which may not be the case for a large firm that has fairly extensive influence on demand for its product. For example, demand for automobiles in any period is related to demand in the previous period, and is therefore not random. When this situation exists, selection of a random number to represent demand may not be appropriate. In the case of the cakes, demand patterns such as concentrations of purchases on Mondays and Thursdays could definitely influence the assumption of randomness. As a result, the demand variable would have to be modified to reflect the known influences.

Second, whenever one is dealing with simulated demand conditions, the potential for sampling error exists. For example, if only days 4 and 5 were examined, the conclusion would be to use decision rule 1. If concepts of probability have been used to generate demand conditions, we must realize that probability is a long-run phenomenon and sample sizes need to be large enough to minimize random error. To compensate for the possibility of sampling error and nonrandomness of a variable, data from the actual population rather than from a theoretical random population might be selected. With these data, confidence intervals might be used, rather than fixed estimates of demand. This leads us to a discussion of system simulation.

SYSTEM-SIMULATION MODELS

Rather than generating variables randomly, system simulation generally calls for drawing samples from the actual population. For example, in a simulation of the impact of a particular television commercial on consumers, a group of 1,000 potential customers could be exposed to alternative forms of television commercials. Each customer would provide data regarding prior brand exposure, television-viewing habits, source credibility, and consumption patterns. Over a period of days, the participants could then be shown differing forms of a commercial (exogenous), and their reactions to the message could be monitored (endogenous). The measures used could be pupil dilation, attitudes, and product perceptions. Preset decision rules would indicate when the commercial message had obtained the desired responses. Until these responses were found, the message and/or environment could be altered according to the direction the undesired responses were taking.

In addition to changes in message content derived from this simulation, there might be modifications in media decisions and marketing objectives. This method differs from the Monte Carlo technique in that it involves responses from actual customers rather than random responses. The method could be modified over time to make it possible to develop a set of hypothetical consumers with prescribed sets of attitudes and reactions. Predictions could be made of how the hypothetical group would have responded to changes in the message. The collection of data from 1,000 people would be unnecessary if the hypothetical group adequately reflected the actual population.

The results of simulations of this type can include predictions of how the general population might react to the commercial message. These predictions might take the form of confidence intervals. The method differs from a simple random sample in that viewing conditions are simulated (as in a studio) and reactions are measured after alternative message modifications but before exposure of the general population to the message.

HEURISTIC MODELS

Heuristic models are used to simulate actual decision processes that cannot easily be formulated mathematically. Although they do not provide an algorithm that necessarily yields optimum decisions, they do tend to formalize the reasoning processes and rules to be used in a complex decision-making situation. One of the basic purposes of heuristics, besides providing a sense of order, is to impose rules of thumb that will allow time-saving elimination of potential alternatives.

As an example, in establishing the best number of sales territories to have in a region, one method would be to examine all possible combinations and select the combination that yielded the largest expected profit. Heuristics might allow the incrementation of territories, one at a time; profit evaluations and additions would be continued until no additional profit improvement was found. Heuristics provides a flexibility in analysis of a large-scale problem that is lacking in other types of simulation or common quantitative techniques.

Allocation of Sales Territories

Consider the problem just mentioned: the optimum number of sales territories to have in a particular region. Our firm is basing its decision upon the following set of heuristics.

1. Sales territories tend to change in terms of potential business, competition, and costs of operation. Some existing territories are characterized by either too much business potential to be handled optimally or else too little potential to allow an adequate profit contribution. Heuristics will allow the firm to redesign the territories without having to consider all the possible combinations of territories that can be formed. We know that territories need to be located near the concentrations of our customers, which correspond to the population hubs within our market.

2. Profit will be used as a basic criterion for deciding whether a territory is worth adding to the sales system. Because we are interested in long-run viability, however, it is necessary to forecast profits for at least a five-year period in order to anticipate changes in demand and profit conditions within the territories.

3. The territories will be considered on an incremental basis, with the merits of additions, mergers, and subdivisions decided solely upon the basis of profits. Although it is sometimes desirable to operate territories with a negative profit contribution for purposes of prestige, competitive blockage, and market penetration, cases of this sort are unusual and can be handled individually.

A flow diagram is very useful in implementing this heuristic model. The decision sequence is illustrated in Figure 18-2. In step 1 the various bits of input information are defined. Next, from the infinite number of possible territory sites, the N territories that will provide the largest profits are selected, on the basis of proximity to customer concentrations. Next, possible subdivision of these territories should be investigated, using the criterion of profit contribution to the entire sales system. And if basic territories or subdivided territories yield losses over the five-year period, they should be eliminated, unless included for ancillary reasons.

In the next steps, mergers of territories are considered, one at a time, and eliminated if they do not provide an improvement in system profit. Finally, the current customers in territories that have been eliminated need to be reassigned to new or existing territories, and the profit contributions need to be reassessed.

Allocation of Effort Within a Sales Territory

Flow charts such as the one shown in Figure 18-2 can be prepared at several levels of generality. Figure 18-2 represents an aggregate heuristic flow chart designed to aid in gross territory allocations. After the territorial allocations have been made comes the question of how to allocate effort within a single territory or a group of territories. Many models make use of a single criterion, such as time or cost, in allocating sales effort within a territory; however, few consider effort allocation along more than one dimension simultaneously.

An interesting and very applicable heuristic model has been developed by Cloonan.[1] In his program Cloonan utilizes the concept of opportunity costs to measure when it is practicable to leave the minimum-cost sales

---

[1] James B. Cloonan, "An Analysis of Sales Tours," in *Proceedings of the 4th International Conference on Operational Research*, ed. David B. Hertz and Jacques Melse, Wiley, New York, 1966.

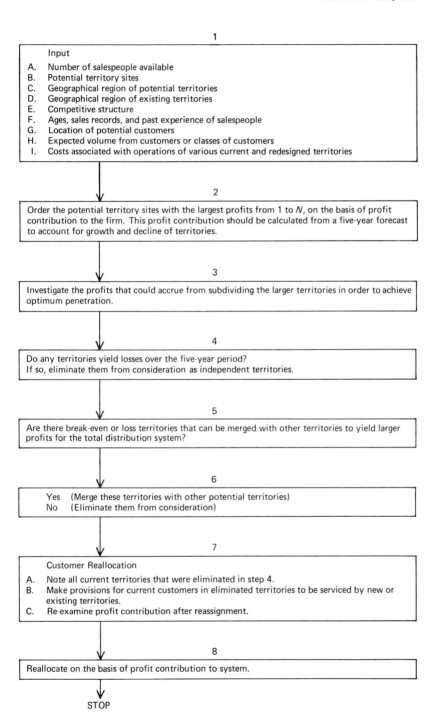

1

Input

A. Number of salespeople available
B. Potential territory sites
C. Geographical region of potential territories
D. Geographical region of existing territories
E. Competitive structure
F. Ages, sales records, and past experience of salespeople
G. Location of potential customers
H. Expected volume from customers or classes of customers
I. Costs associated with operations of various current and redesigned territories

2

Order the potential territory sites with the largest profits from 1 to N, on the basis of profit contribution to the firm. This profit contribution should be calculated from a five-year forecast to account for growth and decline of territories.

3

Investigate the profits that could accrue from subdividing the larger territories in order to achieve optimum penetration.

4

Do any territories yield losses over the five-year period?
If so, eliminate them from consideration as independent territories.

5

Are there break-even or loss territories that can be merged with other territories to yield larger profits for the total distribution system?

6

Yes (Merge these territories with other potential territories)
No (Eliminate them from consideration)

7

Customer Reallocation

A. Note all current territories that were eliminated in step 4.
B. Make provisions for current customers in eliminated territories to be serviced by new or existing territories.
C. Re-examine profit contribution after reassignment.

8

Reallocate on the basis of profit contribution to system.

STOP

Figure 18-2 Flow diagram for redesign of sales territories

route. Taken into account are the time and money losses derived from leaving the minimum-cost route, as well as the value of the call. The author hypothesizes that the value of a call is related not only to how long it has been since a call was last made on that customer, but also to the type of account.

Cloonan develops a heuristic flow diagram that uses the following terms.

N = number of accounts in tour.

$TT(N \times N)$ = matrix of distances between accounts expressed in time.

$CT(N \times 1)$ = duration of a sales call on each account.

$JE(N \times 1)$ = time (months) since last call on each account ($12 \geq JE \geq 1$).

$G(N \times 12)$ = value of a call on any account as a function of JE.

$GMAX$ = the maximum value of G (in this model G is maximum when $JE = 12$).

VO = a critical-value ratio established by management on the basis of available time.

TN = the accumulated value of sales calls.

TR = the accumulated travel time.

TC = the accumulated calling time.

X = present location of salesman.

Y = account being evaluated for the next call.

Z = account after Y, used to establish opportunity cost.

VN = value, $f(G)$, of a call on account Y.

OT = opportunity cost of travel to Y.

VR = the ratio $VN/(OT+CT)$.

Through use of these terms, a flow diagram was developed, as shown in Figure 18-3. The routing problem is expressed in terms of the opportunity cost and value relationships. Specifically, Cloonan states that the value of a call is related to the time since the last call in the following way:

$$V_{iT} = (at - bt^2 + c)V_{im},$$

where

V_{iT} = value of call on customer i at time T,

t = time since last call on customer i,

V_{im} = maximum value of a call on customer i,

a, b, c = positive constants.[2]

As illustrated in Figure 18-3, the central goal is to evaluate the opportunity

---

[2] D. B. Montgomery and G. L. Urban, *Management Science in Marketing*, Prentice-Hall, Englewood Cliffs, N.J., 1969, p. 283.

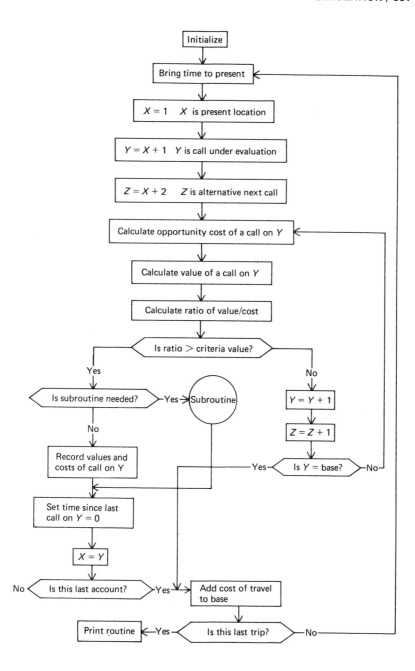

Figure 18-3 Flow diagram for sales tours (SOURCE: James B. Cloonan, "An Analysis of Sales Tours," in *Proceedings of the 4th International Conference on Operational Research,* ed. David B. Hertz and Jacques Melse, Wiley, New York, 1966, pp. 284–292. Reprinted by permission of the publisher.)

cost of a call. This opportunity cost is the net difference in calling and travel time between X, the present location of the salesperson; Y, the account under examination; and Z, the next account in the route. The alternative route is compared to the minimum-cost route, X to Z with no stop at Y.

The *value* of a particular call on an account is defined as the present value of the possible streams of future profits multiplied by the probabilities of these streams of profits. Cloonan states that, although this is a good theoretical definition of value, it may be nearly unworkable in practice. More pragmatically, a ranking may be made on a relative basis. For example, account B may be judged twice as important as account A. Although Cloonan did not specifically discuss them, other methods of analyzing customer potential can be used, including historical analysis and market surveys.

Costs are evaluated in terms of units of time, the important components being travel time, calling time, and travel expenses. Only variable costs are considered in the model, although it could be expanded to include fixed costs.

The primary value of a heuristic approach such as that shown in Figure 18-3 is that it helps to structure a decision-making procedure. The benefits of explicitly treating variables such as opportunity costs and value should be apparent when this method is compared to more arbitrary ones. We can see that, once this method was implemented in an individual territory, it could be expanded to include regions and the total market.

GAME MODELS

In recent years simulation gaming has been utilized in many diverse situations.[3] One of the more practical and well-received uses has been business gaming. Information and techniques from business games are commonly being examined by the marketing, production, finance, and personnel departments of corporations. In fact, all areas of business represent potential applications of gaming models.

Both the academic and the business world routinely use gaming as an aid in developing the ability to make various decisions. Businesses frequently use simulations depicting their own operations, but sometimes the game involves an entirely different industry or another decision framework. Regardless of which business game is chosen, management has generally

---

[3] This section on simulation gaming has been adapted from material provided by Dr. Edwin C. Hackleman, coauthor, with Louis E. Boone, of the simulation game *Marketing Strategy: A Marketing Decision Game.*

found it quite useful as a device for demonstrating the interplay of many variables, and for giving the players a chance to see how the outcomes of their decisions are influenced by the decisions of others.

One of the reasons for the increase in popularity of business simulations over the last twenty years is their ability to present a dynamic decision environment. For example, industry simulations have received particular attention. These games force the players to analyze many facets of the market—the products to be produced and marketed, the present and potential customers, pricing possibilities, promotional mixes and expenditures, channels of distribution, and so on—while anticipating and reacting to the decisions of competitors in the industry. All of the system components collectively determine the sales, costs, and profits of the firms competing in the industry.

Even though high-speed computers with vast capacities can be employed to handle large masses of data and complex system relationships, no business game has been constructed to duplicate an existing industry exactly. The reason is that the system relationships specified in the simulation model are inexact representations of the actual industry. For example, the exact relationship between sales and advertising policy is almost always unknown; as a result, the system relationship specified in the model is only an approximation. Still, much of the excitement of actual competition is provided, the players "learn by doing," and they obtain invaluable experience in making corporate decisions in a competitive environment.

Marketing Strategy: A Marketing Decision Game by Boone and Hackleman[4] has been used by thousands of students as a learning device. It provides a typical illustration of a business game that allows students to apply what they have learned about marketing management, accounting, marketing research, and economic analysis.

Marketing Strategy simulates an automotive industry (or system) composed of five companies, each producing a product line of three automobile models. Simulated competition may proceed for a number of years of operation; information regarding earnings and sales is provided quarterly for each company in the industry. These years of simulated operation require only a small amount of processing time on the computer.

Each company or management team is usually composed of three to five players who must work together to establish company objectives and to assign responsibilities to each member of the staff. Management must plot its strategy by selecting the automobiles to be produced and marketed,

---

[4] Louis E. Boone and Edwin C. Hackleman, *Marketing Strategy: A Marketing Decision Game*, rev. ed., Merrill, Columbus, Ohio, 1975.

the price to be charged for each model, the number of units of each model to be produced each quarter, the gross amount of advertising desired, the specific advertising allocations to the three models, and the number and allocations of automotive dealerships for the three models. Advertising and dealerships must be allocated across four different geographical regions, each with a different sales potential.

In addition, each company may purchase sales forecasts, consumer preference studies for the various models, and surveillance information about the actions of competitors. The form for making the purchases is shown in Figure 18-4. The "research" information is examined carefully and used as a guide to decisions during the competition.

The quarterly decisions required as input in Marketing Strategy are shown in Figure 18-5. As in the previous figure, card columns are indicated, because the information is transferred to computer decision cards. The output from Marketing Strategy is sufficient for each management team to construct an income statement and balance sheet for the quarter. These financial statements are used to analyze the efficacy of past decisions and are mandatory for making decisions for the next quarter.

The activities are made realistic by the inclusion of a number of stochastic and fixed exogenous variables. Each can have a substantial impact on endogenous variables. The dynamic nature of Marketing Strategy is revealed quickly: profit leadership in the industry typically changes hands several times during the course of play.

SIMULATION AND ANALYTICAL MODELS

In other sections of this text, material has been presented pertaining to topics such as Markov chains, queuing, and inventory models. Simulation can be applied to complex situations in which standard applications of these analytical techniques are impractical. The following sections briefly summarize how simulation can be expanded for use with these already familiar techniques.

Markov Chains
The reader will recall that a system, in the Markov sense, can be broken down into a set of mutually exclusive states, and that a transition probability matrix can completely define the behavior of a first-order Markov system. Rather than generating the transition probabilities in the manner shown in Chapter 15, we can simulate the Markov chains. Simulation, especially when computerized, allows stationarity assumptions to be relaxed, and

ADVANCED MARKETING RESEARCH AUTHORIZATION FORM

Period_____   Industry   ☐ Col. 1 ⌐Card Three⌐

                           Company   ☐ Col. 2

Economic Forecasts:

A. Quarterly Sales Index for Next Quarter   ☐ Col. 3
   Cost: $500,000

B. Annual Sales Forecast for the Industry   ☐ Col. 4
   Cost: $1,500,000

C. Quarterly Sales Index for Next Quarter (Regions)
   Cost: $200,000 each
           Northeast Region   ☐ Col. 5
           Southern Region   ☐ Col. 6
           North Central Region   ☐ Col. 7
           Western Region   ☐ Col. 8

D. Projected Percentage Size of the Automobile
   Submarkets   ☐ Col. 9
   Cost: $500,000

Competitive Analysis—Distribution

A. Current Total Number of Retail Outlets
   Used by Each Company in the Industry   ☐ Col. 10
   Cost: $500,000

B. Current Number of Retail Outlets Used for
   Each Model
   Cost: $400,000 each
           Company 1   ☐ Col. 11
           Company 2   ☐ Col. 12
           Company 3   ☐ Col. 13
           Company 4   ☐ Col. 14
           Company 5   ☐ Col. 15

C. Current Number of Retail Outlets Used in
   Each Region
   Cost: $300,000 each
           Company 1   ☐ Col. 16
           Company 2   ☐ Col. 17
           Company 3   ☐ Col. 18
           Company 4   ☐ Col. 19
           Company 5   ☐ Col. 20

Figure 18-4 Marketing research authorization form for the game Marketing Strategy (SOURCE: Louis E. Boone and Edwin C. Hackleman, *Marketing Strategy: A Marketing Decision Game,* rev. ed., Merrill, Columbus, Ohio, 1975. Reprinted by permission of the publisher and authors.)

Competitive Analysis—Advertising

A. Current Total Advertising Expenditures by
Each Company in the Industry   ☐ Col. 21
   Cost: $500,000

B. Current Advertising Expenditures for Each Model
   Cost: $400,000 each
                  Company 1   ☐ Col. 22
                  Company 2   ☐ Col. 23
                  Company 3   ☐ Col. 24
                  Company 4   ☐ Col. 25
                  Company 5   ☐ Col. 26

C. Current Advertising Expenditures in Each Region
   Cost: $300,000
                  Company 1   ☐ Col. 27
                  Company 2   ☐ Col. 28
                  Company 3   ☐ Col. 29
                  Company 4   ☐ Col. 30
                  Company 5   ☐ Col. 31

CONSUMER PREFERENCE STUDIES FOR THE AUTO MODELS

Directions: For each study you wish to purchase, underline the auto model name
and place the first letter of the model name in the box beginning with Col. 32. There
are sufficient boxes for each of the 15 models. The models do not have to be listed
in any order.

Models for Which Studies are Available:

Youth Economy Market		_Young Executive Market_	
Asteroid	Cannon	Fatari	Hawk
Blazer	Dakota	Goliath	Intrepid
Enterprise		Juggernaut	

Family Market
Keynote   Moonbeam
Lancet   Nemesis
Orbiter

Cost: $500,000 for each model study purchased.

☐ Col. 32
☐ Col. 33
☐ Col. 34
☐ Col. 35
☐ Col. 36
☐ Col. 37
☐ Col. 38
☐ Col. 39
☐ Col. 40
☐ Col. 41
☐ Col. 42
☐ Col. 43
☐ Col. 44
☐ Col. 45
☐ Col. 46

TOTAL MARKETING RESEARCH EXPENDITURES $_____

Figure 18-4 _(cont.)_

ADVANCED MANAGEMENT DECISION FORM

Period _____   Industry   ☐ Col. 1   [Card One]

Authorized Signature _____ Company   ☐ Col. 2

MODEL 1 DECISIONS

Model Name_____First Letter   Col. 3
Retail Price   Col. 4–7
Units Produced   Col. 8–13

Numbers of Dealers Allocated to Model 1

Northeast Region   Col. 14–17
Southern Region   Col. 18–21
North Central Region   Col. 22–25
Western Region   Col. 26–29

Advertising Allocated to Model 1 (in millions)

Northeast Region   Col. 30–32
Southern Region   Col. 33–35
North Central Region   Col. 36–38
Western Region   Col. 39–41

MODEL 2 DECISIONS

Model Name_____First Letter   Col. 42
Retail Price   Col. 43–46
Units Produced   Col. 47–52

Number of Dealers Allocated to Model 2

Northeast Region   Col. 53–56
Southern Region   Col. 57–60
North Central Region   Col. 61–64
Western Region   Col. 65–68

Advertising Allocated to Model 2 (in millions)

Northeast Region   Col. 69–71
Southern Region   Col. 72–74
North Central Region   Col. 75–77
Western Region   Col. 78–80

Figure 18-5 Management decision form for the game Marketing Strategy (SOURCE: Louis E. Boone and Edwin C. Hackleman, *Marketing Strategy: A Marketing Decision Game,* rev. ed., Merill, Columbus, Ohio, 1975. Reprinted by permission of the publisher and authors.)

Industry ☐ Col. 1   ⬡ Card Two

Company ☐ Col. 2

MODEL 3 DECISIONS

Model Name _____First Letter   ☐ Col. 3

Retail Price   Col. 4–7

Units Produced   Col. 9–13

Number of Dealers Allocated to Model 3

Northeast Region   Col. 15–17

Southern Region   Col. 18–21

North Central Region   Col. 22–25

Western Region   Col. 26–29

Advertising Allocated to Model 3 (in millions)

Northeast Region   Col. 30–32

Southern Region   Col. 33–35

North Central Region   Col. 36–38

Western Region   Col. 39–41

DECISION SUMMARY

PRODUCTION SCHEDULE:

	Model 1	Model 2	Model 3
Available in Inventory	_____	_____	_____
Scheduled Production	_____	_____	_____
Available for Sale	_____	_____	_____

DEALER EXPENSES:

_____ × $2000 = $ _____
Number

Dealers Terminated:

_____ × $3000 = $ _____

Dealers Added:

_____ × $3000 = $ _____

Dealers Shifted to New Model:

_____ × $3000 = $ _____

TOTAL ADVERTISING EXPENDITURES: $ _____

Figure 18-5 *(cont.)*

probabilities do not necessarily have to be assumed to progress to a steady state. The simulation of Markov processes can be accomplished by uniform random-number generation for numbers ranging between zero and one. If we define a system as being in a state A at the beginning of one period and state B at the beginning of the next period, the random number that is generated will specify a transition from state A to state B if it is above the transition probability for shifting from A to B. The same is true for transitions from B to A. The computer program can then count the frequency with which each of the finite states A and B is represented. This technique can be expanded to include multiple states, multiple periods, and transition probabilities that are not stationary.

Queuing

Some special types of simulations have been used for job-shop or production-line problems. The simulation usually involves generating random arrivals of jobs to be done sequentially. The processing times are usually assumed to be stochastic—in other words, they vary. The technique can be applied to personnel allocation, assembly-line balancing, machine loading, delivery, and other important functions. Through use of computer simulation, decisions regarding production processes and layout can be made before full-scale implementation, and tests for improvements can be made after implementation.

Inventory Control

Monte Carlo simulation similar to that used in the muffler example can be applied to a wide variety of inventory problems. Random processes that simulate usage can generate appropriate out-of-stock costs; safety stocks and carrying costs can then be estimated using conventional analytical methods, which allow for minimization of overall inventory costs. Simulation offers an opportunity to experiment with various decision rules so as to optimize inventory-control decisions.

THE ROLE OF THE COMPUTER IN SIMULATION

Computers take on a very important role in Monte Carlo, system, and game simulations, and in testing decision rules in heuristic simulations. Large-scale Monte Carlo simulations can be accomplished only with a machine. The computer can generate random numbers such as those shown in Table 18-2 for use in simulation of any random process. In addition, the necessary iterations can be done readily with standard computer programs.

In game simulations, the computer can allow the manipulation of exogenous variables and system relationships within the model. Exogenous variables can either be generated randomly or be set by management as inputs into the system. The ability to interact with a computer often makes simulation more realistic and permits more complex decision settings. In the Marketing Strategy game, for example, sales may result from the interaction of price, advertising, and number of dealers allocated (exogenous, controllable) but may be influenced heavily by competitive actions and market demand (exogenous, uncontrollable). We need not assume that competitive strategies and sales potentials are totally unknown; the firm can buy consumer-preference information, sales forecasts, and surveillance information. This brings realism to the model and allows the adjustment of controllable variables on the basis of additional information, a procedure which ties in closely with the Bayesian methods discussed in Chapter 4. We can quickly see that one of the biggest advantages of a computer is its ability to compact into a few minutes of processing decisions that might otherwise take months or years to make.

Recently, a group of simulation computer languages that greatly simplify the writing of simulation programs have been developed. Examples are DYNAMO, GASP, GPSS II, SIMSCRIPT, SIMLATE, and SIMPAC. These languages were developed to allow the rapid conversion of a simulation problem into an operational computer program. Each of these languages has a special purpose. For example, GPSS (General Purpose Systems Simulator) was designed to apply to a broad class of simulations that make use of a fairly standard set of procedures. GPSS, along with SIMSCRIPT and GASP, has found wide application in production and inventory scheduling, as well as in queuing. The languages DYNAMO and SIMLATE are used in more aggregate economic simulations in which there is a large set of interacting, simultaneous equations. These aggregate simulations can be expanded to national and even international dimensions.

As the possible interactions between variables grow, and as these interactions are investigated through collection of additional information, the simulation becomes very complex. Preprogrammed, high-speed, electronic computers not only make a simulation of this type feasible, but they also allow for specification of additional variables, leading to increased clarity and realism.

THE PROPER APPLICATION OF SIMULATION

Simulation can be applied to inventory control, warehouse location and operations, scheduling, assembly-line balancing, queuing, executive training, and other situations. The user of simulation techniques has to be well grounded in fundamental statistics; pertinent areas of knowledge include experimental design, random processes, sampling, and parameter estimation. Further, to use simulation properly, a knowledge of computers is necessary.

The question will often arise, "Should quantitative analysis or simulation be employed to solve a problem?" The answer, in general, is to use quantitative analysis whenever possible. This includes Markov analysis, linear programming, and dynamic programming. In noncomplex as well as in some complex decision settings, quantitative techniques will consume less time and money. As the number of variables, the difficulty, and/or the expense increases, however, there should be a greater inclination to use simulation.

STUDY SUGGESTIONS

1. One of the major tasks for most students at the end of a term is planning and preparation for final examinations. It is to the benefit of most to make a paper-and-pencil flow diagram of the preparation period so that they will be systematic in study. However, when we think about it, a simplified heuristic approach to the problem can be quite useful. For your final examination period, draw a flow diagram that contains a set of useful heuristic decision rules. (*Note:* Don't forget that there are some easily defined system components, system variables, parameters, and so on. For example, you could define as a system parameter the day upon which a final exam is to be given; you could define current grades, necessary preparation times, and so on.)

2. Business games have been very important instructional tools over the last few years. Take the operations of a single local supermarket as an example. Spell out in precise detail what you feel the system, system components, system variables (endogenous and exogenous), system parameters, and relationships are for a simulation of the operations of this supermarket. What benefits could a simulation containing your definitions have for a supermarket operator? What limitations would there be?

3. In many college classes, students are asked to use the computer. Assume that in your class there are 50 students and each has been asked to run a computer problem on the terminal located within your building. This terminal services one student at a time. For the purpose of completing the analysis, your class has been allocated a two-hour block of time on next Friday. Establish a hypothetical discrete distribution of times required to service the students after arrival (these times will differ from student to student). Using a random-number process, simulate the arrivals of the students during the two-hour period. Then report the length of the line of waiting students during the simulated period, the average waiting time, and other important results. Finally, state whether the two-hour reserved period should be longer, shorter, or remain the same.

4. Obtain a recipe for baking a cake or a similar set of directions. Would you say that this set of directions is a model? Set up an objective of baking n cakes, or the equivalent. Establish a flow diagram for the production of the n cakes, or the equivalent. Be sure that you carefully define system components and other important parts of the process.

   Upon completion, would you still say the recipe is a model, and if so, is it a simulation model?

5. The designs of production processes demand some of the most difficult management decisions. Try to design a simplified model of a production process using tape and/or scissors and/or cards. Be careful to define the necessary basic terminology.

   Now, as a class project, implement this simulation with a group of fellow students. What modifications have to be made in order to accomplish your objectives? What benefits would this method have for training production-system designers? What limitations?

SUPPLEMENTARY READINGS

Basil, B. C., P. R. Cone, and J. A. Fleming. *Executive Decision Making Through Simulation.* Merrill, Columbus, Ohio, 1965.

Bonini, C. P. *Simulation of Information and Decision Systems in the Firm.* Prentice-Hall, Englewood Cliffs, N.J., 1963.

Charafas, D. N. *Systems and Simulation.* Academic Press, New York, 1965.

Greenlaw, P. S., L. W. Herron, and R. H. Rawden. *Business Simulation: In Industrial and Universal Education.* Prentice-Hall, Englewood Cliffs, N.J., 1962.

Harling, J. "Simulation Techniques in Operations Research: A Review." *Operations Research*, 6, No. 3 (1958), 307–319.

Jackson, J. R. *Simulation as Experimental Mathematics.* Research Report No. 72, Management Sciences Research Project. University of California at Los Angeles, June 1961.

Meier, R., W. T. Newell, and H. L. Pazer. *Simulation in Business and Economics.* Prentice-Hall, Englewood Cliffs, N.J., 1969.

Mize, J. H., and J. G. Cox. *Essentials of Simulation.* Prentice-Hall, Englewood Cliffs, N.J., 1968.

Naylor, T. H., J. L. Balintfy, D. S. Burdick, and D. Chu. *Computer Simulation Techniques.* Wiley, New York, 1966.

Shuchman, A. *Scientific Decision Making in Business.* Holt, Rinehart, and Winston, New York, 1963.

Tocher, K. D. *The Art of Simulation.* Van Nostrand, Princeton, N.J., 1963.

Appendices

Appendix A
Areas Under
the Normal Curve

The entries in the following table represent the proportion of the total area under a normal curve which falls between the mean and Z standard deviations from the mean. For example, when $X - \mu = 10$ and $\sigma = 5$, $Z = \frac{X - \mu}{\sigma} = \frac{10}{5} = 2.00$. The proportion of area from μ to X can be found in the table under 2.00 and equals .4772. The area beyond 2.00 is equal to .5000 − .4772, or .0228. If Z is 1.76, for example, the correct entry is found by moving down to 1.70 in the left-hand column and over to .06 in the top row. The correct proportion is found to be .4608.

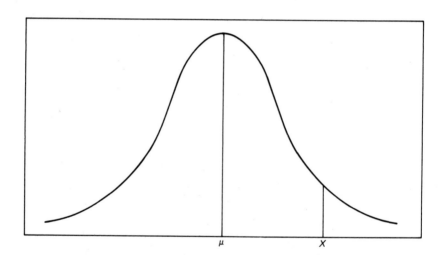

Z	.00	.01	.02	.03	.04	.05	.06	.07	.08	.09
0.0	0.0	0.0040	0.0080	0.0120	0.0160	0.0199	0.0239	0.0279	0.0319	0.0359
0.10	0.0398	0.0438	0.0478	0.0517	0.0557	0.0596	0.0636	0.0675	0.0714	0.0753
0.20	0.0793	0.0832	0.0871	0.0910	0.0948	0.0987	0.1026	0.1064	0.1103	0.1141
0.30	0.1179	0.1217	0.1255	0.1293	0.1331	0.1368	0.1406	0.1443	0.1480	0.1517
0.40	0.1554	0.1591	0.1628	0.1664	0.1700	0.1736	0.1772	0.1808	0.1844	0.1879
0.50	0.1915	0.1950	0.1985	0.2019	0.2054	0.2088	0.2123	0.2157	0.2190	0.2224
0.60	0.2257	0.2291	0.2324	0.2357	0.2389	0.2422	0.2454	0.2486	0.2517	0.2549
0.70	0.2580	0.2611	0.2642	0.2673	0.2703	0.2734	0.2764	0.2793	0.2823	0.2852
0.80	0.2881	0.2910	0.2939	0.2967	0.2995	0.3023	0.3051	0.3078	0.3106	0.3133
0.90	0.3159	0.3186	0.3212	0.3238	0.3264	0.3289	0.3315	0.3340	0.3365	0.3389
1.00	0.3413	0.3438	0.3461	0.3485	0.3508	0.3531	0.3554	0.3577	0.3599	0.3621
1.10	0.3643	0.3665	0.3686	0.3708	0.3729	0.3749	0.3770	0.3790	0.3810	0.3830
1.20	0.3849	0.3869	0.3888	0.3907	0.3925	0.3943	0.3962	0.3980	0.3997	0.4015
1.30	0.4032	0.4049	0.4066	0.4082	0.4099	0.4115	0.4131	0.4147	0.4162	0.4177
1.40	0.4192	0.4207	0.4222	0.4236	0.4251	0.4265	0.4279	0.4292	0.4306	0.4319
1.50	0.4332	0.4345	0.4357	0.4370	0.4382	0.4394	0.4406	0.4418	0.4429	0.4441
1.60	0.4452	0.4463	0.4474	0.4484	0.4495	0.4505	0.4515	0.4525	0.4535	0.4545
1.70	0.4554	0.4564	0.4573	0.4582	0.4591	0.4599	0.4608	0.4616	0.4625	0.4633
1.80	0.4641	0.4649	0.4656	0.4664	0.4671	0.4678	0.4686	0.4693	0.4699	0.4706
1.90	0.4713	0.4719	0.4726	0.4732	0.4738	0.4744	0.4750	0.4756	0.4761	0.4767
2.00	0.4772	0.4778	0.4783	0.4788	0.4793	0.4798	0.4803	0.4808	0.4812	0.4817
2.10	0.4821	0.4826	0.4830	0.4834	0.4838	0.4842	0.4846	0.4850	0.4854	0.4857
2.20	0.4861	0.4864	0.4868	0.4871	0.4875	0.4878	0.4881	0.4884	0.4887	0.4890
2.30	0.4893	0.4896	0.4898	0.4901	0.4904	0.4906	0.4909	0.4911	0.4913	0.4916
2.40	0.4918	0.4920	0.4922	0.4925	0.4927	0.4929	0.4931	0.4932	0.4934	0.4936
2.50	0.4938	0.4940	0.4941	0.4943	0.4945	0.4946	0.4948	0.4949	0.4951	0.4952
2.60	0.4953	0.4955	0.4956	0.4957	0.4959	0.4960	0.4961	0.4962	0.4963	0.4964
2.70	0.4965	0.4966	0.4967	0.4968	0.4969	0.4970	0.4971	0.4972	0.4973	0.4974
2.80	0.4974	0.4975	0.4976	0.4977	0.4977	0.4978	0.4979	0.4979	0.4980	0.4981
2.90	0.4981	0.4982	0.4982	0.4983	0.4984	0.4984	0.4985	0.4985	0.4986	0.4986
3.00	0.4986	0.4987	0.4987	0.4988	0.4988	0.4989	0.4989	0.4989	0.4990	0.4990
3.10	0.4990	0.4991	0.4991	0.4991	0.4992	0.4992	0.4992	0.4992	0.4993	0.4993
3.20	0.4993	0.4993	0.4994	0.4994	0.4994	0.4994	0.4994	0.4995	0.4995	0.4995
3.30	0.4995	0.4995	0.4995	0.4996	0.4996	0.4996	0.4996	0.4996	0.4996	0.4997
3.40	0.4997	0.4997	0.4997	0.4997	0.4997	0.4997	0.4997	0.4997	0.4997	0.4998
3.50	0.4998	0.4998	0.4998	0.4998	0.4998	0.4998	0.4998	0.4998	0.4998	0.4998

Appendix B
Binomial
Probabilities—
Noncumulative

The following table shows the probabilities for the number of successes r, in n trials, for certain values of p, the probability of success on a single trial

$$P(r = r_0 \mid n, p)$$

p

n	r	.95	.90	.85	.80	.75	.70	.65	.60	.55	.50	.45	.40	.35	.30	.25	.20	.15	.10	.05
1	0	.0500	.1000	.1500	.2000	.2500	.3000	.3500	.4000	.4500	.5000	.5500	.6000	.6500	.7000	.7500	.8000	.8500	.9000	.9500
	1	.9500	.9000	.8500	.8000	.7500	.7000	.6500	.6000	.5500	.5000	.4500	.4000	.3500	.3000	.2500	.2000	.1500	.1000	.0500
2	0	.0025	.0100	.0225	.0400	.0625	.0900	.1225	.1600	.2025	.2500	.3025	.3600	.4225	.4900	.5625	.6400	.7225	.8100	.9025
	1	.0950	.1800	.2550	.3200	.3750	.4200	.4550	.4800	.4950	.5000	.4950	.4800	.4550	.4200	.3750	.3200	.2550	.1800	.0950
	2	.9025	.8100	.7225	.6400	.5625	.4900	.4225	.3600	.3025	.2500	.2025	.1600	.1225	.0900	.0625	.0400	.0225	.0100	.0025
3	0	.0001	.0010	.0034	.0080	.0156	.0270	.0429	.0640	.0911	.1250	.1664	.2160	.2746	.3430	.4219	.5120	.6141	.7290	.8574
	1	.0071	.0270	.0574	.0960	.1406	.1890	.2389	.2880	.3341	.3750	.4084	.4320	.4436	.4410	.4219	.3840	.3251	.2430	.1354
	2	.1354	.2430	.3251	.3840	.4219	.4410	.4436	.4320	.4084	.3750	.3341	.2880	.2389	.1890	.1406	.0960	.0574	.0270	.0071
	3	.8574	.7290	.6141	.5120	.4219	.3430	.2746	.2160	.1664	.1250	.0911	.0640	.0429	.0270	.0156	.0080	.0034	.0010	.0001
4	0	.0000	.0001	.0005	.0016	.0039	.0081	.0150	.0256	.0410	.0625	.0915	.1296	.1785	.2401	.3164	.4096	.5220	.6561	.8145
	1	.0005	.0036	.0115	.0256	.0469	.0756	.1115	.1536	.2005	.2500	.2995	.3456	.3845	.4116	.4219	.4096	.3685	.2916	.1715
	2	.0135	.0486	.0975	.1536	.2109	.2646	.3105	.3456	.3675	.3750	.3675	.3456	.3105	.2646	.2109	.1536	.0975	.0486	.0135
	3	.1715	.2916	.3685	.4096	.4219	.4116	.3845	.3456	.2995	.2500	.2005	.1536	.1115	.0756	.0469	.0256	.0115	.0036	.0005
	4	.8145	.6561	.5220	.4096	.3164	.2401	.1785	.1296	.0915	.0625	.0410	.0256	.0150	.0081	.0039	.0016	.0005	.0001	.0000
5	0	.0000	.0000	.0001	.0003	.0010	.0024	.0053	.0102	.0185	.0313	.0503	.0778	.1160	.1681	.2373	.3277	.4437	.5905	.7738
	1	.0000	.0005	.0022	.0064	.0146	.0284	.0488	.0768	.1128	.1563	.2059	.2592	.3124	.3601	.3955	.4096	.3915	.3280	.2036
	2	.0011	.0081	.0244	.0512	.0879	.1323	.1811	.2304	.2757	.3125	.3369	.3456	.3364	.3087	.2637	.2048	.1382	.0729	.0214
	3	.0214	.0729	.1382	.2048	.2637	.3087	.3364	.3456	.3369	.3125	.2757	.2304	.1811	.1323	.0879	.0512	.0244	.0081	.0011
	4	.2036	.3280	.3915	.4096	.3955	.3601	.3124	.2592	.2059	.1563	.1128	.0768	.0488	.0284	.0146	.0064	.0022	.0005	.0000
	5	.7738	.5905	.4437	.3277	.2373	.1681	.1160	.0778	.0503	.0312	.0185	.0102	.0053	.0024	.0010	.0003	.0001	.0000	.0000
6	0	.0000	.0000	.0000	.0001	.0002	.0007	.0018	.0041	.0083	.0156	.0277	.0467	.0754	.1176	.1780	.2621	.3771	.5314	.7351
	1	.0000	.0001	.0004	.0015	.0044	.0102	.0205	.0369	.0609	.0938	.1359	.1866	.2437	.3025	.3560	.3932	.3993	.3543	.2321
	2	.0001	.0012	.0055	.0154	.0330	.0595	.0951	.1382	.1861	.2344	.2780	.3110	.3280	.3241	.2966	.2458	.1762	.0984	.0305
	3	.0021	.0146	.0415	.0819	.1318	.1852	.2355	.2765	.3032	.3125	.3032	.2765	.2355	.1852	.1318	.0819	.0415	.0146	.0021
	4	.0305	.0984	.1762	.2458	.2966	.3241	.3280	.3110	.2780	.2344	.1861	.1382	.0951	.0595	.0330	.0154	.0055	.0012	.0001
	5	.2321	.3543	.3993	.3932	.3560	.3025	.2437	.1866	.1359	.0938	.0609	.0369	.0205	.0102	.0044	.0015	.0004	.0001	.0000
	6	.7351	.5314	.3771	.2621	.1780	.1176	.0754	.0467	.0277	.0156	.0083	.0041	.0018	.0007	.0002	.0001	.0000	.0000	.0000
7	0	.0000	.0000	.0000	.0000	.0001	.0002	.0006	.0016	.0037	.0078	.0152	.0280	.0490	.0824	.1335	.2097	.3206	.4783	.6983
	1	.0000	.0000	.0001	.0004	.0013	.0036	.0084	.0172	.0320	.0547	.0872	.1306	.1848	.2471	.3115	.3670	.3960	.3720	.2573
	2	.0000	.0002	.0012	.0043	.0115	.0250	.0466	.0774	.1172	.1641	.2140	.2613	.2985	.3177	.3115	.2753	.2097	.1240	.0406
	3	.0002	.0026	.0109	.0287	.0577	.0972	.1442	.1935	.2388	.2734	.2918	.2903	.2679	.2269	.1730	.1147	.0617	.0230	.0036
	4	.0036	.0230	.0617	.1147	.1730	.2269	.2679	.2903	.2918	.2734	.2388	.1935	.1442	.0972	.0577	.0287	.0109	.0026	.0002

n	r										p									
		.05	.10	.15	.20	.25	.30	.35	.40	.45	.50	.55	.60	.65	.70	.75	.80	.85	.90	.95
	5	.0000	.0002	.0012	.0043	.0115	.0250	.0466	.0774	.1172	.1641	.2140	.2613	.2985	.3177	.3115	.2753	.2097	.1240	.0406
	6	.0000	.0000	.0001	.0004	.0013	.0036	.0084	.0172	.0320	.0547	.0872	.1306	.1848	.2471	.3115	.3670	.3960	.3720	.2573
	7	.0000	.0000	.0000	.0000	.0001	.0002	.0006	.0016	.0037	.0078	.0152	.0280	.0490	.0824	.1335	.2097	.3206	.4783	.6983
8	0	.6634	.4305	.2725	.1678	.1001	.0576	.0319	.0168	.0084	.0039	.0017	.0007	.0002	.0001	.0000	.0000	.0000	.0000	.0000
	1	.2793	.3826	.3847	.3355	.2670	.1977	.1373	.0896	.0548	.0313	.0164	.0079	.0033	.0012	.0004	.0001	.0000	.0000	.0000
	2	.0515	.1488	.2376	.2936	.3115	.2965	.2587	.2090	.1569	.1094	.0703	.0413	.0217	.0100	.0038	.0011	.0002	.0000	.0000
	3	.0054	.0331	.0839	.1468	.2076	.2541	.2786	.2787	.2568	.2188	.1719	.1239	.0808	.0467	.0231	.0092	.0026	.0004	.0000
	4	.0004	.0046	.0185	.0459	.0865	.1361	.1875	.2322	.2627	.2734	.2627	.2322	.1875	.1361	.0865	.0459	.0185	.0046	.0004
	5	.0000	.0004	.0026	.0092	.0231	.0467	.0808	.1239	.1719	.2187	.2568	.2787	.2786	.2541	.2076	.1468	.0839	.0331	.0054
	6	.0000	.0000	.0002	.0011	.0038	.0100	.0217	.0413	.0703	.1094	.1569	.2090	.2587	.2965	.3115	.2936	.2376	.1488	.0515
	7	.0000	.0000	.0000	.0001	.0004	.0012	.0033	.0079	.0164	.0312	.0548	.0896	.1373	.1977	.2670	.3355	.3847	.3826	.2793
	8	.0000	.0000	.0000	.0000	.0000	.0001	.0002	.0007	.0017	.0039	.0084	.0168	.0319	.0576	.1001	.1678	.2725	.4305	.6634
9	0	.6302	.3874	.2316	.1342	.0751	.0404	.0207	.0101	.0046	.0020	.0008	.0003	.0001	.0000	.0000	.0000	.0000	.0000	.0000
	1	.2985	.3874	.3679	.3020	.2253	.1556	.1004	.0605	.0339	.0176	.0083	.0035	.0013	.0004	.0001	.0000	.0000	.0000	.0000
	2	.0629	.1722	.2597	.3020	.3003	.2668	.2162	.1612	.1110	.0703	.0407	.0212	.0098	.0039	.0012	.0003	.0000	.0000	.0000
	3	.0077	.0446	.1069	.1762	.2336	.2668	.2716	.2508	.2119	.1641	.1160	.0743	.0424	.0210	.0087	.0028	.0006	.0001	.0000
	4	.0006	.0074	.0283	.0661	.1168	.1715	.2194	.2508	.2600	.2461	.2128	.1672	.1181	.0735	.0389	.0165	.0050	.0008	.0000
	5	.0000	.0008	.0050	.0165	.0389	.0735	.1181	.1672	.2128	.2461	.2600	.2508	.2194	.1715	.1168	.0661	.0283	.0074	.0006
	6	.0000	.0001	.0006	.0028	.0087	.0210	.0424	.0743	.1160	.1641	.2119	.2508	.2716	.2668	.2336	.1762	.1069	.0446	.0077
	7	.0000	.0000	.0000	.0003	.0012	.0039	.0098	.0212	.0407	.0703	.1110	.1612	.2162	.2668	.3003	.3020	.2597	.1722	.0629
	8	.0000	.0000	.0000	.0000	.0001	.0004	.0013	.0035	.0083	.0176	.0339	.0605	.1004	.1556	.2253	.3020	.3679	.3874	.2985
	9	.0000	.0000	.0000	.0000	.0000	.0000	.0001	.0003	.0008	.0020	.0046	.0101	.0207	.0404	.0751	.1342	.2316	.3874	.6302
10	0	.5987	.3487	.1969	.1074	.0563	.0282	.0135	.0060	.0025	.0010	.0003	.0001	.0000	.0000	.0000	.0000	.0000	.0000	.0000
	1	.3151	.3874	.3474	.2684	.1877	.1211	.0725	.0403	.0207	.0098	.0042	.0016	.0005	.0001	.0000	.0000	.0000	.0000	.0000
	2	.0746	.1937	.2759	.3020	.2816	.2335	.1757	.1209	.0763	.0439	.0229	.0106	.0043	.0014	.0004	.0001	.0000	.0000	.0000
	3	.0105	.0574	.1298	.2013	.2503	.2668	.2522	.2150	.1665	.1172	.0746	.0425	.0212	.0090	.0031	.0008	.0001	.0000	.0000
	4	.0010	.0112	.0401	.0881	.1460	.2001	.2377	.2508	.2384	.2051	.1596	.1115	.0689	.0368	.0162	.0055	.0012	.0001	.0000
	5	.0001	.0015	.0085	.0264	.0584	.1029	.1536	.2007	.2340	.2461	.2340	.2007	.1536	.1029	.0584	.0264	.0085	.0015	.0001
	6	.0000	.0001	.0012	.0055	.0162	.0368	.0689	.1115	.1596	.2051	.2384	.2508	.2377	.2001	.1460	.0881	.0401	.0112	.0010
	7	.0000	.0000	.0001	.0008	.0031	.0090	.0212	.0425	.0746	.1172	.1665	.2150	.2522	.2668	.2503	.2013	.1298	.0574	.0105
	8	.0000	.0000	.0000	.0001	.0004	.0014	.0043	.0106	.0229	.0439	.0763	.1209	.1757	.2335	.2816	.3020	.2759	.1937	.0746
	9	.0000	.0000	.0000	.0000	.0000	.0001	.0005	.0016	.0042	.0098	.0207	.0403	.0725	.1211	.1877	.2684	.3474	.3874	.3151
	10	.0000	.0000	.0000	.0000	.0000	.0000	.0000	.0001	.0003	.0010	.0025	.0060	.0135	.0282	.0563	.1074	.1969	.3487	.5987

p

n	r	.05	.10	.15	.20	.25	.30	.35	.40	.45	.50	.55	.60	.65	.70	.75	.80	.85	.90	.95
11	0	.5688	.3138	.1673	.0859	.0422	.0198	.0088	.0036	.0014	.0005	.0002	.0000	.0000	.0000	.0000	.0000	.0000	.0000	.0000
	1	.3293	.3835	.3248	.2362	.1549	.0932	.0518	.0266	.0125	.0054	.0021	.0007	.0002	.0000	.0000	.0000	.0000	.0000	.0000
	2	.0867	.2131	.2866	.2953	.2581	.1998	.1395	.0887	.0513	.0269	.0126	.0052	.0018	.0005	.0001	.0000	.0000	.0000	.0000
	3	.0137	.0710	.1517	.2215	.2581	.2568	.2254	.1774	.1259	.0806	.0462	.0234	.0102	.0037	.0011	.0002	.0000	.0000	.0000
	4	.0014	.0158	.0536	.1107	.1721	.2201	.2428	.2365	.2060	.1611	.1128	.0701	.0379	.0173	.0064	.0017	.0003	.0000	.0000
	5	.0001	.0025	.0132	.0388	.0803	.1321	.1830	.2207	.2360	.2256	.1931	.1471	.0985	.0566	.0268	.0097	.0023	.0003	.0000
	6	.0000	.0003	.0023	.0097	.0268	.0566	.0985	.1471	.1931	.2256	.2360	.2207	.1830	.1321	.0803	.0388	.0132	.0025	.0001
	7	.0000	.0000	.0003	.0017	.0064	.0173	.0379	.0701	.1128	.1611	.2060	.2365	.2428	.2201	.1721	.1107	.0536	.0158	.0014
	8	.0000	.0000	.0000	.0002	.0011	.0037	.0102	.0234	.0462	.0806	.1259	.1774	.2254	.2568	.2581	.2215	.1517	.0710	.0137
	9	.0000	.0000	.0000	.0000	.0001	.0005	.0018	.0052	.0126	.0269	.0513	.0887	.1395	.1998	.2581	.2953	.2866	.2131	.0867
	10	.0000	.0000	.0000	.0000	.0000	.0000	.0002	.0007	.0021	.0054	.0125	.0266	.0518	.0932	.1549	.2362	.3248	.3835	.3293
	11	.0000	.0000	.0000	.0000	.0000	.0000	.0000	.0000	.0002	.0005	.0014	.0036	.0088	.0198	.0422	.0859	.1673	.3138	.5688
12	0	.5404	.2824	.1422	.0687	.0317	.0138	.0057	.0022	.0008	.0002	.0001	.0000	.0000	.0000	.0000	.0000	.0000	.0000	.0000
	1	.3413	.3766	.3012	.2062	.1267	.0712	.0368	.0174	.0075	.0029	.0010	.0003	.0001	.0000	.0000	.0000	.0000	.0000	.0000
	2	.0988	.2301	.2924	.2835	.2323	.1678	.1088	.0639	.0339	.0161	.0068	.0025	.0008	.0002	.0000	.0000	.0000	.0000	.0000
	3	.0173	.0852	.1720	.2362	.2581	.2397	.1954	.1419	.0923	.0537	.0277	.0125	.0048	.0015	.0004	.0001	.0000	.0000	.0000
	4	.0021	.0213	.0683	.1329	.1936	.2311	.2367	.2128	.1700	.1208	.0762	.0420	.0199	.0078	.0024	.0005	.0001	.0000	.0000
	5	.0002	.0038	.0193	.0532	.1032	.1585	.2039	.2270	.2225	.1934	.1489	.1009	.0591	.0291	.0115	.0033	.0006	.0000	.0000
	6	.0000	.0005	.0040	.0155	.0401	.0792	.1281	.1766	.2124	.2256	.2124	.1766	.1281	.0792	.0401	.0155	.0040	.0005	.0000
	7	.0000	.0000	.0006	.0033	.0115	.0291	.0591	.1009	.1489	.1934	.2225	.2270	.2039	.1585	.1032	.0532	.0193	.0038	.0002
	8	.0000	.0000	.0001	.0005	.0024	.0078	.0199	.0420	.0762	.1208	.1700	.2128	.2367	.2311	.1936	.1329	.0683	.0213	.0021
	9	.0000	.0000	.0000	.0001	.0004	.0015	.0048	.0125	.0277	.0537	.0923	.1419	.1954	.2397	.2581	.2362	.1720	.0852	.0173
	10	.0000	.0000	.0000	.0000	.0000	.0002	.0008	.0025	.0068	.0161	.0339	.0639	.1088	.1678	.2323	.2835	.2924	.2301	.0988
	11	.0000	.0000	.0000	.0000	.0000	.0000	.0001	.0003	.0010	.0029	.0075	.0174	.0368	.0712	.1267	.2062	.3012	.3766	.3413
	12	.0000	.0000	.0000	.0000	.0000	.0000	.0000	.0000	.0001	.0002	.0008	.0022	.0057	.0138	.0317	.0687	.1422	.2824	.5404
13	0	.5133	.2542	.1209	.0550	.0238	.0097	.0037	.0013	.0004	.0001	.0000	.0000	.0000	.0000	.0000	.0000	.0000	.0000	.0000
	1	.3512	.3672	.2774	.1787	.1029	.0540	.0259	.0113	.0045	.0016	.0005	.0001	.0000	.0000	.0000	.0000	.0000	.0000	.0000
	2	.1109	.2448	.2937	.2680	.2059	.1388	.0836	.0453	.0220	.0095	.0036	.0012	.0003	.0001	.0000	.0000	.0000	.0000	.0000
	3	.0214	.0997	.1900	.2457	.2517	.2181	.1651	.1107	.0660	.0349	.0162	.0065	.0022	.0006	.0001	.0000	.0000	.0000	.0000
	4	.0028	.0277	.0838	.1535	.2097	.2337	.2222	.1845	.1350	.0873	.0495	.0243	.0101	.0034	.0009	.0001	.0000	.0000	.0000
	5	.0003	.0055	.0266	.0691	.1258	.1803	.2154	.2214	.1989	.1571	.1089	.0656	.0336	.0142	.0047	.0011	.0001	.0000	.0000
	6	.0000	.0008	.0063	.0230	.0559	.1030	.1546	.1968	.2169	.2095	.1775	.1312	.0833	.0442	.0186	.0058	.0011	.0001	.0000
	7	.0000	.0001	.0011	.0058	.0186	.0442	.0833	.1312	.1775	.2095	.2169	.1968	.1546	.1030	.0559	.0230	.0063	.0008	.0000
	8	.0000	.0000	.0001	.0011	.0047	.0142	.0336	.0656	.1089	.1571	.1989	.2214	.2154	.1803	.1258	.0691	.0266	.0055	.0003
	9	.0000	.0000	.0000	.0001	.0009	.0034	.0101	.0243	.0495	.0873	.1350	.1845	.2222	.2337	.2097	.1535	.0838	.0277	.0028
	10	.0000	.0000	.0000	.0000	.0001	.0006	.0022	.0065	.0162	.0349	.0660	.1107	.1651	.2181	.2517	.2457	.1900	.0997	.0214
	11	.0000	.0000	.0000	.0000	.0000	.0001	.0003	.0012	.0036	.0095	.0220	.0453	.0836	.1388	.2059	.2680	.2937	.2448	.1109
	12	.0000	.0000	.0000	.0000	.0000	.0000	.0000	.0001	.0005	.0016	.0045	.0113	.0259	.0540	.1029	.1787	.2774	.3672	.3512
	13	.0000	.0000	.0000	.0000	.0000	.0000	.0000	.0000	.0000	.0001	.0004	.0013	.0037	.0097	.0238	.0550	.1209	.2542	.5133

n	r	.05	.10	.15	.20	.25	.30	.35	.40	.45	.50	.55	.60	.65	.70	.75	.80	.85	.90	.95
											p									
14	0	.4877	.2288	.1028	.0440	.0178	.0068	.0024	.0008	.0002	.0001	.0000	.0000	.0000	.0000	.0000	.0000	.0000	.0000	.0000
	1	.3593	.3559	.2539	.1539	.0832	.0407	.0181	.0073	.0027	.0009	.0002	.0001	.0000	.0000	.0000	.0000	.0000	.0000	.0000
	2	.1229	.2570	.2912	.2501	.1802	.1134	.0634	.0317	.0141	.0056	.0019	.0005	.0001	.0000	.0000	.0000	.0000	.0000	.0000
	3	.0259	.1142	.2056	.2501	.2402	.1943	.1366	.0845	.0462	.0222	.0093	.0033	.0010	.0002	.0000	.0000	.0000	.0000	.0000
	4	.0037	.0349	.0998	.1720	.2202	.2290	.2022	.1549	.1040	.0611	.0312	.0136	.0049	.0014	.0003	.0000	.0000	.0000	.0000
	5	.0004	.0078	.0352	.0860	.1468	.1963	.2178	.2066	.1701	.1222	.0762	.0408	.0183	.0066	.0018	.0003	.0000	.0000	.0000
	6	.0000	.0013	.0093	.0322	.0734	.1262	.1759	.2066	.2088	.1833	.1398	.0918	.0510	.0232	.0082	.0020	.0003	.0000	.0000
	7	.0000	.0002	.0019	.0092	.0280	.0618	.1082	.1574	.1952	.2095	.1952	.1574	.1082	.0618	.0280	.0092	.0019	.0002	.0000
	8	.0000	.0000	.0003	.0020	.0082	.0232	.0510	.0918	.1398	.1833	.2088	.2066	.1759	.1262	.0734	.0322	.0093	.0013	.0000
	9	.0000	.0000	.0000	.0003	.0018	.0066	.0183	.0408	.0762	.1222	.1701	.2066	.2178	.1963	.1468	.0860	.0352	.0078	.0004
	10	.0000	.0000	.0000	.0000	.0003	.0014	.0049	.0136	.0312	.0611	.1040	.1549	.2022	.2290	.2202	.1720	.0998	.0349	.0037
	11	.0000	.0000	.0000	.0000	.0000	.0002	.0010	.0033	.0093	.0222	.0462	.0845	.1366	.1943	.2402	.2501	.2056	.1142	.0259
	12	.0000	.0000	.0000	.0000	.0000	.0000	.0001	.0005	.0019	.0056	.0141	.0317	.0634	.1134	.1802	.2501	.2912	.2570	.1229
	13	.0000	.0000	.0000	.0000	.0000	.0000	.0000	.0001	.0002	.0009	.0027	.0073	.0181	.0407	.0832	.1539	.2539	.3559	.3593
	14	.0000	.0000	.0000	.0000	.0000	.0000	.0000	.0000	.0000	.0001	.0002	.0008	.0024	.0068	.0178	.0440	.1028	.2288	.4877
15	0	.4633	.2059	.0874	.0352	.0134	.0047	.0016	.0005	.0001	.0000	.0000	.0000	.0000	.0000	.0000	.0000	.0000	.0000	.0000
	1	.3658	.3432	.2312	.1319	.0668	.0305	.0126	.0047	.0016	.0005	.0001	.0000	.0000	.0000	.0000	.0000	.0000	.0000	.0000
	2	.1348	.2669	.2856	.2309	.1559	.0916	.0476	.0219	.0090	.0032	.0010	.0003	.0001	.0000	.0000	.0000	.0000	.0000	.0000
	3	.0307	.1285	.2184	.2501	.2252	.1700	.1110	.0634	.0318	.0139	.0052	.0016	.0004	.0001	.0000	.0000	.0000	.0000	.0000
	4	.0049	.0428	.1156	.1876	.2252	.2186	.1792	.1268	.0780	.0417	.0191	.0074	.0024	.0006	.0001	.0000	.0000	.0000	.0000
	5	.0006	.0105	.0449	.1032	.1651	.2061	.2123	.1859	.1404	.0916	.0515	.0245	.0096	.0030	.0007	.0001	.0000	.0000	.0000
	6	.0000	.0019	.0132	.0430	.0917	.1472	.1906	.2066	.1914	.1527	.1048	.0612	.0298	.0116	.0034	.0007	.0001	.0000	.0000
	7	.0000	.0003	.0030	.0138	.0393	.0811	.1319	.1771	.2013	.1964	.1647	.1181	.0710	.0348	.0131	.0035	.0005	.0000	.0000
	8	.0000	.0000	.0005	.0035	.0131	.0348	.0710	.1181	.1647	.1964	.2013	.1771	.1319	.0811	.0393	.0138	.0030	.0003	.0000
	9	.0000	.0000	.0001	.0007	.0034	.0116	.0298	.0612	.1048	.1527	.1914	.2066	.1906	.1472	.0917	.0430	.0132	.0019	.0000
	10	.0000	.0000	.0000	.0001	.0007	.0030	.0096	.0245	.0515	.0916	.1404	.1859	.2123	.2061	.1651	.1032	.0449	.0105	.0006
	11	.0000	.0000	.0000	.0000	.0001	.0006	.0024	.0074	.0191	.0417	.0780	.1268	.1792	.2186	.2252	.1876	.1156	.0428	.0049
	12	.0000	.0000	.0000	.0000	.0000	.0001	.0004	.0016	.0052	.0139	.0318	.0634	.1110	.1700	.2252	.2501	.2184	.1285	.0307
	13	.0000	.0000	.0000	.0000	.0000	.0000	.0001	.0003	.0010	.0032	.0090	.0219	.0476	.0916	.1559	.2309	.2856	.2669	.1348
	14	.0000	.0000	.0000	.0000	.0000	.0000	.0000	.0000	.0001	.0005	.0016	.0047	.0126	.0305	.0668	.1319	.2312	.3432	.3658
	15	.0000	.0000	.0000	.0000	.0000	.0000	.0000	.0000	.0000	.0000	.0001	.0005	.0016	.0047	.0134	.0352	.0874	.2059	.4633
16	0	.4401	.1853	.0743	.0281	.0100	.0033	.0010	.0003	.0001	.0000	.0000	.0000	.0000	.0000	.0000	.0000	.0000	.0000	.0000
	1	.3706	.3294	.2097	.1126	.0535	.0228	.0087	.0030	.0009	.0002	.0001	.0000	.0000	.0000	.0000	.0000	.0000	.0000	.0000
	2	.1463	.2745	.2775	.2111	.1336	.0732	.0353	.0150	.0056	.0018	.0005	.0001	.0000	.0000	.0000	.0000	.0000	.0000	.0000
	3	.0359	.1423	.2285	.2463	.2079	.1465	.0888	.0468	.0215	.0085	.0029	.0008	.0002	.0000	.0000	.0000	.0000	.0000	.0000
	4	.0061	.0514	.1311	.2001	.2252	.2040	.1553	.1014	.0572	.0278	.0115	.0040	.0011	.0002	.0000	.0000	.0000	.0000	.0000

_p_

n	r	.05	.10	.15	.20	.25	.30	.35	.40	.45	.50	.55	.60	.65	.70	.75	.80	.85	.90	.95
	5	.0008	.0137	.0555	.1201	.1802	.2099	.2008	.1623	.1123	.0667	.0337	.0142	.0049	.0013	.0002	.0000	.0000	.0000	.0000
	6	.0001	.0028	.0180	.0550	.1101	.1649	.1982	.1983	.1684	.1222	.0755	.0392	.0167	.0056	.0014	.0002	.0000	.0000	.0000
	7	.0000	.0004	.0045	.0197	.0524	.1010	.1524	.1889	.1969	.1746	.1318	.0840	.0442	.0185	.0058	.0012	.0001	.0000	.0000
	8	.0000	.0001	.0009	.0055	.0197	.0487	.0923	.1417	.1812	.1964	.1812	.1417	.0923	.0487	.0197	.0055	.0009	.0001	.0000
	9	.0000	.0000	.0001	.0012	.0058	.0185	.0442	.0840	.1318	.1746	.1969	.1889	.1524	.1010	.0524	.0197	.0045	.0004	.0000
	10	.0000	.0000	.0000	.0002	.0014	.0056	.0167	.0392	.0755	.1222	.1684	.1983	.1982	.1649	.1101	.0550	.0180	.0028	.0001
	11	.0000	.0000	.0000	.0000	.0002	.0013	.0049	.0142	.0337	.0667	.1123	.1623	.2008	.2099	.1802	.1201	.0555	.0137	.0008
	12	.0000	.0000	.0000	.0000	.0000	.0002	.0011	.0040	.0115	.0278	.0572	.1014	.1553	.2040	.2252	.2001	.1311	.0514	.0061
	13	.0000	.0000	.0000	.0000	.0000	.0000	.0002	.0008	.0029	.0085	.0215	.0468	.0888	.1465	.2079	.2463	.2285	.1423	.0359
	14	.0000	.0000	.0000	.0000	.0000	.0000	.0000	.0001	.0005	.0018	.0056	.0150	.0353	.0732	.1336	.2111	.2775	.2745	.1463
	15	.0000	.0000	.0000	.0000	.0000	.0000	.0000	.0000	.0001	.0002	.0009	.0030	.0087	.0228	.0535	.1126	.2096	.3294	.3706
	16	.0000	.0000	.0000	.0000	.0000	.0000	.0000	.0000	.0000	.0000	.0001	.0003	.0010	.0033	.0100	.0281	.0742	.1853	.4401
17	0	.4181	.1668	.0631	.0225	.0075	.0023	.0007	.0002	.0000	.0000	.0000	.0000	.0000	.0000	.0000	.0000	.0000	.0000	.0000
	1	.3741	.3150	.1893	.0957	.0426	.0169	.0060	.0019	.0005	.0001	.0000	.0000	.0000	.0000	.0000	.0000	.0000	.0000	.0000
	2	.1575	.2800	.2673	.1914	.1136	.0581	.0260	.0102	.0035	.0010	.0003	.0001	.0000	.0000	.0000	.0000	.0000	.0000	.0000
	3	.0415	.1556	.2359	.2393	.1893	.1245	.0701	.0341	.0144	.0052	.0016	.0004	.0001	.0000	.0000	.0000	.0000	.0000	.0000
	4	.0076	.0605	.1457	.2093	.2209	.1868	.1320	.0796	.0411	.0182	.0068	.0021	.0005	.0001	.0000	.0000	.0000	.0000	.0000
	5	.0010	.0175	.0668	.1361	.1914	.2081	.1849	.1379	.0875	.0472	.0215	.0081	.0024	.0006	.0001	.0000	.0000	.0000	.0000
	6	.0001	.0039	.0236	.0680	.1276	.1784	.1991	.1839	.1432	.0944	.0525	.0242	.0090	.0026	.0005	.0001	.0000	.0000	.0000
	7	.0000	.0007	.0065	.0267	.0668	.1201	.1685	.1927	.1841	.1484	.1008	.0571	.0263	.0095	.0025	.0004	.0000	.0000	.0000
	8	.0000	.0001	.0014	.0084	.0279	.0644	.1134	.1606	.1883	.1855	.1540	.1070	.0611	.0276	.0093	.0021	.0003	.0000	.0000
	9	.0000	.0000	.0003	.0021	.0093	.0276	.0611	.1070	.1540	.1855	.1883	.1606	.1134	.0644	.0279	.0084	.0014	.0001	.0000
	10	.0000	.0000	.0000	.0004	.0025	.0095	.0263	.0571	.1008	.1484	.1841	.1927	.1685	.1201	.0668	.0267	.0065	.0007	.0000
	11	.0000	.0000	.0000	.0001	.0005	.0026	.0090	.0242	.0525	.0944	.1432	.1839	.1991	.1784	.1276	.0680	.0236	.0039	.0001
	12	.0000	.0000	.0000	.0000	.0001	.0006	.0024	.0081	.0215	.0472	.0875	.1379	.1849	.2081	.1914	.1361	.0668	.0175	.0010
	13	.0000	.0000	.0000	.0000	.0000	.0001	.0005	.0021	.0068	.0182	.0411	.0796	.1320	.1868	.2209	.2093	.1457	.0605	.0076
	14	.0000	.0000	.0000	.0000	.0000	.0000	.0001	.0004	.0016	.0052	.0144	.0341	.0701	.1245	.1893	.2393	.2359	.1556	.0415
	15	.0000	.0000	.0000	.0000	.0000	.0000	.0000	.0001	.0003	.0010	.0035	.0102	.0260	.0581	.1136	.1914	.2673	.2800	.1575
	16	.0000	.0000	.0000	.0000	.0000	.0000	.0000	.0000	.0000	.0001	.0005	.0019	.0060	.0169	.0426	.0957	.1893	.3150	.3741
	17	.0000	.0000	.0000	.0000	.0000	.0000	.0000	.0000	.0000	.0000	.0000	.0002	.0007	.0023	.0075	.0225	.0631	.1668	.4181
18	0	.3972	.1501	.0536	.0180	.0056	.0016	.0004	.0001	.0000	.0000	.0000	.0000	.0000	.0000	.0000	.0000	.0000	.0000	.0000
	1	.3763	.3002	.1704	.0811	.0338	.0126	.0042	.0012	.0003	.0001	.0000	.0000	.0000	.0000	.0000	.0000	.0000	.0000	.0000
	2	.1683	.2835	.2556	.1723	.0958	.0458	.0190	.0069	.0022	.0006	.0001	.0000	.0000	.0000	.0000	.0000	.0000	.0000	.0000
	3	.0473	.1680	.2406	.2297	.1704	.1046	.0547	.0246	.0095	.0031	.0009	.0002	.0001	.0000	.0000	.0000	.0000	.0000	.0000
	4	.0093	.0700	.1592	.2153	.2130	.1681	.1104	.0614	.0291	.0117	.0039	.0011	.0002	.0000	.0000	.0000	.0000	.0000	.0000

p

n	r	.05	.10	.15	.20	.25	.30	.35	.40	.45	.50	.55	.60	.65	.70	.75	.80	.85	.90	.95
	5	.0014	.0218	.0787	.1507	.1988	.2017	.1664	.1146	.0666	.0327	.0134	.0045	.0012	.0002	.0000	.0000	.0000	.0000	.0000
	6	.0002	.0052	.0301	.0816	.1436	.1873	.1941	.1655	.1181	.0708	.0354	.0145	.0047	.0012	.0002	.0000	.0000	.0000	.0000
	7	.0000	.0010	.0091	.0350	.0820	.1376	.1792	.1892	.1657	.1214	.0742	.0374	.0151	.0046	.0010	.0001	.0000	.0000	.0000
	8	.0000	.0002	.0022	.0120	.0376	.0811	.1327	.1734	.1864	.1669	.1248	.0771	.0385	.0149	.0042	.0008	.0001	.0000	.0000
	9	.0000	.0000	.0004	.0033	.0139	.0386	.0794	.1284	.1694	.1855	.1694	.1284	.0794	.0386	.0139	.0033	.0004	.0000	.0000
	10	.0000	.0000	.0001	.0008	.0042	.0149	.0385	.0771	.1248	.1669	.1864	.1734	.1327	.0811	.0376	.0120	.0022	.0002	.0000
	11	.0000	.0000	.0000	.0001	.0010	.0046	.0151	.0374	.0742	.1214	.1657	.1892	.1792	.1376	.0820	.0350	.0091	.0010	.0000
	12	.0000	.0000	.0000	.0000	.0002	.0012	.0047	.0145	.0354	.0708	.1181	.1655	.1941	.1873	.1436	.0816	.0301	.0052	.0002
	13	.0000	.0000	.0000	.0000	.0000	.0002	.0012	.0045	.0134	.0327	.0666	.1146	.1664	.2017	.1988	.1507	.0787	.0218	.0014
	14	.0000	.0000	.0000	.0000	.0000	.0000	.0002	.0011	.0039	.0117	.0291	.0614	.1104	.1681	.2130	.2153	.1592	.0700	.0093
	15	.0000	.0000	.0000	.0000	.0000	.0000	.0000	.0002	.0009	.0031	.0095	.0246	.0547	.1046	.1704	.2297	.2406	.1680	.0473
	16	.0000	.0000	.0000	.0000	.0000	.0000	.0000	.0000	.0001	.0006	.0022	.0069	.0190	.0458	.0958	.1723	.2556	.2835	.1684
	17	.0000	.0000	.0000	.0000	.0000	.0000	.0000	.0000	.0000	.0001	.0003	.0012	.0042	.0126	.0338	.0811	.1704	.3002	.3763
	18	.0000	.0000	.0000	.0000	.0000	.0000	.0000	.0000	.0000	.0000	.0000	.0001	.0004	.0016	.0056	.0180	.0536	.1501	.3972
19	0	.3774	.1351	.0456	.0144	.0042	.0011	.0003	.0001	.0000	.0000	.0000	.0000	.0000	.0000	.0000	.0000	.0000	.0000	.0000
	1	.3774	.2852	.1529	.0685	.0268	.0093	.0029	.0008	.0002	.0000	.0000	.0000	.0000	.0000	.0000	.0000	.0000	.0000	.0000
	2	.1787	.2852	.2428	.1540	.0803	.0358	.0138	.0046	.0013	.0003	.0001	.0000	.0000	.0000	.0000	.0000	.0000	.0000	.0000
	3	.0533	.1796	.2428	.2182	.1517	.0869	.0422	.0175	.0062	.0018	.0005	.0001	.0000	.0000	.0000	.0000	.0000	.0000	.0000
	4	.0112	.0798	.1714	.2182	.2023	.1491	.0909	.0467	.0203	.0074	.0022	.0005	.0001	.0000	.0000	.0000	.0000	.0000	.0000
	5	.0018	.0266	.0907	.1636	.2023	.1916	.1468	.0933	.0497	.0222	.0082	.0024	.0006	.0001	.0000	.0000	.0000	.0000	.0000
	6	.0002	.0069	.0374	.0955	.1574	.1916	.1844	.1451	.0949	.0518	.0233	.0085	.0024	.0005	.0001	.0000	.0000	.0000	.0000
	7	.0000	.0014	.0122	.0443	.0974	.1525	.1844	.1797	.1443	.0961	.0529	.0237	.0083	.0022	.0004	.0000	.0000	.0000	.0000
	8	.0000	.0002	.0032	.0166	.0487	.0981	.1489	.1797	.1771	.1442	.0970	.0532	.0233	.0077	.0018	.0003	.0000	.0000	.0000
	9	.0000	.0000	.0007	.0051	.0198	.0514	.0980	.1464	.1771	.1762	.1449	.0976	.0528	.0220	.0066	.0013	.0001	.0000	.0000
	10	.0000	.0000	.0001	.0013	.0066	.0220	.0528	.0976	.1449	.1762	.1771	.1464	.0980	.0514	.0198	.0051	.0007	.0000	.0000
	11	.0000	.0000	.0000	.0003	.0018	.0077	.0233	.0532	.0970	.1442	.1771	.1797	.1489	.0981	.0487	.0166	.0032	.0002	.0000
	12	.0000	.0000	.0000	.0000	.0004	.0022	.0083	.0237	.0529	.0961	.1443	.1797	.1844	.1525	.0974	.0443	.0122	.0014	.0000
	13	.0000	.0000	.0000	.0000	.0001	.0005	.0024	.0085	.0233	.0518	.0949	.1451	.1844	.1916	.1574	.0955	.0374	.0069	.0002
	14	.0000	.0000	.0000	.0000	.0000	.0001	.0006	.0024	.0082	.0222	.0497	.0933	.1468	.1916	.2023	.1637	.0907	.0266	.0018
	15	.0000	.0000	.0000	.0000	.0000	.0000	.0001	.0005	.0022	.0074	.0203	.0467	.0909	.1491	.2023	.2182	.1714	.0798	.0112
	16	.0000	.0000	.0000	.0000	.0000	.0000	.0000	.0001	.0005	.0018	.0062	.0175	.0422	.0869	.1517	.2182	.2428	.1796	.0533
	17	.0000	.0000	.0000	.0000	.0000	.0000	.0000	.0000	.0001	.0003	.0013	.0046	.0138	.0358	.0803	.1540	.2428	.2852	.1787
	18	.0000	.0000	.0000	.0000	.0000	.0000	.0000	.0000	.0000	.0000	.0002	.0008	.0029	.0093	.0268	.0685	.1529	.2852	.3774
	19	.0000	.0000	.0000	.0000	.0000	.0000	.0000	.0000	.0000	.0000	.0000	.0001	.0003	.0011	.0042	.0144	.0456	.1351	.3774
20	0	.3585	.1216	.0388	.0115	.0032	.0008	.0002	.0000	.0000	.0000	.0000	.0000	.0000	.0000	.0000	.0000	.0000	.0000	.0000
	1	.3774	.2702	.1368	.0576	.0211	.0068	.0020	.0005	.0001	.0000	.0000	.0000	.0000	.0000	.0000	.0000	.0000	.0000	.0000
	2	.1887	.2852	.2293	.1369	.0669	.0278	.0100	.0031	.0008	.0002	.0000	.0000	.0000	.0000	.0000	.0000	.0000	.0000	.0000
	3	.0596	.1901	.2428	.2054	.1339	.0716	.0323	.0123	.0040	.0011	.0002	.0000	.0000	.0000	.0000	.0000	.0000	.0000	.0000
	4	.0133	.0898	.1821	.2182	.1897	.1304	.0738	.0350	.0139	.0046	.0013	.0003	.0000	.0000	.0000	.0000	.0000	.0000	.0000

p

n	r	.05	.10	.15	.20	.25	.30	.35	.40	.45	.50	.55	.60	.65	.70	.75	.80	.85	.90	.95
	5	.0022	.0319	.1028	.1746	.2023	.1789	.1272	.0746	.0365	.0148	.0049	.0013	.0003	.0000	.0000	.0000	.0000	.0000	.0000
	6	.0003	.0089	.0454	.1091	.1686	.1916	.1712	.1244	.0746	.0370	.0150	.0049	.0012	.0002	.0000	.0000	.0000	.0000	.0000
	7	.0000	.0020	.0160	.0545	.1124	.1643	.1844	.1659	.1221	.0739	.0366	.0146	.0045	.0010	.0002	.0000	.0000	.0000	.0000
	8	.0000	.0004	.0046	.0222	.0609	.1144	.1614	.1797	.1623	.1201	.0727	.0355	.0136	.0039	.0008	.0001	.0000	.0000	.0000
	9	.0000	.0001	.0011	.0074	.0271	.0654	.1158	.1597	.1771	.1602	.1185	.0710	.0336	.0120	.0030	.0005	.0000	.0000	.0000
	10	.0000	.0000	.0002	.0020	.0099	.0308	.0686	.1171	.1593	.1762	.1593	.1171	.0686	.0308	.0099	.0020	.0002	.0000	.0000
	11	.0000	.0000	.0000	.0005	.0030	.0120	.0336	.0710	.1185	.1602	.1771	.1597	.1158	.0654	.0271	.0074	.0011	.0001	.0000
	12	.0000	.0000	.0000	.0001	.0008	.0039	.0136	.0355	.0727	.1201	.1623	.1797	.1614	.1144	.0609	.0222	.0046	.0004	.0000
	13	.0000	.0000	.0000	.0000	.0002	.0010	.0045	.0146	.0366	.0739	.1221	.1659	.1844	.1643	.1124	.0545	.0160	.0020	.0000
	14	.0000	.0000	.0000	.0000	.0000	.0002	.0012	.0049	.0150	.0370	.0746	.1244	.1712	.1916	.1686	.1091	.0454	.0089	.0003
	15	.0000	.0000	.0000	.0000	.0000	.0000	.0003	.0013	.0049	.0148	.0365	.0746	.1272	.1789	.2023	.1746	.1028	.0319	.0022
	16	.0000	.0000	.0000	.0000	.0000	.0000	.0000	.0003	.0013	.0046	.0139	.0350	.0738	.1304	.1897	.2182	.1821	.0898	.0133
	17	.0000	.0000	.0000	.0000	.0000	.0000	.0000	.0000	.0002	.0011	.0040	.0123	.0323	.0716	.1339	.2054	.2428	.1901	.0596
	18	.0000	.0000	.0000	.0000	.0000	.0000	.0000	.0000	.0000	.0002	.0008	.0031	.0100	.0278	.0669	.1369	.2293	.2852	.1887
	19	.0000	.0000	.0000	.0000	.0000	.0000	.0000	.0000	.0000	.0000	.0001	.0005	.0020	.0068	.0211	.0576	.1368	.2702	.3774
	20	.0000	.0000	.0000	.0000	.0000	.0000	.0000	.0000	.0000	.0000	.0000	.0000	.0002	.0008	.0032	.0115	.0388	.1216	.3585
21	0	.3406	.1094	.0329	.0092	.0024	.0006	.0001	.0000	.0000	.0000	.0000	.0000	.0000	.0000	.0000	.0000	.0000	.0000	.0000
	1	.3764	.2553	.1221	.0484	.0166	.0050	.0013	.0003	.0001	.0000	.0000	.0000	.0000	.0000	.0000	.0000	.0000	.0000	.0000
	2	.1981	.2837	.2155	.1211	.0555	.0215	.0072	.0020	.0005	.0001	.0000	.0000	.0000	.0000	.0000	.0000	.0000	.0000	.0000
	3	.0660	.1996	.2408	.1917	.1172	.0585	.0245	.0086	.0026	.0006	.0001	.0000	.0000	.0000	.0000	.0000	.0000	.0000	.0000
	4	.0156	.0998	.1912	.2156	.1757	.1128	.0593	.0259	.0095	.0029	.0007	.0001	.0000	.0000	.0000	.0000	.0000	.0000	.0000
	5	.0028	.0377	.1147	.1833	.1992	.1643	.1085	.0588	.0263	.0097	.0029	.0007	.0001	.0000	.0000	.0000	.0000	.0000	.0000
	6	.0004	.0112	.0540	.1222	.1770	.1878	.1558	.1045	.0574	.0259	.0094	.0027	.0006	.0001	.0000	.0000	.0000	.0000	.0000
	7	.0000	.0027	.0204	.0655	.1265	.1725	.1798	.1493	.1007	.0554	.0247	.0087	.0024	.0005	.0001	.0000	.0000	.0000	.0000
	8	.0000	.0005	.0063	.0286	.0738	.1294	.1694	.1742	.1442	.0970	.0529	.0229	.0077	.0019	.0003	.0000	.0000	.0000	.0000
	9	.0000	.0001	.0016	.0103	.0355	.0801	.1318	.1677	.1704	.1402	.0933	.0497	.0206	.0063	.0013	.0002	.0000	.0000	.0000
	10	.0000	.0000	.0003	.0031	.0142	.0412	.0852	.1341	.1673	.1682	.1369	.0894	.0458	.0176	.0047	.0008	.0001	.0000	.0000
	11	.0000	.0000	.0001	.0008	.0047	.0176	.0458	.0894	.1369	.1682	.1673	.1342	.0852	.0412	.0142	.0031	.0003	.0000	.0000
	12	.0000	.0000	.0000	.0002	.0013	.0063	.0206	.0497	.0933	.1402	.1704	.1677	.1318	.0801	.0355	.0103	.0016	.0001	.0000
	13	.0000	.0000	.0000	.0000	.0003	.0019	.0077	.0229	.0529	.0970	.1442	.1742	.1694	.1294	.0738	.0286	.0063	.0005	.0000
	14	.0000	.0000	.0000	.0000	.0001	.0005	.0024	.0087	.0247	.0554	.1007	.1493	.1798	.1725	.1265	.0655	.0204	.0027	.0000
	15	.0000	.0000	.0000	.0000	.0000	.0001	.0006	.0027	.0094	.0259	.0574	.1045	.1558	.1878	.1770	.1222	.0540	.0112	.0004
	16	.0000	.0000	.0000	.0000	.0000	.0000	.0001	.0007	.0029	.0097	.0263	.0588	.1085	.1643	.1992	.1833	.1147	.0377	.0028
	17	.0000	.0000	.0000	.0000	.0000	.0000	.0000	.0001	.0007	.0029	.0095	.0259	.0593	.1128	.1757	.2156	.1912	.0998	.0156
	18	.0000	.0000	.0000	.0000	.0000	.0000	.0000	.0000	.0001	.0006	.0026	.0086	.0245	.0585	.1172	.1917	.2408	.1996	.0660
	19	.0000	.0000	.0000	.0000	.0000	.0000	.0000	.0000	.0000	.0001	.0005	.0020	.0072	.0215	.0555	.1211	.2155	.2837	.1981
	20	.0000	.0000	.0000	.0000	.0000	.0000	.0000	.0000	.0000	.0000	.0001	.0003	.0013	.0050	.0166	.0484	.1221	.2553	.3764
	21	.0000	.0000	.0000	.0000	.0000	.0000	.0000	.0000	.0000	.0000	.0000	.0000	.0001	.0006	.0024	.0092	.0329	.1094	.3406

p

n	r	.05	.10	.15	.20	.25	.30	.35	.40	.45	.50	.55	.60	.65	.70	.75	.80	.85	.90	.95
22	0	.3235	.0985	.0280	.0074	.0018	.0004	.0001	.0000	.0000	.0000	.0000	.0000	.0000	.0000	.0000	.0000	.0000	.0000	.0000
	1	.3746	.2407	.1087	.0406	.0131	.0037	.0009	.0002	.0000	.0000	.0000	.0000	.0000	.0000	.0000	.0000	.0000	.0000	.0000
	2	.2070	.2808	.2015	.1065	.0458	.0166	.0051	.0014	.0003	.0001	.0000	.0000	.0000	.0000	.0000	.0000	.0000	.0000	.0000
	3	.0726	.2080	.2370	.1775	.1017	.0474	.0184	.0060	.0016	.0004	.0001	.0000	.0000	.0000	.0000	.0000	.0000	.0000	.0000
	4	.0182	.1098	.1987	.2108	.1611	.0965	.0471	.0190	.0064	.0017	.0004	.0001	.0000	.0000	.0000	.0000	.0000	.0000	.0000
	5	.0034	.0439	.1262	.1898	.1933	.1489	.0913	.0456	.0187	.0063	.0017	.0004	.0001	.0000	.0000	.0000	.0000	.0000	.0000
	6	.0005	.0138	.0631	.1344	.1826	.1808	.1393	.0862	.0434	.0178	.0058	.0015	.0003	.0000	.0000	.0000	.0000	.0000	.0000
	7	.0001	.0035	.0255	.0768	.1391	.1771	.1714	.1314	.0812	.0407	.0163	.0051	.0012	.0002	.0000	.0000	.0000	.0000	.0000
	8	.0000	.0007	.0084	.0360	.0869	.1423	.1730	.1642	.1246	.0762	.0374	.0144	.0042	.0009	.0001	.0000	.0000	.0000	.0000
	9	.0000	.0001	.0023	.0140	.0451	.0949	.1449	.1703	.1586	.1186	.0711	.0336	.0122	.0032	.0006	.0001	.0000	.0000	.0000
	10	.0000	.0000	.0005	.0046	.0195	.0529	.1015	.1476	.1687	.1542	.1129	.0656	.0294	.0097	.0022	.0003	.0000	.0000	.0000
	11	.0000	.0000	.0001	.0012	.0071	.0247	.0596	.1073	.1506	.1682	.1506	.1073	.0596	.0247	.0071	.0012	.0001	.0000	.0000
	12	.0000	.0000	.0000	.0003	.0022	.0097	.0294	.0656	.1129	.1542	.1687	.1476	.1015	.0529	.0195	.0046	.0005	.0000	.0000
	13	.0000	.0000	.0000	.0001	.0006	.0032	.0122	.0336	.0711	.1186	.1586	.1703	.1449	.0949	.0451	.0140	.0023	.0001	.0000
	14	.0000	.0000	.0000	.0000	.0001	.0009	.0042	.0144	.0374	.0762	.1246	.1642	.1730	.1423	.0869	.0360	.0084	.0007	.0000
	15	.0000	.0000	.0000	.0000	.0000	.0002	.0012	.0051	.0163	.0407	.0812	.1314	.1714	.1771	.1391	.0768	.0255	.0035	.0001
	16	.0000	.0000	.0000	.0000	.0000	.0000	.0003	.0015	.0058	.0178	.0434	.0862	.1393	.1808	.1826	.1344	.0631	.0138	.0005
	17	.0000	.0000	.0000	.0000	.0000	.0000	.0001	.0004	.0017	.0063	.0163	.0456	.0913	.1489	.1933	.1898	.1262	.0439	.0034
	18	.0000	.0000	.0000	.0000	.0000	.0000	.0000	.0001	.0004	.0017	.0064	.0190	.0471	.0965	.1611	.2108	.1987	.1098	.0182
	19	.0000	.0000	.0000	.0000	.0000	.0000	.0000	.0000	.0001	.0004	.0016	.0060	.0184	.0474	.1017	.1775	.2370	.2080	.0726
	20	.0000	.0000	.0000	.0000	.0000	.0000	.0000	.0000	.0000	.0001	.0003	.0014	.0051	.0166	.0458	.1065	.2015	.2808	.2070
	21	.0000	.0000	.0000	.0000	.0000	.0000	.0000	.0000	.0000	.0000	.0000	.0002	.0009	.0037	.0131	.0406	.1087	.2407	.3746
	22	.0000	.0000	.0000	.0000	.0000	.0000	.0000	.0000	.0000	.0000	.0000	.0000	.0001	.0004	.0018	.0074	.0280	.0985	.3235
23	0	.3074	.0886	.0238	.0059	.0013	.0003	.0000	.0000	.0000	.0000	.0000	.0000	.0000	.0000	.0000	.0000	.0000	.0000	.0000
	1	.3721	.2265	.0966	.0339	.0103	.0027	.0006	.0001	.0000	.0000	.0000	.0000	.0000	.0000	.0000	.0000	.0000	.0000	.0000
	2	.2154	.2768	.1875	.0933	.0376	.0127	.0037	.0009	.0002	.0000	.0000	.0000	.0000	.0000	.0000	.0000	.0000	.0000	.0000
	3	.0794	.2153	.2317	.1633	.0878	.0382	.0138	.0041	.0010	.0002	.0000	.0000	.0000	.0000	.0000	.0000	.0000	.0000	.0000
	4	.0209	.1196	.2044	.2042	.1463	.0818	.0371	.0138	.0042	.0011	.0002	.0000	.0000	.0000	.0000	.0000	.0000	.0000	.0000
	5	.0042	.0505	.1371	.1940	.1853	.1332	.0758	.0350	.0132	.0040	.0010	.0002	.0000	.0000	.0000	.0000	.0000	.0000	.0000
	6	.0007	.0168	.0726	.1455	.1853	.1712	.1225	.0700	.0323	.0120	.0036	.0008	.0001	.0000	.0000	.0000	.0000	.0000	.0000
	7	.0001	.0045	.0311	.0883	.1500	.1782	.1602	.1133	.0642	.0292	.0106	.0029	.0006	.0001	.0000	.0000	.0000	.0000	.0000
	8	.0000	.0010	.0110	.0442	.1000	.1527	.1725	.1511	.1051	.0585	.0258	.0088	.0023	.0004	.0000	.0000	.0000	.0000	.0000
	9	.0000	.0002	.0032	.0184	.0555	.1091	.1548	.1679	.1433	.0974	.0525	.0221	.0070	.0016	.0002	.0000	.0000	.0000	.0000
	10	.0000	.0000	.0008	.0064	.0259	.0655	.1167	.1567	.1642	.1364	.0899	.0464	.0182	.0052	.0010	.0001	.0000	.0000	.0000
	11	.0000	.0000	.0002	.0019	.0102	.0332	.0743	.1234	.1587	.1612	.1299	.0823	.0400	.0142	.0034	.0005	.0000	.0000	.0000
	12	.0000	.0000	.0000	.0005	.0034	.0142	.0400	.0823	.1299	.1612	.1587	.1234	.0743	.0332	.0102	.0019	.0002	.0000	.0000
	13	.0000	.0000	.0000	.0001	.0010	.0052	.0182	.0464	.0899	.1364	.1642	.1567	.1167	.0655	.0259	.0064	.0008	.0000	.0000
	14	.0000	.0000	.0000	.0000	.0002	.0016	.0070	.0221	.0525	.0974	.1433	.1679	.1548	.1091	.0555	.0184	.0032	.0002	.0000

p

n	r	.95	.90	.85	.80	.75	.70	.65	.60	.55	.50	.45	.40	.35	.30	.25	.20	.15	.10	.05
	15	.0000	.0010	.0110	.0442	.1000	.1527	.1725	.1511	.1051	.0584	.0258	.0088	.0023	.0004	.0000	.0000	.0000	.0000	.0000
	16	.0000	.0045	.0311	.0883	.1500	.1782	.1602	.1133	.0642	.0292	.0106	.0029	.0006	.0001	.0000	.0000	.0000	.0000	.0000
	17	.0007	.0168	.0726	.1455	.1853	.1712	.1225	.0700	.0323	.0120	.0036	.0008	.0001	.0000	.0000	.0000	.0000	.0000	.0000
	18	.0042	.0505	.1371	.1940	.1853	.1331	.0758	.0350	.0132	.0040	.0010	.0002	.0000	.0000	.0000	.0000	.0000	.0000	.0000
	19	.0209	.1196	.2044	.2042	.1463	.0818	.0371	.0138	.0042	.0011	.0002	.0000	.0000	.0000	.0000	.0000	.0000	.0000	.0000
24	0	.0000	.0000	.0000	.0000	.0000	.0000	.0000	.0000	.0000	.0000	.0000	.0000	.0000	.0002	.0010	.0047	.0202	.0798	.2920
	1	.0000	.0000	.0000	.0000	.0000	.0000	.0000	.0000	.0000	.0000	.0000	.0001	.0004	.0020	.0080	.0283	.0857	.2127	.3688
	2	.0000	.0000	.0000	.0000	.0000	.0000	.0000	.0000	.0000	.0000	.0001	.0006	.0026	.0097	.0308	.0815	.1739	.2718	.2232
	3	.0000	.0000	.0000	.0000	.0000	.0000	.0000	.0000	.0000	.0001	.0007	.0028	.0102	.0305	.0752	.1493	.2251	.2215	.0862
	4	.0000	.0000	.0000	.0000	.0000	.0000	.0000	.0000	.0001	.0006	.0028	.0099	.0289	.0687	.1316	.1960	.2085	.1292	.0238
	5	.0000	.0000	.0000	.0000	.0000	.0000	.0000	.0001	.0006	.0025	.0091	.0265	.0622	.1177	.1755	.1960	.1472	.0574	.0050
	6	.0000	.0000	.0000	.0000	.0000	.0000	.0001	.0004	.0021	.0080	.0237	.0560	.1061	.1598	.1853	.1552	.0822	.0202	.0008
	7	.0000	.0000	.0000	.0000	.0000	.0000	.0003	.0017	.0067	.0206	.0499	.0960	.1470	.1761	.1588	.0998	.0373	.0058	.0001
	8	.0000	.0000	.0000	.0000	.0000	.0002	.0012	.0053	.0174	.0438	.0867	.1360	.1682	.1604	.1125	.0530	.0140	.0014	.0000
	9	.0000	.0000	.0000	.0000	.0001	.0008	.0039	.0141	.0378	.0779	.1261	.1612	.1610	.1222	.0667	.0236	.0044	.0003	.0000
	10	.0000	.0000	.0000	.0000	.0004	.0026	.0109	.0318	.0694	.1169	.1548	.1612	.1300	.0785	.0333	.0088	.0012	.0000	.0000
	11	.0000	.0000	.0000	.0002	.0016	.0079	.0258	.0608	.1079	.1488	.1612	.1367	.0891	.0428	.0141	.0028	.0003	.0000	.0000
	12	.0000	.0000	.0000	.0008	.0051	.0199	.0520	.0988	.1429	.1612	.1429	.0988	.0520	.0199	.0051	.0008	.0000	.0000	.0000
	13	.0000	.0000	.0003	.0028	.0141	.0428	.0891	.1367	.1612	.1488	.1079	.0608	.0258	.0079	.0016	.0002	.0000	.0000	.0000
	14	.0000	.0000	.0012	.0088	.0333	.0785	.1300	.1612	.1548	.1169	.0694	.0318	.0109	.0026	.0004	.0000	.0000	.0000	.0000
	15	.0000	.0003	.0044	.0236	.0667	.1222	.1610	.1612	.1261	.0779	.0378	.0141	.0039	.0008	.0001	.0000	.0000	.0000	.0000
	16	.0000	.0014	.0140	.0530	.1125	.1604	.1682	.1360	.0867	.0438	.0174	.0053	.0012	.0002	.0000	.0000	.0000	.0000	.0000
	17	.0001	.0058	.0373	.0998	.1588	.1761	.1470	.0960	.0499	.0206	.0067	.0017	.0003	.0000	.0000	.0000	.0000	.0000	.0000
	18	.0008	.0202	.0822	.1552	.1853	.1598	.1061	.0560	.0237	.0080	.0021	.0004	.0001	.0000	.0000	.0000	.0000	.0000	.0000
	19	.0050	.0574	.1472	.1960	.1755	.1177	.0622	.0265	.0091	.0025	.0006	.0001	.0000	.0000	.0000	.0000	.0000	.0000	.0000
	20	.0238	.1292	.2085	.1960	.1316	.0687	.0289	.0099	.0028	.0006	.0001	.0000	.0000	.0000	.0000	.0000	.0000	.0000	.0000
	21	.0862	.2215	.2251	.1493	.0752	.0305	.0102	.0028	.0007	.0001	.0000	.0000	.0000	.0000	.0000	.0000	.0000	.0000	.0000
	22	.2232	.2718	.1739	.0815	.0308	.0097	.0026	.0006	.0001	.0000	.0000	.0000	.0000	.0000	.0000	.0000	.0000	.0000	.0000
	23	.3688	.2127	.0857	.0283	.0080	.0020	.0004	.0001	.0000	.0000	.0000	.0000	.0000	.0000	.0000	.0000	.0000	.0000	.0000
	24	.2920	.0798	.0202	.0047	.0010	.0002	.0000	.0000	.0000	.0000	.0000	.0000	.0000	.0000	.0000	.0000	.0000	.0000	.0000
25	0	.0000	.0000	.0000	.0000	.0000	.0000	.0000	.0000	.0000	.0000	.0000	.0000	.0000	.0001	.0008	.0038	.0172	.0718	.2774
	1	.0000	.0000	.0000	.0000	.0000	.0000	.0000	.0000	.0000	.0000	.0000	.0000	.0003	.0014	.0063	.0236	.0759	.1994	.3650
	2	.0000	.0000	.0000	.0000	.0000	.0000	.0000	.0000	.0000	.0000	.0000	.0004	.0018	.0074	.0251	.0708	.1607	.2659	.2305
	3	.0000	.0000	.0000	.0000	.0000	.0000	.0000	.0000	.0000	.0001	.0004	.0019	.0076	.0243	.0641	.1358	.2174	.2265	.0930
	4	.0000	.0000	.0000	.0000	.0000	.0000	.0000	.0000	.0001	.0004	.0018	.0071	.0224	.0572	.1175	.1867	.2110	.1384	.0269

n	r									*p*										
		.05	.10	.15	.20	.25	.30	.35	.40	.45	.50	.55	.60	.65	.70	.75	.80	.85	.90	.95
	5	.0060	.0646	.1564	.1960	.1645	.1030	.0506	.0199	.0063	.0016	.0003	.0000	.0000	.0000	.0000	.0000	.0000	.0000	.0000
	6	.0010	.0239	.0920	.1633	.1828	.1472	.0908	.0442	.0172	.0053	.0013	.0002	.0000	.0000	.0000	.0000	.0000	.0000	.0000
	7	.0001	.0072	.0441	.1108	.1654	.1712	.1327	.0800	.0381	.0143	.0042	.0009	.0001	.0000	.0000	.0000	.0000	.0000	.0000
	8	.0000	.0018	.0175	.0623	.1241	.1651	.1607	.1200	.0701	.0322	.0115	.0031	.0006	.0001	.0000	.0000	.0000	.0000	.0000
	9	.0000	.0004	.0058	.0294	.0781	.1336	.1635	.1511	.1084	.0609	.0266	.0088	.0021	.0004	.0000	.0000	.0000	.0000	.0000
	10	.0000	.0001	.0016	.0118	.0417	.0916	.1409	.1612	.1419	.0974	.0520	.0212	.0064	.0013	.0002	.0000	.0000	.0000	.0000
	11	.0000	.0000	.0004	.0040	.0189	.0536	.1034	.1465	.1583	.1328	.0867	.0434	.0161	.0042	.0007	.0001	.0000	.0000	.0000
	12	.0000	.0000	.0001	.0012	.0074	.0268	.0650	.1139	.1511	.1550	.1236	.0760	.0350	.0115	.0025	.0003	.0000	.0000	.0000
	13	.0000	.0000	.0000	.0003	.0025	.0115	.0350	.0760	.1236	.1550	.1511	.1140	.0650	.0268	.0074	.0012	.0001	.0000	.0000
	14	.0000	.0000	.0000	.0001	.0007	.0042	.0161	.0434	.0867	.1328	.1583	.1465	.1034	.0536	.0189	.0040	.0004	.0000	.0000
	15	.0000	.0000	.0000	.0000	.0002	.0013	.0064	.0212	.0520	.0974	.1419	.1612	.1409	.0916	.0417	.0118	.0016	.0001	.0000
	16	.0000	.0000	.0000	.0000	.0000	.0004	.0021	.0088	.0266	.0609	.1084	.1511	.1635	.1336	.0781	.0294	.0058	.0004	.0000
	17	.0000	.0000	.0000	.0000	.0000	.0001	.0006	.0031	.0115	.0322	.0701	.1200	.1607	.1651	.1241	.0623	.0175	.0018	.0000
	18	.0000	.0000	.0000	.0000	.0000	.0000	.0001	.0009	.0042	.0143	.0381	.0800	.1327	.1712	.1654	.1108	.0441	.0072	.0001
	19	.0000	.0000	.0000	.0000	.0000	.0000	.0000	.0002	.0013	.0053	.0172	.0442	.0908	.1472	.1828	.1633	.0920	.0239	.0010
	20	.0000	.0000	.0000	.0000	.0000	.0000	.0000	.0000	.0003	.0016	.0063	.0199	.0506	.1030	.1645	.1960	.1564	.0646	.0060
	21	.0000	.0000	.0000	.0000	.0000	.0000	.0000	.0000	.0001	.0004	.0018	.0071	.0224	.0572	.1175	.1867	.2110	.1384	.0269
	22	.0000	.0000	.0000	.0000	.0000	.0000	.0000	.0000	.0000	.0001	.0004	.0019	.0076	.0243	.0641	.1358	.2174	.2265	.0930
	23	.0000	.0000	.0000	.0000	.0000	.0000	.0000	.0000	.0000	.0000	.0001	.0004	.0018	.0074	.0251	.0708	.1607	.2659	.2305
	24	.0000	.0000	.0000	.0000	.0000	.0000	.0000	.0000	.0000	.0000	.0000	.0000	.0003	.0014	.0063	.0236	.0759	.1994	.3650
	25	.0000	.0000	.0000	.0000	.0000	.0000	.0000	.0000	.0000	.0000	.0000	.0000	.0000	.0001	.0008	.0038	.0172	.0718	.2774

Appendix C
Binomial
Probabilities—
Cumulative

The following table shows the probabilities for *r or more* successes in *n* trials for certain values of *p*, the probability of success on a single trial.

$$P(r \geq r_0 \mid n, p)$$

							p				
n	r	.05	.10	.15	.20	.25	.30	.35	.40	.45	.50
1	0	1.0000	1.0000	1.0000	1.0000	1.0000	1.0000	1.0000	1.0000	1.0000	1.0000
	1	0.0500	0.1000	0.1500	0.2000	0.2500	0.3000	0.3500	0.4000	0.4500	0.5000
2	0	1.0000	1.0000	1.0000	1.0000	1.0000	1.0000	1.0000	1.0000	1.0000	1.0000
	1	0.0975	0.1900	0.2775	0.3600	0.4375	0.5100	0.5775	0.6400	0.6975	0.7500
	2	0.0025	0.0100	0.0225	0.0400	0.0625	0.0900	0.1225	0.1600	0.2025	0.2500
3	0	1.0000	1.0000	1.0000	1.0000	1.0000	1.0000	1.0000	1.0000	1.0000	1.0000
	1	0.1426	0.2710	0.3859	0.4880	0.5781	0.6570	0.7254	0.7840	0.8336	0.8750
	2	0.0072	0.0280	0.0607	0.1040	0.1562	0.2160	0.2817	0.3520	0.4252	0.5000
	3	0.0001	0.0010	0.0034	0.0080	0.0156	0.0270	0.0429	0.0640	0.0911	0.1250
4	0	1.0000	1.0000	1.0000	1.0000	1.0000	1.0000	1.0000	1.0000	1.0000	1.0000
	1	0.1855	0.3439	0.4780	0.5904	0.6836	0.7599	0.8215	0.8704	0.9085	0.9375
	2	0.0140	0.0523	0.1095	0.1808	0.2617	0.3483	0.4370	0.5248	0.6090	0.6875
	3	0.0005	0.0037	0.0120	0.0272	0.0508	0.0837	0.1265	0.1792	0.2415	0.3125
	4	0.0000	0.0001	0.0005	0.0016	0.0039	0.0081	0.0150	0.0256	0.0410	0.0625
5	0	1.0000	1.0000	1.0000	1.0000	1.0000	1.0000	1.0000	1.0000	1.0000	1.0000
	1	0.2262	0.4095	0.5563	0.6723	0.7627	0.8319	0.8840	0.9222	0.9497	0.9687
	2	0.0226	0.0815	0.1648	0.2627	0.3672	0.4718	0.5716	0.6630	0.7438	0.8125
	3	0.0012	0.0086	0.0266	0.0579	0.1035	0.1631	0.2352	0.3174	0.4069	0.5000
	4	0.0000	0.0005	0.0022	0.0067	0.0156	0.0308	0.0540	0.0870	0.1312	0.1875
	5	0.0000	0.0000	0.0001	0.0003	0.0010	0.0024	0.0053	0.0102	0.0185	0.0312
6	0	1.0000	1.0000	1.0000	1.0000	1.0000	1.0000	1.0000	1.0000	1.0000	1.0000
	1	0.2649	0.4686	0.6229	0.7379	0.8220	0.8824	0.9246	0.9533	0.9723	0.9844
	2	0.0328	0.1143	0.2235	0.3446	0.4661	0.5798	0.6809	0.7667	0.8364	0.8906
	3	0.0022	0.0158	0.0473	0.0989	0.1694	0.2557	0.3529	0.4557	0.5585	0.6562
	4	0.0001	0.0013	0.0059	0.0170	0.0376	0.0705	0.1174	0.1792	0.2553	0.3437
	5	0.0000	0.0001	0.0004	0.0016	0.0046	0.0109	0.0223	0.0410	0.0692	0.1094
	6	0.0000	0.0000	0.0000	0.0001	0.0002	0.0007	0.0018	0.0041	0.0083	0.0156
7	0	1.0000	1.0000	1.0000	1.0000	1.0000	1.0000	1.0000	1.0000	1.0000	1.0000
	1	0.3017	0.5217	0.6794	0.7903	0.8665	0.9176	0.9510	0.9720	0.9848	0.9922
	2	0.0444	0.1497	0.2834	0.4233	0.5551	0.6706	0.7662	0.8414	0.8976	0.9375
	3	0.0038	0.0257	0.0738	0.1480	0.2436	0.3529	0.4677	0.5801	0.6836	0.7734
	4	0.0002	0.0027	0.0121	0.0333	0.0706	0.1260	0.1998	0.2898	0.3917	0.5000
	5	0.0000	0.0002	0.0012	0.0047	0.0129	0.0288	0.0556	0.0963	0.1529	0.2266
	6	0.0000	0.0000	0.0001	0.0004	0.0013	0.0038	0.0090	0.0188	0.0357	0.0625
	7	0.0000	0.0000	0.0000	0.0000	0.0001	0.0002	0.0006	0.0016	0.0037	0.0078
8	0	1.0000	1.0000	1.0000	1.0000	1.0000	1.0000	1.0000	1.0000	1.0000	1.0000
	1	0.3366	0.5695	0.7275	0.8322	0.8999	0.9424	0.9681	0.9832	0.9916	0.9961
	2	0.0572	0.1869	0.3428	0.4967	0.6329	0.7447	0.8309	0.8936	0.9368	0.9648
	3	0.0058	0.0381	0.1052	0.2031	0.3215	0.4482	0.5722	0.6846	0.7799	0.8555
	4	0.0004	0.0050	0.0214	0.0563	0.1138	0.1941	0.2936	0.4059	0.5230	0.6367
	5	0.0000	0.0004	0.0029	0.0104	0.0273	0.0580	0.1061	0.1737	0.2604	0.3633
	6	0.0000	0.0000	0.0002	0.0012	0.0042	0.0113	0.0253	0.0498	0.0885	0.1445
	7	0.0000	0.0000	0.0000	0.0001	0.0004	0.0013	0.0036	0.0085	0.0181	0.0352
	8	0.0000	0.0000	0.0000	0.0000	0.0000	0.0001	0.0002	0.0007	0.0017	0.0039
9	0	1.0000	1.0000	1.0000	1.0000	1.0000	1.0000	1.0000	1.0000	1.0000	1.0000
	1	0.3698	0.6126	0.7684	0.8658	0.9249	0.9596	0.9793	0.9899	0.9954	0.9980
	2	0.0712	0.2252	0.4005	0.5638	0.6997	0.8040	0.8789	0.9295	0.9615	0.9805
	3	0.0084	0.0530	0.1409	0.2618	0.3993	0.5372	0.6627	0.7682	0.8505	0.9102
	4	0.0006	0.0083	0.0339	0.0856	0.1657	0.2703	0.3911	0.5174	0.6386	0.7461

p

.55	.60	.65	.70	.75	.80	.85	.90	.95
1.0000	1.0000	1.0000	1.0000	1.0000	1.0000	1.0000	1.0000	1.0000
0.5500	0.6000	0.6500	0.7000	0.7500	0.8000	0.8500	0.9000	0.9500
1.0000	1.0000	1.0000	1.0000	1.0000	1.0000	1.0000	1.0000	1.0000
0.7975	0.8400	0.8775	0.9100	0.9375	0.9600	0.9775	0.9900	0.9975
0.3025	0.3600	0.4225	0.4900	0.5625	0.6400	0.7225	0.8100	0.9025
1.0000	1.0000	1.0000	1.0000	1.0000	1.0000	1.0000	1.0000	1.0000
0.9089	0.9360	0.9571	0.9730	0.9844	0.9920	0.9966	0.9990	0.9999
0.5747	0.6480	0.7182	0.7840	0.8437	0.8960	0.9392	0.9720	0.9927
0.1664	0.2160	0.2746	0.3430	0.4219	0.5120	0.6141	0.7290	0.8574
1.0000	1.0000	1.0000	1.0000	1.0000	1.0000	1.0000	1.0000	1.0000
0.9590	0.9744	0.9850	0.9919	0.9961	0.9984	0.9995	0.9999	1.0000
0.7585	0.8208	0.8735	0.9163	0.9492	0.9728	0.9880	0.9963	0.9995
0.3910	0.4752	0.5630	0.6517	0.7383	0.8192	0.8905	0.9477	0.9860
0.0915	0.1296	0.1785	0.2401	0.3164	0.4096	0.5220	0.6561	0.8145
1.0000	1.0000	1.0000	1.0000	1.0000	1.0000	1.0000	1.0000	1.0000
0.9815	0.9898	0.9947	0.9976	0.9990	0.9997	0.9999	1.0000	1.0000
0.8688	0.9130	0.9460	0.9692	0.9844	0.9933	0.9978	0.9995	1.0000
0.5931	0.6826	0.7648	0.8369	0.8965	0.9421	0.9734	0.9914	0.9988
0.2562	0.3370	0.4284	0.5282	0.6328	0.7373	0.8352	0.9185	0.9774
0.0503	0.0778	0.1160	0.1681	0.2373	0.3277	0.4437	0.5905	0.7738
1.0000	1.0000	1.0000	1.0000	1.0000	1.0000	1.0000	1.0000	1.0000
0.9917	0.9959	0.9982	0.9993	0.9998	0.9999	1.0000	1.0000	1.0000
0.9308	0.9590	0.9777	0.9891	0.9954	0.9984	0.9996	0.9999	1.0000
0.7447	0.8208	0.8826	0.9295	0.9624	0.9830	0.9941	0.9987	0.9999
0.4415	0.5443	0.6471	0.7443	0.8306	0.9011	0.9527	0.9841	0.9978
0.1636	0.2333	0.3191	0.4202	0.5339	0.6554	0.7765	0.8857	0.9672
0.0277	0.0467	0.0754	0.1176	0.1780	0.2621	0.3771	0.5314	0.7351
1.0000	1.0000	1.0000	1.0000	1.0000	1.0000	1.0000	1.0000	1.0000
0.9963	0.9984	0.9994	0.9998	0.9999	1.0000	1.0000	1.0000	1.0000
0.9643	0.9812	0.9910	0.9962	0.9987	0.9996	0.9999	1.0000	1.0000
0.8471	0.9037	0.9444	0.9712	0.9871	0.9953	0.9988	0.9998	1.0000
0.6083	0.7102	0.8002	0.8740	0.9294	0.9667	0.9879	0.9973	0.9998
0.3164	0.4199	0.5323	0.6471	0.7564	0.8520	0.9262	0.9743	0.9962
0.1024	0.1586	0.2338	0.3294	0.4449	0.5767	0.7166	0.8503	0.9556
0.0152	0.0280	0.0490	0.0824	0.1335	0.2097	0.3206	0.4783	0.6983
1.0000	1.0000	1.0000	1.0000	1.0000	1.0000	1.0000	1.0000	1.0000
0.9983	0.9993	0.9998	0.9999	1.0000	1.0000	1.0000	1.0000	1.0000
0.9819	0.9915	0.9964	0.9987	0.9996	0.9999	1.0000	1.0000	1.0000
0.9115	0.9502	0.9747	0.9887	0.9958	0.9988	0.9998	1.0000	1.0000
0.7396	0.8263	0.8939	0.9420	0.9727	0.9896	0.9971	0.9996	1.0000
0.4770	0.5941	0.7064	0.8059	0.8862	0.9437	0.9786	0.9950	0.9996
0.2201	0.3154	0.4278	0.5518	0.6785	0.7969	0.8948	0.9619	0.9942
0.0632	0.1064	0.1691	0.2553	0.3671	0.5033	0.6572	0.8131	0.9428
0.0084	0.0168	0.0319	0.0576	0.1001	0.1678	0.2725	0.4305	0.6634
1.0000	1.0000	1.0000	1.0000	1.0000	1.0000	1.0000	1.0000	1.0000
0.9992	0.9997	0.9999	1.0000	1.0000	1.0000	1.0000	1.0000	1.0000
0.9909	0.9962	0.9986	0.9996	0.9999	1.0000	1.0000	1.0000	1.0000
0.9502	0.9750	0.9888	0.9957	0.9987	0.9997	1.0000	1.0000	1.0000
0.8342	0.9006	0.9464	0.9747	0.9900	0.9969	0.9994	0.9999	1.0000

p

n	r	.05	.10	.15	.20	.25	.30	.35	.40	.45	.50
	5	0.0000	0.0009	0.0056	0.0196	0.0489	0.0988	0.1717	0.2666	0.3786	0.5000
	6	0.0000	0.0001	0.0006	0.0031	0.0100	0.0253	0.0536	0.0994	0.1658	0.2539
	7	0.0000	0.0000	0.0000	0.0003	0.0013	0.0043	0.0112	0.0250	0.0498	0.0898
	8	0.0000	0.0000	0.0000	0.0000	0.0001	0.0004	0.0014	0.0038	0.0091	0.0195
	9	0.0000	0.0000	0.0000	0.0000	0.0000	0.0000	0.0001	0.0003	0.0008	0.0020
10	0	1.0000	1.0000	1.0000	1.0000	1.0000	1.0000	1.0000	1.0000	1.0000	1.0000
	1	0.4013	0.6513	0.8031	0.8926	0.9437	0.9718	0.9865	0.9940	0.9975	0.9990
	2	0.0861	0.2639	0.4557	0.6242	0.7560	0.8507	0.9140	0.9536	0.9767	0.9893
	3	0.0115	0.0702	0.1798	0.3222	0.4744	0.6172	0.7384	0.8327	0.9004	0.9453
	4	0.0010	0.0128	0.0500	0.1209	0.2241	0.3504	0.4862	0.6177	0.7340	0.8281
	5	0.0001	0.0016	0.0099	0.0328	0.0781	0.1503	0.2485	0.3669	0.4956	0.6230
	6	0.0000	0.0001	0.0014	0.0064	0.0197	0.0473	0.0949	0.1662	0.2616	0.3770
	7	0.0000	0.0000	0.0001	0.0009	0.0035	0.0106	0.0260	0.0548	0.1020	0.1719
	8	0.0000	0.0000	0.0000	0.0001	0.0004	0.0016	0.0048	0.0123	0.0274	0.0547
	9	0.0000	0.0000	0.0000	0.0000	0.0000	0.0001	0.0005	0.0017	0.0045	0.0107
	10	0.0000	0.0000	0.0000	0.0000	0.0000	0.0000	0.0000	0.0001	0.0003	0.0010
11	0	1.0000	1.0000	1.0000	1.0000	1.0000	1.0000	1.0000	1.0000	1.0000	1.0000
	1	0.4312	0.6862	0.8327	0.9141	0.9578	0.9802	0.9912	0.9964	0.9986	0.9995
	2	0.1019	0.3026	0.5078	0.6779	0.8029	0.8870	0.9394	0.9698	0.9861	0.9941
	3	0.0152	0.0896	0.2212	0.3826	0.5448	0.6873	0.7999	0.8811	0.9348	0.9673
	4	0.0016	0.0185	0.0694	0.1611	0.2867	0.4304	0.5744	0.7037	0.8089	0.8867
	5	0.0001	0.0028	0.0159	0.0504	0.1146	0.2103	0.3317	0.4672	0.6029	0.7256
	6	0.0000	0.0003	0.0027	0.0117	0.0343	0.0782	0.1487	0.2465	0.3669	0.5000
	7	0.0000	0.0000	0.0003	0.0020	0.0076	0.0216	0.0501	0.0994	0.1738	0.2744
	8	0.0000	0.0000	0.0000	0.0002	0.0012	0.0043	0.0122	0.0293	0.0610	0.1133
	9	0.0000	0.0000	0.0000	0.0000	0.0001	0.0006	0.0020	0.0059	0.0148	0.0327
	10	0.0000	0.0000	0.0000	0.0000	0.0000	0.0000	0.0002	0.0007	0.0022	0.0059
	11	0.0000	0.0000	0.0000	0.0000	0.0000	0.0000	0.0000	0.0000	0.0002	0.0005
12	0	1.0000	1.0000	1.0000	1.0000	1.0000	1.0000	1.0000	1.0000	1.0000	1.0000
	1	0.4596	0.7176	0.8578	0.9313	0.9683	0.9862	0.9943	0.9978	0.9992	0.9998
	2	0.1184	0.3410	0.5565	0.7251	0.8416	0.9150	0.9576	0.9804	0.9917	0.9968
	3	0.0196	0.1109	0.2642	0.4417	0.6093	0.7472	0.8487	0.9166	0.9579	0.9807
	4	0.0022	0.0256	0.0922	0.2054	0.3512	0.5075	0.6533	0.7747	0.8655	0.9270
	5	0.0002	0.0043	0.0239	0.0726	0.1576	0.2763	0.4167	0.5618	0.6956	0.8062
	6	0.0000	0.0005	0.0046	0.0194	0.0544	0.1178	0.2127	0.3348	0.4731	0.6128
	7	0.0000	0.0001	0.0007	0.0039	0.0143	0.0386	0.0846	0.1582	0.2607	0.3872
	8	0.0000	0.0000	0.0001	0.0006	0.0028	0.0095	0.0255	0.0573	0.1117	0.1938
	9	0.0000	0.0000	0.0000	0.0001	0.0004	0.0017	0.0056	0.0153	0.0356	0.0730
	10	0.0000	0.0000	0.0000	0.0000	0.0000	0.0002	0.0008	0.0028	0.0079	0.0193
	11	0.0000	0.0000	0.0000	0.0000	0.0000	0.0000	0.0001	0.0003	0.0011	0.0032
	12	0.0000	0.0000	0.0000	0.0000	0.0000	0.0000	0.0000	0.0000	0.0001	0.0002
13	0	1.0000	1.0000	1.0000	1.0000	1.0000	1.0000	1.0000	1.0000	1.0000	1.0000
	1	0.4867	0.7458	0.8791	0.9450	0.9762	0.9903	0.9963	0.9987	0.9996	0.9999
	2	0.1354	0.3787	0.6017	0.7664	0.8733	0.9363	0.9704	0.9874	0.9951	0.9983
	3	0.0245	0.1339	0.3080	0.4983	0.6674	0.7975	0.8868	0.9421	0.9731	0.9888
	4	0.0031	0.0342	0.1180	0.2527	0.4157	0.5794	0.7217	0.8314	0.9071	0.9539
	5	0.0003	0.0065	0.0342	0.0991	0.2060	0.3457	0.4995	0.6470	0.7720	0.8666
	6	0.0000	0.0009	0.0075	0.0300	0.0802	0.1654	0.2841	0.4256	0.5732	0.7095
	7	0.0000	0.0001	0.0013	0.0070	0.0243	0.0624	0.1295	0.2288	0.3563	0.5000
	8	0.0000	0.0000	0.0002	0.0012	0.0056	0.0182	0.0462	0.0977	0.1788	0.2905
	9	0.0000	0.0000	0.0000	0.0002	0.0010	0.0040	0.0126	0.0321	0.0698	0.1334

p

.55	.60	.65	.70	.75	.80	.85	.90	.95
0.6214	0.7334	0.8283	0.9012	0.9511	0.9804	0.9944	0.9991	1.0000
0.3614	0.4826	0.6089	0.7297	0.8343	0.9144	0.9661	0.9917	0.9994
0.1495	0.2318	0.3373	0.4628	0.6007	0.7382	0.8591	0.9470	0.9916
0.0385	0.0705	0.1211	0.1960	0.3003	0.4362	0.5995	0.7748	0.9288
0.0046	0.0101	0.0207	0.0404	0.0751	0.1342	0.2316	0.3874	0.6302
1.0000	1.0000	1.0000	1.0000	1.0000	1.0000	1.0000	1.0000	1.0000
0.9997	0.9999	1.0000	1.0000	1.0000	1.0000	1.0000	1.0000	1.0000
0.9955	0.9983	0.9995	0.9999	1.0000	1.0000	1.0000	1.0000	1.0000
0.9726	0.9877	0.9952	0.9984	0.9996	0.9999	1.0000	1.0000	1.0000
0.8980	0.9452	0.9740	0.9894	0.9965	0.9991	0.9999	1.0000	1.0000
0.7384	0.8338	0.9051	0.9526	0.9803	0.9936	0.9986	0.9999	1.0000
0.5044	0.6331	0.7515	0.8497	0.9219	0.9672	0.9901	0.9984	0.9999
0.2660	0.3823	0.5138	0.6496	0.7759	0.8791	0.9500	0.9872	0.9990
0.0996	0.1673	0.2616	0.3828	0.5256	0.6778	0.8202	0.9298	0.9885
0.0233	0.0464	0.0860	0.1493	0.2440	0.3758	0.5443	0.7361	0.9139
0.0025	0.0060	0.0135	0.0282	0.0563	0.1074	0.1969	0.3487	0.5987
1.0000	1.0000	1.0000	1.0000	1.0000	1.0000	1.0000	1.0000	1.0000
0.9998	1.0000	1.0000	1.0000	1.0000	1.0000	1.0000	1.0000	1.0000
0.9978	0.9993	0.9998	1.0000	1.0000	1.0000	1.0000	1.0000	1.0000
0.9852	0.9941	0.9980	0.9994	0.9999	1.0000	1.0000	1.0000	1.0000
0.9390	0.9707	0.9878	0.9957	0.9988	0.9998	1.0000	1.0000	1.0000
0.8262	0.9006	0.9499	0.9784	0.9924	0.9980	0.9997	1.0000	1.0000
0.6331	0.7535	0.8513	0.9218	0.9657	0.9883	0.9973	0.9997	1.0000
0.3971	0.5328	0.6683	0.7897	0.8854	0.9496	0.9841	0.9972	0.9999
0.1911	0.2963	0.4255	0.5696	0.7133	0.8389	0.9306	0.9815	0.9984
0.0652	0.1189	0.2001	0.3127	0.4552	0.6174	0.7788	0.9104	0.9848
0.0139	0.0302	0.0606	0.1130	0.1971	0.3221	0.4922	0.6974	0.8981
0.0014	0.0036	0.0088	0.0198	0.0422	0.0859	0.1673	0.3138	0.5688
1.0000	1.0000	1.0000	1.0000	1.0000	1.0000	1.0000	1.0000	1.0000
0.9999	1.0000	1.0000	1.0000	1.0000	1.0000	1.0000	1.0000	1.0000
0.9989	0.9997	0.9999	1.0000	1.0000	1.0000	1.0000	1.0000	1.0000
0.9921	0.9972	0.9992	0.9998	1.0000	1.0000	1.0000	1.0000	1.0000
0.9644	0.9847	0.9944	0.9983	0.9996	0.9999	1.0000	1.0000	1.0000
0.8883	0.9427	0.9745	0.9905	0.9972	0.9994	0.9999	1.0000	1.0000
0.7393	0.8418	0.9154	0.9614	0.9857	0.9961	0.9993	0.9999	1.0000
0.5269	0.6652	0.7873	0.8821	0.9456	0.9806	0.9954	0.9995	1.0000
0.3044	0.4382	0.5833	0.7237	0.8424	0.9274	0.9761	0.9957	0.9998
0.1345	0.2253	0.3467	0.4925	0.6488	0.7946	0.9078	0.9744	0.9978
0.0421	0.0834	0.1513	0.2528	0.3907	0.5583	0.7358	0.8891	0.9804
0.0083	0.0196	0.0424	0.0850	0.1584	0.2749	0.4435	0.6590	0.8816
0.0008	0.0022	0.0057	0.0138	0.0317	0.0687	0.1422	0.2824	0.5404
1.0000	1.0000	1.0000	1.0000	1.0000	1.0000	1.0000	1.0000	1.0000
1.0000	1.0000	1.0000	1.0000	1.0000	1.0000	1.0000	1.0000	1.0000
0.9995	0.9999	1.0000	1.0000	1.0000	1.0000	1.0000	1.0000	1.0000
0.9959	0.9987	0.9997	0.9999	1.0000	1.0000	1.0000	1.0000	1.0000
0.9797	0.9922	0.9975	0.9993	0.9999	1.0000	1.0000	1.0000	1.0000
0.9301	0.9679	0.9874	0.9960	0.9990	0.9998	1.0000	1.0000	1.0000
0.8212	0.9023	0.9538	0.9818	0.9943	0.9988	0.9998	1.0000	1.0000
0.6437	0.7712	0.8705	0.9376	0.9757	0.9930	0.9987	0.9999	1.0000
0.4268	0.5744	0.7159	0.8346	0.9198	0.9700	0.9925	0.9991	1.0000
0.2279	0.3530	0.5005	0.6543	0.7940	0.9009	0.9658	0.9935	0.9997

p

n	r	.05	.10	.15	.20	.25	.30	.35	.40	.45	.50
	10	0.0000	0.0000	0.0000	0.0000	0.0001	0.0007	0.0025	0.0078	0.0203	0.0461
	11	0.0000	0.0000	0.0000	0.0000	0.0000	0.0001	0.0003	0.0013	0.0041	0.0112
	12	0.0000	0.0000	0.0000	0.0000	0.0000	0.0000	0.0000	0.0001	0.0005	0.0017
	13	0.0000	0.0000	0.0000	0.0000	0.0000	0.0000	0.0000	0.0000	0.0000	0.0001
14	0	1.0000	1.0000	1.0000	1.0000	1.0000	1.0000	1.0000	1.0000	1.0000	1.0000
	1	0.5123	0.7712	0.8972	0.9560	0.9822	0.9932	0.9976	0.9992	0.9998	0.9999
	2	0.1530	0.4154	0.6433	0.8021	0.8990	0.9525	0.9795	0.9919	0.9971	0.9991
	3	0.0301	0.1584	0.3521	0.5519	0.7189	0.8392	0.9161	0.9602	0.9830	0.9935
	4	0.0042	0.0441	0.1465	0.3018	0.4787	0.6448	0.7795	0.8757	0.9368	0.9713
	5	0.0004	0.0092	0.0467	0.1298	0.2585	0.4158	0.5773	0.7207	0.8328	0.9102
	6	0.0000	0.0015	0.0115	0.0439	0.1117	0.2195	0.3595	0.5141	0.6627	0.7880
	7	0.0000	0.0002	0.0022	0.0116	0.0383	0.0933	0.1836	0.3075	0.4539	0.6047
	8	0.0000	0.0000	0.0003	0.0024	0.0103	0.0315	0.0753	0.1501	0.2586	0.3953
	9	0.0000	0.0000	0.0000	0.0004	0.0022	0.0083	0.0243	0.0583	0.1189	0.2120
	10	0.0000	0.0000	0.0000	0.0000	0.0003	0.0017	0.0060	0.0175	0.0426	0.0898
	11	0.0000	0.0000	0.0000	0.0000	0.0000	0.0002	0.0011	0.0039	0.0114	0.0287
	12	0.0000	0.0000	0.0000	0.0000	0.0000	0.0000	0.0001	0.0006	0.0022	0.0065
	13	0.0000	0.0000	0.0000	0.0000	0.0000	0.0000	0.0000	0.0001	0.0003	0.0009
	14	0.0000	0.0000	0.0000	0.0000	0.0000	0.0000	0.0000	0.0000	0.0000	0.0001
15	0	1.0000	1.0000	1.0000	1.0000	1.0000	1.0000	1.0000	1.0000	1.0000	1.0000
	1	0.5367	0.7941	0.9126	0.9648	0.9866	0.9953	0.9984	0.9995	0.9999	1.0000
	2	0.1710	0.4510	0.6814	0.8329	0.9198	0.9647	0.9858	0.9948	0.9983	0.9995
	3	0.0362	0.1841	0.3958	0.6020	0.7639	0.8732	0.9383	0.9729	0.9893	0.9963
	4	0.0055	0.0556	0.1773	0.3518	0.5387	0.7031	0.8273	0.9095	0.9576	0.9824
	5	0.0006	0.0127	0.0617	0.1642	0.3135	0.4845	0.6481	0.7827	0.8796	0.9408
	6	0.0001	0.0022	0.0168	0.0611	0.1484	0.2784	0.4357	0.5968	0.7392	0.8491
	7	0.0000	0.0003	0.0036	0.0181	0.0566	0.1311	0.2452	0.3902	0.5478	0.6964
	8	0.0000	0.0000	0.0006	0.0042	0.0173	0.0500	0.1132	0.2131	0.3465	0.5000
	9	0.0000	0.0000	0.0001	0.0008	0.0042	0.0152	0.0422	0.0950	0.1818	0.3036
	10	0.0000	0.0000	0.0000	0.0001	0.0008	0.0037	0.0124	0.0338	0.0769	0.1509
	11	0.0000	0.0000	0.0000	0.0000	0.0001	0.0007	0.0028	0.0093	0.0255	0.0592
	12	0.0000	0.0000	0.0000	0.0000	0.0000	0.0001	0.0005	0.0019	0.0063	0.0176
	13	0.0000	0.0000	0.0000	0.0000	0.0000	0.0000	0.0001	0.0003	0.0011	0.0037
	14	0.0000	0.0000	0.0000	0.0000	0.0000	0.0000	0.0000	0.0000	0.0001	0.0005
	15	0.0000	0.0000	0.0000	0.0000	0.0000	0.0000	0.0000	0.0000	0.0000	0.0000
16	0	1.0000	1.0000	1.0000	1.0000	1.0000	1.0000	1.0000	1.0000	1.0000	1.0000
	1	0.5599	0.8147	0.9257	0.9719	0.9900	0.9967	0.9990	0.9997	0.9999	1.0000
	2	0.1892	0.4853	0.7161	0.8593	0.9365	0.9739	0.9902	0.9967	0.9990	0.9997
	3	0.0429	0.2108	0.4386	0.6482	0.8029	0.9006	0.9549	0.9817	0.9934	0.9979
	4	0.0070	0.0684	0.2101	0.4019	0.5950	0.7541	0.8661	0.9349	0.9719	0.9894
	5	0.0009	0.0170	0.0791	0.2018	0.3698	0.5501	0.7108	0.8334	0.9147	0.9616
	6	0.0001	0.0033	0.0235	0.0817	0.1897	0.3402	0.5100	0.6712	0.8024	0.8949
	7	0.0000	0.0005	0.0056	0.0267	0.0796	0.1753	0.3119	0.4728	0.6340	0.7727
	8	0.0000	0.0001	0.0011	0.0070	0.0271	0.0744	0.1594	0.2839	0.4371	0.5982
	9	0.0000	0.0000	0.0002	0.0015	0.0075	0.0257	0.0671	0.1423	0.2559	0.4018
	10	0.0000	0.0000	0.0000	0.0002	0.0016	0.0071	0.0229	0.0583	0.1241	0.2272
	11	0.0000	0.0000	0.0000	0.0000	0.0003	0.0016	0.0062	0.0191	0.0486	0.1051
	12	0.0000	0.0000	0.0000	0.0000	0.0000	0.0003	0.0013	0.0049	0.0149	0.0384
	13	0.0000	0.0000	0.0000	0.0000	0.0000	0.0000	0.0002	0.0009	0.0035	0.0106
	14	0.0000	0.0000	0.0000	0.0000	0.0000	0.0000	0.0000	0.0001	0.0006	0.0021
	15	0.0000	0.0000	0.0000	0.0000	0.0000	0.0000	0.0000	0.0000	0.0001	0.0003
	16	0.0000	0.0000	0.0000	0.0000	0.0000	0.0000	0.0000	0.0000	0.0000	0.0000

p

.55	.60	.65	.70	.75	.80	.85	.90	.95
0.0929	0.1686	0.2783	0.4206	0.5842	0.7473	0.8820	0.9658	0.9969
0.0269	0.0579	0.1132	0.2025	0.3326	0.5016	0.6920	0.8661	0.9755
0.0049	0.0126	0.0296	0.0637	0.1267	0.2336	0.3983	0.6213	0.8646
0.0004	0.0013	0.0037	0.0097	0.0238	0.0550	0.1209	0.2542	0.5133
1.0000	1.0000	1.0000	1.0000	1.0000	1.0000	1.0000	1.0000	1.0000
1.0000	1.0000	1.0000	1.0000	1.0000	1.0000	1.0000	1.0000	1.0000
0.9997	0.9999	1.0000	1.0000	1.0000	1.0000	1.0000	1.0000	1.0000
0.9978	0.9994	0.9999	1.0000	1.0000	1.0000	1.0000	1.0000	1.0000
0.9886	0.9961	0.9989	0.9998	1.0000	1.0000	1.0000	1.0000	1.0000
0.9574	0.9825	0.9940	0.9983	0.9997	1.0000	1.0000	1.0000	1.0000
0.8811	0.9417	0.9757	0.9917	0.9978	0.9996	1.0000	1.0000	1.0000
0.7414	0.8499	0.9247	0.9685	0.9897	0.9976	0.9997	1.0000	1.0000
0.5461	0.6924	0.8164	0.9067	0.9617	0.9884	0.9978	0.9998	1.0000
0.3373	0.4859	0.6405	0.7805	0.8883	0.9561	0.9885	0.9985	1.0000
0.1672	0.2793	0.4227	0.5842	0.7415	0.8702	0.9533	0.9908	0.9996
0.0632	0.1243	0.2205	0.3552	0.5213	0.6982	0.8535	0.9559	0.9958
0.0170	0.0398	0.0839	0.1608	0.2811	0.4480	0.6479	0.8416	0.9699
0.0029	0.0081	0.0205	0.0475	0.1010	0.1979	0.3567	0.5846	0.8470
0.0002	0.0008	0.0024	0.0068	0.0178	0.0440	0.1028	0.2288	0.4877
1.0000	1.0000	1.0000	1.0000	1.0000	1.0000	1.0000	1.0000	1.0000
1.0000	1.0000	1.0000	1.0000	1.0000	1.0000	1.0000	1.0000	1.0000
0.9999	1.0000	1.0000	1.0000	1.0000	1.0000	1.0000	1.0000	1.0000
0.9989	0.9997	0.9999	1.0000	1.0000	1.0000	1.0000	1.0000	1.0000
0.9937	0.9981	0.9995	0.9999	1.0000	1.0000	1.0000	1.0000	1.0000
0.9745	0.9906	0.9972	0.9993	0.9999	1.0000	1.0000	1.0000	1.0000
0.9231	0.9662	0.9876	0.9963	0.9992	0.9999	1.0000	1.0000	1.0000
0.8182	0.9049	0.9578	0.9848	0.9958	0.9992	0.9999	1.0000	1.0000
0.6535	0.7869	0.8868	0.9500	0.9827	0.9958	0.9994	1.0000	1.0000
0.4522	0.6098	0.7548	0.8689	0.9434	0.9819	0.9964	0.9997	1.0000
0.2608	0.4032	0.5643	0.7216	0.8516	0.9389	0.9832	0.9977	0.9999
0.1204	0.2173	0.3519	0.5155	0.6865	0.8358	0.9383	0.9873	0.9994
0.0424	0.0905	0.1727	0.2969	0.4613	0.6482	0.8227	0.9444	0.9945
0.0107	0.0271	0.0617	0.1268	0.2361	0.3980	0.6042	0.8159	0.9638
0.0017	0.0052	0.0142	0.0353	0.0802	0.1671	0.3186	0.5490	0.8290
0.0001	0.0005	0.0016	0.0047	0.0134	0.0352	0.0874	0.2059	0.4633
1.0000	1.0000	1.0000	1.0000	1.0000	1.0000	1.0000	1.0000	1.0000
1.0000	1.0000	1.0000	1.0000	1.0000	1.0000	1.0000	1.0000	1.0000
0.9999	1.0000	1.0000	1.0000	1.0000	1.0000	1.0000	1.0000	1.0000
0.9994	0.9999	1.0000	1.0000	1.0000	1.0000	1.0000	1.0000	1.0000
0.9965	0.9991	0.9998	1.0000	1.0000	1.0000	1.0000	1.0000	1.0000
0.9851	0.9951	0.9987	0.9997	1.0000	1.0000	1.0000	1.0000	1.0000
0.9514	0.9809	0.9938	0.9984	0.9997	1.0000	1.0000	1.0000	1.0000
0.8759	0.9417	0.9771	0.9929	0.9984	0.9998	1.0000	1.0000	1.0000
0.7441	0.8577	0.9329	0.9743	0.9925	0.9985	0.9998	1.0000	1.0000
0.5629	0.7161	0.8406	0.9256	0.9729	0.9930	0.9989	0.9999	1.0000
0.3660	0.5272	0.6881	0.8247	0.9204	0.9733	0.9944	0.9995	1.0000
0.1976	0.3288	0.4900	0.6598	0.8103	0.9183	0.9765	0.9967	0.9999
0.0853	0.1666	0.2892	0.4499	0.6302	0.7982	0.9209	0.9830	0.9991
0.0281	0.0651	0.1339	0.2459	0.4050	0.5981	0.7899	0.9316	0.9930
0.0066	0.0183	0.0451	0.0994	0.1971	0.3518	0.5614	0.7892	0.9571
0.0010	0.0033	0.0098	0.0261	0.0635	0.1407	0.2839	0.5147	0.8108
0.0001	0.0003	0.0010	0.0033	0.0100	0.0281	0.0742	0.1853	0.4401

$$p$$

n	r	.05	.10	.15	.20	.25	.30	.35	.40	.45	.50
17	0	1.0000	1.0000	1.0000	1.0000	1.0000	1.0000	1.0000	1.0000	1.0000	1.0000
	1	0.5819	0.8332	0.9369	0.9775	0.9925	0.9977	0.9993	0.9998	1.0000	1.0000
	2	0.2078	0.5182	0.7475	0.8818	0.9499	0.9807	0.9933	0.9979	0.9994	0.9999
	3	0.0503	0.2382	0.4802	0.6904	0.8363	0.9226	0.9673	0.9877	0.9959	0.9988
	4	0.0088	0.0826	0.2444	0.4511	0.6470	0.7981	0.8972	0.9536	0.9815	0.9936
	5	0.0012	0.0221	0.0987	0.2418	0.4261	0.6113	0.7652	0.8740	0.9404	0.9755
	6	0.0001	0.0047	0.0319	0.1057	0.2347	0.4032	0.5803	0.7361	0.8529	0.9283
	7	0.0000	0.0008	0.0083	0.0377	0.1071	0.2248	0.3812	0.5522	0.7098	0.8338
	8	0.0000	0.0001	0.0017	0.0109	0.0402	0.1046	0.2128	0.3595	0.5257	0.6855
	9	0.0000	0.0000	0.0003	0.0026	0.0124	0.0403	0.0994	0.1989	0.3374	0.5000
	10	0.0000	0.0000	0.0000	0.0005	0.0031	0.0127	0.0383	0.0919	0.1834	0.3145
	11	0.0000	0.0000	0.0000	0.0001	0.0006	0.0032	0.0120	0.0348	0.0826	0.1662
	12	0.0000	0.0000	0.0000	0.0000	0.0001	0.0007	0.0030	0.0106	0.0301	0.0717
	13	0.0000	0.0000	0.0000	0.0000	0.0000	0.0001	0.0006	0.0025	0.0086	0.0245
	14	0.0000	0.0000	0.0000	0.0000	0.0000	0.0000	0.0001	0.0005	0.0019	0.0064
	15	0.0000	0.0000	0.0000	0.0000	0.0000	0.0000	0.0000	0.0001	0.0003	0.0012
	16	0.0000	0.0000	0.0000	0.0000	0.0000	0.0000	0.0000	0.0000	0.0000	0.0001
	17	0.0000	0.0000	0.0000	0.0000	0.0000	0.0000	0.0000	0.0000	0.0000	0.0000
18	0	1.0000	1.0000	1.0000	1.0000	1.0000	1.0000	1.0000	1.0000	1.0000	1.0000
	1	0.6028	0.8499	0.9464	0.9820	0.9944	0.9984	0.9996	0.9999	1.0000	1.0000
	2	0.2265	0.5497	0.7759	0.9009	0.9605	0.9858	0.9954	0.9987	0.9997	0.9999
	3	0.0581	0.2662	0.5203	0.7287	0.8647	0.9400	0.9764	0.9918	0.9975	0.9993
	4	0.0109	0.0982	0.2798	0.4990	0.6943	0.8354	0.9217	0.9672	0.9880	0.9962
	5	0.0015	0.0282	0.1206	0.2836	0.4813	0.6673	0.8114	0.9058	0.9589	0.9846
	6	0.0002	0.0064	0.0419	0.1329	0.2825	0.4656	0.6450	0.7912	0.8923	0.9519
	7	0.0000	0.0012	0.0118	0.0513	0.1390	0.2783	0.4509	0.6257	0.7742	0.8811
	8	0.0000	0.0002	0.0027	0.0163	0.0569	0.1407	0.2717	0.4366	0.6085	0.7597
	9	0.0000	0.0000	0.0005	0.0043	0.0193	0.0596	0.1391	0.2632	0.4221	0.5927
	10	0.0000	0.0000	0.0001	0.0009	0.0054	0.0210	0.0597	0.1347	0.2527	0.4073
	11	0.0000	0.0000	0.0000	0.0002	0.0012	0.0061	0.0212	0.0576	0.1280	0.2403
	12	0.0000	0.0000	0.0000	0.0000	0.0002	0.0014	0.0062	0.0203	0.0537	0.1189
	13	0.0000	0.0000	0.0000	0.0000	0.0000	0.0003	0.0014	0.0058	0.0183	0.0481
	14	0.0000	0.0000	0.0000	0.0000	0.0000	0.0000	0.0003	0.0013	0.0049	0.0154
	15	0.0000	0.0000	0.0000	0.0000	0.0000	0.0000	0.0000	0.0002	0.0010	0.0038
	16	0.0000	0.0000	0.0000	0.0000	0.0000	0.0000	0.0000	0.0000	0.0001	0.0007
	17	0.0000	0.0000	0.0000	0.0000	0.0000	0.0000	0.0000	0.0000	0.0000	0.0001
	18	0.0000	0.0000	0.0000	0.0000	0.0000	0.0000	0.0000	0.0000	0.0000	0.0000
19	0	1.0000	1.0000	1.0000	1.0000	1.0000	1.0000	1.0000	1.0000	1.0000	1.0000
	1	0.6226	0.8649	0.9544	0.9856	0.9958	0.9989	0.9997	0.9999	1.0000	1.0000
	2	0.2453	0.5797	0.8015	0.9171	0.9690	0.9896	0.9969	0.9992	0.9998	1.0000
	3	0.0665	0.2946	0.5587	0.7631	0.8887	0.9538	0.9830	0.9945	0.9985	0.9996
	4	0.0132	0.1150	0.3158	0.5449	0.7369	0.8668	0.9409	0.9770	0.9923	0.9978
	5	0.0020	0.0352	0.1444	0.3267	0.5346	0.7178	0.8500	0.9304	0.9720	0.9904
	6	0.0002	0.0086	0.0537	0.1631	0.3322	0.5261	0.7032	0.8371	0.9223	0.9682
	7	0.0000	0.0017	0.0163	0.0676	0.1749	0.3345	0.5188	0.6919	0.8273	0.9165
	8	0.0000	0.0003	0.0041	0.0233	0.0775	0.1820	0.3344	0.5122	0.6831	0.8204
	9	0.0000	0.0000	0.0008	0.0067	0.0287	0.0839	0.1855	0.3325	0.5060	0.6762
	10	0.0000	0.0000	0.0001	0.0016	0.0089	0.0326	0.0875	0.1861	0.3290	0.5000
	11	0.0000	0.0000	0.0000	0.0003	0.0023	0.0105	0.0347	0.0885	0.1841	0.3238
	12	0.0000	0.0000	0.0000	0.0000	0.0005	0.0028	0.0114	0.0352	0.0871	0.1796
	13	0.0000	0.0000	0.0000	0.0000	0.0001	0.0006	0.0031	0.0116	0.0342	0.0835
	14	0.0000	0.0000	0.0000	0.0000	0.0000	0.0001	0.0007	0.0031	0.0109	0.0318
	15	0.0000	0.0000	0.0000	0.0000	0.0000	0.0000	0.0001	0.0006	0.0028	0.0096
	16	0.0000	0.0000	0.0000	0.0000	0.0000	0.0000	0.0000	0.0001	0.0005	0.0022
	17	0.0000	0.0000	0.0000	0.0000	0.0000	0.0000	0.0000	0.0000	0.0001	0.0004
	18	0.0000	0.0000	0.0000	0.0000	0.0000	0.0000	0.0000	0.0000	0.0000	0.0000
	19	0.0000	0.0000	0.0000	0.0000	0.0000	0.0000	0.0000	0.0000	0.0000	0.0000

p

.55	.60	.65	.70	.75	.80	.85	.90	.95
1.0000	1.0000	1.0000	1.0000	1.0000	1.0000	1.0000	1.0000	1.0000
1.0000	1.0000	1.0000	1.0000	1.0000	1.0000	1.0000	1.0000	1.0000
1.0000	1.0000	1.0000	1.0000	1.0000	1.0000	1.0000	1.0000	1.0000
0.9997	0.9999	1.0000	1.0000	1.0000	1.0000	1.0000	1.0000	1.0000
0.9981	0.9995	0.9999	1.0000	1.0000	1.0000	1.0000	1.0000	1.0000
0.9914	0.9975	0.9994	0.9999	1.0000	1.0000	1.0000	1.0000	1.0000
0.9699	0.9894	0.9970	0.9993	0.9999	1.0000	1.0000	1.0000	1.0000
0.9174	0.9652	0.9880	0.9968	0.9994	0.9999	1.0000	1.0000	1.0000
0.8166	0.9081	0.9617	0.9873	0.9969	0.9995	1.0000	1.0000	1.0000
0.6626	0.8011	0.9006	0.9597	0.9876	0.9974	0.9997	1.0000	1.0000
0.4743	0.6405	0.7872	0.8954	0.9598	0.9891	0.9983	0.9999	1.0000
0.2902	0.4478	0.6188	0.7752	0.8929	0.9623	0.9917	0.9992	1.0000
0.1471	0.2639	0.4197	0.5968	0.7653	0.8943	0.9681	0.9953	0.9999
0.0596	0.1260	0.2348	0.3887	0.5739	0.7582	0.9013	0.9779	0.9988
0.0184	0.0464	0.1028	0.2019	0.3530	0.5489	0.7556	0.9174	0.9912
0.0041	0.0123	0.0327	0.0774	0.1637	0.3096	0.5198	0.7618	0.9497
0.0006	0.0021	0.0067	0.0193	0.0501	0.1182	0.2525	0.4818	0.7922
0.0000	0.0002	0.0007	0.0023	0.0075	0.0225	0.0631	0.1668	0.4181
1.0000	1.0000	1.0000	1.0000	1.0000	1.0000	1.0000	1.0000	1.0000
1.0000	1.0000	1.0000	1.0000	1.0000	1.0000	1.0000	1.0000	1.0000
1.0000	1.0000	1.0000	1.0000	1.0000	1.0000	1.0000	1.0000	1.0000
0.9999	1.0000	1.0000	1.0000	1.0000	1.0000	1.0000	1.0000	1.0000
0.9990	0.9998	1.0000	1.0000	1.0000	1.0000	1.0000	1.0000	1.0000
0.9951	0.9987	0.9997	1.0000	1.0000	1.0000	1.0000	1.0000	1.0000
0.9817	0.9942	0.9986	0.9997	1.0000	1.0000	1.0000	1.0000	1.0000
0.9463	0.9797	0.9938	0.9986	0.9998	1.0000	1.0000	1.0000	1.0000
0.8720	0.9423	0.9788	0.9939	0.9988	0.9998	1.0000	1.0000	1.0000
0.7473	0.8653	0.9403	0.9790	0.9946	0.9991	0.9999	1.0000	1.0000
0.5778	0.7368	0.8609	0.9404	0.9806	0.9957	0.9995	1.0000	1.0000
0.3915	0.5634	0.7283	0.8593	0.9430	0.9837	0.9973	0.9998	1.0000
0.2258	0.3743	0.5491	0.7217	0.8610	0.9487	0.9882	0.9988	1.0000
0.1077	0.2088	0.3550	0.5344	0.7174	0.8671	0.9581	0.9936	0.9998
0.0411	0.0942	0.1886	0.3327	0.5187	0.7164	0.8794	0.9718	0.9985
0.0120	0.0328	0.0783	0.1645	0.3057	0.5010	0.7202	0.9018	0.9891
0.0025	0.0082	0.0236	0.0600	0.1353	0.2713	0.4797	0.7338	0.9419
0.0003	0.0013	0.0046	0.0142	0.0395	0.0991	0.2240	0.4503	0.7735
0.0000	0.0001	0.0004	0.0016	0.0056	0.0180	0.0536	0.1501	0.3972
1.0000	1.0000	1.0000	1.0000	1.0000	1.0000	1.0000	1.0000	1.0000
1.0000	1.0000	1.0000	1.0000	1.0000	1.0000	1.0000	1.0000	1.0000
1.0000	1.0000	1.0000	1.0000	1.0000	1.0000	1.0000	1.0000	1.0000
0.9999	1.0000	1.0000	1.0000	1.0000	1.0000	1.0000	1.0000	1.0000
0.9995	0.9999	1.0000	1.0000	1.0000	1.0000	1.0000	1.0000	1.0000
0.9972	0.9994	0.9999	1.0000	1.0000	1.0000	1.0000	1.0000	1.0000
0.9891	0.9969	0.9993	0.9999	1.0000	1.0000	1.0000	1.0000	1.0000
0.9658	0.9884	0.9969	0.9994	0.9999	1.0000	1.0000	1.0000	1.0000
0.9129	0.9648	0.9886	0.9972	0.9995	0.9999	1.0000	1.0000	1.0000
0.8159	0.9115	0.9653	0.9895	0.9977	0.9997	1.0000	1.0000	1.0000
0.6710	0.8139	0.9125	0.9674	0.9911	0.9984	0.9999	1.0000	1.0000
0.4940	0.6675	0.8145	0.9161	0.9712	0.9933	0.9992	1.0000	1.0000
0.3169	0.4878	0.6656	0.8180	0.9225	0.9767	0.9959	0.9997	1.0000
0.1727	0.3081	0.4812	0.6655	0.8251	0.9324	0.9837	0.9983	1.0000
0.0777	0.1629	0.2968	0.4739	0.6678	0.8369	0.9463	0.9914	0.9998
0.0280	0.0696	0.1500	0.2822	0.4654	0.6733	0.8556	0.9648	0.9980
0.0077	0.0230	0.0591	0.1332	0.2631	0.4551	0.6841	0.8850	0.9868
0.0015	0.0055	0.0170	0.0462	0.1113	0.2369	0.4413	0.7054	0.9335
0.0002	0.0008	0.0031	0.0104	0.0310	0.0829	0.1985	0.4203	0.7547
0.0000	0.0001	0.0003	0.0011	0.0042	0.0144	0.0456	0.1351	0.3773

p

n	r	.05	.10	.15	.20	.25	.30	.35	.40	.45	.50
20	0	1.0000	1.0000	1.0000	1.0000	1.0000	1.0000	1.0000	1.0000	1.0000	1.0000
	1	0.6415	0.8784	0.9612	0.9885	0.9968	0.9992	0.9998	1.0000	1.0000	1.0000
	2	0.2642	0.6083	0.8244	0.9308	0.9757	0.9924	0.9979	0.9995	0.9999	1.0000
	3	0.0755	0.3231	0.5951	0.7939	0.9087	0.9645	0.9879	0.9964	0.9991	0.9998
	4	0.0159	0.1330	0.3523	0.5885	0.7748	0.8929	0.9556	0.9840	0.9951	0.9987
	5	0.0026	0.0432	0.1702	0.3704	0.5852	0.7625	0.8818	0.9490	0.9811	0.9941
	6	0.0003	0.0113	0.0673	0.1958	0.3828	0.5836	0.7546	0.8744	0.9447	0.9793
	7	0.0000	0.0024	0.0219	0.0867	0.2142	0.3920	0.5834	0.7500	0.8701	0.9423
	8	0.0000	0.0004	0.0059	0.0321	0.1018	0.2277	0.3990	0.5841	0.7480	0.8684
	9	0.0000	0.0001	0.0013	0.0100	0.0409	0.1133	0.2376	0.4044	0.5857	0.7483
	10	0.0000	0.0000	0.0002	0.0026	0.0139	0.0480	0.1218	0.2447	0.4086	0.5881
	11	0.0000	0.0000	0.0000	0.0006	0.0039	0.0171	0.0532	0.1275	0.2493	0.4119
	12	0.0000	0.0000	0.0000	0.0001	0.0009	0.0051	0.0196	0.0565	0.1308	0.2517
	13	0.0000	0.0000	0.0000	0.0000	0.0002	0.0013	0.0060	0.0210	0.0580	0.1316
	14	0.0000	0.0000	0.0000	0.0000	0.0000	0.0003	0.0015	0.0065	0.0214	0.0577
	15	0.0000	0.0000	0.0000	0.0000	0.0000	0.0000	0.0003	0.0016	0.0064	0.0207
	16	0.0000	0.0000	0.0000	0.0000	0.0000	0.0000	0.0000	0.0003	0.0015	0.0059
	17	0.0000	0.0000	0.0000	0.0000	0.0000	0.0000	0.0000	0.0000	0.0003	0.0013
	18	0.0000	0.0000	0.0000	0.0000	0.0000	0.0000	0.0000	0.0000	0.0000	0.0002
	19	0.0000	0.0000	0.0000	0.0000	0.0000	0.0000	0.0000	0.0000	0.0000	0.0000
	20	0.0000	0.0000	0.0000	0.0000	0.0000	0.0000	0.0000	0.0000	0.0000	0.0000
21	0	1.0000	1.0000	1.0000	1.0000	1.0000	1.0000	1.0000	1.0000	1.0000	1.0000
	1	0.6594	0.8906	0.9671	0.9908	0.9976	0.9994	0.9999	1.0000	1.0000	1.0000
	2	0.2830	0.6353	0.8450	0.9424	0.9810	0.9944	0.9985	0.9997	0.9999	1.0000
	3	0.0849	0.3516	0.6295	0.8213	0.9255	0.9729	0.9914	0.9976	0.9994	0.9999
	4	0.0189	0.1520	0.3887	0.6296	0.8083	0.9144	0.9669	0.9890	0.9969	0.9993
	5	0.0032	0.0522	0.1975	0.4140	0.6326	0.8016	0.9076	0.9630	0.9874	0.9964
	6	0.0004	0.0144	0.0827	0.2307	0.4334	0.6373	0.7991	0.9043	0.9611	0.9867
	7	0.0000	0.0033	0.0287	0.1085	0.2564	0.4495	0.6433	0.7998	0.9036	0.9608
	8	0.0000	0.0006	0.0083	0.0431	0.1299	0.2770	0.4635	0.6505	0.8029	0.9054
	9	0.0000	0.0001	0.0020	0.0144	0.0561	0.1476	0.2941	0.4763	0.6587	0.8083
	10	0.0000	0.0000	0.0004	0.0041	0.0206	0.0676	0.1623	0.3086	0.4883	0.6682
	11	0.0000	0.0000	0.0001	0.0010	0.0064	0.0264	0.0772	0.1744	0.3210	0.5000
	12	0.0000	0.0000	0.0000	0.0002	0.0017	0.0087	0.0313	0.0849	0.1841	0.3318
	13	0.0000	0.0000	0.0000	0.0000	0.0004	0.0024	0.0108	0.0352	0.0908	0.1917
	14	0.0000	0.0000	0.0000	0.0000	0.0001	0.0006	0.0031	0.0123	0.0379	0.0946
	15	0.0000	0.0000	0.0000	0.0000	0.0000	0.0001	0.0007	0.0036	0.0132	0.0392
	16	0.0000	0.0000	0.0000	0.0000	0.0000	0.0000	0.0001	0.0008	0.0037	0.0133
	17	0.0000	0.0000	0.0000	0.0000	0.0000	0.0000	0.0000	0.0002	0.0008	0.0036
	18	0.0000	0.0000	0.0000	0.0000	0.0000	0.0000	0.0000	0.0000	0.0001	0.0007
	19	0.0000	0.0000	0.0000	0.0000	0.0000	0.0000	0.0000	0.0000	0.0000	0.0001
	20	0.0000	0.0000	0.0000	0.0000	0.0000	0.0000	0.0000	0.0000	0.0000	0.0000
	21	0.0000	0.0000	0.0000	0.0000	0.0000	0.0000	0.0000	0.0000	0.0000	0.0000
22	0	1.0000	1.0000	1.0000	1.0000	1.0000	1.0000	1.0000	1.0000	1.0000	1.0000
	1	0.6765	0.9015	0.9720	0.9926	0.9982	0.9996	0.9999	1.0000	1.0000	1.0000
	2	0.3018	0.6608	0.8633	0.9520	0.9851	0.9959	0.9990	0.9998	1.0000	1.0000
	3	0.0948	0.3800	0.6618	0.8455	0.9393	0.9793	0.9939	0.9984	0.9997	0.9999
	4	0.0222	0.1719	0.4248	0.6680	0.8376	0.9319	0.9755	0.9924	0.9980	0.9996
	5	0.0040	0.0621	0.2262	0.4571	0.6765	0.8354	0.9284	0.9734	0.9917	0.9978
	6	0.0006	0.0182	0.0999	0.2674	0.4832	0.6866	0.8371	0.9278	0.9729	0.9915
	7	0.0001	0.0044	0.0368	0.1330	0.3006	0.5058	0.6978	0.8416	0.9295	0.9738
	8	0.0000	0.0009	0.0114	0.0561	0.1615	0.3287	0.5264	0.7102	0.8482	0.9331
	9	0.0000	0.0001	0.0030	0.0201	0.0746	0.1865	0.3534	0.5460	0.7236	0.8569

p

.55	.60	.65	.70	.75	.80	.85	.90	.95
1.0000	1.0000	1.0000	1.0000	1.0000	1.0000	1.0000	1.0000	1.0000
1.0000	1.0000	1.0000	1.0000	1.0000	1.0000	1.0000	1.0000	1.0000
1.0000	1.0000	1.0000	1.0000	1.0000	1.0000	1.0000	1.0000	1.0000
1.0000	1.0000	1.0000	1.0000	1.0000	1.0000	1.0000	1.0000	1.0000
0.9997	0.9999	1.0000	1.0000	1.0000	1.0000	1.0000	1.0000	1.0000
0.9985	0.9997	0.9999	1.0000	1.0000	1.0000	1.0000	1.0000	1.0000
0.9936	0.9984	0.9997	1.0000	1.0000	1.0000	1.0000	1.0000	1.0000
0.9786	0.9935	0.9985	0.9997	1.0000	1.0000	1.0000	1.0000	1.0000
0.9420	0.9790	0.9940	0.9987	0.9998	1.0000	1.0000	1.0000	1.0000
0.8692	0.9435	0.9804	0.9949	0.9991	0.9999	1.0000	1.0000	1.0000
0.7507	0.8725	0.9468	0.9829	0.9961	0.9994	1.0000	1.0000	1.0000
0.5914	0.7553	0.8782	0.9520	0.9861	0.9974	0.9997	1.0000	1.0000
0.4143	0.5956	0.7624	0.8867	0.9591	0.9900	0.9987	0.9999	1.0000
0.2520	0.4159	0.6010	0.7723	0.8982	0.9679	0.9941	0.9996	1.0000
0.1299	0.2500	0.4166	0.6080	0.7858	0.9133	0.9781	0.9976	1.0000
0.0553	0.1256	0.2454	0.4164	0.6172	0.8042	0.9327	0.9887	0.9997
0.0189	0.0510	0.1182	0.2375	0.4148	0.6296	0.8298	0.9568	0.9974
0.0049	0.0160	0.0444	0.1071	0.2252	0.4114	0.6477	0.8670	0.9841
0.0009	0.0036	0.0121	0.0355	0.0913	0.2061	0.4049	0.6769	0.9245
0.0001	0.0005	0.0021	0.0076	0.0243	0.0692	0.1756	0.3917	0.7358
0.0000	0.0000	0.0002	0.0008	0.0032	0.0115	0.0388	0.1216	0.3585
1.0000	1.0000	1.0000	1.0000	1.0000	1.0000	1.0000	1.0000	1.0000
1.0000	1.0000	1.0000	1.0000	1.0000	1.0000	1.0000	1.0000	1.0000
1.0000	1.0000	1.0000	1.0000	1.0000	1.0000	1.0000	1.0000	1.0000
1.0000	1.0000	1.0000	1.0000	1.0000	1.0000	1.0000	1.0000	1.0000
0.9999	1.0000	1.0000	1.0000	1.0000	1.0000	1.0000	1.0000	1.0000
0.9992	0.9998	1.0000	1.0000	1.0000	1.0000	1.0000	1.0000	1.0000
0.9963	0.9992	0.9999	1.0000	1.0000	1.0000	1.0000	1.0000	1.0000
0.9868	0.9964	0.9993	0.9999	1.0000	1.0000	1.0000	1.0000	1.0000
0.9621	0.9877	0.9969	0.9994	0.9999	1.0000	1.0000	1.0000	1.0000
0.9092	0.9648	0.9892	0.9976	0.9996	1.0000	1.0000	1.0000	1.0000
0.8159	0.9151	0.9687	0.9913	0.9983	0.9998	1.0000	1.0000	1.0000
0.6790	0.8256	0.9228	0.9736	0.9936	0.9990	0.9999	1.0000	1.0000
0.5117	0.6914	0.8377	0.9324	0.9794	0.9959	0.9996	1.0000	1.0000
0.3413	0.5237	0.7059	0.8523	0.9438	0.9856	0.9980	0.9999	1.0000
0.1971	0.3495	0.5365	0.7230	0.8701	0.9569	0.9917	0.9994	1.0000
0.0964	0.2002	0.3567	0.5505	0.7436	0.8915	0.9713	0.9967	1.0000
0.0389	0.0957	0.2009	0.3627	0.5666	0.7693	0.9173	0.9856	0.9996
0.0126	0.0370	0.0924	0.1984	0.3674	0.5860	0.8025	0.9478	0.9968
0.0031	0.0110	0.0331	0.0856	0.1917	0.3704	0.6113	0.8480	0.9811
0.0006	0.0024	0.0086	0.0271	0.0745	0.1787	0.3705	0.6484	0.9151
0.0001	0.0003	0.0014	0.0056	0.0190	0.0576	0.1550	0.3647	0.7170
0.0000	0.0000	0.0001	0.0006	0.0024	0.0092	0.0329	0.1094	0.3406
1.0000	1.0000	1.0000	1.0000	1.0000	1.0000	1.0000	1.0000	1.0000
1.0000	1.0000	1.0000	1.0000	1.0000	1.0000	1.0000	1.0000	1.0000
1.0000	1.0000	1.0000	1.0000	1.0000	1.0000	1.0000	1.0000	1.0000
1.0000	1.0000	1.0000	1.0000	1.0000	1.0000	1.0000	1.0000	1.0000
0.9999	1.0000	1.0000	1.0000	1.0000	1.0000	1.0000	1.0000	1.0000
0.9995	0.9999	1.0000	1.0000	1.0000	1.0000	1.0000	1.0000	1.0000
0.9979	0.9996	0.9999	1.0000	1.0000	1.0000	1.0000	1.0000	1.0000
0.9920	0.9981	0.9996	1.0000	1.0000	1.0000	1.0000	1.0000	1.0000
0.9757	0.9929	0.9984	0.9998	1.0000	1.0000	1.0000	1.0000	1.0000
0.9383	0.9785	0.9942	0.9989	0.9999	1.0000	1.0000	1.0000	1.0000

p

n	r	.05	.10	.15	.20	.25	.30	.35	.40	.45	.50
	10	0.0000	0.0000	0.0007	0.0061	0.0295	0.0916	0.2084	0.3756	0.5650	0.7383
	11	0.0000	0.0000	0.0001	0.0016	0.0100	0.0387	0.1070	0.2280	0.3963	0.5841
	12	0.0000	0.0000	0.0000	0.0003	0.0029	0.0140	0.0474	0.1207	0.2457	0.4159
	13	0.0000	0.0000	0.0000	0.0001	0.0007	0.0043	0.0180	0.0551	0.1328	0.2617
	14	0.0000	0.0000	0.0000	0.0000	0.0001	0.0011	0.0058	0.0215	0.0617	0.1431
	15	0.0000	0.0000	0.0000	0.0000	0.0000	0.0002	0.0016	0.0070	0.0243	0.0669
	16	0.0000	0.0000	0.0000	0.0000	0.0000	0.0000	0.0003	0.0019	0.0080	0.0262
	17	0.0000	0.0000	0.0000	0.0000	0.0000	0.0000	0.0001	0.0004	0.0021	0.0085
	18	0.0000	0.0000	0.0000	0.0000	0.0000	0.0000	0.0000	0.0001	0.0005	0.0022
	19	0.0000	0.0000	0.0000	0.0000	0.0000	0.0000	0.0000	0.0000	0.0001	0.0004
	20	0.0000	0.0000	0.0000	0.0000	0.0000	0.0000	0.0000	0.0000	0.0000	0.0001
	21	0.0000	0.0000	0.0000	0.0000	0.0000	0.0000	0.0000	0.0000	0.0000	0.0000
	22	0.0000	0.0000	0.0000	0.0000	0.0000	0.0000	0.0000	0.0000	0.0000	0.0000
23	0	1.0000	1.0000	1.0000	1.0000	1.0000	1.0000	1.0000	1.0000	1.0000	1.0000
	1	0.6926	0.9114	0.9762	0.9941	0.9987	0.9997	0.9999	1.0000	1.0000	1.0000
	2	0.3206	0.6849	0.8796	0.9602	0.9884	0.9970	0.9993	0.9999	1.0000	1.0000
	3	0.1052	0.4080	0.6920	0.8668	0.9508	0.9843	0.9957	0.9990	0.9998	1.0000
	4	0.0258	0.1927	0.4604	0.7035	0.8630	0.9462	0.9819	0.9948	0.9988	0.9998
	5	0.0049	0.0731	0.2560	0.4993	0.7168	0.8644	0.9449	0.9810	0.9945	0.9987
	6	0.0008	0.0226	0.1189	0.3053	0.5315	0.7312	0.8691	0.9460	0.9814	0.9947
	7	0.0001	0.0058	0.0463	0.1598	0.3463	0.5601	0.7466	0.8760	0.9490	0.9827
	8	0.0000	0.0012	0.0152	0.0715	0.1963	0.3819	0.5864	0.7627	0.8848	0.9534
	9	0.0000	0.0002	0.0042	0.0273	0.0963	0.2291	0.4140	0.6116	0.7797	0.8950
	10	0.0000	0.0000	0.0010	0.0089	0.0408	0.1201	0.2592	0.4438	0.6364	0.7976
	11	0.0000	0.0000	0.0002	0.0025	0.0149	0.0546	0.1425	0.2871	0.4722	0.6612
	12	0.0000	0.0000	0.0000	0.0006	0.0046	0.0214	0.0682	0.1636	0.3135	0.5000
	13	0.0000	0.0000	0.0000	0.0001	0.0012	0.0072	0.0283	0.0813	0.1836	0.3388
	14	0.0000	0.0000	0.0000	0.0000	0.0003	0.0021	0.0100	0.0349	0.0937	0.2024
	15	0.0000	0.0000	0.0000	0.0000	0.0001	0.0005	0.0030	0.0128	0.0411	0.1050
	16	0.0000	0.0000	0.0000	0.0000	0.0000	0.0001	0.0008	0.0040	0.0153	0.0466
	17	0.0000	0.0000	0.0000	0.0000	0.0000	0.0000	0.0002	0.0010	0.0048	0.0173
	18	0.0000	0.0000	0.0000	0.0000	0.0000	0.0000	0.0000	0.0002	0.0012	0.0053
	19	0.0000	0.0000	0.0000	0.0000	0.0000	0.0000	0.0000	0.0000	0.0002	0.0013
	20	0.0000	0.0000	0.0000	0.0000	0.0000	0.0000	0.0000	0.0000	0.0000	0.0002
	21	0.0000	0.0000	0.0000	0.0000	0.0000	0.0000	0.0000	0.0000	0.0000	0.0000
	22	0.0000	0.0000	0.0000	0.0000	0.0000	0.0000	0.0000	0.0000	0.0000	0.0000
	23	0.0000	0.0000	0.0000	0.0000	0.0000	0.0000	0.0000	0.0000	0.0000	0.0000
24	0	1.0000	1.0000	1.0000	1.0000	1.0000	1.0000	1.0000	1.0000	1.0000	1.0000
	1	0.7080	0.9202	0.9798	0.9953	0.9990	0.9998	1.0000	1.0000	1.0000	1.0000
	2	0.3392	0.7075	0.8941	0.9669	0.9910	0.9978	0.9995	0.9999	1.0000	1.0000
	3	0.1159	0.4357	0.7202	0.8855	0.9602	0.9881	0.9970	0.9993	0.9999	1.0000
	4	0.0298	0.2143	0.4951	0.7361	0.8850	0.9576	0.9867	0.9965	0.9992	0.9999
	5	0.0060	0.0851	0.2866	0.5401	0.7533	0.8889	0.9578	0.9865	0.9964	0.9992
	6	0.0010	0.0277	0.1394	0.3441	0.5778	0.7712	0.8956	0.9600	0.9873	0.9967
	7	0.0001	0.0075	0.0572	0.1889	0.3926	0.6114	0.7894	0.9040	0.9636	0.9887
	8	0.0000	0.0017	0.0199	0.0892	0.2338	0.4353	0.6425	0.8081	0.9137	0.9680
	9	0.0000	0.0003	0.0059	0.0362	0.1213	0.2750	0.4743	0.6721	0.8270	0.9242
	10	0.0000	0.0001	0.0015	0.0126	0.0547	0.1528	0.3133	0.5109	0.7009	0.8463
	11	0.0000	0.0000	0.0003	0.0038	0.0213	0.0742	0.1833	0.3498	0.5461	0.7294
	12	0.0000	0.0000	0.0001	0.0010	0.0072	0.0314	0.0942	0.2130	0.3849	0.5806
	13	0.0000	0.0000	0.0000	0.0002	0.0021	0.0115	0.0423	0.1143	0.2420	0.4194
	14	0.0000	0.0000	0.0000	0.0000	0.0005	0.0036	0.0164	0.0535	0.1341	0.2706
	15	0.0000	0.0000	0.0000	0.0000	0.0001	0.0010	0.0055	0.0217	0.0648	0.1537
	16	0.0000	0.0000	0.0000	0.0000	0.0000	0.0002	0.0016	0.0075	0.0269	0.0758
	17	0.0000	0.0000	0.0000	0.0000	0.0000	0.0000	0.0004	0.0022	0.0095	0.0320
	18	0.0000	0.0000	0.0000	0.0000	0.0000	0.0000	0.0001	0.0005	0.0028	0.0113
	19	0.0000	0.0000	0.0000	0.0000	0.0000	0.0000	0.0000	0.0001	0.0007	0.0033

p

	.55	.60	.65	.70	.75	.80	.85	.90	.95
10	0.8672	0.9449	0.9820	0.9957	0.9993	0.9999	1.0000	1.0000	1.0000
11	0.7543	0.8793	0.9526	0.9860	0.9971	0.9996	1.0000	1.0000	1.0000
12	0.6037	0.7719	0.8930	0.9613	0.9900	0.9984	0.9999	1.0000	1.0000
13	0.4350	0.6243	0.7916	0.9084	0.9705	0.9939	0.9993	1.0000	1.0000
14	0.2764	0.4540	0.6466	0.8135	0.9254	0.9799	0.9970	0.9999	1.0000
15	0.1518	0.2898	0.4736	0.6712	0.8385	0.9439	0.9886	0.9991	1.0000
16	0.0705	0.1584	0.3022	0.4942	0.6994	0.8670	0.9632	0.9956	0.9999
17	0.0271	0.0722	0.1629	0.3134	0.5168	0.7326	0.9001	0.9818	0.9994
18	0.0083	0.0266	0.0716	0.1645	0.3235	0.5429	0.7738	0.9379	0.9960
19	0.0020	0.0076	0.0245	0.0681	0.1624	0.3320	0.5752	0.8281	0.9778
20	0.0003	0.0016	0.0061	0.0207	0.0606	0.1545	0.3382	0.6200	0.9052
21	0.0000	0.0002	0.0010	0.0041	0.0149	0.0480	0.1367	0.3392	0.6981
22	0.0000	0.0000	0.0001	0.0004	0.0018	0.0074	0.0280	0.0985	0.3235
0	1.0000	1.0000	1.0000	1.0000	1.0000	1.0000	1.0000	1.0000	1.0000
1	1.0000	1.0000	1.0000	1.0000	1.0000	1.0000	1.0000	1.0000	1.0000
2	1.0000	1.0000	1.0000	1.0000	1.0000	1.0000	1.0000	1.0000	1.0000
3	1.0000	1.0000	1.0000	1.0000	1.0000	1.0000	1.0000	1.0000	1.0000
4	1.0000	1.0000	1.0000	1.0000	1.0000	1.0000	1.0000	1.0000	1.0000
5	0.9997	1.0000	1.0000	1.0000	1.0000	1.0000	1.0000	1.0000	1.0000
6	0.9988	0.9998	1.0000	1.0000	1.0000	1.0000	1.0000	1.0000	1.0000
7	0.9952	0.9990	0.9998	1.0000	1.0000	1.0000	1.0000	1.0000	1.0000
8	0.9847	0.9960	0.9992	0.9999	1.0000	1.0000	1.0000	1.0000	1.0000
9	0.9589	0.9872	0.9970	0.9995	0.9999	1.0000	1.0000	1.0000	1.0000
10	0.9063	0.9651	0.9900	0.9979	0.9997	1.0000	1.0000	1.0000	1.0000
11	0.8164	0.9186	0.9717	0.9928	0.9988	0.9999	1.0000	1.0000	1.0000
12	0.6865	0.8364	0.9318	0.9785	0.9953	0.9994	1.0000	1.0000	1.0000
13	0.5278	0.7129	0.8575	0.9454	0.9851	0.9975	0.9998	1.0000	1.0000
14	0.3636	0.5562	0.7408	0.8799	0.9592	0.9911	0.9990	1.0000	1.0000
15	0.2203	0.3884	0.5860	0.7709	0.9037	0.9727	0.9958	0.9998	1.0000
16	0.1152	0.2373	0.4136	0.6181	0.8037	0.9285	0.9848	0.9988	1.0000
17	0.0510	0.1240	0.2534	0.4399	0.6537	0.8402	0.9537	0.9942	0.9999
18	0.0186	0.0540	0.1309	0.2688	0.4685	0.6947	0.8811	0.9774	0.9992
19	0.0055	0.0190	0.0551	0.1356	0.2832	0.5007	0.7440	0.9269	0.9951
20	0.0012	0.0052	0.0181	0.0538	0.1370	0.2965	0.5396	0.8073	0.9742
21	0.0002	0.0010	0.0043	0.0157	0.0492	0.1332	0.3080	0.5920	0.8948
22	0.0000	0.0001	0.0007	0.0030	0.0116	0.0398	0.1204	0.3151	0.6794
23	0.0000	0.0000	0.0000	0.0003	0.0013	0.0059	0.0238	0.0886	0.3074
0	1.0000	1.0000	1.0000	1.0000	1.0000	1.0000	1.0000	1.0000	1.0000
1	1.0000	1.0000	1.0000	1.0000	1.0000	1.0000	1.0000	1.0000	1.0000
2	1.0000	1.0000	1.0000	1.0000	1.0000	1.0000	1.0000	1.0000	1.0000
3	1.0000	1.0000	1.0000	1.0000	1.0000	1.0000	1.0000	1.0000	1.0000
4	1.0000	1.0000	1.0000	1.0000	1.0000	1.0000	1.0000	1.0000	1.0000
5	0.9999	1.0000	1.0000	1.0000	1.0000	1.0000	1.0000	1.0000	1.0000
6	0.9993	0.9999	1.0000	1.0000	1.0000	1.0000	1.0000	1.0000	1.0000
7	0.9972	0.9995	0.9999	1.0000	1.0000	1.0000	1.0000	1.0000	1.0000
8	0.9905	0.9978	0.9996	1.0000	1.0000	1.0000	1.0000	1.0000	1.0000
9	0.9731	0.9925	0.9984	0.9998	1.0000	1.0000	1.0000	1.0000	1.0000
10	0.9352	0.9783	0.9945	0.9990	0.9999	1.0000	1.0000	1.0000	1.0000
11	0.8659	0.9465	0.9836	0.9964	0.9995	1.0000	1.0000	1.0000	1.0000
12	0.7580	0.8857	0.9577	0.9885	0.9979	0.9998	1.0000	1.0000	1.0000
13	0.6151	0.7870	0.9058	0.9686	0.9928	0.9990	0.9999	1.0000	1.0000
14	0.4539	0.6502	0.8167	0.9258	0.9787	0.9962	0.9997	1.0000	1.0000
15	0.2991	0.4891	0.6866	0.8472	0.9453	0.9874	0.9985	0.9999	1.0000
16	0.1730	0.3279	0.5257	0.7250	0.8787	0.9638	0.9941	0.9997	1.0000
17	0.0863	0.1919	0.3575	0.5647	0.7662	0.9108	0.9801	0.9983	1.0000
18	0.0364	0.0960	0.2105	0.3886	0.6074	0.8111	0.9428	0.9925	0.9999
19	0.0127	0.0400	0.1044	0.2288	0.4222	0.6559	0.8606	0.9723	0.9990

p

n	r	.05	.10	.15	.20	.25	.30	.35	.40	.45	.50
	20	0.0000	0.0000	0.0000	0.0000	0.0000	0.0000	0.0000	0.0000	0.0001	0.0008
	21	0.0000	0.0000	0.0000	0.0000	0.0000	0.0000	0.0000	0.0000	0.0000	0.0001
	22	0.0000	0.0000	0.0000	0.0000	0.0000	0.0000	0.0000	0.0000	0.0000	0.0000
	23	0.0000	0.0000	0.0000	0.0000	0.0000	0.0000	0.0000	0.0000	0.0000	0.0000
	24	0.0000	0.0000	0.0000	0.0000	0.0000	0.0000	0.0000	0.0000	0.0000	0.0000
25	0	1.0000	1.0000	1.0000	1.0000	1.0000	1.0000	1.0000	1.0000	1.0000	1.0000
	1	0.7226	0.9282	0.9828	0.9962	0.9992	0.9999	1.0000	1.0000	1.0000	1.0000
	2	0.3576	0.7288	0.9069	0.9726	0.9930	0.9984	0.9997	0.9999	1.0000	1.0000
	3	0.1271	0.4629	0.7463	0.9018	0.9679	0.9910	0.9979	0.9996	0.9999	1.0000
	4	0.0341	0.2364	0.5289	0.7660	0.9038	0.9668	0.9903	0.9976	0.9995	0.9999
	5	0.0072	0.0980	0.3179	0.5793	0.7863	0.9095	0.9679	0.9905	0.9977	0.9995
	6	0.0012	0.0334	0.1615	0.3833	0.6217	0.8065	0.9174	0.9706	0.9914	0.9980
	7	0.0002	0.0095	0.0695	0.2200	0.4389	0.6593	0.8266	0.9264	0.9742	0.9927
	8	0.0000	0.0023	0.0255	0.1091	0.2735	0.4881	0.6939	0.8464	0.9361	0.9784
	9	0.0000	0.0005	0.0080	0.0468	0.1494	0.3231	0.5332	0.7265	0.8660	0.9461
	10	0.0000	0.0001	0.0021	0.0173	0.0713	0.1894	0.3697	0.5754	0.7576	0.8852
	11	0.0000	0.0000	0.0005	0.0056	0.0297	0.0978	0.2288	0.4142	0.6157	0.7878
	12	0.0000	0.0000	0.0001	0.0015	0.0107	0.0442	0.1254	0.2677	0.4574	0.6550
	13	0.0000	0.0000	0.0000	0.0004	0.0034	0.0175	0.0604	0.1538	0.3063	0.5000
	14	0.0000	0.0000	0.0000	0.0001	0.0009	0.0060	0.0255	0.0778	0.1827	0.3450
	15	0.0000	0.0000	0.0000	0.0000	0.0002	0.0018	0.0093	0.0344	0.0960	0.2122
	16	0.0000	0.0000	0.0000	0.0000	0.0000	0.0005	0.0029	0.0132	0.0440	0.1148
	17	0.0000	0.0000	0.0000	0.0000	0.0000	0.0001	0.0008	0.0043	0.0174	0.0539
	18	0.0000	0.0000	0.0000	0.0000	0.0000	0.0000	0.0002	0.0012	0.0058	0.0216
	19	0.0000	0.0000	0.0000	0.0000	0.0000	0.0000	0.0000	0.0003	0.0016	0.0073
	20	0.0000	0.0000	0.0000	0.0000	0.0000	0.0000	0.0000	0.0001	0.0004	0.0020
	21	0.0000	0.0000	0.0000	0.0000	0.0000	0.0000	0.0000	0.0000	0.0001	0.0005
	22	0.0000	0.0000	0.0000	0.0000	0.0000	0.0000	0.0000	0.0000	0.0000	0.0001
	23	0.0000	0.0000	0.0000	0.0000	0.0000	0.0000	0.0000	0.0000	0.0000	0.0000
	24	0.0000	0.0000	0.0000	0.0000	0.0000	0.0000	0.0000	0.0000	0.0000	0.0000
	25	0.0000	0.0000	0.0000	0.0000	0.0000	0.0000	0.0000	0.0000	0.0000	0.0000

p

.55	.60	.65	.70	.75	.80	.85	.90	.95
0.0036	0.0134	0.0422	0.1111	0.2466	0.4599	0.7134	0.9149	0.9940
0.0008	0.0035	0.0133	0.0424	0.1150	0.2639	0.5049	0.7857	0.9702
0.0001	0.0007	0.0030	0.0119	0.0398	0.1145	0.2798	0.5643	0.8841
0.0000	0.0001	0.0005	0.0022	0.0090	0.0331	0.1059	0.2925	0.6608
0.0000	0.0000	0.0000	0.0002	0.0010	0.0047	0.0202	0.0798	0.2920
1.0000	1.0000	1.0000	1.0000	1.0000	1.0000	1.0000	1.0000	1.0000
1.0000	1.0000	1.0000	1.0000	1.0000	1.0000	1.0000	1.0000	1.0000
1.0000	1.0000	1.0000	1.0000	1.0000	1.0000	1.0000	1.0000	1.0000
1.0000	1.0000	1.0000	1.0000	1.0000	1.0000	1.0000	1.0000	1.0000
1.0000	1.0000	1.0000	1.0000	1.0000	1.0000	1.0000	1.0000	1.0000
0.9999	1.0000	1.0000	1.0000	1.0000	1.0000	1.0000	1.0000	1.0000
0.9996	0.9999	1.0000	1.0000	1.0000	1.0000	1.0000	1.0000	1.0000
0.9984	0.9997	1.0000	1.0000	1.0000	1.0000	1.0000	1.0000	1.0000
0.9942	0.9988	0.9998	1.0000	1.0000	1.0000	1.0000	1.0000	1.0000
0.9826	0.9957	0.9992	0.9999	1.0000	1.0000	1.0000	1.0000	1.0000
0.9560	0.9868	0.9971	0.9995	1.0000	1.0000	1.0000	1.0000	1.0000
0.9040	0.9656	0.9907	0.9982	0.9998	1.0000	1.0000	1.0000	1.0000
0.8173	0.9222	0.9745	0.9940	0.9991	0.9999	1.0000	1.0000	1.0000
0.6937	0.8462	0.9396	0.9825	0.9966	0.9996	1.0000	1.0000	1.0000
0.5426	0.7323	0.8746	0.9558	0.9893	0.9985	0.9999	1.0000	1.0000
0.3843	0.5858	0.7712	0.9022	0.9703	0.9944	0.9995	1.0000	1.0000
0.2424	0.4246	0.6303	0.8106	0.9287	0.9827	0.9979	0.9999	1.0000
0.1340	0.2735	0.4668	0.6769	0.8506	0.9532	0.9920	0.9995	1.0000
0.0638	0.1535	0.3061	0.5118	0.7265	0.8909	0.9745	0.9977	1.0000
0.0258	0.0736	0.1734	0.3407	0.5611	0.7800	0.9305	0.9905	0.9998
0.0086	0.0294	0.0826	0.1935	0.3783	0.6167	0.8385	0.9666	0.9988
0.0023	0.0095	0.0320	0.0905	0.2137	0.4207	0.6821	0.9020	0.9928
0.0005	0.0024	0.0097	0.0332	0.0962	0.2340	0.4711	0.7636	0.9659
0.0001	0.0004	0.0021	0.0090	0.0321	0.0982	0.2537	0.5371	0.8729
0.0000	0.0001	0.0003	0.0016	0.0070	0.0274	0.0931	0.2712	0.6424
0.0000	0.0000	0.0000	0.0001	0.0008	0.0038	0.0172	0.0718	0.2774

Appendix D
Poisson
Distribution—
Noncumulative

The entries in the following table represent the individual-term Poisson probabilities for the number of occurrences X per unit of measurement for certain values of m, the mean number of occurrences per unit of measurement.

$$P(X = X_0 \mid m)$$

POISSON DISTRIBUTION—NONCUMULATIVE / 403

X	.001	.002	.003	.004	.005	.006	.007	.008	.009	.010	.011	.012	.013	.014	.015	.016	.017	.018	.019
0	.9990	.9980	.9970	.9960	.9950	.9940	.9930	.9920	.9910	.9901	.9891	.9881	.9871	.9861	.9851	.9841	.9831	.9822	.9812
1	.0010	.0020	.0030	.0040	.0050	.0060	.0070	.0079	.0089	.0099	.0109	.0119	.0128	.0138	.0148	.0157	.0167	.0177	.0186
2	.0000	.0000	.0000	.0000	.0000	.0000	.0000	.0000	.0000	.0000	.0001	.0001	.0001	.0001	.0001	.0001	.0001	.0002	.0002

X	.020	.030	.040	.050	.060	.070	.080	.090	.100	.110	.120	.130	.140	.150	.160	.170	.180	.190	.200
0	.9802	.9704	.9608	.9512	.9418	.9324	.9231	.9139	.9048	.8958	.8869	.8781	.8694	.8607	.8521	.8437	.8353	.8270	.8187
1	.0196	.0291	.0384	.0476	.0565	.0653	.0738	.0823	.0905	.0985	.1064	.1142	.1217	.1291	.1363	.1434	.1503	.1571	.1637
2	.0002	.0004	.0008	.0012	.0017	.0023	.0030	.0037	.0045	.0054	.0064	.0074	.0085	.0097	.0109	.0122	.0135	.0149	.0164
3	.0000	.0000	.0000	.0000	.0000	.0001	.0001	.0001	.0002	.0002	.0003	.0003	.0004	.0005	.0006	.0007	.0008	.0009	.0011
4	.0000	.0000	.0000	.0000	.0000	.0000	.0000	.0000	.0000	.0000	.0000	.0000	.0000	.0000	.0000	.0000	.0000	.0000	.0001

X	.210	.220	.230	.240	.250	.260	.270	.280	.290	.300	.310	.320	.330	.340	.350	.360	.370	.380	.390
0	.8106	.8025	.7945	.7866	.7788	.7711	.7634	.7558	.7483	.7408	.7334	.7261	.7189	.7118	.7047	.6977	.6907	.6839	.6771
1	.1702	.1766	.1827	.1888	.1947	.2005	.2061	.2116	.2170	.2222	.2274	.2324	.2372	.2420	.2466	.2512	.2556	.2599	.2641
2	.0179	.0194	.0210	.0227	.0243	.0261	.0278	.0296	.0315	.0333	.0352	.0372	.0391	.0411	.0432	.0452	.0473	.0494	.0515
3	.0013	.0014	.0016	.0018	.0020	.0023	.0025	.0028	.0030	.0033	.0036	.0040	.0043	.0047	.0050	.0054	.0058	.0063	.0067
4	.0001	.0001	.0001	.0001	.0001	.0001	.0002	.0002	.0002	.0003	.0003	.0003	.0004	.0004	.0004	.0005	.0005	.0006	.0007
5	.0000	.0000	.0000	.0000	.0000	.0000	.0000	.0000	.0000	.0000	.0000	.0000	.0000	.0000	.0000	.0000	.0000	.0000	.0001

X	0.40	0.45	0.50	0.55	0.60	0.65	0.70	0.75	0.80	0.85	0.90	0.95	1.00	1.05	1.10	1.15	1.20	1.25	1.30
0	.6703	.6376	.6065	.5769	.5488	.5220	.4966	.4724	.4493	.4274	.4066	.3867	.3679	.3499	.3329	.3166	.3012	.2865	.2725
1	.2681	.2869	.3033	.3173	.3293	.3393	.3476	.3543	.3595	.3633	.3659	.3674	.3679	.3674	.3662	.3641	.3614	.3581	.3543
2	.0536	.0646	.0758	.0873	.0988	.1103	.1217	.1329	.1438	.1544	.1647	.1745	.1839	.1929	.2014	.2094	.2169	.2238	.2303
3	.0072	.0097	.0126	.0160	.0198	.0239	.0284	.0332	.0383	.0437	.0494	.0553	.0613	.0675	.0738	.0803	.0867	.0933	.0998
4	.0007	.0011	.0016	.0022	.0030	.0039	.0050	.0062	.0077	.0093	.0111	.0131	.0153	.0177	.0203	.0231	.0260	.0291	.0324
5	.0001	.0001	.0002	.0002	.0004	.0005	.0007	.0009	.0012	.0016	.0020	.0025	.0031	.0037	.0045	.0053	.0062	.0073	.0084
6	.0000	.0000	.0000	.0000	.0000	.0001	.0001	.0001	.0002	.0002	.0003	.0004	.0005	.0007	.0008	.0010	.0012	.0015	.0018
7	.0000	.0000	.0000	.0000	.0000	.0000	.0000	.0000	.0000	.0000	.0000	.0001	.0001	.0001	.0001	.0002	.0002	.0003	.0003
8	.0000	.0000	.0000	.0000	.0000	.0000	.0000	.0000	.0000	.0000	.0000	.0000	.0000	.0000	.0000	.0000	.0000	.0001	.0001

m

X	1.4	1.5	1.6	1.7	1.8	1.9	2.0	2.1	2.2	2.3	2.4	2.5	2.6	2.7	2.8	2.9	3.0	3.1	3.2
0	.2466	.2231	.2019	.1827	.1653	.1496	.1353	.1225	.1108	.1003	.0907	.0821	.0743	.0672	.0608	.0550	.0498	.0450	.0408
1	.3452	.3347	.3230	.3106	.2975	.2842	.2707	.2572	.2438	.2306	.2177	.2052	.1931	.1815	.1703	.1596	.1494	.1397	.1304
2	.2417	.2510	.2584	.2640	.2678	.2700	.2707	.2700	.2681	.2652	.2613	.2565	.2510	.2450	.2384	.2314	.2240	.2165	.2087
3	.1128	.1255	.1378	.1496	.1607	.1710	.1804	.1890	.1966	.2033	.2090	.2138	.2176	.2205	.2225	.2237	.2240	.2237	.2226
4	.0395	.0471	.0551	.0636	.0723	.0812	.0902	.0992	.1082	.1169	.1254	.1336	.1414	.1488	.1557	.1622	.1680	.1733	.1781
5	.0111	.0141	.0176	.0216	.0260	.0309	.0361	.0417	.0476	.0538	.0602	.0668	.0735	.0804	.0872	.0940	.1008	.1075	.1140
6	.0026	.0035	.0047	.0061	.0078	.0098	.0120	.0146	.0174	.0206	.0241	.0278	.0319	.0362	.0407	.0455	.0504	.0555	.0608
7	.0005	.0008	.0011	.0015	.0020	.0027	.0034	.0044	.0055	.0068	.0083	.0099	.0118	.0139	.0163	.0188	.0216	.0246	.0278
8	.0001	.0001	.0002	.0003	.0005	.0006	.0009	.0011	.0015	.0019	.0025	.0031	.0038	.0047	.0057	.0068	.0081	.0095	.0111
9	.0000	.0000	.0000	.0001	.0001	.0001	.0002	.0003	.0004	.0005	.0007	.0009	.0011	.0014	.0018	.0022	.0027	.0033	.0040
10	.0000	.0000	.0000	.0000	.0000	.0000	.0000	.0001	.0001	.0001	.0002	.0002	.0003	.0004	.0005	.0006	.0008	.0010	.0013
11	.0000	.0000	.0000	.0000	.0000	.0000	.0000	.0000	.0000	.0000	.0000	.0000	.0001	.0001	.0001	.0002	.0002	.0003	.0004
12	.0000	.0000	.0000	.0000	.0000	.0000	.0000	.0000	.0000	.0000	.0000	.0000	.0000	.0001	.0001	.0000	.0001	.0001	.0001

X	3.3	3.4	3.5	3.6	3.7	3.8	3.9	4.0	4.1	4.2	4.3	4.4	4.5	4.6	4.7	4.8	4.9	5.0	5.1
0	.0369	.0334	.0302	.0273	.0247	.0224	.0202	.0183	.0166	.0150	.0136	.0123	.0111	.0101	.0091	.0082	.0074	.0067	.0061
1	.1217	.1135	.1057	.0984	.0915	.0850	.0789	.0733	.0679	.0630	.0583	.0540	.0500	.0462	.0427	.0395	.0365	.0337	.0311
2	.2008	.1929	.1850	.1771	.1692	.1615	.1539	.1465	.1393	.1323	.1254	.1188	.1125	.1063	.1005	.0948	.0894	.0842	.0793
3	.2209	.2186	.2158	.2125	.2087	.2046	.2001	.1954	.1904	.1852	.1798	.1743	.1687	.1631	.1574	.1517	.1460	.1404	.1348
4	.1823	.1858	.1888	.1912	.1931	.1944	.1951	.1954	.1951	.1944	.1933	.1917	.1898	.1875	.1849	.1820	.1789	.1755	.1719
5	.1203	.1264	.1322	.1377	.1429	.1477	.1522	.1563	.1600	.1633	.1662	.1687	.1708	.1725	.1738	.1747	.1753	.1755	.1753
6	.0662	.0716	.0771	.0826	.0881	.0936	.0989	.1042	.1093	.1143	.1191	.1237	.1281	.1323	.1362	.1398	.1432	.1462	.1490
7	.0312	.0348	.0385	.0425	.0466	.0508	.0551	.0595	.0640	.0686	.0732	.0778	.0824	.0869	.0914	.0959	.1002	.1044	.1086
8	.0129	.0148	.0169	.0191	.0215	.0241	.0269	.0298	.0328	.0360	.0393	.0428	.0463	.0500	.0537	.0575	.0614	.0653	.0692
9	.0047	.0056	.0066	.0076	.0089	.0102	.0116	.0132	.0150	.0168	.0188	.0209	.0232	.0255	.0280	.0307	.0334	.0363	.0392
10	.0016	.0019	.0023	.0028	.0033	.0039	.0045	.0053	.0061	.0071	.0081	.0092	.0104	.0118	.0132	.0147	.0164	.0181	.0200
11	.0005	.0006	.0007	.0009	.0011	.0013	.0016	.0019	.0023	.0027	.0032	.0037	.0043	.0049	.0056	.0064	.0073	.0082	.0093
12	.0001	.0002	.0002	.0003	.0003	.0004	.0005	.0006	.0008	.0009	.0011	.0013	.0016	.0019	.0022	.0026	.0030	.0034	.0039
13	.0000	.0000	.0001	.0001	.0001	.0001	.0002	.0002	.0002	.0003	.0004	.0005	.0006	.0007	.0008	.0009	.0011	.0013	.0015
14	.0000	.0000	.0000	.0000	.0000	.0000	.0000	.0001	.0001	.0001	.0001	.0001	.0002	.0002	.0003	.0003	.0004	.0005	.0006
15	.0000	.0000	.0000	.0000	.0000	.0000	.0000	.0000	.0000	.0000	.0000	.0000	.0001	.0001	.0001	.0001	.0001	.0002	.0002
16	.0000	.0000	.0000	.0000	.0000	.0000	.0000	.0000	.0000	.0000	.0000	.0000	.0000	.0000	.0000	.0000	.0000	.0000	.0001

m

X	5.2	5.3	5.4	5.5	5.6	5.7	5.8	5.9	6.0	6.1	6.2	6.3	6.4	6.5	6.6	6.7	6.8	6.9	7.0
0	.0055	.0050	.0045	.0041	.0037	.0033	.0030	.0027	.0025	.0022	.0020	.0018	.0017	.0015	.0014	.0012	.0011	.0010	.0009
1	.0287	.0265	.0244	.0225	.0207	.0191	.0176	.0162	.0149	.0137	.0126	.0116	.0106	.0098	.0090	.0082	.0076	.0070	.0064
2	.0746	.0701	.0659	.0618	.0580	.0544	.0509	.0477	.0446	.0417	.0390	.0364	.0340	.0318	.0296	.0276	.0258	.0240	.0223
3	.1293	.1239	.1185	.1133	.1082	.1033	.0985	.0938	.0892	.0848	.0806	.0765	.0726	.0688	.0652	.0617	.0584	.0552	.0521
4	.1681	.1641	.1600	.1558	.1515	.1472	.1428	.1383	.1339	.1294	.1249	.1205	.1162	.1118	.1076	.1034	.0992	.0952	.0912
5	.1748	.1740	.1728	.1714	.1697	.1678	.1656	.1632	.1606	.1579	.1549	.1519	.1487	.1454	.1420	.1385	.1349	.1314	.1277
6	.1515	.1537	.1555	.1571	.1584	.1594	.1601	.1605	.1606	.1605	.1601	.1595	.1586	.1575	.1562	.1546	.1529	.1511	.1490
7	.1125	.1163	.1200	.1234	.1267	.1298	.1326	.1353	.1377	.1399	.1418	.1435	.1450	.1462	.1472	.1480	.1486	.1489	.1490
8	.0731	.0771	.0810	.0849	.0887	.0925	.0962	.0998	.1033	.1066	.1099	.1130	.1160	.1188	.1215	.1240	.1263	.1284	.1304
9	.0423	.0454	.0486	.0519	.0552	.0586	.0620	.0654	.0688	.0723	.0757	.0791	.0825	.0858	.0891	.0923	.0954	.0985	.1014
10	.0220	.0241	.0262	.0285	.0309	.0334	.0359	.0386	.0413	.0441	.0469	.0498	.0528	.0558	.0588	.0618	.0649	.0679	.0710
11	.0104	.0116	.0129	.0143	.0157	.0173	.0190	.0207	.0225	.0244	.0265	.0285	.0307	.0330	.0353	.0377	.0401	.0426	.0452
12	.0045	.0051	.0058	.0065	.0073	.0082	.0092	.0102	.0113	.0124	.0137	.0150	.0164	.0179	.0194	.0210	.0227	.0245	.0263
13	.0018	.0021	.0024	.0028	.0032	.0036	.0041	.0046	.0052	.0058	.0065	.0073	.0081	.0089	.0099	.0108	.0119	.0130	.0142
14	.0007	.0008	.0009	.0011	.0013	.0015	.0017	.0019	.0022	.0025	.0029	.0033	.0037	.0041	.0046	.0052	.0058	.0064	.0071
15	.0002	.0003	.0003	.0004	.0005	.0006	.0007	.0008	.0009	.0010	.0012	.0014	.0016	.0018	.0020	.0023	.0026	.0029	.0033
16	.0001	.0001	.0001	.0001	.0002	.0002	.0002	.0003	.0003	.0004	.0005	.0005	.0006	.0007	.0008	.0010	.0011	.0013	.0014
17	.0000	.0000	.0000	.0000	.0001	.0001	.0001	.0001	.0001	.0001	.0002	.0002	.0002	.0003	.0003	.0004	.0004	.0005	.0006
18	.0000	.0000	.0000	.0000	.0000	.0000	.0000	.0000	.0000	.0000	.0000	.0001	.0001	.0001	.0001	.0001	.0001	.0002	.0002
19	.0000	.0000	.0000	.0000	.0000	.0000	.0000	.0000	.0000	.0000	.0000	.0000	.0000	.0000	.0000	.0001	.0001	.0001	.0001

X	7.5	8.0	8.5	9.0	9.5	10.0	10.5	11.0	11.5	12.0	12.5	13.0	13.5	14.0	14.5	15.0	20.0	25.0	30.0
0	.0006	.0003	.0002	.0001	.0001	.0000	.0000	.0000	.0000	.0000	.0000	.0000	.0000	.0000	.0000	.0000	.0000	.0000	.0000
1	.0041	.0027	.0017	.0011	.0007	.0005	.0003	.0002	.0001	.0001	.0000	.0000	.0000	.0000	.0000	.0000	.0000	.0000	.0000
2	.0156	.0107	.0074	.0050	.0034	.0023	.0015	.0010	.0007	.0004	.0003	.0002	.0001	.0001	.0001	.0000	.0000	.0000	.0000
3	.0389	.0286	.0208	.0150	.0107	.0076	.0053	.0037	.0026	.0018	.0012	.0008	.0006	.0004	.0003	.0002	.0000	.0000	.0000
4	.0729	.0573	.0443	.0337	.0254	.0189	.0139	.0102	.0074	.0053	.0038	.0027	.0019	.0013	.0009	.0006	.0000	.0000	.0000
5	.1094	.0916	.0752	.0607	.0483	.0378	.0293	.0224	.0170	.0127	.0095	.0070	.0051	.0037	.0027	.0019	.0001	.0000	.0000
6	.1367	.1221	.1066	.0911	.0764	.0631	.0513	.0411	.0325	.0255	.0197	.0152	.0115	.0087	.0065	.0048	.0002	.0000	.0000
7	.1465	.1396	.1294	.1171	.1037	.0901	.0769	.0646	.0535	.0437	.0353	.0281	.0222	.0174	.0135	.0104	.0005	.0000	.0000
8	.1373	.1396	.1375	.1318	.1232	.1126	.1009	.0888	.0769	.0655	.0551	.0457	.0375	.0304	.0244	.0194	.0013	.0000	.0001
9	.1144	.1241	.1299	.1318	.1300	.1251	.1177	.1085	.0982	.0874	.0765	.0661	.0563	.0473	.0394	.0324	.0029	.0001	.0001
10	.0858	.0993	.1104	.1186	.1235	.1251	.1236	.1194	.1129	.1048	.0956	.0859	.0760	.0663	.0571	.0486	.0058	.0004	.0000
11	.0585	.0722	.0853	.0970	.1067	.1137	.1180	.1194	.1181	.1144	.1087	.1015	.0932	.0844	.0753	.0663	.0106	.0008	.0000
12	.0366	.0481	.0604	.0728	.0844	.0948	.1032	.1094	.1131	.1144	.1132	.1099	.1049	.0984	.0910	.0829	.0176	.0017	.0001
13	.0211	.0296	.0395	.0504	.0617	.0729	.0834	.0926	.1001	.1056	.1089	.1099	.1089	.1060	.1014	.0956	.0271	.0033	.0002
14	.0113	.0169	.0240	.0324	.0419	.0521	.0625	.0728	.0822	.0905	.0972	.1021	.1050	.1060	.1051	.1024	.0387	.0059	.0005

m

	7.5	8.0	8.5	9.0	9.5	10.0	10.5	11.0	11.5	12.0	12.5	13.0	13.5	14.0	14.5	15.0	20.0	25.0	30.0
15	.0057	.0090	.0136	.0194	.0265	.0347	.0438	.0534	.0630	.0724	.0810	.0885	.0945	.0989	.1016	.1024	.0516	.0099	.0010
16	.0026	.0045	.0072	.0109	.0157	.0217	.0287	.0367	.0453	.0543	.0633	.0719	.0798	.0866	.0920	.0960	.0646	.0155	.0019
17	.0012	.0021	.0036	.0058	.0088	.0128	.0177	.0237	.0306	.0383	.0465	.0550	.0633	.0713	.0785	.0847	.0760	.0227	.0034
18	.0005	.0009	.0017	.0029	.0046	.0071	.0104	.0145	.0196	.0255	.0323	.0397	.0475	.0554	.0632	.0706	.0844	.0316	.0057
19	.0002	.0004	.0008	.0014	.0023	.0037	.0057	.0084	.0119	.0161	.0213	.0272	.0337	.0409	.0483	.0557	.0888	.0415	.0089
20	.0001	.0002	.0003	.0006	.0011	.0019	.0030	.0046	.0068	.0097	.0133	.0177	.0228	.0286	.0350	.0418	.0888	.0519	.0134
21	.0000	.0001	.0001	.0003	.0005	.0009	.0015	.0024	.0037	.0055	.0079	.0109	.0146	.0191	.0242	.0299	.0846	.0618	.0192
22	.0000	.0000	.0000	.0001	.0002	.0004	.0007	.0012	.0020	.0030	.0045	.0065	.0090	.0121	.0159	.0204	.0769	.0702	.0261
23	.0000	.0000	.0000	.0000	.0001	.0002	.0003	.0006	.0010	.0016	.0024	.0037	.0053	.0074	.0100	.0133	.0669	.0763	.0341
24	.0000	.0000	.0000	.0000	.0000	.0001	.0001	.0003	.0005	.0008	.0013	.0020	.0030	.0043	.0061	.0083	.0557	.0795	.0426
25	.0000	.0000	.0000	.0000	.0000	.0000	.0001	.0001	.0002	.0004	.0006	.0010	.0016	.0024	.0035	.0050	.0446	.0795	.0511
26	.0000	.0000	.0000	.0000	.0000	.0000	.0000	.0000	.0001	.0002	.0003	.0005	.0008	.0013	.0020	.0029	.0343	.0765	.0590
27	.0000	.0000	.0000	.0000	.0000	.0000	.0000	.0000	.0000	.0001	.0001	.0002	.0004	.0007	.0011	.0016	.0254	.0708	.0655
28	.0000	.0000	.0000	.0000	.0000	.0000	.0000	.0000	.0000	.0000	.0001	.0001	.0002	.0003	.0005	.0009	.0181	.0632	.0702
29	.0000	.0000	.0000	.0000	.0000	.0000	.0000	.0000	.0000	.0000	.0000	.0000	.0001	.0002	.0003	.0004	.0125	.0545	.0726
30	.0000	.0000	.0000	.0000	.0000	.0000	.0000	.0000	.0000	.0000	.0000	.0000	.0000	.0001	.0001	.0002	.0083	.0454	.0726
31	.0000	.0000	.0000	.0000	.0000	.0000	.0000	.0000	.0000	.0000	.0000	.0000	.0000	.0000	.0001	.0001	.0054	.0366	.0703
32	.0000	.0000	.0000	.0000	.0000	.0000	.0000	.0000	.0000	.0000	.0000	.0000	.0000	.0000	.0000	.0001	.0034	.0286	.0659
33	.0000	.0000	.0000	.0000	.0000	.0000	.0000	.0000	.0000	.0000	.0000	.0000	.0000	.0000	.0000	.0000	.0020	.0217	.0599
34	.0000	.0000	.0000	.0000	.0000	.0000	.0000	.0000	.0000	.0000	.0000	.0000	.0000	.0000	.0000	.0000	.0012	.0159	.0529
35	.0000	.0000	.0000	.0000	.0000	.0000	.0000	.0000	.0000	.0000	.0000	.0000	.0000	.0000	.0000	.0000	.0007	.0114	.0453
36	.0000	.0000	.0000	.0000	.0000	.0000	.0000	.0000	.0000	.0000	.0000	.0000	.0000	.0000	.0000	.0000	.0004	.0079	.0378
37	.0000	.0000	.0000	.0000	.0000	.0000	.0000	.0000	.0000	.0000	.0000	.0000	.0000	.0000	.0000	.0000	.0002	.0053	.0306
38	.0000	.0000	.0000	.0000	.0000	.0000	.0000	.0000	.0000	.0000	.0000	.0000	.0000	.0000	.0000	.0000	.0001	.0035	.0242
39	.0000	.0000	.0000	.0000	.0000	.0000	.0000	.0000	.0000	.0000	.0000	.0000	.0000	.0000	.0000	.0000	.0001	.0023	.0186
40	.0000	.0000	.0000	.0000	.0000	.0000	.0000	.0000	.0000	.0000	.0000	.0000	.0000	.0000	.0000	.0000	.0000	.0014	.0139
41	.0000	.0000	.0000	.0000	.0000	.0000	.0000	.0000	.0000	.0000	.0000	.0000	.0000	.0000	.0000	.0000	.0000	.0009	.0102
42	.0000	.0000	.0000	.0000	.0000	.0000	.0000	.0000	.0000	.0000	.0000	.0000	.0000	.0000	.0000	.0000	.0000	.0005	.0073
43	.0000	.0000	.0000	.0000	.0000	.0000	.0000	.0000	.0000	.0000	.0000	.0000	.0000	.0000	.0000	.0000	.0000	.0003	.0051
44	.0000	.0000	.0000	.0000	.0000	.0000	.0000	.0000	.0000	.0000	.0000	.0000	.0000	.0000	.0000	.0000	.0000	.0002	.0035
45	.0000	.0000	.0000	.0000	.0000	.0000	.0000	.0000	.0000	.0000	.0000	.0000	.0000	.0000	.0000	.0000	.0000	.0001	.0023
46	.0000	.0000	.0000	.0000	.0000	.0000	.0000	.0000	.0000	.0000	.0000	.0000	.0000	.0000	.0000	.0000	.0000	.0001	.0015
47	.0000	.0000	.0000	.0000	.0000	.0000	.0000	.0000	.0000	.0000	.0000	.0000	.0000	.0000	.0000	.0000	.0000	.0000	.0010
48	.0000	.0000	.0000	.0000	.0000	.0000	.0000	.0000	.0000	.0000	.0000	.0000	.0000	.0000	.0000	.0000	.0000	.0000	.0006
49	.0000	.0000	.0000	.0000	.0000	.0000	.0000	.0000	.0000	.0000	.0000	.0000	.0000	.0000	.0000	.0000	.0000	.0000	.0004
50	.0000	.0000	.0000	.0000	.0000	.0000	.0000	.0000	.0000	.0000	.0000	.0000	.0000	.0000	.0000	.0000	.0000	.0000	.0002
51	.0000	.0000	.0000	.0000	.0000	.0000	.0000	.0000	.0000	.0000	.0000	.0000	.0000	.0000	.0000	.0000	.0000	.0000	.0001
52	.0000	.0000	.0000	.0000	.0000	.0000	.0000	.0000	.0000	.0000	.0000	.0000	.0000	.0000	.0000	.0000	.0000	.0000	.0001

Appendix E
Poisson
Distribution—
Cumulative

The entries in the following table represent the Poisson probabilities for *X or more* occurrences per unit of measurement for certain values of *m*, the mean number of occurrences per unit of measurement.

$$P(X \geq X_0 \,|\, m)$$

m

X	0.015	0.014	0.013	0.012	0.011	0.010	0.009	0.008	0.007	0.006	0.005	0.004	0.003	0.002	0.001
0	1.0000	1.0000	1.0000	1.0000	1.0000	1.0000	1.0000	1.0000	1.0000	1.0000	1.0000	1.0000	1.0000	1.0000	1.0000
1	0.0149	0.0139	0.0129	0.0119	0.0109	0.0099	0.0090	0.0080	0.0070	0.0060	0.0050	0.0040	0.0030	0.0020	0.0010
2	0.0001	0.0001	0.0001	0.0001	0.0001	0.0000	0.0000	0.0000	0.0000	0.0000	0.0000	0.0000	0.0000	0.0000	0.0000

X	0.120	0.110	0.100	0.090	0.080	0.070	0.060	0.050	0.040	0.030	0.020	0.019	0.018	0.017	0.016
0	1.0000	1.0000	1.0000	1.0000	1.0000	1.0000	1.0000	1.0000	1.0000	1.0000	1.0000	1.0000	1.0000	1.0000	1.0000
1	0.1131	0.1042	0.0952	0.0861	0.0769	0.0676	0.0582	0.0488	0.0392	0.0296	0.0198	0.0188	0.0178	0.0169	0.0159
2	0.0066	0.0056	0.0047	0.0038	0.0030	0.0023	0.0017	0.0012	0.0008	0.0004	0.0002	0.0002	0.0002	0.0001	0.0001
3	0.0003	0.0002	0.0002	0.0001	0.0001	0.0001	0.0000	0.0000	0.0000	0.0000	0.0000	0.0000	0.0000	0.0000	0.0000

X	0.270	0.260	0.250	0.240	0.230	0.220	0.210	0.200	0.190	0.180	0.170	0.160	0.150	0.140	0.130
0	1.0000	1.0000	1.0000	1.0000	1.0000	1.0000	1.0000	1.0000	1.0000	1.0000	1.0000	1.0000	1.0000	1.0000	1.0000
1	0.2356	0.2289	0.2212	0.2134	0.2055	0.1975	0.1894	0.1813	0.1730	0.1647	0.1563	0.1479	0.1393	0.1306	0.1219
2	0.0305	0.0285	0.0265	0.0246	0.0227	0.0209	0.0192	0.0175	0.0159	0.0144	0.0129	0.0115	0.0102	0.0089	0.0078
3	0.0027	0.0024	0.0022	0.0019	0.0017	0.0015	0.0013	0.0011	0.0010	0.0008	0.0007	0.0006	0.0005	0.0004	0.0003
4	0.0002	0.0001	0.0001	0.0001	0.0001	0.0001	0.0001	0.0001	0.0000	0.0000	0.0000	0.0000	0.0000	0.0000	0.0000

X	0.500	0.450	0.400	0.390	0.380	0.370	0.360	0.350	0.340	0.330	0.320	0.310	0.300	0.290	0.280
0	1.0000	1.0000	1.0000	1.0000	1.0000	1.0000	1.0000	1.0000	1.0000	1.0000	1.0000	1.0000	1.0000	1.0000	1.0000
1	0.3935	0.3624	0.3297	0.3229	0.3161	0.3093	0.3023	0.2953	0.2882	0.2811	0.2738	0.2666	0.2592	0.2517	0.2442
2	0.0902	0.0754	0.0615	0.0589	0.0563	0.0537	0.0512	0.0487	0.0462	0.0438	0.0415	0.0392	0.0369	0.0347	0.0326
3	0.0144	0.0109	0.0079	0.0074	0.0069	0.0064	0.0059	0.0055	0.0051	0.0047	0.0043	0.0039	0.0036	0.0033	0.0030
4	0.0017	0.0012	0.0008	0.0007	0.0006	0.0006	0.0005	0.0005	0.0004	0.0004	0.0003	0.0003	0.0003	0.0002	0.0002
5	0.0002	0.0001	0.0001	0.0001	0.0000	0.0000	0.0000	0.0000	0.0000	0.0000	0.0000	0.0000	0.0000	0.0000	0.0000

X	1.250	1.200	1.150	1.100	1.050	1.000	0.950	0.900	0.850	0.800	0.750	0.700	0.650	0.600	0.550
0	1.0000	1.0000	1.0000	1.0000	1.0000	1.0000	1.0000	1.0000	1.0000	1.0000	1.0000	1.0000	1.0000	1.0000	1.0000
1	0.7134	0.6988	0.6833	0.6671	0.6500	0.6321	0.6133	0.5934	0.5726	0.5507	0.5276	0.5034	0.4780	0.4512	0.4231
2	0.3553	0.3373	0.3192	0.3009	0.2826	0.2642	0.2458	0.2275	0.2093	0.1912	0.1734	0.1558	0.1386	0.1219	0.1057
3	0.1315	0.1205	0.1098	0.0996	0.0897	0.0803	0.0713	0.0629	0.0549	0.0474	0.0405	0.0341	0.0283	0.0231	0.0185
4	0.0382	0.0337	0.0296	0.0257	0.0222	0.0190	0.0161	0.0135	0.0111	0.0091	0.0073	0.0058	0.0044	0.0034	0.0025
5	0.0091	0.0077	0.0065	0.0054	0.0045	0.0036	0.0029	0.0023	0.0018	0.0014	0.0011	0.0008	0.0006	0.0004	0.0003
6	0.0018	0.0015	0.0012	0.0009	0.0007	0.0006	0.0004	0.0003	0.0003	0.0002	0.0001	0.0001	0.0001	0.0000	0.0000
7	0.0003	0.0002	0.0002	0.0001	0.0001	0.0001	0.0001	0.0000	0.0000	0.0000	0.0000	0.0000	0.0000	0.0000	0.0000

m

X	2.700	2.600	2.500	2.400	2.300	2.200	2.100	2.000	1.900	1.800	1.700	1.600	1.500	1.400	1.300
0	1.0000	1.0000	1.0000	1.0000	1.0000	1.0000	1.0000	1.0000	1.0000	1.0000	1.0000	1.0000	1.0000	1.0000	1.0000
1	0.9328	0.9257	0.9179	0.9093	0.8997	0.8892	0.8775	0.8647	0.8504	0.8347	0.8173	0.7981	0.7769	0.7534	0.7275
2	0.7513	0.7326	0.7127	0.6916	0.6691	0.6454	0.6204	0.5940	0.5662	0.5372	0.5068	0.4751	0.4422	0.4082	0.3732
3	0.5063	0.4815	0.4562	0.4303	0.4040	0.3773	0.3504	0.3233	0.2963	0.2694	0.2428	0.2166	0.1912	0.1665	0.1429
4	0.2859	0.2640	0.2424	0.2213	0.2006	0.1806	0.1614	0.1429	0.1253	0.1087	0.0932	0.0788	0.0656	0.0537	0.0431
5	0.1371	0.1226	0.1088	0.0959	0.0837	0.0725	0.0621	0.0527	0.0441	0.0364	0.0296	0.0237	0.0186	0.0143	0.0107
6	0.0567	0.0490	0.0420	0.0357	0.0300	0.0249	0.0204	0.0166	0.0132	0.0104	0.0080	0.0060	0.0045	0.0032	0.0022
7	0.0205	0.0172	0.0142	0.0116	0.0094	0.0075	0.0059	0.0045	0.0034	0.0026	0.0019	0.0013	0.0009	0.0006	0.0004
8	0.0066	0.0053	0.0042	0.0033	0.0026	0.0020	0.0015	0.0011	0.0008	0.0006	0.0004	0.0003	0.0002	0.0001	0.0001
9	0.0019	0.0015	0.0011	0.0009	0.0006	0.0005	0.0003	0.0002	0.0002	0.0001	0.0001	0.0000	0.0000	0.0000	0.0000
10	0.0005	0.0004	0.0003	0.0002	0.0001	0.0001	0.0001	0.0000	0.0000	0.0000	0.0000	0.0000	0.0000	0.0000	0.0000
11	0.0001	0.0001	0.0000	0.0000	0.0000	0.0000	0.0000	0.0000	0.0000	0.0000	0.0000	0.0000	0.0000	0.0000	0.0000

X	4.200	4.100	4.000	3.900	3.800	3.700	3.600	3.500	3.400	3.300	3.200	3.100	3.000	2.900	2.800
0	1.0000	1.0000	1.0000	1.0000	1.0000	1.0000	1.0000	1.0000	1.0000	1.0000	1.0000	1.0000	1.0000	1.0000	1.0000
1	0.9850	0.9834	0.9817	0.9797	0.9776	0.9753	0.9727	0.9698	0.9666	0.9631	0.9592	0.9549	0.9502	0.9450	0.9392
2	0.9220	0.9155	0.9084	0.9008	0.8926	0.8838	0.8743	0.8641	0.8532	0.8414	0.8288	0.8153	0.8009	0.7854	0.7689
3	0.7897	0.7762	0.7619	0.7469	0.7311	0.7146	0.6973	0.6792	0.6603	0.6406	0.6201	0.5988	0.5768	0.5540	0.5305
4	0.6046	0.5858	0.5665	0.5467	0.5265	0.5058	0.4848	0.4634	0.4416	0.4197	0.3975	0.3752	0.3528	0.3304	0.3081
5	0.4101	0.3907	0.3711	0.3516	0.3321	0.3128	0.2936	0.2745	0.2558	0.2374	0.2194	0.2018	0.1847	0.1682	0.1523
6	0.2468	0.2307	0.2148	0.1994	0.1844	0.1699	0.1559	0.1424	0.1295	0.1171	0.1054	0.0943	0.0839	0.0742	0.0651
7	0.1325	0.1213	0.1107	0.1005	0.0909	0.0818	0.0733	0.0653	0.0578	0.0510	0.0446	0.0388	0.0335	0.0287	0.0244
8	0.0639	0.0573	0.0511	0.0454	0.0401	0.0352	0.0308	0.0267	0.0231	0.0198	0.0168	0.0142	0.0119	0.0099	0.0081
9	0.0279	0.0245	0.0213	0.0185	0.0160	0.0137	0.0117	0.0099	0.0083	0.0069	0.0057	0.0047	0.0038	0.0031	0.0024
10	0.0111	0.0095	0.0081	0.0069	0.0058	0.0048	0.0040	0.0033	0.0027	0.0022	0.0018	0.0014	0.0011	0.0009	0.0007
11	0.0040	0.0034	0.0028	0.0023	0.0019	0.0016	0.0013	0.0010	0.0008	0.0006	0.0005	0.0004	0.0003	0.0002	0.0002
12	0.0013	0.0011	0.0009	0.0007	0.0006	0.0005	0.0004	0.0003	0.0002	0.0002	0.0001	0.0001	0.0001	0.0001	0.0000
13	0.0004	0.0003	0.0003	0.0002	0.0002	0.0001	0.0001	0.0001	0.0001	0.0000	0.0000	0.0000	0.0000	0.0000	0.0000
14	0.0001	0.0001	0.0001	0.0000	0.0000	0.0000	0.0000	0.0000	0.0000	0.0000	0.0000	0.0000	0.0000	0.0000	0.0000

X	5.700	5.600	5.500	5.400	5.300	5.200	5.100	5.000	4.900	4.800	4.700	4.600	4.500	4.400	4.300
0	1.0000	1.0000	1.0000	1.0000	1.0000	1.0000	1.0000	1.0000	1.0000	1.0000	1.0000	1.0000	1.0000	1.0000	1.0000
1	0.9966	0.9963	0.9959	0.9955	0.9950	0.9945	0.9939	0.9933	0.9925	0.9918	0.9909	0.9899	0.9889	0.9877	0.9864
2	0.9776	0.9756	0.9734	0.9711	0.9685	0.9658	0.9628	0.9596	0.9561	0.9523	0.9482	0.9437	0.9389	0.9337	0.9281
3	0.9232	0.9176	0.9116	0.9052	0.8984	0.8912	0.8835	0.8753	0.8667	0.8575	0.8477	0.8374	0.8264	0.8149	0.8026
4	0.8199	0.8094	0.7983	0.7867	0.7746	0.7619	0.7487	0.7350	0.7206	0.7058	0.6903	0.6743	0.6577	0.6406	0.6228

m

X	5.700	5.600	5.500	5.400	5.300	5.200	5.100	5.000	4.900	4.800	4.700	4.600	4.500	4.400	4.300
5	0.6728	0.6578	0.6425	0.6267	0.6105	0.5939	0.5769	0.5595	0.5418	0.5237	0.5054	0.4868	0.4679	0.4488	0.4296
6	0.5050	0.4881	0.4711	0.4539	0.4365	0.4191	0.4016	0.3840	0.3665	0.3490	0.3316	0.3142	0.2971	0.2801	0.2633
7	0.3456	0.3297	0.3139	0.2983	0.2829	0.2676	0.2526	0.2378	0.2233	0.2092	0.1954	0.1820	0.1689	0.1564	0.1442
8	0.2158	0.2030	0.1905	0.1783	0.1665	0.1551	0.1440	0.1334	0.1231	0.1133	0.1040	0.0950	0.0866	0.0786	0.0710
9	0.1234	0.1143	0.1056	0.0973	0.0894	0.0819	0.0748	0.0681	0.0618	0.0558	0.0503	0.0451	0.0403	0.0358	0.0317
10	0.0648	0.0591	0.0538	0.0487	0.0440	0.0397	0.0356	0.0318	0.0283	0.0251	0.0222	0.0195	0.0171	0.0149	0.0129
11	0.0314	0.0282	0.0252	0.0225	0.0200	0.0177	0.0156	0.0137	0.0120	0.0104	0.0090	0.0078	0.0067	0.0057	0.0048
12	0.0141	0.0125	0.0110	0.0096	0.0084	0.0073	0.0063	0.0054	0.0047	0.0040	0.0034	0.0029	0.0024	0.0020	0.0017
13	0.0059	0.0051	0.0044	0.0038	0.0033	0.0028	0.0024	0.0020	0.0017	0.0014	0.0012	0.0010	0.0008	0.0007	0.0005
14	0.0023	0.0020	0.0017	0.0014	0.0012	0.0010	0.0008	0.0007	0.0006	0.0005	0.0004	0.0003	0.0003	0.0002	0.0002
15	0.0008	0.0007	0.0006	0.0005	0.0004	0.0003	0.0003	0.0002	0.0002	0.0001	0.0001	0.0001	0.0001	0.0001	0.0000
16	0.0003	0.0002	0.0002	0.0001	0.0001	0.0001	0.0001	0.0001	0.0001	0.0000	0.0000	0.0000	0.0000	0.0000	0.0000
17	0.0001	0.0001	0.0000	0.0000	0.0000	0.0000	0.0000	0.0000	0.0000	0.0000	0.0000	0.0000	0.0000	0.0000	0.0000

X	8.000	7.500	7.000	6.900	6.800	6.700	6.600	6.500	6.400	6.300	6.200	6.100	6.000	5.900	5.800
0	1.0000	1.0000	1.0000	1.0000	1.0000	1.0000	1.0000	1.0000	1.0000	1.0000	1.0000	1.0000	1.0000	1.0000	1.0000
1	0.9996	0.9994	0.9991	0.9990	0.9989	0.9988	0.9986	0.9985	0.9983	0.9982	0.9980	0.9978	0.9975	0.9973	0.9970
2	0.9969	0.9953	0.9927	0.9920	0.9913	0.9905	0.9897	0.9887	0.9877	0.9866	0.9854	0.9841	0.9826	0.9811	0.9794
3	0.9862	0.9797	0.9704	0.9680	0.9656	0.9629	0.9600	0.9570	0.9537	0.9502	0.9464	0.9423	0.9380	0.9334	0.9285
4	0.9576	0.9408	0.9182	0.9129	0.9072	0.9012	0.8948	0.8881	0.8811	0.8736	0.8658	0.8575	0.8488	0.8396	0.8300
5	0.9003	0.8679	0.8270	0.8177	0.8080	0.7978	0.7873	0.7763	0.7649	0.7531	0.7408	0.7281	0.7149	0.7013	0.6873
6	0.8087	0.7585	0.6993	0.6863	0.6730	0.6593	0.6453	0.6310	0.6163	0.6012	0.5859	0.5702	0.5543	0.5381	0.5217
7	0.6866	0.6218	0.5503	0.5353	0.5201	0.5047	0.4892	0.4735	0.4577	0.4418	0.4258	0.4098	0.3937	0.3776	0.3616
8	0.5470	0.4753	0.4013	0.3864	0.3715	0.3567	0.3419	0.3272	0.3127	0.2982	0.2840	0.2699	0.2560	0.2424	0.2290
9	0.4074	0.3380	0.2709	0.2580	0.2452	0.2327	0.2204	0.2084	0.1967	0.1852	0.1741	0.1633	0.1528	0.1426	0.1328
10	0.2833	0.2236	0.1695	0.1595	0.1498	0.1404	0.1314	0.1226	0.1142	0.1061	0.0984	0.0910	0.0839	0.0772	0.0708
11	0.1841	0.1377	0.0985	0.0916	0.0849	0.0786	0.0726	0.0668	0.0614	0.0563	0.0514	0.0469	0.0426	0.0386	0.0349
12	0.1119	0.0792	0.0533	0.0490	0.0448	0.0409	0.0373	0.0339	0.0307	0.0277	0.0250	0.0224	0.0201	0.0179	0.0159
13	0.0638	0.0427	0.0270	0.0245	0.0221	0.0199	0.0179	0.0160	0.0143	0.0127	0.0113	0.0100	0.0088	0.0078	0.0068
14	0.0341	0.0216	0.0128	0.0114	0.0102	0.0091	0.0080	0.0071	0.0062	0.0055	0.0048	0.0042	0.0036	0.0031	0.0027
15	0.0172	0.0102	0.0057	0.0050	0.0044	0.0039	0.0034	0.0030	0.0026	0.0022	0.0019	0.0016	0.0014	0.0012	0.0010
16	0.0082	0.0046	0.0024	0.0021	0.0018	0.0016	0.0013	0.0012	0.0010	0.0008	0.0007	0.0006	0.0005	0.0004	0.0004
17	0.0037	0.0019	0.0010	0.0008	0.0007	0.0006	0.0005	0.0004	0.0004	0.0003	0.0003	0.0002	0.0002	0.0001	0.0001
18	0.0016	0.0008	0.0004	0.0003	0.0003	0.0002	0.0002	0.0001	0.0001	0.0001	0.0001	0.0001	0.0001	0.0000	0.0000
19	0.0006	0.0003	0.0001	0.0001	0.0001	0.0001	0.0001	0.0000	0.0000	0.0000	0.0000	0.0000	0.0000	0.0000	0.0000
20	0.0002	0.0001	0.0000	0.0000	0.0000	0.0000	0.0000	0.0000	0.0000	0.0000	0.0000	0.0000	0.0000	0.0000	0.0000
21	0.0001	0.0000	0.0000	0.0000	0.0000	0.0000	0.0000	0.0000	0.0000	0.0000	0.0000	0.0000	0.0000	0.0000	0.0000

m

X	8.500	9.000	9.500	10.000	10.500	11.000	11.500	12.000	12.500	13.000	13.500	14.000	14.500	15.000	20.000
0	1.0000	1.0000	1.0000	1.0000	1.0000	1.0000	1.0000	1.0000	1.0000	1.0000	1.0000	1.0000	1.0000	1.0000	1.0000
1	0.9998	0.9999	0.9999	1.0000	1.0000	1.0000	1.0000	1.0000	1.0000	1.0000	1.0000	1.0000	1.0000	1.0000	1.0000
2	0.9981	0.9988	0.9992	0.9995	0.9997	0.9998	0.9999	0.9999	0.9999	1.0000	1.0000	1.0000	1.0000	1.0000	1.0000
3	0.9907	0.9938	0.9958	0.9972	0.9982	0.9988	0.9992	0.9995	0.9997	0.9998	0.9999	0.9999	0.9999	1.0000	1.0000
4	0.9699	0.9788	0.9851	0.9897	0.9928	0.9951	0.9966	0.9977	0.9984	0.9989	0.9993	0.9995	0.9997	0.9998	1.0000
5	0.9256	0.9450	0.9597	0.9707	0.9789	0.9849	0.9893	0.9924	0.9947	0.9963	0.9974	0.9982	0.9987	0.9991	1.0000
6	0.8504	0.8843	0.9115	0.9329	0.9496	0.9625	0.9723	0.9797	0.9852	0.9893	0.9923	0.9945	0.9961	0.9972	1.0000
7	0.7438	0.7932	0.8350	0.8699	0.8984	0.9214	0.9397	0.9542	0.9654	0.9741	0.9807	0.9858	0.9895	0.9924	0.9998
8	0.6144	0.6761	0.7313	0.7798	0.8215	0.8568	0.8863	0.9105	0.9302	0.9460	0.9585	0.9684	0.9761	0.9820	0.9998
9	0.4769	0.5443	0.6082	0.6672	0.7206	0.7680	0.8094	0.8450	0.8751	0.9002	0.9210	0.9379	0.9516	0.9625	0.9980
10	0.3470	0.4126	0.4782	0.5421	0.6029	0.6595	0.7112	0.7576	0.7986	0.8342	0.8647	0.8906	0.9122	0.9301	0.9950
11	0.2366	0.2940	0.3547	0.4170	0.4793	0.5401	0.5983	0.6528	0.7029	0.7483	0.7888	0.8243	0.8551	0.8815	0.9892
12	0.1513	0.1970	0.2480	0.3032	0.3613	0.4207	0.4802	0.5384	0.5942	0.6468	0.6955	0.7400	0.7799	0.8152	0.9787
13	0.0909	0.1242	0.1636	0.2084	0.2580	0.3113	0.3671	0.4240	0.4810	0.5369	0.5907	0.6415	0.6889	0.7324	0.9610
14	0.0514	0.0739	0.1019	0.1355	0.1746	0.2187	0.2670	0.3185	0.3722	0.4270	0.4818	0.5355	0.5875	0.6368	0.9339
15	0.0274	0.0415	0.0600	0.0835	0.1121	0.1460	0.1847	0.2280	0.2750	0.3249	0.3767	0.4296	0.4824	0.5343	0.8952
16	0.0138	0.0220	0.0335	0.0487	0.0683	0.0926	0.1217	0.1556	0.1940	0.2364	0.2822	0.3306	0.3808	0.4319	0.8435
17	0.0066	0.0111	0.0177	0.0270	0.0396	0.0559	0.0764	0.1013	0.1307	0.1645	0.2025	0.2441	0.2888	0.3359	0.7790
18	0.0030	0.0053	0.0089	0.0143	0.0219	0.0322	0.0458	0.0630	0.0842	0.1095	0.1391	0.1728	0.2103	0.2511	0.7030
19	0.0013	0.0024	0.0043	0.0072	0.0115	0.0177	0.0262	0.0374	0.0519	0.0698	0.0916	0.1174	0.1470	0.1805	0.6186
20	0.0005	0.0011	0.0020	0.0035	0.0058	0.0093	0.0143	0.0213	0.0306	0.0427	0.0579	0.0765	0.0988	0.1248	0.5298
21	0.0002	0.0004	0.0009	0.0016	0.0028	0.0047	0.0075	0.0116	0.0173	0.0250	0.0351	0.0479	0.0638	0.0830	0.4410
22	0.0001	0.0002	0.0004	0.0007	0.0013	0.0023	0.0038	0.0061	0.0094	0.0141	0.0204	0.0288	0.0396	0.0531	0.3563
23	0.0000	0.0001	0.0001	0.0003	0.0006	0.0010	0.0018	0.0030	0.0049	0.0076	0.0115	0.0167	0.0237	0.0327	0.2794
24	0.0000	0.0000	0.0001	0.0001	0.0002	0.0005	0.0008	0.0015	0.0025	0.0040	0.0062	0.0093	0.0137	0.0195	0.2126
25	0.0000	0.0000	0.0000	0.0000	0.0001	0.0002	0.0004	0.0007	0.0012	0.0020	0.0032	0.0050	0.0076	0.0112	0.1568
26	0.0000	0.0000	0.0000	0.0000	0.0000	0.0001	0.0002	0.0003	0.0006	0.0010	0.0016	0.0026	0.0041	0.0062	0.1122
27	0.0000	0.0000	0.0000	0.0000	0.0000	0.0000	0.0001	0.0001	0.0003	0.0005	0.0008	0.0013	0.0021	0.0033	0.0779
28	0.0000	0.0000	0.0000	0.0000	0.0000	0.0000	0.0000	0.0000	0.0001	0.0002	0.0004	0.0006	0.0011	0.0017	0.0525
29	0.0000	0.0000	0.0000	0.0000	0.0000	0.0000	0.0000	0.0000	0.0000	0.0001	0.0002	0.0003	0.0005	0.0009	0.0344
30	0.0000	0.0000	0.0000	0.0000	0.0000	0.0000	0.0000	0.0000	0.0000	0.0000	0.0001	0.0001	0.0002	0.0004	0.0219
31	0.0000	0.0000	0.0000	0.0000	0.0000	0.0000	0.0000	0.0000	0.0000	0.0000	0.0000	0.0001	0.0001	0.0002	0.0135
32	0.0000	0.0000	0.0000	0.0000	0.0000	0.0000	0.0000	0.0000	0.0000	0.0000	0.0000	0.0000	0.0000	0.0001	0.0081
33	0.0000	0.0000	0.0000	0.0000	0.0000	0.0000	0.0000	0.0000	0.0000	0.0000	0.0000	0.0000	0.0000	0.0000	0.0048
34	0.0000	0.0000	0.0000	0.0000	0.0000	0.0000	0.0000	0.0000	0.0000	0.0000	0.0000	0.0000	0.0000	0.0000	0.0027

	m	
X	25.000	30.000
0	1.0000	1.0000
1	1.0000	1.0000
2	1.0000	1.0000
3	1.0000	1.0000
4	1.0000	1.0000
5	1.0000	1.0000
6	1.0000	1.0000
7	1.0000	1.0000
8	1.0000	1.0000
9	0.9999	1.0000
10	0.9998	1.0000
11	0.9994	1.0000
12	0.9986	0.9999
13	0.9968	0.9998
14	0.9935	0.9996
15	0.9876	0.9991
16	0.9777	0.9980
17	0.9622	0.9961
18	0.9395	0.9927
19	0.9079	0.9871
20	0.8664	0.9781
21	0.8145	0.9647
22	0.7527	0.9456
23	0.6825	0.9194
24	0.6061	0.8854
25	0.5266	0.8428
26	0.4471	0.7916
27	0.3706	0.7327
28	0.2998	0.6671
29	0.2366	0.5969
30	0.1821	0.5243
31	0.1367	0.4516
32	0.1001	0.3814
33	0.0715	0.3155
34	0.0498	0.2556
35	0.0338	0.2027
36	0.0225	0.1574
37	0.0146	0.1196
38	0.0092	0.0890
39	0.0057	0.0649
40	0.0034	0.0463
41	0.0020	0.0323
42	0.0012	0.0221
43	0.0007	0.0148
44	0.0004	0.0097
45	0.0002	0.0063
46	0.0001	0.0040
47	0.0001	0.0025
48	0.0000	0.0015
49	0.0000	0.0009
50	0.0000	0.0005
51	0.0000	0.0003
52	0.0000	0.0002
53	0.0000	0.0001

Index

Index

Risk, 57
Routing, 108
Row procedures, 46

Saddle point, 162–163
Sample, 10
  random restricted, 10–11
  random unrestricted, 10
Scientific approach, 1
  implementation, 7
  information collection, 1–2
  problem definition, 2
  selecting best alternative, 6–7
  selecting courses of action, 2–3
  testing alternatives, 3–6
Sensitivity analysis, 237–254
  steps, 245–247
Sequential Bayesian analysis, 70, 80–82
Set, 9
Simplex algorithm, 220–235
Simultaneous equations, 44
Square matrix, 37
Standard deviation units, 28–31
State of nature, 57
Stochastic models, 349
Strategies
  admissible, 79, 162
  dominated, 79, 162
  Hurwicz, 174
  inadmissible, 79
  Laplace, 173
  Maximax, 174

minimax, 162, 174
Minimax regret, 172
mixed, 164
pure, 81, 164
Symmetric matrix, 42
System, 348
  components, 348
  parameters, 348
  relationships, 348
  simulation, 356
  states, 348
  variables, 348

Trade-offs, 89–103
Transportation problems, 255–272

Uncertainty, 57
  dynamic programming, 114
  inventory, 120
  subjective probabilities, 66–68
Unit matrix, 41
Urban, G. L., 360

Variation of parameters, 98, 102
Vogel approximation, 263–265

Weighted averages, 58

Zero-one programming, 335–343
  assignment problem, 336, 342
  knapsack problem, 337
  traveling salesman problem, 340

109K